HISTORY OF SCOTS AND ENGLISH LAND LAW

Based on

C. D'O. FARRAN

Principles of Scots and English Land Law

(W. Green, Edinburgh, 1958)

GEOGRAPHICAL PUBLICATIONS LIMITED
THE KEEP, BERKHAMSTED, HERTS, U.K.

British Library Cataloguing in Publication Data

Kolbert, Colin Francis
    History of Scots and English land law. – (Studies
    in land economy).
    1. Real property – Great Britain
    I. Title   II. Mackay, N A M   III. Farran, Charles
    d'Olivier. Principles of Scots and English land law.
    Adaptations   IV. Series
    346′ .41′043   KD829

    ISBN 0 900394 19 6

Made and printed in Great Britain by
William Clowes & Sons Limited, London, Beccles, and Colchester

STUDIES IN LAND ECONOMY

HISTORY OF SCOTS AND ENGLISH LAND LAW

by

C. F. KOLBERT

of Lincoln's Inn, Barrister-at-Law
Fellow and Tutor of Magdalene College, Cambridge
and University Lecturer in the
Department of Land Economy, Cambridge

and

N. A. M. MACKAY

Writer to the Signet
Sometime Commoner of
Worcester College, Oxford

GEOGRAPHICAL PUBLICATIONS LIMITED

STUDIES IN LAND ECONOMY

The Department of Land Economy of the University of Cambridge has embarked on a publication policy made possible by financial support from the Department's Development Fund and authorised by the Managers. Besides a series of *Occasional Papers*, published by the Department itself, the policy has a second objective: the publication of *Studies in Land Economy*, a series of books concerned with past and present land affairs. Authors will be selected for their scholarship and knowledge, however specialised or local, and will not be exclusively drawn from members of the University or staff of the Department. Joint publication with other universities and institutions is welcomed and encouraged.

First in the series was D. R. Denman (1973) *The King's Vista: A Land Reform which has Changed the Face of Persia*, followed by D. M. Turner (1977) *An Approach to Land Values*, and S. Millward (ed) (1977) *Urban Harvest* (a joint publication with the University of Salford). The *History of Scots and English Land Law* is thus the fourth, and it provides another variation: the updating and expansion of the late Dr Farran's leading text on comparative land law. Other works in the series will follow, under the imprint of Geographical Publications Limited.

University of Cambridge
August 1977

D. R. Denman
Professor of Land Economy

Her Majesty Queen Elizabeth II as feudal superior of Glenormiston receiving the render of one red rose from her vassal, Mr S. E. Denman, on 1 July 1966 (*see* pp. 63, 370–1)

(*Photograph copyright* The Scotsman Publications Ltd)

Contents

APPENDICES

Preface

The late Dr Farran's *Principles of Scots and English Land Law*, on which this work is based, was published by Green's of Edinburgh in 1958. The years since then have seen much change in the law and in politics generally, not least in the relationships between England and Scotland. With the rise of nationalism and talk of the separation of Scotland, dissolution of the Union being advocated in some quarters and 'devolution' in others (a Bill on this subject being before Parliament as we write), we think it well to turn attention to one aspect of our common heritage. An examination of the development of the land laws of these two realms within the United Kingdom sheds much light on the long history which we share and shows that what we have in common is probably more than that which divides us – though the general ignorance of each others' system which Scots and English lawyers usually profess might lead one to assume otherwise. Conveyancers, especially, often claim total mystification about practices across the Border.

Dr Farran's researches are far too valuable and important a contribution to the history of the law of Scotland (which has yet to be written) to be allowed to languish amongst out-of-print books. They are kept alive in the present volume, though we have revised, extended and up-dated them and added several completely new chapters.

There are many to whom we owe thanks for help of all description but we are especially grateful to Professor Donald Denman for his encouragement throughout the project; to Madame Farran; to the library staffs of the Squire Law Library, Cambridge, of Lincoln's Inn and of the Signet Library, all of whom cheerfully made many journeys to their dustiest and remotest vaults in response to our requests; to Mrs R. Easthope, Miss Iris Elkington and Mrs J. Webb, for their skilled typing of the manuscript; to Dr Derek Nicholls of the Department of Land Economy, Cambridge, for the care he lavished on the proofs; to Mr Andrew Wallace-Hadrill, Fellow of Magdalene College, for help with translations; and to Mrs Audrey Clark of Geographical Publications Ltd whose minute attention to detail has even caused two pedants to spell mediaeval in the 'modern' manner.

St Mary Magdalene Day, 1977   C. F. K. and N. A. M. M.

Table of Cases

Table of Statutes

Abbreviations

A.P.S.	Acts of the Parliament of Scotland, 1124–1707
Balfour, *Practicks*	Sir James Balfour of Pittendreich, *Practicks: or a system of the more Ancient Laws of Scotland* (1754; and Stair Society, 1962)
Bell, *Principles*	Professor G. J. Bell, *Principles of the Law of Scotland* (10th edn 1899)
Bl.Comm.	Sir William Blackstone, *Commentaries on the Laws of England* (1st edn 1765)
Bracton	Henry de Bracton, *De Legibus et Consuetudinibus Angliae* (thought to have been written before 1257)
C.L.J.	Cambridge Law Journal (1921–)
Cheshire	G. C. Cheshire, *Modern Law of Real Property* (12th edn by E. H. Burn, 1976)
Craig	Sir Thomas Craig, *Ius Feudale* (translation by Lord President Clyde (2 vols), 1934)
Craigie	J. Craigie, *Scottish Law of Conveyancing: Heritable Rights* (3rd edn 1899)
Co.Litt.	*Coke upon Littleton* (19th edn 1832) (Littleton's *Tenures* was first printed about 1481; Sir Edward Coke's commentary was published in 1628)
D.N.B.	*Dictionary of National Biography*
E.H.R.	English Historical Review (1886–)
Erskine	Professor John Erskine of Carnock, *An Institute of the Law of Scotland* (8th edn 1871)
Fearne, *Contingent Remainders*	Charles Fearne, *Essay on the Learning of Contingent Remainders and Executory Devises* (1772; 10th edn 1844)
Gloag and Henderson	W. M. Gloag and R. C. Henderson, *Introduction to the Law of Scotland* (7th edn 1968)
Grant, *S.E.D.S.*	I. F. Grant, *The Social and Economic Development of Scotland before 1603*
Green's *Encyclopaedia*	*Encyclopaedia of the Laws of Scotland*, edited

	by Viscount Dunedin, published by Green, Edinburgh, 1926
Halliday	J. M. Halliday, *The Conveyancing and Feudal Reform (Scotland) Act 1970* (1st edn 1970)
H.E.L.	Sir W. S. Holdsworth, *A History of English Law.*
Jur. Rev.	Juridical Review (1889–)
Kenny	Kenny's *Outlines of Criminal Law* (19th edn by J. W. C. Turner, 1966)
L.Q.R.	Law Quarterly Review (1886–)
Lord Kames, *Elucidations*	Henry Home (Lord Kames), *Elucidations respecting the Law of Scotland* (1777)
M.	W. M. Morison's *Dictionary of Decisions* (22 vols)
M.L.R.	Modern Law Review (1937–)
McDouall, *Institute*	Andrew McDouall (Lord Bankton), *An Institute of the Laws of Scotland in Civil Rights: with Observations upon the Agreement or Diversity between them and the Laws of England. In four books after the General Method of the Viscount of Stair's Institutions* (1752)
Mackay, *Stair*	Aeneas J. G. Mackay, *Memoirs of Sir James Dalrymple, First Viscount Stair, President of the Court of Session in Scotland* (1873)
Megarry and Wade	The Hon. Sir Robert Megarry and H. W. R. Wade, *The Law of Real Property* (4th edn 1975)
Omond, *Lord Advocates*	G. W. T. Omond, *The Lord Advocates of Scotland from the close of the 15th Century to the passing of the Reform Bill* (2 vols, 1883: second series, 1834–1880, 1914)
P. & M.	Sir F. Pollock and F. W. Maitland, *History of English Law before the time of Edward I* (2nd edn 1898)
Paterson, *Compendium*	James Paterson, *A Compendium of English and Scotch Law stating their differences, with a Dictionary of Parallel Terms and Phrases* (1860)
Regiam Majestatem	*Regiam Majestatem*, Lord Cooper's Edition (Stair Society, Vol 11)
Ross, *Lectures*	Walter Ross, *Lectures on the History and Practice of the Law of Scotland relative to*

	Conveyancing and Legal Diligence (2 vols, 1822)
Sources	*The Sources and Literature of Scots Law* (Stair Society, Vol 1)
Stair	Sir James Dalrymple (Viscount Stair), *Institutions of the Law of Scotland* (1681 : 5th edn 1832)
S.H.R.	Scottish Historical Review (1904–)
Walker	D. M. Walker, *Principles of Scottish Private Law.* (2 vols, 2nd edn 1975)
Whitelocke, *Memorials*	Sir Bulstrode Whitelocke, Lord Commissioner, *Memorials of English Affairs, or an Historical Account of what passed from the beginning of the reign of Charles I to Charles II, his happy Restauration* (1682) *New Edition with many additions never before printed,* 1732)

Introduction

Scots and English lawyers tend to be particularly suspicious of one another. Although the two countries employ in social converse what is ostensibly the same language, the legal terminology of each is formidably foreign to the other party. An English lawyer who dares to open a Scots law book discovers an alien world of pursuers and spuilzies and assoilzied defenders; nor is the Scots man of law much more at home with torts and emblements, replevin and champerty.

Stories ranging from the sublime to the ridiculous have been told of the ignorance of Scots and English lawyers of one another's systems. Thus Blackstone apparently believed that the notorious *jus primae noctis* was known to medieval Scotland under the name of 'merchet', while Cosmo Innes was none too sure that it had not existed in England.[1] In fact merchet was known to England as well as Scotland, but its connection with the *jus primae noctis* has been exploded.

Yet ever since the accession of a Scottish family to the English throne there have been those on both sides of the Border who have advocated a unification of our legal systems. Two men as fundamentally unlike as James VI of Scotland and Oliver Cromwell shared this desire.[2] James called a conference of lawyers to inquire how the laws of the two countries might be unified.[3] Bacon, however, saw that 'men love to hold their own as they have held, and the difference of this law carrieth no mark of separation'.[4] A united kingdom, in his view, did not necessarily imply a unified system of private law. Our own is not the only state whose history has proved the truth of this observation.

1   Bl. Comm., ii, 6; Innes, *Scotch Legal Antiquities*, 53.
2   As to Cromwell, *see* Omond, *Lord Advocates*, 164.
3   Craig, *Epistle Dedicatory* to *Ius Feudale*, p. ix.
4   *Works*, 1824 edn., iv, 287–304.

In the course of time men have come to recognise that English and Scots law can and some would say should exist as separate systems within a single state, but that is no reason for virtually complete mutual ignorance being if not cultivated, at least consciously preserved, between them. To a Scot must go the credit of having wished to remedy the deficiency. Lord Kames wrote in the eighteenth century, when relations between the two countries were not particularly happy:

> I have often reflected upon it as an unhappy circumstance, that different parts of the same kingdom should be governed by different laws. This imperfection could not be remedied in the union betwixt England and Scotland; for what nation will tamely surrender its laws any more than its liberties? But if the thing is unavoidable, its bad consequences were not altogether so. These might have been prevented, and may yet be prevented, by establishing publick professors of both laws, and giving suitable encouragement for carrying on together the study of both ... The proposed plan has great advantages, not only by removing or lessening the foresaid inconvenience, but by introducing the best method of studying law, for I know none more rational, than a careful judicious comparison of the laws of different countries ... A regular institute of the common law of this island, deducing historically the changes which that law has undergone in the two nations, would be a valuable present to the public; because it would make the study of both laws a task easy and agreeable. Such an institute it is true, is an undertaking too great for any one hand. But if men of knowledge and genius would undertake particular branches, a general system might in time be completed from their works.[5]

Two hundred years have gone by and no men of 'knowledge and genius' have taken up Lord Kames's challenge. Rather than wait any longer for their appearance the late Dr Farran made a start in the field of land law which was chosen because it is the branch of law in which England and Scotland, although starting from the same basis (that of the derivative tenure of all land from the Crown), have developed most individually and shown most divergence from one another. While it may no longer be the most important branch of our legal systems, land law was for long considered to be so, since for centuries the land law determined the very structure of society.

5 Lord Kames, *Historical Law Tracts*, p. xii.

Consequently it has had lavished on it in both countries an abundance of attention, both favourable and the reverse, which has sometimes aided its orderly development, at other times has caused unnecessary complications. However as a result of many centuries of detailed attention it is easier to discern the historical stages of the development of land law than of most other branches of law.

It is often stated that one of the purposes of the comparative study of legal systems is to help prepare the way for an eventual unification of the systems studied. Let it be made clear at once that nothing could be further from our present purpose. After all, English land law has a very ancient and venerable tradition behind it and is one of the most characteristic and important offshoots of the Common Law, so that there seems no reason at all why England should be made to adopt Scots land law or any variant of it. The land law of Scotland has just as long and venerable a history, is just as intrinsically Scottish: it would be equally unthinkable to impose English real property law upon Scotland.

The purpose of the present inquiry is not, therefore, to prepare the case for unification, but merely to help each to understand the other. 'Wer eine Religion kennt, kennt keine', was the motto of one who had as great a knowledge of the world's religious systems as anyone has ever had.[6] However annoyed the adherents of any particular religion may have been by this dictum, it is nothing to the wrath of most lawyers at a similar one about their *Rechtssystem*. Yet for many generations in both England and Scotland, students have profited, despite their grumbles, from being put through a course of ancient Roman law as well as that of their own time and country. Unfortunately much of the value of this has generally been lost hitherto by a failure to teach Roman law as a comparative subject alongside the equivalent topic in Scots or English law – or, better still, both. It is even more likely that if the timescale is right and we examine our own legal system contemporaneously with another, we may be able to throw some light on each. On the other hand to compare, say, ancient Chinese law with that of a modern European community would probably be of more limited value; for one would not know whether a similarity or difference arose by accident, or whether it was attributable to the different social or historical

6   Muller, *The Sacred Books of the East.*

conditions under which they had to operate. The same is true to a lesser extent of Rome and modern Britain, although there the existence of modern Civil law systems makes the effort well worth while. But in taking Scots and English law as our subject the gulf is far less great. The two have operated in the same island over more or less the same length of time and under comparable, though by no means identical, social and historical conditions.

Such an examination of legal systems necessarily implies an historical approach. While it may be diverting and temporarily of some practical value to place side by side the rules of two or more countries as they exist at any particular moment,[7] it is not likely to be a wholly satisfactory exercise for, apart from the probability that any system may change, one needs also to know how far resemblances and differences are ancient and deep-rooted and how far they are modern and accidental. 'Il faut éclaircir l'histoire par les lois et les lois par l'histoire.'[8]

Before beginning, we must point out that one of the sharpest distinctions between English and Scots law is to be seen in the general nature of their history. English law has developed slowly and regularly, advancing ponderously from one foot to another, ever glancing backwards to observe the tracks it has made. This has made the development of English law ideal to study and easy to record. Not surprisingly, histories of English law abound.

Scots law, on the other hand, has developed erratically making many false starts and changes of mind; careless of inconsistency, but anxious to secure the best from whatever source it may come. For example, jury trial in civil cases, which had been unknown in Scotland, was introduced from England in 1815 and tried until 1868, but found not to suit the Scots courts. It survives only in a few special cases,[9] and even this has been regretted. Scots law has been described as a knitting together of many scattered threads as variegated as the

---

7   As in Paterson, *Compendium of English and Scots Law* (1860). The *Institute* of McDouall (Lord Bankton) (1752) is a more truly comparative work, as the full title indicates: *An Institute of the Laws of Scotland in Civil Rights: with Observations upon the Agreement or Diversity between them and the Laws of England. In four books after the General Method of the Viscount of Stair's Institutions.*

8   Montesquieu, *L'Esprit des Lois*, ii, 21, 2.

9   MacGillivray, 'The Influence of English Law', *Sources* (Stair Society, Vol I), 222–3.

national tartan.[10] For this reason a history of Scots law must necessarily be harder to write than one of English law. Its writer would have to be well versed in the history of the Roman, Canon, English, French, Dutch, Norse, Celtic and other systems of law, and would have to trace all the varied institutions of Scots law back to their often confused origins. This, together with the fact that Scotland, when all is said and done, is a very small country, explains why Scotland has not yet produced a Maitland or a Holdsworth.

It has thus been necessary to glean the Scots materials for this comparative study from a variety of scattered sources. The old *Regiam Majestatem* copied from Glanvil assists us sometimes. Often we are compelled to begin with the *Jus Feudale* of Craig,[11] who wrote about 1600. His work does not purport to be a history of Scots land law. It consists of the received continental law of the feudalists with some references to Scots and English rules, but its history is often so naïve as to be palpably suspect.[12] Stair's great treatise of the mid-seventeenth century, and Erskine's of the next, are magnificent compilations, but their concern is with the law as it stood – or ought to have been standing – in their own day. Indeed Craig, Stair and Erskine can be viewed in a very real sense as creating, not as re-cording, Scots legal history. The high renown of their writings was itself one cause for the irregular development of Scots law. It was easy and natural to start afresh from them rather than to search antiquity for lost or dubious precedents. Furthermore, conditions in medieval Scotland were far from those necessary to orderly legal development. What law there was was mostly *jus non scriptum*.[13]

With Lord Kames himself we come to one who took an intelligent interest in the history of legal institutions. But he was, like Black-stone, on the bench and had neither the time nor the materials for a systematic survey. Dalrymple's *Essay towards a general history of feudal property in Great Britain*, published in 1757, was an early attempt at such a study. But anyone writing in the eighteenth century could have only very limited knowledge of the legal history of either country, and his work does not pretend to be much more than a

10   Mackintosh, *Roman Law in Modern Practice*, 5.
11   Girvan, 'Feudal Law', *Sources* (Stair Society, Vol 1), 193.
12   Innes, *Scotch Legal Antiquities*, 3.
13   Maitland, *Cambridge Modern History*, ii, 53.

literary essay. With Ross, however, we get a more genuinely historical approach. His *Lectures*, published in 1792, are of great interest and value, but he was concerned only with a narrow subject, being more interested in the origin and history of particular clauses to be found in deeds than in the development of legal theory. Cosmo Innes has perhaps the best claim to be considered Scotland's legal historian. His works, especially *Scotch Legal Antiquities* (1872), contain a great deal that is interesting about our own and other branches of Scots law. Finally, all interested in Scots law owe a deep debt of gratitude to the Stair Society for their fine series of works dealing with the sources of Scots legal history.

This absence of any real history of Scots land law has made it necessary to break fresh ground in this work, although it is not primarily intended as such a history. Material which up to now has been difficult of access and in many cases long out of print, has been brought together for the first time. Little of it has ever been systematically considered by any legal historian. The treatment of English law is necessarily more derivative, but it is hoped that some light may be thrown on this subject as a result of comparing it with parallel trends in Scotland. The main interest throughout has been in the comparison of the development of the two systems and in the deductions to be drawn from such a comparison.

As only a few readers are likely to be conversant with the laws of both countries, it has been necessary to set out at some length matters which may seem elementary on the English side to the English reader, and on the Scots side to the Scot. Thus, in order that the latter may understand the equitable estate (notoriously a difficult subject for those not trained at the Inns of Court) the medieval origins of the Lord Chancellor's jurisdiction must be explained. Similarly, if we did not explain what may seem obvious to the Scottish reader, English readers might fall into the trap of supposing sasine to be equivalent to seisin. There is, alas, some truth in the gibe that 'the first article of an English lawyer's creed is that English law is so incomparably superior to other systems that the others are hardly worth a glance, and there are few subjects on which England is so contentedly ignorant as Scotland and her institutions'.[14]

14   Lord Cooper, *The Scottish Legal Tradition*, 30.

PART I

THE COMMON FOUNDATION

THE DOCTRINE
OF UNIVERSAL DERIVATIVE TENURE
FROM THE CROWN

Chapters 1 to 9

1 Pre-Feudal Tenures and the Introduction of Feudal Doctrine

The term 'tenure' will have to be used to describe landholding in pre-feudal times, although it is nowadays so firmly linked with feudal notions. Maitland, however, pointed out that the term 'tenure' has no specifically feudal significance.[1] *Tenere* (to hold) is found in connection with the holding of land even where there is as yet no hint of feudal theory. What is characteristically feudal is not tenure of land of itself, but tenure of land from a feudal superior.

PRE-FEUDAL ENGLAND

The oldest and probably for a long time the only really important type of Anglo-Saxon tenure in England was that known as folk-land. This was almost traditionally thought to be the land of the folk, that is *ager publicus*[2]; but Vinogradoff showed that it was an allodial system of customary landholding, in which the land was apparently held of no superior.[3] Its most significant feature was however that it was inalienable out of the holder's family, and centring thus on the family group it did indeed belong in a sense to the folk or kindred. Individual landownership, free from family ties, probably originated with the Church, which was heavily influenced by the ideas of Roman Law. The Romans clearly had in *dominium* an idea of individual ownership and Christianity, too, was a strong force for individualism.

---

1 P. & M., i, 234, note 1.
2 Cf Pollock, *The Land Laws*, Appendix B; Digby, *Introduction to the History of the Law of Real Property*, 3
3 Vinogradoff, *Collected Papers*, i, 91.

The two combined to develop the second form of Anglo-Saxon landholding, book-land.[4]

Book-land was invariably a gift from a superior, and the gift took the form of a written charter, which may itself represent a link with the *carta* reciting *mancipatio*, which had long taken the place of the actual conveyancing ceremony at Rome.[5] At first, grants of book-land were made exclusively to ecclesiastics, but even when later made in favour of laymen they retained a fictional ecclesiastical guise.[6]

Laen-land, the third main type of landholding, was purely derivative. As the name suggests, at first it was a mere loan for a life or lives, three lives becoming common. There were local variants in the north, known as thengage and drengage.[7]

In these institutions it is not difficult to see the budding of the feudal doctrine of universal derivative tenure. It is an easy step forward from the observation that most great men hold their lands by 'book' or charter from the King, and many lesser men in turn hold theirs by laen from them, to the notion that the King's admitted sovereignty over the whole realm must be based on a universal residuary ownership in its soil. Seebohm and other writers[8] have shown that especially in the south and west of England many village communities existed at the Conquest (as some had existed from the earliest Saxon times) which, by means of a rent of honey, corn or money, acknowledged their dependence on the King or on some local lord.

Although events were thus undoubtedly tending towards an eventual evolution of the doctrine of universal dependent tenure, it was not until after the Conquest that the more systematic Norman lawyers actually enunciated it. The Conquest hurried the process of assimilation between English and Continental landholding (which would probably have come about eventually in any case) by the pressure of economic forces.[9] This we can appreciate when we realise

4   The earliest extant book is in Appendix I.
5   Cf Ross, *Lectures*, ii, 65 *et seq.* Arangio-Ruiz, *Instituzioni*, 185.
6   Maitland, *Domesday Book and Beyond*, 243.
7   As to laen-land, see Holdsworth, *H.E.L.*, ii, 70 *et seq.*; Denman, *Origins of Ownership*, 68, 69, 82; and as to thengage and drengage, see Holdsworth, *H.E.L.*, ii, 168.
8   *The English Village Community*, 181–6; Maitland, *Domesday Book and Beyond*, 70 *et seq*; Vinogradoff, *The Growth of the Manor*, 147; Stenton, *English Feudalism*, 114.
9   P. & M., i, 63; Holdsworth, *H.E.L.*, ii, 78.

that the feudal system of landholding found its way almost, if not quite, as effectively into Scotland without any such assistance *vi et armis*. A strong court such as that of the Conqueror and his sons was also long absent in Scotland. Nonetheless feudalism developed there.

The hundred years following the Conquest represent a period of transition towards the universal acceptance and application of the doctrine now under consideration. Some[10] have sought 'to assign the change definitely to the year 1085, citing the Anglo-Saxon Chronicle for 1085,[11] but this is an over-simplification of the position. It is a mistake to look for sudden change by legislation at such a comparatively early period as the eleventh century. The feudal doctrine of tenure was not introduced by decree of the Conqueror at a stroke. Far from imposing immediate and drastic change, the command with which he is credited was to preserve the laws of King Edward in lands as in other things, with the addition of those which he had himself enacted.[12] Nor was this mere words. The Saxon heir of Shirbourne Castle successfully petitioned for it even though it had been donated to a Norman companion-in-arms of William I.[13] It is significant that the original returns of the Domesday inquest were made by the hundred; those of 1166 by the fief.[14] The latter year saw also the birth of the assise of novel disseisin, by which every free tenant, however low down on the feudal ladder, could claim the protection of the royal courts if dispossessed.[15] This plainly flowed according to contemporary ideas from the view that the King was *dominus ultimus*: the chief evidence of lordship – great or small – being the holding of courts for the ultimate dominus of Sovereign lord's tenants, that being part of the feudal superior's obligation of protection in return for his man's oath of fealty.

For a time after the Conquest book-land preserved its name in a few cases, but it was finally merged in the feudal scheme of tenures (usually as frankalmoign) in the course of the twelfth century.[16] In

---

10 E.g. Wright, *Tenures*, 66.
11 Plummer (ed.), *Two Saxon Chronicles*, 217.
12 Robertson, *The Laws of the Kings of England from Edmund to Henry I*, 240.
13 *Case of Tanistry* (1608) Dav Ir 28, 41.
14 Round, *Feudal England*, 236.
15 P. & M., i, 137.
16 P. & M., i, 62.

what had been Northumbria some of the old derivative tenures in thengage and drengage existed till the thirteenth century, proving very difficult to classify under the recognised division of tenures.[17] They are of particular interest to us because up to 1157 Northumbria was in dispute between England and Scotland, being nominally under the Scots monarch, but (in English theory at least) only as tenant from the English King.[18] These tenures were also known to Lowland Scotland. Again, as late as the thirteenth century, a number of free individuals held land for which they could not show a charter, or claim to have been infeft by any lord 'de antiquo conquesto', 'per antiquam tenarum', or simply 'de antiquo'.[19] Very probably these were odd survivals of the old folk-land. But the doctrine of universal derivative tenure was too strongly entrenched by then for anyone to worry about these trifling curiosities. 'Chescune terre Dengleterre est tenue en chef du Roi', said counsel in the Year Books,[20] and neither his contemporaries nor their successors have ever contested it.

PRE-FEUDAL SCOTLAND

So little is known with any certainty about pre-feudal landholding in Scotland and the scanty evidence is so fragmentary that it cannot be considered here in any detail. Until the Anglicisation of the law in southern Scotland, mainly in the reign of Malcolm III (1057–1093) – the contemporary of William the Conqueror, whose wife, St Margaret, was the daughter of Edward the Atheling – there was no real central royal control in Scotland and local magnates probably did more or less as they pleased. The two prime conditions for the orderly development of law, that is some sort of central authority with the power to impose its will, and a period of relative peace in which the tender young plant of the law could put down its roots and begin to flourish, were notably lacking. It seems probable, however,

17   Formerly they had existed all over England: Stenton, *English Feudalism*, Chapter 4; Maitland, 'Northumbrian Tenures', *Collected Papers*, ii, 96.
18   Pease, *The Lords Wardens of the Marches*, 13.
19   Vinogradoff, *Villainage in England*, 199, 452–6.
20   Y.B. 14 & 15 Ed. III (R.S.), 346, *per* R. Thorpe, *arguendo*.

that there were similarities between landholding in 'Scotland proper'[21] in those early times and that which prevailed in Anglo-Saxon England. Indeed, this may be said to be the most clearly defined characteristic of the earliest period of Scottish legal development of which we have any, albeit shadowy, knowledge.

The broad periods of Scottish legal history may be conveniently, though very roughly, distinguished as follows:

1. A period of general similarity with England (though by no means an identical pattern) until the time of Edward I ('The Hammer of the Scots') who set Scotland firmly on its own separate path of legal development.

2. A period of widening divergence as Scotland and England develop their laws separately, lasting from the time of Edward I until the Act of Union, 1707.

3. The period since 1707, during which the House of Lords, as the common Supreme Court, has acted to some extent as a unifying influence. Despite the enthusiasm to unify the laws of the new United Kingdom, Scots law had become and has remained an entirely separate system, especially where land is concerned; and one cannot now foresee a time when union of the laws of England and Scotland is ever likely to be achieved.

In the earliest period, which is our present concern, Scotland could be roughly divided into two parts: the Lowlands, which were heavily Anglicised, and where Anglo-Saxon landholding was probably general; and Scotland proper, north of the Forth, which was a Celtic country. Landholding there was almost certainly on the Celtic customary tribal pattern,[22] as was general also in Ireland, so far as can be ascertained from the Brehon law.[23]

> The phrase 'tribal system' automatically calls up a definite conception of organic development. One imagines the patriarch passing into the wilderness – the increase of his progeny and stock – a gradual localising in their wanderings after pasture and game – the beginnings of the cultivation of the tribal lands – a system of communal agriculture, and, perhaps later, a temporary allotment

21   I.e. truly Celtic Scotland, north of the Firths of Clyde and Forth.
22   Grant, *S.E.D.S.*, 5, 9, 63.
23   Kolbert and O'Brien, *Land Reform in Ireland*, 2–9.

of shares in the common land – the allocation of individual shares to the ruler, the priest, the judge – the enslavement of captives, and malefactors, even of the poorest tribesmen – the emergence of right to the private ownership of land. Such is the commonly accepted idea of the story of the evolution of a tribe, and there is good evidence that the inhabitants of Scotland themselves, or their closest kindred, went through most of these stages.[24]

Later, Miss Grant sounds a warning:

Tribal, or perhaps it would be more correct to say, clannish, the method of landholding in early Scotland doubtless was. This form of social structure is inherent in Celtic culture, which was then predominant over the greater part of the country. The point I am anxious to make is that the word 'system', if it conveys any idea of a settled, organised, uniform condition of affairs, is rather a misleading one.[25]

The introduction of feudalism into Scotland is a very obscure story. It is probable that the Lowlands at any rate became entirely Anglicised some time after the arrival of St Margaret, the English Queen of Malcolm III (1057–1093). James III's Parliament declared a set of rules known as the *Leges Malcolmi* to be the authentic law of the realm, ascribing them to Malcolm II (1005–1034). If these laws were authentic and rightly ascribed, it would mean that feudalism was established in Scotland before it reached England or was fully developed in France, whence it is supposed to have come. Later scholars, notably Lord Kames, contemporary of Lord Hardwicke, L.C., were prepared to believe the *Leges* to be genuine but the work of Malcolm III; more modern research, however, tends to indicate that they are not authentic and that the introduction of feudalism may be ascribed to the reign of David I (1124–1153).[26] This certainly seems reasonable, for not only was he one of the outstanding medieval Kings, he had also an English mother and had lived in England.

---

24 Grant, *S.E.D.S.*, 5, quoting Irish similarities. As to the obscurity of the Brehon Law, *see* Binchy, 'The Linguistic and Historical Value of the Irish Law Tracts' (*Proceedings of the British Academy*, xxix, 4–11) and the remarks of Gavan Duffy, P. in *Foyle and Bann Fisheries Ltd v A-G.* (1949) I.L.T.R. 29 at 41.
25 Grant, *S.E.D.S.*, 9.
26 Hume-Brown, *History of Scotland*, i, 70; Ross, *Lectures*, ii, 60; Girvan, 'Feudal Law', *Sources* (Stair Society, Vol I), 193.

In any case, it must not be thought that feudalism came as a system overnight. Indeed it could extend only very slowly in parts other than the Lowlands, for much of the Highlands was very thinly populated and in any case of very little value to the King.[27] There, Celtic custom almost certainly continued but little is known about it. Even Scottish historians openly rely on Irish sources for that period[28] and those sources are far from clear even for Ireland. However, it is certain that the Celtic custom prevailed for some long time: only in 1493[29] did all the land of Scotland pass even nominally into the hands of the King. It was another story and a long time before that nominal control became a reality. In 1597 James VI imposed feudal theory throughout the realm by statute, but the events of 1745 had first to be faced before Celtic landholding was stamped out by force. After the bloodbath and extermination of suspect Highlanders, the Heritable Jurisdictions Act 1747 recognised those that remained as feudal proprietors. Their Celtic tenants were at a stroke disentitled, for the royal Courts never recognised their customary rights, as had been the case with villeins and copyhold in England. Thus the path was open for the 'clearances'.

UDAL LANDS OF ORKNEY AND SHETLAND

This account of pre-feudal landholding in England and Scotland cannot be closed without some reference to the most remarkable instance of its survival: the udal lands of Orkney and Shetland. Here alone throughout the length and breadth of the United Kingdom, one may still see land held by a customary allodial tenure not unlike the Anglo-Saxon folk-land, acknowledging no feudal superiority or ultimate ownership in the sovereign.

The story began with the settling of 'odel' families from Norway in the islands, where cultivable land was to be had for the taking.[30] In 872 the King of Norway annexed the settled islands. This resulted in their having the Norse system of allodial tenure known as

27 Innes, *Scotch Legal Antiquities*, 154–5.
28 Lang, *History of Scotland*, i, 77 *et seq.* As to the unreliability of those sources, *see* note 23, *ante.*
29 Defeat of the last Lord of the Isles.
30 Hodgkin, *History of the Anglo-Saxons*, ii, 487.

udal tenure. 'Contrasted with the feudal landowner who necessarily held of a superior for service or payment, the odaller held under God alone . . . by right of primal occupancy complete without written title,[31] and subject to neither homage, rent or service. Two obligations the odallers . . . appear to have been under, and these were to the State – to take up arms in defence of their country and to pay the *Skat* or landtax.'[32]

This is not to say, however, that the udal holder was free to do what he liked with the land. As in most primitive systems – including folk-land – the kinsmen had some, albeit rather ill-defined, right of reversion.[33] 'In a sense the odal was inalienable and entailed upon the heirs of the original possessor, the odal-born. Its sale outside the family was justified only by dire necessity[34] and a right of redemption was retained by the vendor and his kinsmen . . . that the odal might ever return to the odal-born.'[35] A word of caution may be tentatively expressed on this, for in the earliest udal land document extant[36] there is no mention whatever either of necessity or of the kindred, and the document seems to show a power of free alienation in the vendor. However, we should not draw any conclusions. The document is included simply because it is the earliest such document in existence; of the facts of the situation to which it relates we know nothing more, not even whether it is typical or extraordinary of its time.

In 1469 Christian I of Denmark and Norway pledged Orkney and Shetland to James III to secure the dowry of his daughter, James's wife. In 1471 Scotland foreclosed and annexed the Isles to the Scots Crown.[37] By the nature of the transaction the Islands remained subject to their own law and this was solemnly confirmed by statute in 1567,[38] a happy contrast to the proceedings of thirty years later

31   Stair, II.3.11; Erskine, II.3.18. But *see Sinclair v Hawick* (1624) M 16393; Udal Land Act 1690, c 61 (A.P.S., ix, 200).
32   Dobie, 'Udal and Feudal', (1931) 43 Jur. Rev. 115 and 'Udal Law', *Sources* (Stair Society, Vol 1), 445 *et seq.*
33   Cf Leviticus, Chapter 25, vv 13 and 23–4; Ruth, Chapter 4, vv 1–10; Jeremiah, Chapter 32, vv 6–25.
34   Ross, *Lectures*, ii, 248.
35   Dobie, 'Udal and Feudal', (1931) 43 Jur. Rev., 117.
36   *See* Appendix IV.
37   A.P.S., ii, 102.
38   A.P.S., iii, 41.

just described. However, a gradual infiltration of feudal charters and feudal, derivative land law generally appears to have taken place, largely through the tyranny of the many Scots donatory earls and the bishops, who rivalled one another in lavish 'grants' of lands that were not really theirs. Indeed, this practice became so general that some nineteenth century observers, notably Sir Walter Scott,[39] considered the udal tenure to be practically extinct.

However, the old tenure of the Islands was not so close to extinction as was then thought and it remains to this day except where the land has been properly feudalised by Crown investiture. The mere long use of feudal conveyancing is not enough to affect the allodial nature of the udaller's title.[40] In the present century two Court of Session cases have recognised the non-feudal nature of the traditional landownership in Orkney and Shetland. In the first *Smith v Lerwick Harbour Trustees*,[41] the contest was as to the ownership of the foreshore between a donee by feudal grant from the Crown as 'Lord of the Shore'[42] and the udal proprietor of the adjacent estate. In the second, *Lord Advocate v Balfour*,[43] the dispute was between a claim of salmon fisheries in the Isles as being *inter regalia* (which they are on the mainland of Scotland, though not in England), and a udal claim based on long-standing custom and occupancy. In both cases the claims of the odallers were preferred to those of the Crown; for the sovereign, not being feudal superior in these islands, cannot claim there the franchises held in the rest of the Kingdom by virtue of the ultimate ownership of the land.

CONCLUSIONS

In so far as it is possible to draw any conclusions from a historical survey such as has been attempted in this chapter the following propositions may be advanced:

1 Landholding in England was a very long-established and

---

39 Lockhart, *Life of Sir Walter Scott*, iii, 145.
40 *Beatton v Gaudie* (1832) 10 S 286
41 (1903) 5 F 680: Drever, 'Udal Law and the Foreshore', (1904) Jur. Rev., 189.
42 In the rest of Scotland, Crown rights in relation to the shore are roughly analogous to those in England: *see* Green's *Encyclopaedia*, title 'Sea' (Part 2, 'Seashore').
43 1907 SC 1360.

effective institution protected by strong laws and the machinery of justice before the arrival of the feudal theory of derivative tenure. Consequently that theory had, as shown in Chapter 8, to accept the earlier customs of landholding very much as they stood and was able only to weave around them its web of lords and fees.[44] The transition from one stage to another was achieved with comparative ease.

2   The earliest form of landholding in Scotland, on the other hand, was founded on rather shadowy Celtic customs unprotected by effective legal institutions. The chief test of possession appears to have been the sword. Law and feudalism seem to have arrived and spread in Scotland more or less simultaneously. Consequently the two became, in a sense, confused; and feudalism refused to come to terms with the older customs of landholding, which had to conform with its rigid tenets, or perish. Only in a few parts of the Anglicised southeast were pre-feudal methods of landholding able to survive for a time. They survive, too, up to the present day in Orkney and Shetland owing to the singular history of those islands being distinct from that of the mainland.

It is the generally accepted view that England was subdued and ravaged by an invader who brought feudalism with him: to the warring Scots, however, feudalism came only by peaceful penetration.

44   Cf Stenton, *English Feudalism*, 114 *et seq.*; Grant, *S.E.D.S.*, 94.

2 The Fundamental Similarity of Scots and English Feudal Law

It is commonly stated that the laws of England and Scotland were extremely similar during the early medieval period, that is from about the reign of David I in Scotland (1124–1153) to that of Edward I in England (1272–1307).[1] This was the opinion expressed by the greatest master of English legal history, when on a rare occasion he turned his attention to Scotland:

> The utmost claimed for the English king was a feudal overlordship, and English law, as English law, had no power north of the Tweed. Nevertheless, we may well doubt whether a man who crossed the river felt that he had passed from the land of one law to the land of another law. . . . If the proper names be omitted we shall hardly now tell a Scottish charter of feoffment from an English,[2] and the few Scottish records of litigation that have come down to us from the thirteenth century might have been written by the clerks of Robert Bruce of Annandale (grandfather of King Robert the Bruce) who was for a time the chief justice of England. . . . It seems clear enough from abundant evidence that, at the outbreak of the war of independence, the law of Scotland, or of southern Scotland, was closely akin to English law.[3]

It is to be noted that the two systems were only 'closely akin', not identical. It would be absurd to suggest a complete assimilation, even in the land law, a branch of law that both countries owed in general to common foreign influences. It seems clear that even in

---

1 E.g. by MacGillivray, 'The Influence of English Law', *Sources* (Stair Society, Vol I), 211–2; Ross, *Lectures*, ii, 125, 161; Preface to A.P.S., i, 4.
2 For specimens *see* Appendix V; Innes, *Scotland in the Middle Ages*, 200–1; Lawrie, *Early Scottish Charters*, 48.
3 P. & M., i, 222.

Lowland Scotland the law was not yet as uniform as in England.[4]
There had been no Bracton to set it in order. Even more important
was the absence of strong central courts such as those at Westminster.
The comparative weakness of the Scots monarchy and the practical
independence of territorial magnates, which found its legal expression
in the mass of local feudal jurisdictions up and down the country,
must have proved a grave obstacle to the development of regularity
in Scots legal institutions. Again, it seems highly probable that the
development of Scots law, even at the centre, lagged quite a long way
behind that taking place in England,[5] so that our hypothetical
English traveller would very probably not find in Scotland the law
he knew in England in his own time, but rather that which his
grandfather had known. This is demonstrated by the fact that the
Regiam Majestatem was based on Glanvil's *Tractatus* at a time when
the latter must already have been very considerably out of date in
England, if not actually superseded by a later work of higher
calibre – that of Bracton which was finished about 1258.[6] The date
of the *Regiam* is uncertain, but Lord Cooper[7] considers about 1250
to be most likely. A passage from Bracton occurs in some manuscripts
of the *Regiam*, but Skene, Thomson and Cooper all ignore it as a
scribal interpolation.[7] It is suggested that this time-lag has been a
constant characteristic of the development of the land law of the
two countries, although not of all branches of law by any means;[8]
and even in the land law there are important exceptions.[9]

It is, however, with the doctrine of universal derivative tenure
that we are at the moment mainly concerned. We may take this as
an example by which to test the general similarity already referred
to; but a warning must first be sounded. Scots legal history is a
subject particularly lacking in the ordered continuity of tradition.[10]
Attempting to trace the medieval history of Scots law is like groping
in a darkness that can be felt.[11] Therefore what follows must be read

4   Campbell, 'Land Tenure in Scotland and England', (1885) 1 LQR 184; P. &
     M., i, 223.
5   Lord Cooper, *Regiam Majestatem*, (Stair Society, Vol 11), 42–3.
6   P. & M., i, 207.
7   *Regiam Majestatem*, (Stair Society, Vol 11), 44.
8   *See* Chapters 17–20.
9   E.g. the registration of sasines, *see* Chapter 26.
10   Mackintosh, *Roman Law in Modern Practice*, 30–31. *See also* Introduction, *supra*.
11   Campbell, 'Land Tenure in Scotland and England', (1885) 1 LQR 406.

on the basis of comparing the English traditional view of tenure
coming down from a time soon after the Conquest with the Scots
view which can only with difficulty be traced further back than
Craig. We must now consider the fundamentals of this dependent
or feudal method of landholding.

'The grand and fundamental maxim of all feudal tenure is this,'
says Blackstone,[12] 'that all lands were originally granted out by the
sovereign, and are therefore holden, either mediately or immediately,
of the Crown.' While everyone must be prepared to admit that this is
a fiction considered as a historical statement,[13] it enunciates a legal
principle that has had extremely important practical consequences on
the history of property in land. It means, for example, that every
claimant to an interest in land (with a few very limited exceptions in
Scotland) must in principle[14] show a title derived from the Crown,
whether by direct royal grant or indirectly through the Crown
grantee's having granted subordinate rights to another and so down,
possibly though a very large number of steps, to the present claimant,
yet always deriving its first spark of life, so to speak, from the
Crown.

But the notion of feudal land tenure in its original form meant a
great deal more than merely that, as a matter of conveyancing, all
titles must flow from the king. It was implicit in the medieval idea of
tenure that with the relation of grantor and grantee of land went that
of feudal lord and man.[15] This lord and man (superior and vassal)
relationship can be well appreciated from what Craig tells us of
feudal loyalty:[16]

> The vassal's duty to respect his superior and to study and advance
> his dignity and interest before those of all others finds its counter-
> part in the superior's obligation to protect the vassal's person,
> property, possessions and good name, without regard to third
> parties. The observance of good faith is universally imperative
> in the discharge of all obligations relative to these matters in

12 Bl. Comm., ii, 52.
13 Even Blackstone (Bl. Comm., ii, 50); but cf the acceptance by Craig and others of
    the Leges Malcolmi.
14 As to this qualification, *see* Chapter 23. For the Scots exceptions *see* Chapters 1
    and 3.
15 P. & M., i, 67, 296–307.
16 Craig, 2, *passim*.

accordance with the terms and tenor of the investiture, or, if these are silent with regard to them, according to local custom.[17]

LORD AND MAN

Before the feudal grantee could enter into enjoyment of the estate granted to him, he had to do fealty or homage to the grantor and 'become his man'. Conversely, the lord could not enjoy a wardship until the infant heir had done homage.[18] Littleton[19] explains that when the tenant does homage to his lord he must be unarmed and bareheaded and the lord seated. The tenant kneels before him on both knees and puts his hands together between the lord's hands and says: 'Jeo deveigne votre home de cest jour en avant, de vie et de membre, et de terrene honour, et a vous serra foial et loial, et foy a vous portera des tenements que ieo claime de tener de vous, salve le foy que ieo doy a nostre Seignior le Roy',[20] and then the lord kisses him.

The Scots form was the same.[21] It was in fact the same throughout western Europe,[22] except for the *salvo*. The *salvo* is very important and distinguishes English feudalism from that of France, and, in effect, Scotland: but *Regiam Majestatem* also mentions the *salvo*.[23]

The words 'Jeo deveigne votre home' caused a practical difficulty in that professed religious had already become 'home de Dieu'. They were therefore excused these words and said instead, 'Jeo vous face homage'.[24] Long before Coke's time this was extended to all ecclesiastical persons, not merely regulars.[25] Consecrated bishops did not owe even this modified homage for lands held in barony, but fealty alone. But bishops-elect did homage before their consecra-

17 Craig, 2.11.1. (Lord Clyde's Translation, Vol 1, 583).
18 Glanvil, IX.4; *Regiam*, II.68.
19 *Tenures*, s 85.
20 Cf the words used at modern coronations: 'I . . . . do become your liege man of life and limb and of earthly worship; and faith and truth I will bear unto you, to live and die, against all manner of folks.' (*Form and Order*, 1953).
21 Craig, 2.12.13.
22 P. & M., i, 297; cf Esmein, *Histoire*, 189–90.
23 *Regiam*, II.62.
24 Littleton, *Tenures*, s 86.
25 Co. Litt. 65b.

tion,[26] a ceremony still observed in England. There were special rules prohibiting women from doing homage, but they could receive it.[27]

Fealty was a simple oath to be faithful and true to the lord and did not involve any ceremony such as kneeling or kissing, or indeed the personal presence of the lord at all.[28] Of course every act of homage involved an oath of fealty as well. Breach of the duty of fidelity to one's lord was very heavily punished in medieval Scotland.[29] In England it was the foundation of the crime of 'petit treason' which, however, survived the feudal relation.[30]

That the English and Scots rules as to homage and fealty were the same may be appreciated from a comparison of the appropriate passages in Glanvil with those in the *Regiam Majestatem*,[31] although modern lawyers tend to underestimate the importance of these ceremonies.[32]

Though homage and fealty were the most significant features of the feudal relationship of lord and vassal, being a reciprocal spiritual bond which went to the very root of feudalism and forming the basis of the honourable association of free men from which flowed all the other mutual obligations, they were not the only important features of that relationship. More important from the point of view of later times were the very varied services which the tenant was bound by the nature of his holding to perform for his superior, and the often highly remunerative incidents or, in Scottish parlance, casualties, to which the lord of land held by certain tenures was entitled. Again the lord, especially in Scotland, had in many cases important rights of jurisdiction over the tenant and his holding. These features will be covered in later chapters.

It must be stressed that this was a reciprocal relationship. The lord, too, owed duties to his vassal. In England, owing to the very early decline of a truly feudal ordering of society, little more came

---

26 Glanvil, IX. 1; *Regiam*, II.64.
27 Glanvil, IX. 1. 3; *Regiam*, II.64, 66.
28 Littleton, *Tenures*, ss 91–3.
29 Grant, *S.E.D.S.*, 95; *see also* Chapter 5.
30 Kenny, 395.
31 Glanvil, IX. 1–6; *Regiam*, II.60–9.
32 Lord Cooper, *Regiam Majestatem*, note to II.60. (Stair Society, Vol 11), 170–1. Cf P. & M., i, 296 *et seq.*; Grant, *S.E.D.S.*, 95 *et seq.*

to be signified by this than the lord's duty to 'warrant' the tenant's title to the land in case of challenge.[33] In Scotland a feudal superior was bound during all the long centuries before the rule of law became an established fact there, to maintain and defend his man in the most literal sense of those words. Miss Grant[34] cites an inquest held at Logie on the feast of St Peter, 1320, to find what rights the Abbot of Dunfermline's men had against him, for example of sanctuary and support (said to be only of grace, but clearly very common) during old age and infirmity. By a law ascribed to Alexander II[35] lords may do battle for their tenants, because the body of a vassal and all his goods ought to be in his superior's protection. Even as late as 1596 the celebrated exploit in which 'Kinmont Willie' was snatched from the clutches of the English in Carlisle Castle itself was the work of his feudal superior, the laird of Buccleuch.[36] By statute a feudal lord in Scotland could be held responsible for the misdeeds of his vassals.[37] It was indeed a 'Mutual ligue and Band'.[38] This point is often wholly misunderstood by modern, and especially continental and socialistic writers who mistakenly use the term 'feudalism' to indicate a condition of slavery or serfdom.[39]

The main features of feudal landholding were thus common to both England and Scotland, being based on the principle of the derivative and dependent tenure of land from the king. But although they agreed on the acceptance of that principle and on its application to all strictly feudal holdings, that is *fiefs* in the French sense,[40] the two legal systems differed in the extent to which they were prepared to extend the principle beyond these to other interests in land. These differences will be examined in the next chapter.

---

33   Glanvil, IX. 4; *Regiam*, I.15 *et seq.*; Littleton, *Tenures*, ss 143–5; Holdsworth, *H.E.L.*, iii, 56, 158; P. & M., ii, 663.
34   *S.E.D.S.*, 81.
35   A.P.S., i, c viii; cf Innes, *Scotland in the Middle Ages*, 214.
36   Chambers, *Domestic Annals of Scotland*, 269; Graham, *Condition of the Border*, Chapter 10.
37   A.P.S., ii, 332; cf Grant, *S.E.D.S.*, 183.
38   Balfour, *Practicks*, 126, c 5, citing *Congiltoun v Hepburn* (1532): cf Bracton f 78b.
39   Kolbert, 'Misuse of the term "Feudalism"', FAO *Land Reform* 1975, No 1, 72.
40   Rough equivalent to English and Scots knights' service and wardholdings respectively. (Esmein, *Histoire*, 195).

3 The English and Scots Approaches to Tenure

DERIVATIVE TENURE

English lawyers, having once grasped the feudal concept of tenure, were prepared to extend it extremely freely, so that for them it was indeed to become the doctrine of *universal* derivative tenure. As Maitland says:[1]

> Not only has every acre of land been brought within its scope, so that the English lawyer can not admit even the bare possibility of land being holden of no one,[2] but the self-same formula has been made to cover relationships which have very little in common. An Earl of Chester, who may at times behave like a sovereign prince, holds his county palatine of the king; the cottier, who like enough is personally unfree, holds his little croft of some mesne lord, or of the king himself.

When, later, economic forces produced a new form of landholding, that of tenant at a rent for a term of years, English law was able to include this within the doctrine. Tenure exists between the termor and his landlord.[3] Even more remarkably, where no temporal service or rent is owed, as in the spiritual holdings, the doctrine was not avoided.[4]

Thus, as we shall see later was also the case with the doctrine of estates, English law, having adopted the notion of feudal tenure as a result of Norman influence, applied it extremely widely, indeed truly universally, to every kind of officially recognised interest in

1 P. & M., i, 212.
2 Challis, *Law of Real Property*, 5.
3 *See* Chapter 8.
4 P. & M., i, 212.

land.[5] This was not in accordance with contemporary continental ideas. Right down to the Revolution of 1789, feudal law in France meant the law of the fief, that is the noble's interest in land, held by homage and military service.[6] But some English writers[7] have perhaps tended to overstate the position, for 'la tenure roturière' (ignoble freehold) 'copie le fief' except in a few special points (homage, for example); while even 'les tenures serviles présentent une grande analogie avec les tenures roturières.'[8]

Maitland has expressed the view that it was this universal application of the doctrine of feudal tenure that caused the comparative simplicity of the medieval English law of land. Stubbs shared this view.[9] Holdsworth refers what he calls the 'great simplification of English land law' also to the extension of the royal courts' jurisdiction over every type of free interest in land. All those who held land by free tenures were protected by the same courts and by the same forms of action.[10] It is obviously an arguable point as to which came first. Did men say, 'All land is held by tenure from the king, therefore his courts should naturally have jurisdiction over it and deal with it on the same basis'; or, remembering that in medieval minds landownership and jurisdiction were inseparably mixed, 'All (free) interests in land are dealt with by the king's courts equally, therefore it must be that he is their ultimate owner'? The latter may be the correct solution, although it seems strange to the modern mind trained to associate jurisdiction with sovereignty rather than with ownership.

Scotland never had the Domesday survey or the Conquest which made it possible. Consequently she escaped a similar drastic standardisation.[11] Moreover, the Scots king's courts failed to obtain the right of universal jurisdiction just referred to until as late as the sixteenth century. An Act in 1457[12] expressly prohibited the Lords of Session from judging in cases of heritage. These were reserved as

---

5   Copyhold was not at first so recognised: *see* Chapter 8.
6   Esmein, *Histoire*, 195 *et seq.*
7   E.g. P. & M., i, 235; Holdsworth, *H.E.L.*, iii, 30.
8   Esmein, *Histoire*, 221.
9   Stubbs, *Constitutional History*, i, 282–3.
10   *H.E.L.*, iii, 30.
11   Grant, *S.E.D.S.*, 65.
12   C 61; A.P.S., ii, 47, ii.

in immediate post-Conquest England for the local feudal courts. But the Act did allow the sheriff a possessory jurisdiction. As in England, this was the first step in the decline of the feudal courts. By 1552 the Court of Session openly declared itself to be competent in matters of title to heritage.[13] Thus the causes which had prevailed in England eventually prevailed in Scotland also; but they were too late to achieve such a universal success as in England.

As a result, Scotland has been considerably more cautious in its application of the doctrine now under consideration. The Scots lawyer can recognise exceptions to the general rule without dismay. He sees moreover little point in preserving the fiction of derivative tenure, unless there is some practical point of advantage to be gained or at least some outward and recognisable sign of its existence. Nor will the conception be needlessly extended to situations and relationships outside the net of true feudal landholding, where admittedly the doctrine must be considered a necessity. The interesting point is that tenure has always had and still has very important practical consequences in Scotland, for example, the payment of feu duties and the enforcement by the superior of feudal conditions both positive and negative which run with the tenure of the land. These conditions can be enforced by feuars who hold their land of the same superior unless they were expressly prohibited in their feu charters from doing so. In England it has been so widely extended as to become a theory and almost nothing more.[14]

We may take as an example of this difference the English and Scots views of a typical settlement, under which the land is to go to *A* for life, then to *B* in tail and then to *C* in fee. The English view at common law of this arrangement is that *A* during his lifetime holds the land (or, rather, his estate in it) of *B*, who holds in turn of *C*, who holds of the feudal superior of the land in question.[15] Before the statute *Quia Emptores* 1290, *C*'s tenure might be of the grantor. By that Act further subinfeudation was prohibited, but this only applied to grants in fee simple. Scots law, on the other hand, takes the view that *B* alone holds the land on a feudal basis – either from the grantor or his superior according to the nature of the grant. There

13 *Weemes v Forbes* (Skene, *De Verborum Significatione*, title 'breve de recto').
14 P. & M., i, 236.
15 Y.B. 21 & 22 Ed. I (R.S.) 641.

being no *Quia Emptores*, subinfeudation was usual in Scotland. *A*, being only a liferenter, has a usufruct or *jus in re aliena*.[16] *C* has in effect a mere *spes successionis* by no means amounting to any feudal holding of the land. Even more striking perhaps is the difference between the English copyholder and the Scots customary tenant. The former, as we shall see, was treated as holding his land of the lord of the manor by the custom of the manor in question. The latter, as we have already seen, was treated by the law as a mere tenant at will. Finally those late arrivals on the feudal scene, the landlord and tenant, for years were in England, and were not in Scotland, treated as being connected by the relationship of tenure.[17]

English and Scots land law, therefore, although they closely resembled one another in their adoption, in the medieval period, of the principle of derivative tenure, differed quite markedly in the extent to which they were prepared to make it a truly universal doctrine. But this will become even more evident when we turn from this general discussion to a more detailed examination of the different relationships in question: for example it comes as a shock to the English legal mind to discover that there are in Scotland exceptions to the doctrine[18].

ALLODIAL LANDS

The clearest and most satisfactory example is the udal landownership of Orkney and Shetland, which has already been discussed. But even on the mainland the law is said to recognise at least three exceptional allodial titles:[19]

1   that of the King and of the Prince of Scotland;
2   that of the Church in certain cases[20];
3   that of the compulsory acquirer of land under certain modern statutes.

16   *See also* Chapter 13.
17   *See* Chapter 8.
18   E.g. Challis, *The Law of Real Property*, 5: 'Hargrave seems to surmise that allodial lands may still exist in Scotland.'
19   Scottish Law Commissioners, 3rd Report, 1837, vi; Erskine, II. III; Dobie, 'Udal Law', *Sources* (Stair Society, Vol I), 462; Green's *Encyclopaedia*, title 'Superior and Vassal'.
20   *See also* Chapter 4.

All British lawyers would, of course agree that the present Queen holds her lands allodially. We must note, however, that many English ones right up to the Union[21] would have denied that the King of Scots did the same. From the time of William the Lion onwards, it was alleged, the Kingdom of Scotland had been held of the King of England as a fee.[22] They could cite repeated acts of homage and the events of Edward I's intervention in support. But the Scots, particularly in the Declaration of Arbroath in 1320, denied the overlordship of the King of England, and claimed that this homage was only for the counties of Cumberland and Huntingdon and other lands held by the kings of Scots in England. If, however, the King of Scots did not hold his lands allodially, then the King of England could scarcely claim to do so either. King John on the 14th May 1213 surrendered his kingdom of England and lordship of Ireland to Pope Innocent III and received them back only after a lapse of several days as a feu at a rent of 1000 marks a year.[23] Moreover, the medieval English kings all did homage to the kings of France, though no doubt claiming to do so merely for their duchies of Normandy and Aquitaine and other French possessions.

Apart from these politico-historical questions, the king in either country must hold allodially, for there is none on earth to whom they owed allegiance. But Craig reminds us that kingdoms are the gift of God and are truly held in fee under Him as a Lord and a Superior.[24]

We may notice in passing a slight but perhaps significant difference between the way in which the two legal systems treated the private property of the monarch as opposed to the hereditary property of the royal house. English law was very reluctant to see the need for any such distinction.[25] Maitland has suggested that to (English) medieval minds it was almost impossible to conceive of the king as an artificial person or corporation sole, distinct from the individual ruler who might be absent or under age or imbecile.[26] Consequently, all the

---

21 *See* Nicolson, *Epistle Dedicatory* to *Leges Marchiarum* (1705). Anderson's *Diplomata et Numismata Scottiae* was prepared then to refute English claims.
22 There is nothing inherently absurd in the idea of a state being a fee. Craig shows (1.3.2; 1.12.6) that many kings held their lands as fees from the Pope and did homage to him: so too, did some of the Emperors (1.3.1).
23 *D.N.B.*, title 'John': Craig, 1.3.2.; P. & M., i, 521.
24 1.12.1.
25 P. & M., i, 511 *et seq.*
26 P. & M., i, 520; Holdsworth, *H.E.L.*, iii, 462 *et seq.* The Scots however, did appreciate the distinction; so also did the French, *see* Esmein, *Histoire*, 328.

king's property was the property of the individual king. What had been his private lands before his accession became by it the king's lands, to be governed by exactly the same rules as those which had come to him with the throne.[27] Even when later it was admitted that he had been a body politic as well as a body natural, he had the same prerogatives in relation to land held in the latter as in the former capacity.[28]

There was, however, and always had been a sentimental distinction between the Ancient Demesne manors of the dynasty, that is those which the Domesday Book records as having belonged to St Edward,[29] and later additions to the royal estates, whether by escheat, forfeiture, purchase or any other means. There was a strong convention that an individual ruler might not part with the Ancient Demesne lands in perpetuity.[30] The customary holders of lands within these manors held by what was in effect a distinct tenure.[31]

Mesne tenants were not to be prejudicially affected by the act of the tenant-in-chief. Consequently on his forfeiture or surrender to the Crown the king was said to hold *ut de honore* rather than *ut de corona* and the tenants did not become technically tenants-in-chief. Challis[32] insists that they did but this is in the teeth of an express decision,[33] which is supported by the words of many royal grants, for example in Charles I's grants to Vermuyden 'in free and common socage and not in chief' as of the manor of Hatfield.[34] When holding *ut de honore* the king did not have special prerogatives, as to wardships.[35] The distinction between *ut de corona* and *ut de honore* was taken as recently as 1922.[36]

---

27   Holdsworth, *H.E.L.*, iii, 462 *et seq.*
28   Holdsworth, *H.E.L.*, iii, 468. *Duchy of Lancaster Case* (1561) 1 Plow 212, 213, *Alcock v Cooke* (1829) 5 Bing 340 at 352, 354.
29   This was the only admissible evidence and it was conclusive. Vinogradoff, *Villainage in England*, 90; Y.B. 33–35 Ed. I (R.S.) 308; 2 & 3 Ed. II (S.S.) 60; 11 & 12 Ed. III (R.S.) 164. However, the rule may not always have been thus; *see* P. & M., i, 399.
30   P. & M., i, 384.
31   I.e. the so-called Ancient Demesne: P. & M., i, 383 *et seq.*; Holdsworth *H.E.L.*, iii, 263 *et seq.* See also Chapter 8, *infra.*
32   *Law of Real Property*, 4.
33   *Estwick's Case* (1613) 12 Co Rep 135; cf Co. Litt. 108a; Viner, *Abridgement*, title 'Tenant in capite'.
34   Reade, *Isle of Axholme*, 73.
35   Co. Litt. 77a.
36   *Re Holliday* [1922] 2 Ch. 698.

In Scotland the distinction was very much more marked. This was in accordance with the continental position.[37] Certain lands were from time to time declared by Parliament to be annexed to the royal dignity.[38] Henceforward they ceased to be the subject-matter of private law and their alienation could only take place by authority of parliament.[39] But this did not prevent the King of Scots from holding other lands *in privato patrimonio* and therein *utitur jure communi*.[40] 'Privatum est,' wrote Craig, 'quod ad eum non iure Coronae, sed per successionem alicui privato, aut alio iure pervenit . . . quod ad eum non ut Principem, sed tanquam Antonium, Arcadium aut Honorium pertinet.'[41] It was this distinction between the king and Henry or Elizabeth that English law refused to admit. The prerogative title to a wardship in Scotland did not apply to the private estates of the king.[42] By the prerogative any minor vassal of the king *as such* was his ward, but among subjects (and the king when taking privately) the wardship went to the eldest superior. The main point was, who was entitled to the fee on the ward's marriage? The king had to be served heir in common form if succeeding in his private capacity under a subject's settlement. He took his public lands *jure coronae* without sasine,[43] but this did not apply to his private lands. Stair[44] cites the case of Charles II succeeding to the sixth Duke of Lennox as his heir. Stair is quite prepared for the king to hold privately of himself in chief, an impossible idea in England.

In this small matter, then, Scots law showed greater maturity than English law in being able to distinguish the king from his office. Modern statutes have created a position not unlike that which prevailed in Scotland for the whole kingdom.[45] By the Act of 1862

37 Craig 1.16.2–3; Esmein, *Histoire*, 328.
38 E.g. A.P.S., ii, 42, 1. Conacher, 'Feudal Tenures in Scotland in the 15th and 16th Centuries' (1936) 48 Jur. Rev. 189; Stair, II.3.35; Erskine, II.6.13 *et seq.*
39 An Act of James II allowed the King (and others) to let lands out on feu farm: A.P.S., ii, 49. This was one factor in the process whereby feu became the predominant tenure in Scotland (*see* Chapter 7, *infra*). See also A.P.S., iv, 131, 4–5; v, 27, 10–11 and *King's Advocate v Morton* (1669) M 7857.
40 Stair, II.4.52; *Bishop of Dumblain v Kinloch* (1676) M 7950, 7952.
41 Craig, 1.16.1.
42 Stair, II.4.51–2.
43 *Murray v Vassals* (1629) M 7789, 9336.
44 Stair, II.4.2.
45 Crown Private Estate Act 1800, extended by Crown Lands Act 1823 and Crown Private Estates Acts 1862 and 1873.

the Queen is expressly authorised to hold of herself as Stair had suggested.[46] It is not quite correct to say that the Queen holds these estates exactly as a subject, for if the power of alienation is not exercised *inter vivos* or by will, the lands in question do not pass according to the ordinary intestate succession rules, but to the successor *jure coronae*, for example to the elder[47] of two daughters only, and so become part of the ordinary – public – estates of the Crown.[48]

Some Scots writers assert that not only the king's lands, but also those of the Prince and Great Steward of Scotland, that is the heir apparent, are held allodially.[49] These lands, the ancestral property of the Stewarts, were settled by Parliament[50] on a limitation almost identical with that by which the Duchy of Cornwall is regulated in England.[51] But these Scots authorities must not be misunderstood. These lands are held allodially only when in the hands of the Sovereign because of the absence of a competent heir apparent, in the English sense of that term.[52] At other times the prince holds them feudally like an ordinary tenant-in-chief of his father or mother. This is made clear by the fact that whereas ward-holding vassals-in-chief could not alienate without the king's consent, such vassals of the prince could do so, like those of other subject superiors.[53] The prerogative rights of wardship referred to earlier belonged to the king in respect of these lands while he held them, but were not enjoyed by the prince, who ranked as a subject for this purpose.[54] But on the other hand vassals of the prince did have the franchise like vassals-in-chief of the Crown.[55]

A very different alleged exception in Scots law to the universality of the doctrine of derivative tenure is said to arise under certain modern statutes relating to the compulsory purchase of land.[56] The

46   Crown Private Estates Act 1862, ss 4, 6.
47   Farran (1953), M.L.R., 140.
48   Chitty, *Prerogatives of the Crown*, 206.
49   E.g. Dobie, 'Udal Law', *Sources* (Stair Society, Vol 1), 461.
50   27th November 1469; *Complete Peerage*, title 'Rothesay'.
51   *The Prince's Case* (1608) 8 Co Rep 1a, 13b; *Complete Peerage* title 'Cornwall'.
52   I.e. one whose claim cannot be defeated by the birth of a nearer heir. For the Scots sense of the term, *see* Bell, *Principles*, s 1677.
53   *Cathcart v Vassals* (1629) M 4176.
54   *Murray v Vassals* (1629) M 7789, 9336.
55   McDouall, *Institute*, II.3.2.
56   Stated to be allodial by Dobie, 'Udal Law', *Sources* (Stair Society, Vol 1). 462; Green's *Encyclopaedia*, title 'Superior and Vassal'.

reason for its establishment has been said to be that 'ground taken for a canal or railway under the powers of an Act of Parliament is a subject to which it is not easy to apply the law of real property in Scotland. Accordingly, the plan . . . has been to give the promoters . . . the full rights and interests of proprietors . . . but to withhold from them everything like a feudal title. They are not intended to hold their right to the soil of a superior.'[57]

The statutes in question do not expressly enact that the compulsory purchaser shall hold allodially. Indeed, s 126 of the Land Clauses Consolidation (Scotland) Act 1845, (the main Act relied on in this connection) expressly states that the statutory title shall not affect or diminish the Right of Superiority in the lands in question, 'Which shall remain entire in the Person granting such Rights and Titles'. By s 80, moreover, the title of compulsory acquirers is to be a 'complete and valid feudal title'. These sections and others in the same Act were considered by the Court of Session in a number of nineteenth century cases in the course of which the Parliamentary counsel who drafted the sections referred to were severely criticised as having had 'but a very misty conception of the relation of superior and vassal'.[58] The Court of Session did not shrink from calling a Statute of the Realm 'self-contradictory and absurd'[59] and 'nonsense.'[60] The settled view came to be that, in spite of ambiguities and errors in the wording of the Act, its effect was to give the compulsory buyer a quasi-allodial title free from all feudal conditions and obligations: that is a title which, while allodial in fact, admits of the theoretical ultimate sovereignty of the Crown. This was an aspect of the matter not clearly dealt with in the cases, which were concerned not with theory, but with the practical effects of superiority as a living force.

This 'settled view' was challenged and reconsidered by the House

---

57 Lord President Inglis (then L.J-C.) in *Macfarlane v Monklands Railway Co* (1864) 2 Macph 529. *See also Heriot's Trust v Caledonian Railway Co* 1915 SC (HL) 52; *Duke of Argyll v L.M.S. Railway Co* 1931 SC 309. Of course, if a company takes by voluntary agreement the ordinary feudal relationship is created: *McCorkindale v Caledonian Railway* (1893) 31 SLR 561.

58 Lord President Inglis in *Macfarlane v Monklands Railway Co* (1864) 2 Macph 519 at 530.

59 *Magistrates of Elgin v Highland Railway Co* (1884) 11 R 950 at 958.

60 *Macfarlane v Monklands Railway Co* (1864) 2 Macph 529 at 531; also 'blundering ignorance', at 529.

of Lords in *Heriot's Trust v Caledonian Railway Company* (1915).[61]
Here a majority in the Inner House had upset the 'settled' view by
ruling that the effect of the statute was not to create an allodial
holding, but merely to effect an automatic and compulsory entry of
the company with the superior of the lands in question, whose
superiority was by other sections rendered virtually worthless from a
financial point of view. On appeal to the House of Lords, the House
lent rather obviously on its Scots member, Lord Dunedin, whose
judgment cautiously avoids a decision on the point of theory now
being considered, calling the matter 'academic'. Lord Atkinson said
'all superiorities . . . *up to that of the Crown* are terminated and
cease any longer to exist.'[62] Lord Haldane, L.C., did not think that
the expression 'feudal' as used in s 80 could be satisfied by the
hypothesis of an allodial title.[63]

The conclusion must be that these lands are not held by a truly
allodial tenure and that there is consequently no breach here in the
universality of the doctrine under consideration. But what is
significant is that the Scots judges have been quite prepared to
consider calmly whether such a breach may or may not exist, not
being firmly prejudiced against such a breach as English judges are.
They also tend to assume, again unlike the English judges, that
where the practical effects of feudal tenure are gone, there must be
an allodial holding. If this were so we should have to conclude that
most of the land in England has been allodial, not feudal, since the
later Middle Ages.

How unnecessary it is to view these holdings under statute as
allodial is shown by the corresponding position in English law.
English lawyers have for so many centuries been familiar with the
idea of the relationship of tenure continuing to exist without any
outward sign of its survival (such as the payment of feu duties or
entry with the superior) that to them the mere absence of these
things does not make it necessary to abandon the doctrine itself.
For them, therefore, there is no significant difference between the
position of companies holding land acquired by compulsory purchase
and those holding theirs as the result of voluntary conveyances.

61   1915 SC (HL) 52; [1915] AC 1046.
62   1915 SC (HL) 52 at 72; [1915] AC 1046 at 1085; (cf Lord Parmoor at 75–6 and
      1090 respectively).
63   1915 SC (HL) 52 at 57; [1915] AC 1046 at 1067.

Unfortunately, however, the extremely academic nature of the doctrine of tenure in modern English law has meant that some points of considerable theoretical importance are a matter of controversy and consequent uncertainty. This is particularly true of the tenurial position of a corporation, the question at issue being whether such a body holds an absolute fee simple of the Queen or mesne lord of the land in question,[64] or holds a conditional fee[65] of the grantor: that is whether, in the language of Scots law, the grant is to be viewed as one *a me* or one *de me*.

The classical writers on English law favoured the latter alternative. Thus Blackstone, closely following Coke,[66] wrote, 'the law doth annex a condition to every such grant, that if the corporation be dissolved the grantor shall have the lands again, because the cause of the grant faileth.' This passage was approved as being good law by a Divisional Court in *Hastings Corporation v Letton*[67] (in which some of the land had been compulsorily acquired) and by the Court of Appeal in *Re Woking Urban Council.*[68]

Why then, it may be asked, is there any controversy? The reason lies in the practical difficulty that, if Blackstone's view were correct, the corporation could not alienate land for a greater period than its own life. Yet alienations by corporations have been held to pass an estate which will outlive the granting body. In spite of the headnote, which is erroneous, this had happened in *Hastings Corporation v Letton*,[69] the first corporation having assigned the land to the one under consideration and then been dissolved. This makes the decision somewhat difficult to follow. Preston's view[70] that the corporation had a conditional fee for enjoyment, but an absolute fee for alienation, has not found much approval: and in *Re Sir*

---

64 The mesne lord tends to be untraceable when tenurial points occur in English cases. In the absence of a known mesne lord tenure in chief of the Crown is presumed. (Y.B. 14 Ed. IV, 5; 3 Hen. VII, 12; 13 Hen. VII, 4; 15 Hen. VII, 7).

65 This is the term usually employed. For the technical, but still important, distinction between conditional and determinable fees, *see* Megarry and Wade, 74–82.

66 Bl. Comm., i, 484–5; Co. Litt., i, 13b. *The Prior of Spalding's Case*, Y.B. 7 Ed. IV, 10–12. *See also Att.-Gen. v Lord Gower* (1740) 9 Mod Rep 224 per Lord Hardwicke, L.C. at 226; *Marriot v Mascal*, 1 Anderson 202.

67 [1908] 1 KB 378.

68 [1914] 1 Ch 300, especially *per* Cozens-Hardy, M.R. *See also Re Higginson and Deane* [1899] 1 QB 325 and *Re Albert Road, Norwood* [1916] 1 Ch 289.

69 [1908] 1 KB 378.

70 Preston, *Essay on Abstracts of Title*, 272. cf Gray, *Perpetuities*, ss 44–51.

Thomas Spencer Wells,[71] the most recent Court of Appeal case on the subject, very cold water has been poured on the doctrine as as whole. Although it was mentioned in argument, none of the Lords Justices considered in their judgments the previous Court of Appeal decision in *Re Woking Urban Council*,[72] which seems against them, but instead they confined their attention to attacks on the decision in *Hastings Corporation v Letton*.[73] The point before them was whether an equity of redemption passed to the Crown or not, so the case is not quite on all fours as a direct authority against the traditional view. The theory adopted was that a body corporate normally takes a fee simple absolute which it can freely alienate.[74] Because of *Quia Emptores* this necessarily implies that the holding is *a me*.

Notwithstanding this case, a County Court judge has shown in a particularly careful judgment that the traditional view may still be preferred.[75] Apart from the old authorities he has in his favour the decision in *Re Woking Urban Council*,[76] and, it would seem, the language of an extremely important modern statute; for the Law of Property Act 1925 s 7 (2) speaks of 'a fee simple vested in a corporation which is liable to determine by reason of the dissolution of the corporation.' The traditional view cannot therefore be considered erroneous and the point remains an open one. It is likely to remain so, as statutes [77] now provide machinery to ensure that a company is not dissolved while assets still remain. If by an oversight any do, they go to the Crown, but this does not apply to a bare legal estate vested in the company as a trustee.[78]

In Scotland the problem under discussion never arises, for when companies take as a result of ordinary conveyances and not under compulsory powers, the grant may be *a me* or *de me* just like any other Scots grant between private individuals. Enough has perhaps

71 [1933] 1 Ch 29.
72 [1914] 1 Ch 300.
73 [1908] 1 KB 378.
74 This view is also held in America, even when the company may by its charter not continue for more than a fixed term of years (*Restatement*; *Property* Vol 1, s 34: *Diamond v Husbands* (1898) 8 Del Ch 205).
75 *British General Insurance Co. Ltd., v Att.-Gen.* [1945] LJNCCR 113, *per* Judge Wethered.
76 [1914] 1 Ch 300.
77 E.g. Companies Act 1948, s 354. *See also* 9 Halsbury's Laws of England (4th ed) para 1398.
78 Companies Act 1948, s 354.

been said to show that even if the acquisition is under compulsory powers, there is no need to destroy the feudal theory so far as the Crown is concerned.

FEUDAL TENURE

We now pass from the actual or alleged exceptions to the doctrine of universal derivative tenure to a consideration of the various types of tenure by which land might be held on a feudal basis under the two systems. Before commencing a detailed examination of these tenures, it must be explained that their traditional grouping according to the services to be rendered, so familiar to the modern student, is by no means as early as might be expected.

The classical division of tenures in English law was not fully developed in the time of Bracton.[79] Even Littleton treats burgage as a tenure distinct from socage.[80] This, although well in accord with the Scots view, does not represent the received English law of later times, which treats burgage only as a variety of socage. Exactly the same is true of barony, which in Bracton's time was treated as distinct from knight's service, yet became merged in that tenure in classical English law. In Scotland it retained much more independence, as did feu farm, whose English equivalent (fee farm) was merged in socage, again contrary to Bracton's view. Here, as so often in this investigation, we see Scotland retaining pre-Edward I law, which has been extensively modified in England. In Scotland, contrariwise, the *Regiam Majestatem* speaks of socage as a distinct tenure,[81] which the later Scots law has declined to do. Probably it was not until the time of Craig that the Scots tenures were finally classified under the modern headings.[82]

Much more than a mere question of classification is involved in this point. Many of the fixed rules as to the incidents of particular tenures were not fully developed when the whole institution of tenure ceased to be of practical importance in England.[83] The same

79 P. & M., i, 239.
80 *Tenures*, s 162; as to burgage, *see* Chapter 7.
81 *Regiam*, II.21. Primogeniture, however, did not apply, as in England in Glanvil's time, and succession was by all the sons.
82 As to which see Stair, II.3.13.
83 Potter, *Historical Introduction to English Law*, 476.

was also true of Scotland, where some very important questions of feudal law, especially as to the effect of forfeiture, were not fully answered until after the Rising of 1745 which caused the abolition of ward-holding and indeed of most of the practical substance of feudalism itself for almost all but conveyancing purposes. In Scotland, 'the variety and confusion of tenures previous to the Feu-Farm Act of 1457 has never been fully appreciated. Every possible combination of lease and ward and blench-farm holding seems to have been adopted.'[84]

The distinction between the various tenures probably originated in the different types of tenant who happened to be holding the land.[85] Thus if the king gave land to a faithful warrior, he naturally looked for service of a military nature from the holder of that land. If, on the other hand, it was given to his personal chef, the services to be expected would be of a culinary nature. William I granted the manor of Addington to his chief cook on the Conquest expedition for the service of cooking each king a plate of porridge on his coronation day.[86] Then again, if the lord of a manor granted to his serfs a piece of land within the manor, he would expect to receive servile or 'unfree' services in return. Finally, if one had received a special favour through the intercession of a saint or of a religious community, one would give lands to the saint or convent without demanding any earthly service, though no doubt expecting the spiritual service to continue. These spiritual tenures form the subject of the next chapter.

84   Grant, *S.E.D.S.*, 39.
85   This survived in the case of frankalmoign, which throughout its history was never open to laymen.
86   *Crown and Empire, The Times* 1937, 70.

4 The Spiritual Tenures

The first tenures which we shall consider are those of a purely ecclesiastical character: frankalmoign and tenure by divine service in England, mortification and the allegedly allodial kirk lands in Scotland. These tenures are taken first, although they are neither the most common, nor the most typically feudal, because they are undoubtedly the oldest and the nearest to the allodial and pre-feudal tenures which we have so far considered. The giving of lands to God and his priests is a very ancient human trait.[1] Such gifts are apt to prove much more permanent than temporal holdings, because the donee does not have to produce an unbroken succession of issue, is unlikely to commit treason or be bankrupted, is never under age or insane, and usually owes no secular service for default in which the land might be seized.

ENGLISH LAW

Land held by the Anglo-Saxon clergy as book-land passed through to the Norman era with at first even its name unaltered. Many English churches, the humble as well as the cathedrals and their closes, are still in the hands of lineal successors of the original donees in pre-Conquest times. But this very continuity created a problem for the Norman lawyers with their theory of the universal derivation of all landholding from the king and the consequent subjection of all landholders to his jurisdiction. The abbots and bishops often claimed to hold their lands in absolute *alodium*, free from all secular burdens. Some could even produce charters from William I's Saxon predecessors to this effect.[2] Indeed they tried to go further and argued that

1 Genesis, Chapter 47, vv 19–26.
2 P. & M., i, 60.

the lands they held were *res sacrae*[3] subject to no human law or jurisdiction other than that of the Vicar of Christ.[4]

What was in effect a compromise was achieved in England. The Church came to agree that in theory she held her frankalmoign lands of the Crown, but that no temporal services or even fealty could be claimed for them.[5] The only control which the royal courts had over the matter in the early Middle Ages was that they insisted that whether the land was held in frankalmoign and therefore immune from their jurisdiction or not should be found as a fact by a lay tribunal.[6] If both parties to a dispute agreed that the lands were frankalmoign, the royal courts could not intervene.[7] But the Church courts had lost much ground even by Bracton's time.[8] Whether frankalmoign lands owed any spiritual services, such as an obligation to say masses for the souls of the donor and his relations, was a matter of conscience and spiritual discipline to be dealt with by the Ordinary or spiritual superior of the donee, rather than by normal processes of law. But the donee or his heir could lodge a complaint in the church court and so move the Ordinary to action.[9] Throughout its history no lay tenant could ever hold his land in frankalmoign. Accordingly, if a holder in frankalmoign alienated to a layman, the donee held in socage. Later this was so even though the alienation was to another ecclesiastical body.[10] The test of frankalmoign was whether the grant was *in liberam eleemosinam.*[11]

Later medieval lawyers drew a distinction between frankalmoign, the essential characteristic of which was, in the view of the law, the absence of any defined feudal services, and what Littleton calls 'Tenure per Divine Service', where some definite service, albeit of a

3   An inspiration from the Roman Law's classification of property: Gaius, *Institutes*, II.3–9; Justinian, *Institutes*, 2.1.7, 8, 10.
4   Ross, *Lectures*, ii, 37 quotes French examples. For the English position *see* P. & M., i. 250.
5   Littleton, *Tenures*, s 135.
6   This was the famous Assize, *Utrum.* (P. & M., i, 247 *et seq.*). For an apparent Scots equivalent of this assize *see Regiam*, II. 34; but also Lord Cooper's note (Stair Society, Vol 11), 146.
7   Glanvil, XII.25; XIII.23, 24.
8   P. & M., i. 248.
9   Littleton, *Tenures*, s 136, as explained by Coke.
10   Littleton, *Tenures*, s 138.
11   *Ibid.*, s 133; cf P. & M., i, 241 *et seq.*; Holdsworth, *H.E.L.*, iii, 34; Chew, *Ecclesiastical Tenants-in-Chief.*

spiritual nature, had been stipulated; for example, to say a mass with a particular intention every Friday or to sing a particular service on a fixed date every year.[12] Laymen could hold by this tenure.[13] For land held by it, in Littleton's time, the lord could claim fealty and even, if necessary, distrain for the non-performance of the agreed services.[14]

Perhaps the most interesting feature of frankalmoign tenure[15] is that it appears by a legislative miscarriage to have survived to the present day.[16] The Tenures Abolition Act 1660 which abolished the military tenures in England expressly safeguarded frankalmoign from its operation.[17] When it was desired to convert the surviving examples of frankalmoign into socage in 1925, this was not done by express words. Instead the odd plan was adopted of repealing the appropriate part of section 7 of the 1660 Act just mentioned.[18] This merely put frankalmoign at the mercy of the rest of that statute, which, in the view of many writers, was powerless to harm it, since an Act for the abolition of military tenures could not affect the least military of all tenures.[19] The matter remained in dispute and probably the better view is that the 1925 repealing Act is expressly stated only to relate to deaths after 1925.[20] However, the remnant of the Tenures Abolition Act 1660 was wholly repealed by the Statute Law (Repeals) Act 1969.[21] The point is largely academic, but it seems that the coming of the Tenures Abolition Act 1660 s 7 was not in any case needed in relation to frankalmoign, because the substantive provisions of that Act did not extend to frankalmoign, in which no new tenure would be created, save by the Crown, since *Quia Emptores* 1290.[22]

---

12 Littleton, *Tenures*, s 137.
13 Blount, *Antient Tenures*, 51.
14 Littleton, *Tenures*, s 137. There was a writ *Cessavit de cantaria*: P. & M., i, 240.
15 Tenure by Divine Service may have been within the terms of the Tenures Abolition Act 1660: *see* Potter, *Historical Introduction to English Law*, 482.
16 This is the view of most modern writers, e.g. Megarry and Wade, 33; Cheshire, 86.
17 12 Car II, c 24, s 7.
18 Administration of Estates Act 1925, 2nd Schedule.
19 This was, for example, Cheshire's view (*Modern Real Property*, 86). It can be argued however, that this is a very open point.
20 Administration of Estates Act 1925, s 54; 2nd Schedule.
21 S1 and Schedule, Part III.
22 *See* 9 Halsbury's *Laws of England* (4th edn), title *Corporations*, para 1353; Co. Litt. 98a; Cheshire, 22, 86.

SCOTS LAW

In Scotland the medieval history of Church landholding was much the same as that in England, except that there were fewer anti-church statutes,[23] the Scots clergy being the allies of the Kings of Scots against their unruly nobles.[24] The Church was among the biggest landowners in Lowland Scotland:[25] Miss Grant shows[26] that for taxation the kirk lands were assessed at one-half of the total of all lands in Scotland, a proportion vastly higher than that in England.

The Scots term equivalent to frankalmoign was 'mortification', which has probably the same derivation as 'mortmain'. The land was dead to the granter, as no service was due and it could never return to him, the church corporations being expected to last for ever. It is often stated that because of this loss of services, the superior had to consent to an alienation. It would seem that this applied only to a grant *a me*, for in a grant *de me* the granter remained liable to the superior for the services.[27] An important difference from England, however, was that even lay corporations could hold by this tenure if they held for a charitable purpose.[28] Because of the vast possessions of the Church and Canon law prohibitions against their permanent alienation, the Church was one important influence by which feuing became a regular feature of the land system of Scotland. Feus at not less than the equivalent of the average annual income from the land were allowed by Canon law and several Scots statutes encouraged the practice.

According to Craig the same distinction from English practice, allowing lay corporations to hold by spiritual tenure, was made in respect of tenure by ascertained divine services, which could be

23   The most important of these statutes in England were the Mortmain Acts which prohibited conveyance of land to the Church without the King's express licence. It seems from Erskine II.1.16 that there was no such restriction in Scotland; but *see also Iter Camerarii* (A.P.S., i, 702).

24   Conacher, 'Feudal Tenures in Scotland in the Fifteenth and Sixteenth Centuries' (1936) 48 Jur. Rev., 189.

25   Innes, *Scotch Legal Antiquities*, Chapter 4.

26   *S.E.D.S.*, 223.

27   P. & M., i, 245. In English law a grant in frankalmoign had to be *de me*. Since no further grants *de me* by subjects were possible after the Statute *Quia Emptores* 1290, no new holding in frankalmoign can have begun after that date, save possibly by Crown grant.

28   *Finoury v Town of Brechin* (1682) M 7982; *Edinburgh Magistrates v Binny* (1694) M 9107; *Ross v Vassals* (1700) M 7985; *Perth Hospital v Campbell* (1724) M 5749.

enforced, if necessary, by distress, as in England where 'they made a subdivision of fees into those which have a fixed service and those in which the service is uncertain'.[29] This approach seems preferable to that of the English law, which denied the term 'divine service' to frankalmoign – a tenure in which *preces et lacrimae* were certainly expected, even if not expressly bargained for, as often happened in Scotland. The mortification *reddendo* even in the eighteenth century was 'redditis inde mihi, heredibus meis et successoribus precibus et lachrymis sive suffragiis.'[30]

The Reformation disturbance of Church landholding in Scotland was even more violent than in south Britain. By an Act of 1587 all lands mortified to religious corporations, except the manses and glebes of the parish clergy, were declared to be forfeited and annexed to the Crown because the cause of their grant – the saying of masses – had now become illegal.[31] Many were erected into temporal lordships and distributed among the royal favourites; but these lords of erection did not enjoy them for very long, for by another Act in 1633 the lands were revested in the Crown.[32] However, the lords who acquiesced in this were allowed to continue to receive the feu duties.

After the final abolition of episcopacy in 1690 the manses and glebes of parish churches represent the sole remnant of the vast landed possessions of the medieval church. These are still mortified fees on the same basis as in medieval times and are therefore not really allodial.[33] 'It might seem,' points out Andrew McDouall (Lord Bankton), 'that the manse and glebe hold of no superior, but truly they hold of the king, as other lands do.'[34] He supports this by showing that the liferent-escheat belonged to the Crown if the incumbent incurred it, whereas in ordinary feudal estates this

---

29 Craig, 1.11.21.
30 Mackenzie, *Fees*, 34.
31 Act 1587, c 29; A.P.S., iii, 431 (8).
32 Act 1633, c 10; A.P.S., v 27 (10). *See also* Grant, *S.E.D.S.* as to these Acts.
33 The institutional writers (e.g. Erskine, II.1.7.) in accordance with their Civilian upbringing deal with these lands as if they were *res sacrae* (as to which see Gaius, *Institutes*, II.3–9 and Justinian, *Institutes*, 2.1.7, 8, 10.) but they are nevertheless 'esteemed as holden of the King' (Stair, II.3.40). Cf *Fletcher v Bishop of St Andrews* (1628) B Supp, i, 258; *Spottiswoode v Fraser* (1771) M 8004.
34 McDouall, *Institute*, II.8, 6.

casualty belonged to the superior,[35] who might or might not be the sovereign. In spite, therefore, of some recent statements to the contrary,[36] these lands do not form any exception to the universality of the doctrine of tenure. This is borne out, too, in conveyancing practice.

The modern method of selling a glebe is to obtain a decree of sale under the Glebe Lands (Scotland) Act 1866, s 17 which has the effect of a conveyance by the minister of the parish at the sight of the heritors to the purchaser. An extract of the decree is recorded in the Register of Sasines and the purchaser acquires a feudal title to the lands described in the decree. He holds of the Crown for payment of one penny as if he had been infeft on a Crown Charter in his favour.[37]

The actual sites of parish churches and burial grounds had been held to be vested not in the minister, but in the heritors of the parish,[38] until recent legislation.[39] The settled view is that this was an allodial, not a feudal holding. Stair affirms this,[40] carefully distinguishing the manses and glebes just discussed. In England the church and churchyard was normally vested in the incumbent, but where there is a lay rector the freehold is in him. The vicar has, however, a complete right to the possession for all purposes connected with his spiritual duties.[41] It has never been suggested that this is an allodial holding, which is impossible in English law.

SPIRITUAL MEN: NON-SPIRITUAL TENURE

These exclusively ecclesiastical tenures were not the only tenures by which clerical corporations or individuals could hold land. They

35 *See* Chapter 5.
36 Scottish Law Commissioners, 3rd Report, 1837, p vi; Dobie, 'Udal Law', *Sources* (Stair Society, Vol 1), 462; Green's *Encyclopaedia*, title 'Superior and Vassal'.
37 For the modern law of Tiends, Church, Manse and Glebe, *see* Walker 1328–1331.
38 *Duke of Roxburghe* (1876) 3 R 728, 734; *Steel v Kirk-Session of St Cuthbert's Parish* (1891) 18 R 911, 917, 919.
39 Church of Scotland (Property and Endowments) Act 1925.
40 II.3.4.
41 *Griffin v Deighton and Davis* (1863) LJQB 29 (Church); *Greenslade v Darby* (1868) LR 3 QB 421 (Churchyard).

were under no incapacity to hold by any of the other tenures.[42] All
the prelates who had seats in the House of Lords in either country
did so because they held lands of the king in barony.[43] Professed
religious on the other hand were regarded as civilly dead and
therefore as incapable of holding land, even in frankalmoign or
mortification, as any other property.[44] Abbots and priors could,
however, hold in virtue of their official position.

In the case of ecclesiastics holding by military service, the obligation was to provide a quota of knights rather than to take up arms in
person though not all medieval prelates were averse to a little
suitable recreation on the battlefield. The Abbot of Bury St Edmunds
appeared with his knights at the siege of Windsor in 1193;[45] and
Thomas Rossy, Bishop of Candida Casa, proposed to settle the
Great Schism by personal combat with the Bishop of Norwich.[46]
Anthony Bek, Bishop of Durham, at the head of 500 horse and
1000 foot, joined Edward I in 1295 in his invasion of Scotland. In
1346 Thomas de Hatfield, Bishop of Durham, joined the army which
defeated the Scots at Neville's Cross, where two Scottish bishops
were among those killed.[47] The Primate of Scotland, two bishops
and two abbots were found dead with their king on the tragic field
of Flodden. These martial events bring us to the military tenures,
the subject of the next chapter.

42　As to holding by ecclesiastics in ward or knight's service, see McDouall, *Institute*,
　　II.3, 6; Littleton, *Tenures*, s 140.
43　Co. Litt. 70b.
44　As to the status of religious, see P. & M., i, 433 *et seq.* It is still regarded in some
　　Roman Catholic countries as imposing civil death: see Farran, 'First Impressions
　　of Austrian Law' (1951) 63 Jur. Rev., 156 at 164. English law, however, does not
　　recognise such disability, even in respect of a person domiciled in such a country;
　　Re Selot's Trusts [1902] 1 Ch 488.
45　P. & M., i, 263. In France prelates holding in feudal tenure had to serve in person
　　up to 1410 and again later (Viollet, *Histoire*, 237).
46　*Copiale Prioratus Sanctiandree, Appendix I.*
47　Low, *Diocesan Histories: Durham*, 168, 191.

5 Military Tenures: Knight's Service and Ward Holding

The tenures by military service form at once the most characteristic and, in early times at least, the commonest of the feudal tenures. This is shown by the rule in both countries that whenever a fee was granted without a clear enunciation of the services to be rendered, it was presumed to be held by military service.[1] The law as to these holdings in the two countries was extremely similar. It will therefore be possible to deal with them together, only remarking where necessary on the differences of detail.

The Scots term for tenure by knight's service is 'ward holding'. Although Stair preferred the English term,[2] the Scots one approximates more closely to the real position in England, as the time during which actual military service was demanded of these fees represents only a fraction of the time during which the tenure existed there.[3] Their distinguishing characteristic, once that period was over, consisted in the valuable incidents or casualties, which the lord could claim from or over them, especially during the infancy of the vassal.[4]

Maitland shows in his account[5] of the early history of knight's

---

1 Stair, II.3.31; *Williamson v Thomson* (M 16559). The term 'Services used and wont' also meant military services and implied the other characteristics of ward lands. After the abolition of ward holding by the Tenures Abolition Act 1746 the presumption is in favour of blench. In England there was such a presumption only when homage was owed (Co. Litt. 67b): in other cases, socage was presumed, as it must be now in all cases.
2 II.4.33.
3 Holdsworth observes (*H.E.L.*, iii, 37) that Littleton's account (*Tenures*, s 103 *et seq.*) reads almost as if he was not aware of the original significance of the tenure.
4 But some of these casualties arose in connection with other tenures: *see* Chapters 6–8.
5 P. & M., i, 225 *et seq.*

service in England that the period during which actual knight service was demanded lasted little more than a century.[6] The Plantagenets found it more convenient to take money compositions (often called scutages[7]) from their tenants-in-chief. They used the money to maintain mercenaries whose service was more efficient than that of the feudal host and was not limited to the traditional forty days' service in any one year.[8] Later even this became unworkable and recourse had to be had to Parliament for money grants, with all that that implied.[9] This stage was reached about Edward I's time.[10]

This is in complete contrast to the position in Scotland, where the army continued to be raised on the basis of feudal landholders' levies until well into the sixteenth century. When Mary of Lorraine, regent for James V, proposed the raising of a paid army the public outcry was so great that the project had to be abandoned. As late as 1509 a charter bound the Laird of Grant to supply 'a lance with its supports, *viz.*, three sufficient horsemen, for each £10 of land, in time of war beyond the kingdom'.[11] Medieval Scotland was too poor a country to support a standing army.[12] The Scots kings, however much they may have wished to do so in the interest of public order, never wholly converted their vassals-in-chief to the idea of paying taxes instead of fighting in person attended by their dependant tenants. As Miss Grant says, 'the connection between landholding and military service was the fundamental theory upon which the military

---

6 *Ibid.*, 231, but he refers at p 272 to a case in 1257. In France actual service was apparently demanded as late as the sixteenth century (Viollet, *Histoire*, 257).

7 Maitland thought that this term was improperly applied as between the Crown and its tenants-in-chief (P. & M., i, 268); cf Chew, 37 E.H.R. 32 and 38 E.H.R. 19 and Potter, *Historical Introduction to English Law*, 477. Littleton, *Tenures*, s 95, uses the term 'escuage' (scutagium) of tenants-in-chief.

8 This is the traditional view. Littleton, for example, says (*Tenures*, s 95): '*quant le roy face voyage royal en Escoce, pur subduer les Scotes, donques il que tient per un fee de service de chivaler, covient estre ove le roy pur XL jours bien et convenablement array pur le guerre*'. Maitland, however, maintained that this meant forty days service at the tenant's own expense and that longer service could be required at the King's expense (P. & M., i, 255).

9 Magna Carta 1215 c 12 prohibited scutages save by the common consent ('*nisi per commune concilium*').

10 Holdsworth, *H.E.L.*, iii, 45.

11 Grant, *S.E.D.S.*, 178.

12 *Ibid.*, 95.

organisation of the nation was built.'[13] The survival of military service to vassals is closely linked with the vassal's power of jurisdiction to compel them to serve. Maitland shows that the lack of such jurisdiction very early caused a commutation of the services into money in England at an early date.[14] Indeed, by the fourteenth century even the levy of scutage had ceased.[15]

The dangers of such a situation are obvious and Scotland experienced them to the full. The medieval history of Scotland is one of unending feuds anyone locally or nationally strong enough to do so feeling free to take the law into his own hands. We have already noted this happening in the Highlands, but it continued for a surprisingly long time in the rest of Scotland. Even as late as the Reformation, Gordon of Cluny, wanting some lands at Midstrath and Marywell, besieged the owner with armed men, burnt his house and would have hanged him had he not prudently signed away his rights to the lands. The charter was recorded in the proper way and is now in the Register House.[16] In 1578 a bailie of Edinburgh bought some land in the Lothians but the Laird of Dalhousie killed three of the servants sent to till it, as well as all the plough-oxen.[17] The Lothians had been for centuries the centre of the most civilised part of Scotland. It is hard to imagine such an outrage taking place in the home counties of Elizabethan England. In Scotland it was almost a matter of course. 'Hosting', or the levying of private armies by the feudal holders of land, was finally stamped out only after 1745, though it was declared illegal by an Act of 1716[18] which provided that 'personal attendance, hosting, hunting, watching, and warding' due under any charter were to be discharged by money payments only. But the Jacobites of 1745 declined to recognise what was to them a usurper's statute, and it was suppressed at the same time as ward-holding was abolished. There was, then, no real parallel to the English position, where these tenures continued for five centuries after the military duties for which they were designed had fallen into abeyance.

13 *Ibid.*, 179.
14 P. & M., i, 272.
15 Holdsworth, *H.E.L.*, iii, 44, 45. Megarry and Wade, 16.
16 From a MS history of the Irvines, cited by Grant, *S.E.D.S.*, 274.
17 Grant, *S.E.D.S.*, 189.
18 1 Geo I, c 54, s 10.

INCIDENTS OF MILITARY TENURES

The incidents or casualties to which the superior of lands held by military tenure was entitled were practically identical in both laws, springing from the general feudal law of western Europe. Craig's work, based as it is on Cujas and other feudalists, as well as on the *Libri Feudorum*, clearly demonstrates this. Apart from the rather indefinite obligation of military service in Scotland they represent the economic reason why these tenures lasted so long as they did. Scots lawyers lacked the opportunity to employ such devices as the use to circumvent the snags of holding by these tenures, as there was no separate Court of Equity. This fact preserved their practical importance far longer there than in England.

The aid was the only incident that was likely to fall during the lifetime of an adult tenant, unless he was at fault in some way. It was a payment which the lord could call for from his vassal, at first for undefined purposes. These were settled for England by Magna Carta[19] as being only three: (1) to ransom the lord from imprisonment; (2) for the knighting of the lord's eldest son; and (3) for the dower of his eldest daughter. The age *pur faire fitz chivalier* was fifteen, the age *pur file marier*, seven.[20] In the absence of Magna Carta the indefinition remained in Scotland. The *Regiam Majestatem* allows the lord to claim an aid towards paying his own relief to his superior, but leaves open whether it was claimable to carry on a war or to dower younger daughters.[21] Skene seems to consider these still open questions in his day. (His edition of *Regiam Majestatem* is dated 1609.) Craig refuses dower in theory to any but the eldest daughter;[22] but allows an aid to pay the superior's relief and even in three cases to support a destitute superior. These are:

> First, if his destitute condition is attributable to some act of the vassal; second, if the superior has shown the vassal a generous measure of liberality in excess of his obligations; and third, if

19 1215, c 20. This clause did not appear in subsequent regrants of the Charter and some aids were apparently taken later for other purposes.
20 Co. Litt., 78b.
21 *Regiam*, II.73.
22 Craig, 2.11.22.

the feu is so profitable as to afford support both for the superior and the vassal.[23]

The next casualty was that which arose on the death of a tenant.[24] This shows convincingly that fees were originally granted for life only, and that the heir could not succeed his ancestor in the lands except as the result of a special exercise of favour towards him by the superior.[25] Of course this favour might be stimulated by financial encouragement: thus if the heir was of full age he had to pay what was called in both countries a relief. At first, like any other bargain, this would depend on the resources, financial or otherwise, of the parties.[26] Later, attempts were made in England to settle the relief at a fixed payment per knight's fee or barony.[27] In Scotland precise obligations in terms of knight's fees seem to have been rare, the military service due being left undefined.[28] The amount in ward-fees was one year's value of the land.[29] In non-military fees, where relief was also payable, it became fixed in England as one year's rent and in Scotland at one year's feu duty in addition to the rent or feu duty normally payable.[30] Holdsworth says that in theory reliefs could still be demanded in England,[31] but they were certainly abolished in Scotland by the Feudal Casualties (Scotland) Act 1914.[32]

In Scotland there was another casualty called composition consisting of one year's net rent of the lands[33] and exigible, in the absence of special stipulation, from a singular successor of the vassal on his entry with the superior, after receiving a disposition and instrument of sasine during the lifetime of the vassal. This too

23   Craig, 2.11.24 (Lord Clyde's Translation, Vol 1, 601).
24   Some casualties also arose on the admission of an assignee, but assignment was only rarely possible. *See also* Chapter 24.
25   For this period *see* Craig, 1.4. As to the inheritability of fees in post-Conquest England, see P. & M., i, 314 and Stenton, *The First Century of English Feudalism.*
26   Holdsworth, *H.E.L.,* iii, 59.
27   For amounts payable at various dates see Holdsworth, *H.E.L.,* iii, 60; P. & M., i, 308.
28   Stair, II.3.31; but cf Appendix V, *infra.*
29   Stair, II.4.27; Craig, 2.20.30.
30   Stair, II.4.27; Holdsworth, *H.E.L.,* iii, 60; cf Glanvil, IX.4. *Regiam* II.71 states fixed sums for knight's fees, etc., taken from Glanvil. It is uncertain whether they applied in Scotland other than in the small area with common feudal law with England but this seems to have passed out of memory by Craig's time.
31   *H.E.L.,* ii, 61.
32   S 18.
33   Act 1469, c 36.

was abolished by the Feudal Casualties (Scotland) Act 1914 which also provided formulae for the redemption of relief and composition.[34]

Tenants-in-chief holding directly of the Crown in England had to do more than merely pay relief. The king by his prerogative was entitled to the 'primer seisin', that is to take possession of the lands so held before the heir could come into them and to hold them until such time as that heir had formally proved his title at an inquisition held by a royal official after the death of his predecessor, had done homage, had paid not merely his relief, but the equivalent of the first year's rent and profits from the land, and finally sued for the lands by the process called *ouster le main*.[35] The heirs of all other lands were able to enter without formality on paying the usual relief. Even by Glanvil's day the lord could not interfere with an heir already informally in possession, although he might enter and take a purely formal seisin.[36] This marks a very early divergence of English from Scots and most continental feudal law. It may be linked with the extreme importance of seisin in England, with which we shall deal in Chapter 23.

In Scotland there seems to have been no special right of the king akin to primer seisin,[37] but all heirs, not merely those holding of the Crown, had first to be 'served', that is, to prove their titles to be heir and then enter formally with the superior.[38] Non-entry involved the most serious consequences. It is spoken of in Scotland as a distinct casualty and by some writers as the most important of all.[39] If the heir did not enter, the fee was not extinguished, but on declarator of non-entry (that is, a judgment to that effect), the superior might go into possession of the land himself and take all the profits until the vassal entered, for the superior was entitled to have a vassal and, moreover, a vassal feudally invested: hence the maxim *nulla sasina, nulla terra* and the rules against an abeyance of seisin.[40] After all, if

---

34 Feudal Casualties (Scotland) Act 1914, ss 5, 6 and Schedule A.
35 Holdsworth, *H.E.L.*, iii, 61; Bl. Comm., ii, 66.
36 Glanvil, VII.9; IX.4.
37 Craig, 2.20.25.
38 There were important procedual differences between cases where the Crown was superior and all others. *See also* Chapter 24.
39 Stair, II.4, 18; Craig, 2.19.2.
40 Challis, *The Law of Real Property*, 100, 101; *see also* Chapter 25 *infra*.

the feudal relation did fundamentally rest, as has been suggested, on the reciprocal oath of homage, it is only logical to require this or its equivalent before admitting a new vassal. The English king's prerogative of primer seisin was probably derived from a similar consideration.[41]

INFANT TENANTS

If the heir were unfortunate enough to be still under age at the time of his ancestor's death, the superior was entitled to even more profitable rights. The age in question was early fixed at twenty-one for males in both countries. As to females, it was fourteen in Scotland, the reason being that males were not ready to perform their duty of fighting and counsel until twenty-one, but females were then capable of marriage at this tender age. In England the coming of age of females was long unsettled,[42] but eventually it was fixed at fourteen[43] as in Scotland, although if a girl was once in wardship under fourteen she remained subject to it until sixteen.[44]

To the lord belonged the ward or guardianship of the infant and the absolute control of all the lands held of himself by military tenure,[45] without at first any liability to account for his stewardship on the heir's attaining full age.[46] This right has often been vilified as unjustifiable, but if we consider it from the feudal standpoint just discussed, we can appreciate its logical force. The superior is entitled to have a vassal, for the lands were not granted absolutely, but on the very condition of vassalage. Nor would any vassal do but only one feudally infeft and physically and mentally capable of discharging the military and other services due to the lord from the tenant in consideration for the grant of the land. If the vassal was incapable because of tender years, there was in effect a non-entry,

---

41 Bl. Comm., ii, 66.
42 Bracton, f 86b.
43 Littleton, *Tenures*, s 103.
44 Statute of Westminster I, 1275, c 22.
45 Co. Litt. 77a; P. & M., i, 121; Stair, II.4.48; *Regiam*, II.44.
46 He became liable for waste, in England by Magna Carta 1215, cc 5, 6; in Scotland by Act of 1491, c 25 (A.P.S., ii, 224). He had always been liable to maintain (aliment) the heir.

albeit temporary and involuntary. Then, too, if fees were originally for life only, as has been suggested, the keeping of the fee vacant until the late tenant's heir is old enough to take it represents a considerable concession on the part of the superior.

Craig said that he was in 'considerable doubt'[47] as to the origin of wardships in England but subscribed to the legend that about 1216 the magnates of England conceded to King Henry the wardship of their heirs and of their lands.[48] As to the practice in Scotland, he says, 'It is no doubt possible that our King Malcolm may have brought in the observance of ward from the already well-established customs of other countries.'[49] As long ago as Selden[50] the Henry III story was shown to be apocryphal. What is so remarkable is that the English legend post-dated the origin of these rights to Glanvil, who deals with wardships at length.[51] Why the legendary event was not ascribed to Alfred or at least the Conqueror, seems beyond explanation.

In Scotland the right of wardship was often compounded for a regular annual payment. This early insurance scheme was known as 'taxed ward'. English landowners did not need it because by means of the use they came to be able to avoid this incident altogether.

The lord's other right in relation to an infant tenant, that of marriage, seems less defensible as a general right. Glanvil, however, deals with the lord's right of marriage only in relation to female heirs[52] and it may well have been so restricted at first. If so, it would appear to be a much more reasonable proposition, for the superior could claim with some justice that a young girl was a totally unsuitable tenant for a military fee, unless and until she had a husband to act on her behalf. Another argument was that she might marry into a family antagonistic to the lord, which must have been a very real danger in Scotland, with all its feuds between rival clans and 'bands'.

The right consisted in the privilege of the lord to choose a match

47 Craig, 2.20.3.
48 *Chronica de Melsa*, i, 443. (Craig, 2.20.4).
49 Craig, 2.20.4 (Lord Clyde's Translation, Vol 2, 805).
50 *Notes on Fortiscue*, 44.
51 Glanvil, VII.9.
52 Glanvil, VII.12.

for the young vassal (in later times whether male or female), a highly remunerative privilege in those business-like days. Wardships and marriages, especially those belonging to the Crown, were a form of investment put up to the highest bidder. A nice element of speculation was present as the heir might die before the investor had enjoyed his estates or sold him in marriage. He must provide someone from the same social class as the ward, but only three classes were recognised: the nobility, burgesses and countryfolk. There must not be extreme disparity in age, nor must the proffered spouse suffer from grave physical or mental defects. A widow should not be offered, as by marrying her the youth would lose the possibility of benefit of clergy.[53] The ward could not be absolutely forced to marry the highest bidder, but a refusal involved the heavy penalty called the 'avail' of the marriage, that is, what it was worth in the open market. In the end the avail came to be payable in every case, even if the ward married with the superior's consent[54] or the lord neglected to procure a spouse.[55] Although great care was no doubt taken to prevent an elopement, the law had its answer if such a mishap occurred: double the avail would have to be paid as a penalty.[56] If the unfortunate maid preferred to immure herself in a nunnery, this thwarting of the lord's rights was equally expensive.[57]

When the vassal at length came of age, he was able to sue for the lands out of the hands of the lord, but in Scotland only after due service as heir and paying the same relief as an adult successor.[58] In England he was spared both the formality of service and the payment unless he held in chief of the Crown.[59]

If there was no heir capable of taking under the terms of investiture at all, the English lord was entitled to take the land by escheat *propter defectum sanguinis*. In Scotland the king, not the superior, got the land in this eventuality.

---

53   Co. Litt. 8ob. See *Quoniam Attachiamenta*, c 92 for the penalities on a superior who forced such a marriage.
54   *Campbell v Lord McNaughton* (1677) M 8535; *Arbuthnot v Keiths* (1662) M 8528.
55   *Palmer v Wilder* (1606) 5 Co Rep 126b; *Lord Darcie's Case* (1607) 6 Co Rep 70b.
56   Littleton, *Tenures*, s 110 (following Statute of Merton 1235). *Quoniam Attachiamenta*, c 91.
57   Viner, *Abridgement*, title 'Guardian and Ward', XIV, 191.
58   Craig, 2.20.22.
59   Bl. Comm., ii, 66. If he held directly of the Crown he had to sue out livery and yield half a year's value of the land to the King (Bl. Comm., ii, 76).

ERRANT TENANTS

The last group of feudal incidents arose because of some wrongful act of the vassal. From the earliest days of feudalism, the tenant had to behave properly in relation to the superior or he forfeited the fee.[60] English law knew only one casualty of this type – escheat – but Scots law penalised also what it called recognition, disclamation and purpresture.

Escheat *propter delictum tenentis* was the penalty suffered by the tenant in England who committed felony. This term originally meant a gross breach of the feudal bond created by homage. While it did so it perfectly logically caused the loss of the tenant's whole interest to the lord. Thus if he had an estate in fee simple, the whole fee was lost but if he had only a life interest the escheat would be for his lifetime. Special rules applied to an estate tail.[61] The original justification of escheat *propter delictum tenentis* was that the tenant who held land on condition of fidelity naturally lost it if he was unfaithful; but felony later came to mean any serious crime.[62] Once that stage was reached the logic of escheat to the lord was gone. The felon had offended against the State: therefore, it would seem, he ought to forfeit his lands to the State. But, owing to Magna Carta,[63] the English kings failed to achieve this, except in the case of the supreme offence against the State and the feudal bond alike: high treason. For this, 'forfeiture' was the proper term, rather than escheat. The king had also a strange and logically indefensible prerogative to the 'year, day and waste' of the lands escheating to a mesne lord.[64]

In Scotland the casualty called escheat had a somewhat similar history. The *Quoniam Attachiamenta*[65] shows us a situation akin to that in England, but with one important exception: escheat (as opposed to forfeiture) was for the lifetime of the vassal only.[66] So it

60 *Libri Feudorum*, I. vii.
61 As to which *see* Chapter 12.
62 Holdsworth, *H.E.L.*, ii, 357, 358; iii, 67 *et seq.*; P. & M., ii, 467.
63 Magna Carta 1215, c 38.
64 *Ibid.* '*Nos non tenebimus terras illorum qui convicti fuerint de felonia, nisi per unum annum et unum diem, et tunc reddantur terrae dominis feodorum*'.
65 Cc 18; 48 (17). The King of Scots also enjoyed 'year, day and waste'.
66 Bell, *Principles*, 733.

continued throughout the history of Scots law,[67] despite assertions of Craig to the contrary in certain circumstances.[68] Escheat and forfeiture have now been abolished in both countries.[69]

The penalty of recognition was that which fell if the vassal holding by ward tenure in Scotland alienated more than half of the lands which he held by this tenure of any one superior without that superior's consent.[70] If he alienated by way of substitution, that is by a grant *a me de superiore meo*, not only was this deed void, but he forfeited the whole of his interest in the fee, so that the superior came in by the vacancy. But apparently if *V* (a vassal) alienated properly, say a third of the land he held to *A*, and then another third (improperly) to *B*, the recognition applied to the whole of *V*'s erstwhile holding, notwithstanding the obvious injustice to *A*.[71] It was this sort of injustice arising from the correct application of legal logic that the English system was able to avoid with its separate Court of Equity.

It was for long a point much debated whether a grant by way of subinfeudation, that is *de me*, was an alienation sufficient to incur recognition.[72] It is obviously arguable that the superior can have no cause for complaint, for the same vassal is still holding beneath him.[73] Occasions for a decision on the point do not seem to have arisen, but the view which prevailed was a compromise. If the sub-feu was in mortification, ward, blench or for an illusory service, this was alienation and consequently the fee recognosced to the superior; but if it was in feu farm for a real return, this was no alienation as the superior was not financially endangered.[74]

In England subinfeudation was prohibited by the Act *Quia Emptores* 1290 which, however, made recognition to a subject for ever impossible by requiring all holders of land other than tenants in

---

67   Stair, II.4.61 states the law as in *Quoniam Attachiamenta*; but arson and certain other crimes were treason in Scotland (Stair, II.3.29) and therefore caused forfeiture.
68   Craig, 3.13.15–19.
69   The Forfeiture Act 1870, s 1 abolished forfeiture in both countries and escheat in England; and the Abolition of Ward Holding Act 1746, s 11 abolished escheat for civil rebellion in Scotland.
70   Stair, II.11.17.
71   *Hay v Muirie's Creditors* (1621) M 6513; but Stair doubted this, II.11.17.
72   Craig, 3.3.22.
73   This was Bracton's view (f 45b–46b).
74   Stair, II.11.13. cf Act of 1457, c 71 (A.P.S., ii, 49); P. & M., i, 331 *et seq.*

chief to alienate only by way of substitution.[75] The position before 1290 is one of some doubt,[76] but the Charter of 1217 gave a ruling that the tenant by any tenure must not alienate so much of the fee as to leave insufficient land in his own hands to discharge his services to his lord.[77] The Scots rule was probably merely a rationalisation of this point.[78] But *Quia Emptores* did not apply to tenants-in-chief of the Crown and they could not alienate without the king's permission. The three Edwards seem to have tried to establish a rule of recognition like that in Scotland but Parliament stepped in and allowed the king only a reasonable fine instead of the forfeiture of the fee.[79] The Mortmain Acts introduced a sort of statutory recognition in England by providing that if land was alienated to a religious body contrary to the Acts, it recognosced to the lord.[80] But it was not true recognition, for the lord's consent was irrelevant. The mesne lord must act to take advantage of the recognition, or the next lord above him could do so, and so up to the king. It shows a remarkable and unusual acceptance of feudal theory in England that these gifts were not claimed by the Crown as forfeited, rather than thus allowed to go to the mesne lord. But a Crown licence of dispensation avoided the prohibitions of the Act.

Recognition in the strict sense only applied to ward holdings, but the term was also applied in a more general sense to any feudal misdeed. All tenures were liable to recognosce for such things as armed defiance of the superior.[81] Disclamation and purpresture were really only examples of recognition in this wider sense. The former meant a denial of the superior's title, the latter an encroachment on his lands or rights.[82] It seems remarkable that these comparatively minor misdeeds involved the forfeiture of the whole fee, while a felony or being outlawed caused a liferent escheat only. Neither of them was ever really known in England, presumably

75 As to *Quia Emptores*, see Plucknett, *Legislation of Edward I*; and Chapter 10.
76 P. & M., i, 329 *et seq.* Maitland concluded that 'reasonable' was very uncertain.
77 Magna Carta 1217, c 39. Megarry and Wade, 30–1.
78 Dalrymple, *An Essay towards a General History of Feudal Property* (1757).
79 *Confirmatio Cararum* 1327, cc 12, 13. The king was able to raise considerable revenues by these fines and the fees charged for a licence to alienate: P. & M., i, 336.
80 E.g. *De viris Religiosis* 1279.
81 Stair, II.11.9.
82 Craig, 3.5.2. (disclamation); 3.5.6. (purpresture).

because of the early decline in the mesne lord's feudal courts.[83] The king was well enough served by the law of treason.

Although these incidents have been dealt with in connection with the military holdings, all of them except wardship, marriage and recognition in the strict sense were common to almost all the tenures. Where this is not so, it will be mentioned. Grand serjeanty carried wardship and marriage. Feus were occasionally granted in Scotland with a special clause *cum maritagio*, as in the Crown feus in Strathearn.[84] So, too, a clause *de non alienando sine consensu superiorum* might attach recognition. The Conveyancing (Scotland) Act 1874 prohibited the creation of casualties in new feus and provided for their commutation in existing ones. The Feudal Casualties (Scotland) Act 1914 completed the work by making commutation compulsory.

Before passing to the remaining tenures, it should be noted that the military tenures were converted to socage in England in 1660 and to blench farm or feu farm in Scotland in 1746.[85]

---

83 But a case of 1225 came close to disclamation: Bracton, *Note Book* pl. 1687. However, 'it would be rash to deny that the tenant might lose the land by reviling his lord, particularly if the lord kept a court and the tenant was duly forjudged the land by his peers' (P. & M., i, 305).
84 Craig, 2.21.8–11.
85 Tenures Abolition Act 1660 (also abolishing wardship and marriage in grand serjeanty and such special prerogatives of the Crown as ousterlemain). Abolition of Wardholding Act 1747 (also abolishing the special clauses just referred to).

6 Serjeanty and Blench Holding

The English tenure called 'serjeanty' is nearest to those which have just been considered, although its meaning changed much during the six centuries of its existence and it is hard to frame a definition to cover all the varieties of serjeanty without also covering some examples of socage.[1] One might call it 'tenure by domestic service'.[2] It embraced a vast range of examples of this from the great lords of the Royal Household, who are servants only in the sense that the titles of the offices which they hold represent what were originally menial posts, to actual menials in the service of subjects. Thus, for example, at Glastonbury Abbey the porter, first cook, cellarman and others held lands by the service of discharging those offices.[3] Yet the services by which an estate held in serjeanty might be burdened were not necessarily of a domestic character. They might be to go in some subordinate capacity with the feudal host, or merely to provide some piece of military equipment. The miscellaneous character of the tenure is shown by the fact that it became necessary to subdivide it into grand and petty (or petit) serjeanty, the former being later assimilated to knight's service, implying even the incidents of wardship and marriage,[4] the latter being assimilated to socage. The dividing line was not the same as that between civil and military serjeanties: grand serjeanty involved rendering in person some honorific service (which need

---

1   Holdsworth, *H.E.L.*, iii, 46 *et seq.*; P. & M., i, 282 *et seq.*
2   Holdsworth, *H.E.L.*, iii, 46.
3   Vinogradoff, *Villainage in England*, 324.
4   By Magna Carta 1215, c 44, the dispute whether wardship and marriage were incidents of serjeanty was settled by the compromise: '*Nos non habebimus custodiam heredis vel terrae alicuius, quam tenet de alio per servitium militare, occasione alicuius parvae sergenteriae quam tenet de nobis per servitium reddendi nobis cultellos, vel sagittas, vel huiusmodi*'.

not be of a military nature) to the king,[5] while the tenant in petty serjeanty was bound to perform for the king some service of a non-personal nature.[6] But the distinction between them and between serjeanty and other tenures was shadowy.[7] They probably worked well enough in practice, however, and present difficulties over the distinction stem mainly from trying to impose a modern classification on natural formlessness. The serjeanties represent a practical attempt to meet social needs in a pre-contract society, as do many examples of socage.

By Littleton's day the rules had hardened somewhat arbitrarily. Serjeanty, whether grand or petty, must now be in chief of the Crown.[8] All petty serjeanties were military, consisting in the obligation to supply a bow, sword, lance or 'autres tiels petits choses touchants le guerre,'[9] rather than actual service. It differed only in dignity from socage.[10]

Cosmo Innes declared that Scotland 'had no tenures by serjeanty.'[11] If one insists on the name, that may have been the case, but in fact Scots lands were held in some cases by a *reddendo* exactly corresponding to the services by which lands treated in England as being held by serjeanty were enjoyed. Thus several consisting of subordinate military service[12] or of the provision of 'petits choses touchants le guerre'[13] can be traced from his pages alone. Few better examples of a holding in serjeanty exist than that of the Barony of Penicuik, whose service was blowing six blasts on a hunting horn on the moor of the Burgh of Edinburgh at the king's hunt.[14] Benham

---

5   Megarry and Wade, 16; Littleton, *Tenures*, s 153; Challis, *The Law of Real Property*, 9.
6   Megarry and Wade, 19; Blount, *Antient Tenures*, 73–184.
7   P. & M., i, 287, 323.
8   Littleton, *Tenures*, s 161. Consequently, serjeanties became inalienable without royal licence. (P. & M., i, 334).
9   Littleton, *Tenures*, ss 159–60.
10 *Ibid.*
11 *Scotch Legal Antiquities*, 62. Craig, 1.9.10. remembered a case (*Hamilton v Stewart*) where land was expressly held in petit serjeanty, but it was such a rarity that the lords did not know whether wardship and marriage fell or not and referred the question to Parliament.
12 Innes, *Scotch Legal Antiquities*, 61. There are also examples of grand serjeanty, e.g. to be the king's armour-bearer: Craig, 1.11.12.
13 Innes, *Scotch Legal Antiquities*, 64.
14 *Ibid.*, 68.

in Gloucestershire was held in return for carrying a horn in Brim-
mersfield Park at such time as the king should hunt there.[15]

These are accounted examples of the Scots blench holding,
although scarcely coming within the definition: 'whose *reddendo* is a
small elusory rent as being rather an acknowledgement of, than profit
to, the superior'.[16] The cost of two archers serving at the vassal's
expense might be far from illusory. Still more so was that owed for the
lands of Lochaw, which under a charter from Bruce were held in
return for providing a ship of forty oars for the king's service, with
sufficient men and tackle for forty days.[17] Similarly the men of
Mauldon in Essex anciently held that town by the serjeanty of
finding for the king 'unam navem cum apparatu suo quotiescunque
contigerit dictum regem ire cum exercitu extra regum Angliae per xl.
dies sumptibus suis propriis'.[18] But blench holdings overlap, as it
were, and include many examples which would in England be called
socage. Where, for example, the definition is complied with and
only some token is rendered for the land (usually on the basis of
rendering that token only if it is demanded[19]) this resembles one
type of socage. At one time there was a trend for blench holdings to
be granted by subjects for a substantial money rent,[20] which resembles another type of socage. Finally, if we accept Craig's definition of blench as 'francum feudum',[21] owing no service at all, but
only fealty, this is akin to yet a third class of socage.

Scots blench-holding reddendo clauses display a wealth of variety
and picturesqueness unrivalled south of the Border.[22] A pair of dog
collars, a pound of Zingiber, a wild duck, a mirror, a garlic head, a
load of hay, a pound of gum and a red mantle were among the
miscellaneous objects coming into the Exchequer as late as 1596.[23]

15　Blount, *Antient Tenures*, 132.
16　Stair, II.3.33; cf Bell, *Principles*, 682, 692.
17　Innes, *Scotch Legal Antiquities*, 67.
18　Blount, *Antient Tenures*, 27.
19　If not demanded within the year they fall due, the right to demand them for that
　　year is lost: *Archbishop of St Andrews v Lord Torsonce* (1610) M 15011; *Lord Sempil
　　v Blair* (1627) I Br Supp 232.
20　Conacher, 'Feudal Tenures in Scotland in the Fifteenth and Sixteenth Centuries'
　　(1936) 48 Jur. Rev., 189. Innes, *Scotch Legal Antiquities*, 63–4, notes that his
　　own lands paid 100 shillings in the time of Robert I.
21　Craig, 1.10.30.
22　See Moorehouse, 'Some Legal Survivals', 1949 Contemporary Review, 362. cf
　　Blount *Antient Tenures* as to English services.
23　Innes, *Scotch Legal Antiquities*, 65, citing *Books of the Exchequer* 9 July 1596.

A century later the tributes were being converted into money, but the officials had to know the right value of a white 'plumash' feather (surprisingly the same as that of an ox or cow), a hen, a pound of cummin seed, a long – and also a short – carriage, a boll of kain-lime, a barrel of onions, a pair of doves and a 'sheer day's work'.[24] Other odd renders included a pair of chaplets of white roses[25] (a single chaplet is met with in England[26]) and the eighth part of a neckchain of gold, the weight of a Harry noble.[27] Most curious of all, for the barony of Carnwath, two pairs of shoes, each containing half an ell of English cloth, had to be presented on Midsummer Day to the man who won a foot race.[28] Should the king visit Foulis, he must be presented, so the story goes, with a bucket of snow.[29] But, dealing with a render of a rose, Coke points out that if it were demanded in midwinter the law would not insist on impossibilities.[30] It has even been alleged that in 1495 James IV gave the castle of Sarchiemuir to Sir James Murray for the service of providing a glass of wine, some fruit and a plateful of cakes to be 'tastefully laid out on a table every New Year's Eve at midnight' for the delight of the king's grandmother's ghost.[31]

The English king did not generally receive or require such exotic tributes, but he was entitled to a pair of scarlet hose, a brace of white doves and four and twenty pasties of fresh herrings at their coming in.[32] Blount, writing in 1784, says that these last were still enjoyed by Exchequer officials in his own day.[33] The tenant of Keperland had to hold the king's head, if necessary, every time he crossed the sea.[34]

If we examine the Scots lists carefully, it is immediately clear that

---

24 'A sheer day's work' was valued at four shillings. Innes gives a table of conversions (*Scotch Legal Antiquities*, 65).

25 (For Gask.) *Innes, Scotch Legal Antiquities*, 67.

26 For lands at Tonge. If the lord was not there on Midsummer Day it was to be given to the Statute of the Blessed Virgin in Tonge Church (Blount, *Antient Tenures*, 12).

27 For Birdiesfield and Bellisfield, Blantyre. (Innes, *Scotch Legal Antiquities*, 67).

28 *Ibid.*, 68.

29 Moorehouse, 'Some Legal Survivals', 1949 Contemporary Review, 362.

30 Co. Litt. 92a.

31 Moorehouse, 'Some Legal Survivals', 1949 Contemporary Review, 362.

32 Blount, *Antient Tenures*, 67, 77, 87.

33 *Ibid.*, preface.

34 *Ibid.*, 63; similarly the Scots service for Largo (Innes, *Scotch Legal Antiquities*, 67).

not all blench renders were designed as mere tokens of vassalage. Oxen, sheep, hens, conies, cheese, pepper, butter and eggs have more than a token of usefulness. Sometime the quantity of produce to be supplied is far beyond that appropriate in the case of a mere token, for example the six hundred wains of peat owed for Balmaschennan.[35] It seems impossible that all these rents in kind originally represented the later idea of a symbol acknowledging the feudal dependency of the vassal on the superior. They represented in an economic sense the practical dependence of the medieval king or subject-superior on his vassals for sustenance and the provision of the necessaries of life of many different kinds.[36] Only when the medieval way of life had been drastically modified by the increasing importance of commerce and free contract did they become mere curiosities. Blench holding has, therefore, a more complex origin than is ascribed to it in the institutional writers, although probably there had always been a few cases where land was given for past services or as a royal favour with only a nominal return. Robert III granted the barony of Manor in Peebles for the slaying of an Englishman in single combat.[37] The Dukes of Marlborough and Wellington hold the lands granted to their famous ancestors by the service of bringing a small flag to Windsor on the anniversaries of Blenheim and Waterloo respectively.

Blench holding still exists, the render being now usually of a Scots penny yearly, if demanded. But the older services still remain. George V, George VI and H.M. the Queen have all enjoyed the ancient right of a red rose when visiting their vassal of Glenormiston, near Innerleithen, the last occasion being the render by Mr. Sidney Denman as recently as 1 July 1966.[38]

Serjeanty was within the Tenures Abolition Act 1660, by which all land held by military tenures in England was converted to socage, but the honorific services due from tenants in grand serjeanty were expressly saved.[39] At the coronation in 1937, as at all others on record,

---

35 Innes, *Scotch Legal Antiquities*, 67.
36 Cain and Conveth were the Gaelic equivalent to meet the simpler needs of clan chiefs. See Craig, 1.10.28 and 1.10.33 as to cain-duty; and 1.11.12 as to the English law of corvage.
37 *Ibid.*, 37.
38 See frontispiece; *The Scotsman* 2 July 1966 and Appendix IX *infra*, pp. 370–1.
39 S 7.

the lord of the manor of Worksop was at the king's right hand to support the sceptre when required. In 1953 the lord was a limited company and the Queen appointed someone else to perform the office on behalf of the lord.

The detailed examples mentioned in this chapter show that there was a very close resemblance between the English tenure of serjeanty and the Scots one of blench; and reinforce in striking fashion some of the basic similarity of Scots and English feudal law.[40]

It should now be noted, however, that the Land Tenure Reform (Scotland) Act 1974 provides that although new feus can be created, no annual payment or service can be imposed; but a capital sum can be charged for the grant of a feu.

40   *See* Chapter 2.

7 Socage, Burgage and Feu Farm

Unlike serjeanty and blench, which have always been something of a rarity, the tenures to be discussed in this chapter were, and are, extremely common.

SOCAGE

With the possible exception of frankalmoign, socage is the only tenure by which land can now be held anywhere in England. Its history shows a gradual extension of its scope from modest beginnings to its present universal prevalence. The term 'socage' was never known in Normandy,[1] and there is much to be said for the idea that it is an Anglo-Saxon survival. It is only extremely rarely found in Scotland. The *Regiam Majestatem* mentions it,[2] but it is a very Anglicised work and the term never seems to have reappeared in Scots law. Erskine gives one example 'about four centuries ago' of a holding in *libero sochagio*.[3] When it first appeared in England, socage was the holding of a definite social class, the sokemen, in Domesday Book. Their status was above that of the villein. They were free men, but being mere peasants, they were not worthy to hold by military service. They differed from the *servientes* or holders in serjeanty in that instead of holding by a personal service to be performed on an indefinite number of occasions, they held by a rent, which might consist of money, or of produce, or even of specified labour, of a set amount each year.[4]

It is this element of specification that the lawyers seized upon as

1 P. & M., i, 293.
2 *Regiam*, II.21.
3 Erskine, I.1.35.
4 P. & M., i, 292; Megarry and Wade, 19–22.

the distinguishing characteristic of socage.[5] A holder in socage is one who owes a specified and fixed service. But this definition is obviously a wide one. It enabled socage to spread beyond its original bounds as the holding of the better class of peasantry to embrace at least three different types of holding: (1) where no special service, but fealty alone was owed: since what was owed was specific, said the medieval lawyer, this was a socage holding; (2) where a merely token service was owed as, for example, 'un certein number de capons, ou de gallines, ou un paire de gaunts',[6] this, being specified, was also socage service; (3) where a real rent of money or produce was owed, this was the clearest case of specification, and consequently socage. It became so elastic that a wide range of local customary varieties of tenure could be included within its scope. The most famous of these was gavelkind, by which the major part of the lands in Kent was held. Its chief characteristic was that on the tenant's death, the fee did not descend to the eldest son as heir, but went to all the sons equally. This was far from being its only peculiarity;[7] for example gavelkind was freely devisable and was not forfeited for treason from the traitor's family. It is clearly a Saxon institution. Folk-land also went to all the sons. Gavelkind was converted to ordinary socage in 1925.[8]

More interesting from the present standpoint is the fact that socage, in the course of its extension, swallowed up two tenures once well known in England which have to this day survived in Scotland as distinct tenures in the absence of this over-generalised conception of socage: burgage and feu farm.

BURGAGE

Burgage was treated as a separate tenure in English law as late as Bracton's day.[9] Littleton also discussed 'tenure en burgage' under a heading separate from that of socage; but he showed that the stage

5   E.g. Littleton, *Tenures*, s 117.
6   *Ibid*, s 128. Many of these were originally real rents. Yet tenure by a pair of mail gloves was serjeanty, which illustrates how unreal the distinction became. *See* Chapter 6; cf the renders for blench holdings listed above (Chapter 6).
7   *See* Cheshire, 18.
8   Administration of Estates Act 1925, s 45 (1) (a).
9   Bracton, f 329.

of total assimilation had almost been reached in his day by adding, 'tiel tenure nest forsqz tenure en Socage'.[10] The chief feature of burgage in England was its subjection to the variations of local custom. Because of their early codification in the borough custumals the local incidents of burgage were better able than were the customs of rural areas[11] to stand up to the ironing out of local divergencies, which was the constant aim of the English common law. Thus we find that old right of the kindred to hinder the disposition of a man's holding, which formed so marked a feature of the Saxon folk-land.[12] The lord retained sometimes a right of pre-emption on a burgess's alienation akin to the *retrait féodal* of French and (indirectly) Scots law.[13] Like the Saxon book-land, burgage could generally be devised by will at a time when the common law had stamped this out elsewhere.[14] Most remarkable of all, the very foundation of feudal landholding, fealty, was not demandable in some particularly ancient boroughs, for example Ipswich[15] and Hereford.[16] Often the burgesses were excused aids, reliefs and other feudal payments, but their particular obligations depended on the custom of the borough in which they lived. Almost the only one of these customs to survive the Middle Ages was that known as Borough English which originated in the English part of Nottingham borough, according to which it was not the eldest, but the youngest son of a burgess who succeeded to his land or intestacy.[17] Even this was wiped away in 1925, the tenure becoming common socage at the same time as gavelkind.[18]

Burgage in Scotland springs from essentially the same beginnings. Burghs there were either burghs incorporated by and subject to the king; or burghs of regality or barony, dependent in the same way on subjects. This was, of course, also true of early medieval England;

---

10   Littleton, *Tenures*, s 162.
11   Holdsworth, *H.E.L.*, ii, 372; iii, 269. But many rural customs survived within the manor (*see* Chapter 8).
12   E.g. *Borough Customs* (Selden Society, Vol 21), ii, 61 (Lincoln), cf Preston (62) Northampton (63).
13   E.g. at Whitby, *ibid.*, 60 *et seq.* cf *Leges Quatour Burgorum*, c 95.
14   E.g. at Nottingham and Waterford (*Borough Customs* (Selden Society, Vol 21) ii, 95).
15   *Ibid.*, 83.
16   *Ibid.*, 85.
17   Co. Litt. 165.
18   Administration of Estates Act 1925, s 45 (1) (a).

Whitby, for example, was the town of the Abbey, not of the Crown. But the distinction between royal burghs and other burghs did not survive in England as it did in Scotland. Whereas in England most boroughs held of the king (or a lord) at a money rent, to be raised in turn from the holders of burgage lands within the borough, those in Scotland usually held their lands in return for the less definite duty of 'watching and warding'.[19] This prevented the Scots tenure from merging in feu farm, as the English one had done in socage. The Scots burgage tenants had many privileges: for example, they normally paid no relief, nor did their holdings fall into non-entry or wardship.[20] But if they owed a rent, their obligation would be the same as that of a feu farm tenant, that is to pay a double rent in the relief year or as a fine on alienation. The casualty of liferent-escheat (and forfeiture) was the only one normally found in connection with burgage. Burgage lands were freely alienable without the superior's consent.[21] Many of the detailed customs in the burghs were exactly similar to those found in English boroughs.

The feudal nature of this tenure was never lost sight of in Scotland despite the absence of so many well-known feudal burdens. Even though the bailies of the town granted the infeftments, they did so only as delegates of the sovereign, as is clearly shown by the rule that when the burgh was annihilated by dissolution, the burgage vassals continued to hold of the king.[22] The burgesses did not claim to hold allodially, free from all superiority in the Crown, as seems to have happened in France.[23] When in 1597 the registration of sasines was made compulsory[24] in the country as a whole, burgage holdings were left to be dealt with by the burgh, and separate registers were

---

19 Stair, II.3.38. This was the usual position, but Craig (1.10.31) shows that other services were sometimes owed, e.g. at Inverkeithing where the services 'used and wont' included military services owed under a charter of Robert I. For the English position *see* Holdsworth, *H.E.L.*, iii, 270 *et seq.*; P. & M., i, 295.
20 Stair, II.3.38.
21 This is often said to have been the most essential characteristic of Burgage (*see* e.g. Green's *Encyclopaedia*, title 'Burgage', para. 1077); but English analogies suggest that this may not have been the case everywhere (cf *Leges Quatuor Burgorum*, c 95). Subinfeudation is also said to have been impossible (McDouall, *Institute*, II.3.68) but *see Leges Quatuor Burgorum*, c 114. The Conveyancing (Scotland) Act 1874, s 25 expressly allows it.
22 *Urquhart v Clunes* (1758) M 15079; *Lockhart v Kennedy* (1662) 1 Br Sup 482.
23 Craig, 1.11.36.
24 *See* Chapter 27.

set up in the various burghs. Since land within a burgh need not necessarily be held in burgage, in cases of doubt it was necessary to register in both registers. Not until 1874 was this tenure assimilated for almost all practical purposes to that of feu farm. Although the marginal note reads 'Distinction . . . abolished', there seems no sufficient wording in the Conveyancing (Scotland) Act 1874, s 25 to achieve this. All that is done is to place the two tenures on the same practical basis as regards conveyancing. Yet even after the Act one difference remained: dispositions of burgage were still to be registered in the burgh registers.[25] Burgage is now only found in this watered-down form and only in royal burghs.

BOOKING

A special local variety of burgage, the tenure by booking in Paisley, possessed some interesting features until the Conveyancing (Scotland) Act of 1874. This holding was, for example, a holding from the burgh and not, as in the usual case of burgage, of the Crown in chief. Casualties such as relief and non-entry could be demanded, if not expressly discharged or commuted. Even more remarkable is the method of conveyancing which applied to these tenements. Delivery of sasine did not take place on the site, but through the resignation of the tenement by the delivery of a staff or baton in the council chamber, in the face of the Council at a public meeting. It was then delivered to the alienee in similar fashion. These proceedings were next recorded by the Town Clerk in the minutes and a copy handed to the new tenant. This 'extract booking' constituted his title to the land, although any further dispositions would have to take place in the Council. The analogies with the English tenure of copyhold 'by copy of the Court Roll' are most remarkable, but like that tenure, the peculiarities of 'booking' too are now practically extinct.[26]

The origin of booking is unfortunately very obscure. The matter was discussed at length in *Chalmers v Magistrates of Paisley*.[27] The

25 *See* Green's *Encyclopaedia*, title 'Burgage', para. 1088.
26 Conveyancing (Scotland) Act 1874, s 26. *McCutcheon v McWilliam* (1876) 3 R 565.
27 (1829) 7 S 718.

pursuers submitted a long memorandum[28] in which they show that by the Abbot of Paisley's Charter of 1490 certain lands near the then town boundary were granted to the burgh for the purpose of grazing and taking peat, stones and so on. This was probably intended to be a mere servitude, but a part of the land was soon laid out by the bailies in small plots which were divided among the burgesses, and recorded in the burgh books. When any burgess wished to alienate his plot, he had to get the burgh books altered accordingly: so, too, did an heir. In their memorandum the defenders described all this as mere conjecture, but could only suggest a less probable explanation: that the bailies, wishing to prevent subinfeudation and to develop a cheap method of transferring these lands, had deliberately invented the process of booking. The first of these aims could have been achieved in a simpler and less unusual way by inserting a clause against subinfeudation; nor does the second object appear to have been achieved when the whole Council had to assemble to transfer half a seat in a church. Lord Eldin in the case mentioned refused to be drawn beyond the remark that the origin of booking did not clearly appear. It is perhaps enough for us to note that there is no hint whatsoever of English influence in the development of this mirror-image of copyhold.

FEU FARM

Feu farm, the most characteristic Scots tenure, was long recognised in England as a separate tenure until it, too, was absorbed into socage. Thus grants *in feodi firma* and many variants of these words are very frequently to be found during the century and a half after the Conquest.[29] Bracton, like the Magna Carta before him,[30] refers to it as a distinct tenure.[31] Its essential characteristic was a simple one, that the land was parted with perpetually, but for a fixed 'farm' or rent. Hence the inclination to class it with socage, once the wide definition of the latter had come in. The rent need not be in money and fixed rents of produce or of mixed money and produce were often found.

28   The memoranda referred to are in the Revised Case for the Pursuers at pp 31
     et seq.; for the Defenders at pp 9 *et seq.* (Advocates' Library).
29   *See* P. & M., i, 293 and the instances there cited.
30   Magna Carta 1215, c 43.
31   Bracton, f 85b, 86. (Different rules as to reliefs).

However, by prohibiting subinfeudation the statute *Quia Emptores* dealt fee-farm a blow from which it never recovered in England. No new tenure in perpetuity for a rent was possible after that Act:[32] yet it is still possible on alienating what the Scots would call the *dominium utile* of the premises that one holds of X to retain a rent, which may well be called a 'fee-farm' rent, instead of receiving a lump sum as payment. It was a common practice in the Manchester and Bristol areas. The vital difference from the Scots position is, however, that there is no tenurial relationship between the vendor and purchaser in such a case in England. The purchaser holds directly of X, the lord under whom the vendor held the fee; it is there an *a me* grant and is consequently a rent-charge as opposed to a rent-service, although the practical effects of this distinction are not very considerable nowadays.

Since 1290 feu-holding has been peculiar to Scotland,[33] and the nature of feu holdings remains almost exactly the same as that which formerly prevailed in the southern country. This is at least strongly suggested by the usual Scots *tenendas* being the same as that commonest in England – '*in feudifirma*'.[34] In both countries a relief was payable and in both a payment was generally due on an alienation.[35] A small difference is that the *reddendo* in a Scots feu might consist of services, generally of an agricultural nature.[36] This makes those holdings akin to socage, with which fee-farm (in the old sense) has been consolidated in England.

Grants in return for a money payment were rare before the fourteenth century, although by no means unknown,[37] but in that century the new movement began of granting out lands for an economic return instead of military dependence or the rather crude

32 Perpetual leases are invalid in English law. (Co. Litt. 45b; *Sevenoaks, Maidstone and Tunbridge Railway Co v London, Chatham and Dover Railway Co* (1879) 11 Ch D 625, 635).

33 Grant, *S.E.D.S.*, 265.

34 Bell, *Principles*, 683.

35 Called a composition in Scotland. In England the fine was only payable by tenants-in-chief, at least after *Quia Emptores* 1290 (but by copyhold tenants in manors until 1925).

36 Conacher, 'Feudal Tenures in Scotland in the Fifteenth and Sixteenth Centuries' (1936) 48 Jur. Rev., 189 maintains that it was only in recent times that it became possible to have a feu duty of money alone; but cf the earlier example in Lawrie, *Early Scottish Charters*, C.

37 E.g. the example in note 36, *supra*.

services in kind which were a feature of blench holdings. This development was at first confined to Church lands, for the clergy were forbidden by Canon Law from parting with them completely, nor did they need armed retainers. Yet, good agriculturalists though many of the orders were, they could not farm their vast estates themselves, and the tacksmen, or tenants, of the day were too humble in station and too devoid of financial recources to provide an answer. Accordingly the feu farm arrangement was seized on as providing the best compromise between an ordinary feudal grant and a tack (or lease). Most of the kirk lands in Scotland were feued out in this and the following century, a trend stimulated also by the pressure of papal taxation, which made it essential to have money rather than produce or services.[38]

But the Scots kings could not be expected to fail to observe the financial advantages of the feuing system. They were generally impecunious to a remarkable degree,[39] but they saw that much would be gained if, instead of the very irregular and unsatisfactory income from wardships and other feudal casualties, their vassals were to yield a fixed and regular money rent for their holdings. Many of the vassals probably also welcomed the opportunity to exchange the hated ward system for something more certain and secure, even if heavier on their pockets. The only difficulty was that the Crown lands were inalienable without Parliamentary consent. This was obtained in the famous Act of 1457,[40] which allowed the king and other lords to set their lands in feu. From then on the tendency to substitute feus for ward-holdings or for the very unsatisfactory tacks went on increasing right up to the Union. The poverty of most of the country people meant, however, that they were only able to hold tacks and the feuing movement therefore never became a universal one.[41] Apart from Fife, Strathearn and Bute, where small feu holdings did become fairly common, and the neighbourhood of towns, the holders by the new tenure were mostly the gentry and even great lords did not scruple to hold by it.[42] The new commercial

38 Hannay, 'A Study in Reformation History', 23 S.H.R. 25, 41.
39 Grant, *S.E.D.S.*, 205.
40 A.P.S., ii, 49.   41 Grant, *S.E.D.S.*, 270.
42 E.g. Culqhoun of Luss as early as James III's reign (Exchequer Rolls XIII, 116). In England at a much earlier date a prior held a whole manor for a money rent (P. & M., i, 272).

attitude to landholding naturally made this businesslike tenure popular and the abolition of ward-holding in 1746, which had long been overdue, destroyed the old system altogether.

Thus feu farm has gradually advanced to be the predominant tenure by which land is held in Scotland at the present day, but it is not quite universal, as socage is in England.

8 Copyhold, Kindly Tenancy and Leasehold

COPYHOLD: FREE AND UNFREE TENANTS

The tenures that have so far been considered exist or existed in Scotland and England alike with, comparatively, only minor divergencies of detail. An important English tenure which has no real counterpart in Scots legal history is that originally entitled 'villein tenure', but subsequently 'copyhold' when its original character had been considerably modified.[1]

As the older name suggests, this was probably in origin the tenure of the personally unfree.[2] But even as early as the immediate post-Conquest period free men occasionally held by this unfree tenure or rather, since it was not yet a tenure, held their land in return for 'unfree' services. This meant services of which the nature was not settled beforehand. Thus the man might have to work for his lord on two or three days of the week. Although how much of any particular labour amounted to a 'work' (that is, a supposed day's work) was early fixed by custom, the nature of the work to be done depended entirely on the lord's pleasure. This uncertainty of the services to be rendered was the main distinction between free and unfree tenements.[3] Whilst at least as early as Magna Carta the holder of land by a free tenure could seek the protection of the king's courts if dispossessed or otherwise interfered with in the lawful enjoyment of his land, the royal courts were not prepared to protect the holders in villeinage at such an early date.[4] The three-field

1 Craig, 1.11.32 (Lord Clyde's Translation, Vol 1, 197).
2 Vinogradoff, *Villainage in England*; Holdsworth, *H.E.L.*, iii, 198 *et seq.*
3 P. & M., i, 365 *et seq.*; Simpson, *An Introduction to the History of the Land Law*, 13.
4 There was a hint that they might interfere to protect villeinage in Bracton's day: see *Bestenover v Montcute* (Bracton, *Note Book*, pl. 70, 88) and *William Henry's*

arrangement of the typical English manor called for very close relations between the lord and his tenants and between the tenants themselves. This was a matter most suitably left to the administration of the lord's manor court or court leet.[5] Therefore the holding in villeinage had no standing before the king's courts which treated it as a mere tenancy at the will of the lord. It is tempting to equate the position of the villein with that of the slave at Rome holding a *peculium*, which remained always the lord's property and at the lord's absolute discretion.[6] As Fitzherbert says, 'Ceux del maner teignent lour terres forsque al volunte le seigneur . . . solonque le custome del manor . . . et le franc-tenement est en le seigneur.'[7]

So far as the king's courts were concerned, then, the status of the tenants of land held in villeinage was not so very different from that of the Scots Celtic customary tenants, whose relation to the land was treated by the royal courts there as one of the merest *precarium*.

Wherein lay the difference which was to preserve the one and to destroy the other? In part the answer may be found in the very important phrase 'solonque le custome del manor'. The lord's will was absolute as far as the king's courts were concerned; but in reality that will had to be exercised in accordance with longstanding local custom, which regulated, for example, the lord's rights in respect of heriots[8] and merchet.[9] More often it gave rights to the tenants,

---

son v Bartholomew Eustace's son (*ibid.*, pl. 1103) but it seems to have come to nothing and been forgotten when the question came up again two hundred years later.

5 See Keeton, *Laxton and its Past*.

6 Justinian, *Institutes*, 2.9.1.; Buckland, *Textbook of Roman Law*, 65.

7 *Abridgement*, title 'Faux Jugement', pl. 7.

8 'This heriot is the best live beast or averium which the tenant dies possessed of, sometimes the best inanimate good, under which a jewel or plate may be included' (Bl. Comm., ii, 424). Its explanation seems to lie in the originally servile status of the villein, when he would own nothing for himself but only hold of his lord. It was known in Scotland as herezeld and demanded in some baronies as late as 1753 (Ross, *Lectures*, ii, 176). In England it was usually confined to copyhold, but could by express agreement apply to leaseholds (*Osborne v Sture* (1686) 2 Lut 1361) and by special custom even to freeholds (*Damerell v Protheroe* (1847) 10 QB 20. See also *Copestake v Hoper* [1908] 2 Ch 10 for a surprisingly modern instance). In *Western v Bailey* [1897] 1 QB 86 it was even held to be immaterial that the deceased tenant's best beast, which the lord intended to seize as a heriot, had never even been in the manor. See Megarry and Wade, 25, 37.

9 Merchet was a fine payable by a tenant to give his daughter in marriage or his son into the church, and was a special mark of villeinage (P. & M., i, 368 *et seq.*).

for example, for a widow to have free-bench in her late husband's copyhold.[10] Since the villeinage-holders were in most cases there first and the lord only superimposed on them at a comparatively late stage of development,[11] he was bound as a matter of 'positive morality' to leave them in peaceful possession of their ancient holdings provided that they duly discharged their appointed service. But important though this point undoubtedly was, we must look to some deeper cause for the survival of their rights after the commercial attitude to landholding had replaced the feudal-patriarchal one. This change was fatal to the Celtic customary tenure. So long as the old order prevailed, quite as strong a 'positive morality', the custom of the race or clan, prevented any large-scale evictions. But once the new attitude came in, the old customary obligations were forgotten and as sheep were more profitable inhabitants of the land than cottars, the cottage folk simply had to go elsewhere. This did not happen to any great extent in England, probably because there had been a marked tendency in England to commute the vague agricultural services to money rents. 'The centralized government of England which kept the peace, the insular position of the country which kept it free from foreign invasion, and the rise of the woollen industry, supplied three economic conditions precedent for the transition from a system of natural husbandry to a system of money rents.'[12] These three elements were markedly absent in Scotland. As late as the sixteenth century the government was not strong enough to keep the peace even in the Lothians; the country was constantly invaded or under threat of invasion from England and the wool trade had scarcely begun in Scotland in medieval times.[13]

Once the tenant ceased the render of 'unfree' services and paid instead a fixed sum of money, villein tenure differed from socage in little but its history and the time was obviously near for its protection by the ordinary courts of the land. But before that came

10 Often also used for the widower's right called 'curtesy' in freehold. The widow's right was usually *dum casta* (see Blount, *Antient Tenures*, 44). Dower in gavelkind land was also *dum casta* (Co. Litt. 33b). See Megarry and Wade, 21–2, 154–6, 532.
11 *Warrick v The Queen's College, Oxford* (1871) LR 6 Ch App 716 *per* Lord Hatherley, LC; *see also MacAndrew v Crerar* 1929 SC 699 at 710 *per* Lord Hunter for the same view in Scotland and as to commonties.
12 Holdsworth, *H.E.L.*, iii, 202.
13 Grant, *S.E.D.S.*, 172.

about, a new conveyancing method was introduced within the manor.[14] The tenant was admitted as always in the court of the manor by the lord's steward, but now he demanded and received a record of the proceedings in the form of a copy of that portion of the court roll which related to his holding. Since anyone can pay money, the lords would now often receive assignees, though demanding a fine for the privilege. Formerly this had been uncommon and undesirable because of the close economic relationship of the members of the 'little Commonwealth'[15] of the manor. Conveyance was by surrender into the lord's hands – this at least the lord would insist on – by means of a symbolic rod, and subsequent admission of the asignee in place of the outgoing tenant. The holder by villein services thus became the copyholder of the modern law.

This need not, of course, have meant the recognition of that tenure by the royal courts, as can be appreciated by comparing the position in Scotland, where the rentallers achieved the first step but not the second; but it seems that in England the copyhold system[16] came in about a century before the royal courts first intervened. The precedents were very much against such intervention yet the new court of Chancery could not allow the consciences of lords of the manor to be burdened by unjust actions any more than those of other men.[17] Thus it was through the medium of that great reforming agency, the Chancellor, that copyholds first gained royal recognition and protection.[18] But in an age of keen competition between tribunals, the Common Law courts were bound to follow suit, and they did so by allowing the dispossessed copyholder the action of trespass in the fifteenth century.[19] Furthermore, he was

---

14   '*Recordum currae et rotulum*' first appeared about 1320 (Holdsworth, *H.E.L.*, iii, 206) i.e. before the Black Death, which is often said to have been an important element in changing villeinage to copyhold (e.g. Megarry and Wade, 26–7).

15   Coke's expression (Epilogue to *The Complete Copyholder*). Scott uses the term 'this diminutive republic' of the Kindly Tenants of Lochmaben (as to whom, *see infra*, this chapter.

16   Copyhold was always characterised by these requirements, yet freehold estates could from the earliest times be transferred inter partes without recourse to the superior lord.

17   See Chapter 15 for the early history of Equity.

18   The copyholders of the Manor of Winkfield petitioned the King's Council in 1394 but the first interference with a lord in dealings with his copyholders seems to have been in 1438. (Holdsworth, *H.E.L.*, iii, 208).

19   Y.B. 7 Ed. IV, Mich. Pl. 16; Y.B. 21 Ed. IV Mich. Pl. 27.

allowed the freeholder's action of ejectment in 1588,[20] even though it was the termor's remedy. This marked the completion of the procedural uniformity, which sprang from the application of the doctrine of universal derivative tenure, as understood in England. Henceforth the peculiarities of copyhold were to be mostly of a conveyancing character and as time went on they became more and more anachronistic and anomalous. The chief difficulty was that many farms and estates consisted of mixed copyhold and socage lands. It was therefore necessary on the sale of such property to go through two distinct conveyancing processes, but eventually all copyholds were converted into socage by the steamroller legislation of 1925,[21] though some of the incidents, which were still of value to lord or tenant, were retained and still subsist unless abolished by written agreement of the parties. Those rights are:

1 any right of lord or tenant to mines and minerals;
2 any rights of the lord in respect of fairs, markets and sporting;
3 any tenant's rights of common;
4 any liability of lord or tenant for the upkeep of dykes, ditches, sea-walls, bridges and the like.[22]

The economic conditions which led to the official protection of copyholds in England were lacking in Scotland, as also was the machinery by which that protection was brought about in England, the separate administration of Equity. Indeed at the time when copyholds gained recognition from the courts at Westminster Scotland lacked any national tribunal competent in matters of heritage, though in the remarkable tenure by booking at Paisley she came to something very like the English copyhold. Why it was restricted to this single burgh is a question that must be left to the historian of Scotland's towns.

One institution which undoubtedly assisted the English villeinage to achieve a higher status has not yet been mentioned. The Ancient Demesne lands of the monarchy were throughout the Middle Ages in a very special position. The king was for them not merely supreme

---

20 *Melwich v Luter* (1588) 4 Co Rep 26a.
21 Law of Property Act 1922, ss 128–37 and Schedules 12 and 13.
22 Law of Property Act 1922, ss 128 (2), 138, and 12th Schedule. As to the abolition of copyhold incidents generally, *see* Megarry and Wade, 36–7.

ruler, but also landlord or lord of the manor, though his tenants in the demesne lands did not distinguish between the two capacities. They expected relief from his courts in cases where, had their lord been a subject, the royal courts would not have intervened. Thus they came to enjoy the protection of the little writ of right, the manorial equivalent of its big brother which protected the freeholder in the national courts.[23] Holders in villeinage on these lands therefore enjoyed a greater degree of protection from the law than their peers had elsewhere: not surprisingly therefore claimants pretended (usually in vain) that the manor they held in was mentioned as belonging to St Edward in the Domesday Book.[24]

KINDLY TENANTS

The special position of the ancient demesne landholders does have an opposite number, albeit on a far smaller scale, in Scotland. There, too, in the Saxon Lowlands, and especially in the Border country, what was in effect the English villeinage existed in the medieval period. This was the holding of the *nativi*, who were, at least in origin, serfs *adstricti glebae*. They were allowed to possess certain lands in return for agricultural services on the lord's mains. The grant of a proper legal estate in the land, which could be enforced against the granter, was however by no means contemplated.[25] 'Even the relation of landlord and tenant was deemed too formal to be necessary where there was honour on one side and gratitude upon the other.'[26] The right was a very personal one which implied residence and could in no way be alienated.[27] However, by the goodwill of the landlord, descendants were frequently allowed to succeed their ancestors in the rooms (or smallholdings),

23 P. & M., i, 385 *et seq.*
24 Holdsworth, *H.E.L.*, iii, 204.
25 Carmont, 'The King's Kindlie Tenants of Lochmaben', (1909) 21 Jur. Rev., 323, 324.
26 *Ibid.*, 324.
27 Stair, II.9.21. It was always regarded as a special favour to be treated as a kindly tenant. Mere residence and payment of rent was not enough: *Cassilis' Tutor v Lochinvar* (1581) M 15183. Subletting was not allowed and a sort of recognition applied. (*See Craigie Wallace* (1623) M 7191).

provided that they continued to pay the annual quit rent and sometimes a small fine on the entry of the new tenant.[28] For this reason it seems, they received the 'endearing'[29] name of Kindly Tenants.

In the course of time it became customary for the superior who had a number of such tenants to keep a rental book recording their names and holdings; hence they acquired the alternative title of rentallers.[30] But it would be a mistake to regard them as an exact counterpart of the English copyholders. Unlike their luckier peers to the south, these rentallers lived in a country where until the Court of Session was created in the sixteenth century ejected tenants had small hope of redress, since the administration of justice locally was the duty of the ejecting landowner.[31] This is probably the most fundamental difference between the two countries in the Middle Ages, and by the time that the Scots central courts were effectively established it was too late to save the rentallers of subject-superiors from extinction. They had almost all disappeared with the new feuing policy and the commercial outlook which it both represented and engendered. By the early sixteenth century kindly tenants were usually to be found only on the lands of the Church and on the royal domain.[32] But the cataclysm which swept away the ecclesiastical landowners dealt no more leniently with the kindly tenants. The priests, seeing that their hour was about to strike, endeavoured to realise their property by sale and feu, and in the process a considerable number of their kindly tenants must have been dispossessed. Even worse, however, when the kirk lands fell into the hands of the Lords of Erection, who were quite blatantly anxious to make all they could out of the lands they received, rents were raised to a preposterous

---

28 Carmont, 'The King's Kindlie Tenants of Lochmaben', (1909) 21 Jur. Rev., 323, 325–6.

29 Ross, *Lectures*, ii, 474. There is some doubt as to the derivation of the word 'kindly'. On one argument they were so called because the laird had treated them with kindness. Although this may be the correct explanation (*see* Grant, *S.E.D.S.*, 91), others may be nearer the truth when they say that the tenants were so called because they paid in kind; or because the kindred had a right of succession.

30 The rental roll of Kelso Abbey throws light on conditions on a large estate in 1290: *see* Grant, *S.E.D.S.*, 85 *et seq.*

31 Carmont, 'The King's Kindlie Tenants of Lochmaben', (1909) 21 Jur. Rev., 323, 325.

32 For a few exceptions as late as the eighteenth century, *see ibid.* at 326.

level of extortion to give a pretext for the expulsion of the tenentry, which speedily followed.[33] The king's council and Parliament attempted to stem the tide,[34] but this was by no means a time of implicit obedience to authority. Thus by the late sixteenth century the rentallers on the former church estates had gone the way of those on lay superiors' estates earlier in the century. Official pronouncements that a rentaller was entitled to hold for life, or if 'heirs' were named in the grant, for two lives,[35] came too late to be much more than an academic exercise.

One class of kindly tenant still remained: those who were lucky enough to dwell on the royal estates. They had in their favour (as had their counterparts, the ancient demesne holders in England) the fact that there was an efficient tribunal at their service, which indeed gave judgment that 'an man being rentalled on the king's rental, of any lands and possession, and deceases, leavand behind him a wife and bairns, the bairns ought to be rentalled, and the wife should bruik the same for all the days of her lifetime, allenarly, and has no power to put any other person in the rental'.[36] Armed with this, the king's kindly tenants were able to hold out a little longer than the others. Unhappily, however, the kings of Scots were not the people to sit calmly by while others made substantial profits. The Act of 1587 restricted the rentallers' rights to those of mere life tenants and allowed the sovereign to set the lands in feu.[37] This was done at once, and any kindly tenants surviving into the seventeenth and later centuries were the result of an unusual oversight. One solitary kindly tenant survived on the royal lands in Fife until 1892.[38]

To this extinction there is a notable, though very limited, exception: the king's kindly tenants of the four 'towns' (actually villages) of Lochmaben – Hightae, Smallholm, Heck and Greenhill. Why they survive may well be a matter of local pride. Lochmaben had originally been part of the Bruce family estates, and the valiant Robert

33 Ross, *Lectures*, ii, 479, 480.
34 *See* e.g. the Rentallers Act 1563 (A.P.S., ii, 540, (15)).
35 Erskine, II.6.38. *Galloway v Tailzifer* (1631) M 7194.
36 Ross, *Lectures*, ii, 480.
37 Rentallers, Feuing Act 1587, c 69 (A.P.S., iii, 465 (5)). By the Rentallers Act 1563, c 77 (A.P.S., ii, 540 (15)) the kindly tenants on the former kirk lands were declared to hold only life estates.
38 Carmont, 'The King's Kindlie Tenants of Lochmaben', (1909) 21 Jur. Rev., 323.

led them to exploits of remarkable bravery against the English at Bannockburn.[39] In return he granted them exceptional privileges. They were to enjoy their roums heritably for ever and moreover were given full rights of alienation *inter vivos* or by will, the latter a very singular exemption from the ordinary law of the land. Later kings confirmed these privileges on several different occasions. By virtue of these charters the tenants were able to withstand a very heavy and repeated attack on their holdings by the feudal donatories of Lochmaben Castle, who claimed that these lands had been erected into a barony in their favour.[40] Although gradually becoming fewer, through alienations to adjoining feudal proprietors, some of these remarkable kindly tenancies still remain in being. Their conveyancing is very simple and very similar to that of English copyhold: 'The seller and the buyer have but to agree about the price, and after the buyer pays it over, the two make a visit to the keeper of the roll – the Earl of Mansfield's chamberlain – and request him to strike out the seller's name and enter the buyer's name as a holder of these roums in the roll of kindlie tenants and on a small payment being made for the change, the transaction is closed.'[41]

The kindly tenants of Lochmaben represent what is really the sole Scots equivalent of the great English tenure of copyhold: indeed, they have even survived it. There can be little doubt that their holdings constitute a tenure. In *Marquess of Queensberry v Wright*[42] it was expressly held that they do, and that *dominium utile* of the lands is in the tenants.[43] This is the main test in Scotland of the existence of a tenurial relationship.[44]

---

39   Thomson, 'The Kindly Tenants', *Transactions of Dumfries and Galloway Antiquarian Society*, 1897–8.
40   This litigation lased for over two centuries from 1612. *Kindly Tenants of Lochmaben v Viscount Stormont* (1726) M 15195, affirmed by 1 Pat 77; and *Marquess of Queensberry v Wright* (1838) 16 S 439 are the principal cases.
41   Thomson, *see* note 39 *supra*.
42   (1838) 16 S 439.
43   It was also said (*ibid.* at 444) that 'they have the sole right of property in the lands occupied by them under a different name, but with all the substantial rights of the udal proprietors in Orkney'. If this is meant to suggest that they held allodially it must be erroneous, for the whole point of the kindly tenants cases has been that they held directly of the Crown, and derived their privileged position from that fact.
44   *See* Chapters 11 and 12.

LEASEHOLD

A considerably more difficult question is whether the English lease-hold interest in land should be described as a tenure. The history of that interest in English law and the reasons why it has never obtained recognition as real property will be discussed later in connection with the terms of years considered as an estate.[45] The questions to be determined for the present are whether the lessor-lessee relationship can be properly described as one of tenure, whether the lessee can be said to have a tenement and, to be carefully distinguished from the first, whether 'leasehold tenure' can be correctly included among the species of tenure known to English law. There can be few questions in the land law on which eminent opinion is so divided.

Blackstone,[46] Challis,[47] Cheshire,[48] Digby,[49] Potter,[50] are names to conjure with in English land law, and it would be presumptuous indeed to disagree with them, did not Bracton,[51] Littleton,[52] Coke,[53] Maitland,[54] Holdsworth,[55] Plucknett,[56] Elphinstone,[57] Cotton, L. J.,[58] Megarry and Wade,[59] Simpson,[60]

45 *See* Chapter 14.
46 He nowhere expressly denies that leases are tenements, but it is implicit in his treatment of the subject, e.g. he defines an estate for years as 'a contract for the possession of lands or tenements for some determinate period' (Bl. Comm., ii, 140). This view comes close to the Scots view of tacks: nor is this surprising, for Blackstone drew much on Spelman, who first brought continental feudalists' conceptions to England: *see* Hogg, 'Effects of Tenure on Real Property Law', (1909) 25 LQR 178.
47 *Law of Real Property*, 7, 65, 242 *et seq.* (*see also* Challis, 'Are Leaseholds Tenements?', (1890) 6 LQR 69).
48 Cheshire, 38–9.
49 *Introduction to the History of the Law of Real Property*, 231.
50 *Historical Introduction to English Law*, 486.
51 ii, f 80a.
52 *Tenures*, s 132.
53 Co. Litt., ii, 67b, 93a.
54 P. & M., i, 113, 234.
55 *Historical Introduction to Land Law*, 235.
56 *Concise History of the Common Law*, 572.
57 'Are Leaseholds Tenements?', (1889) 5 LQR 326.
58 *Sheffield Wagon Co v Stratton* (1878) 48 LJQB 35, 36.
59 Megarry and Wade, 45–66.
60 *Historical Introduction to the History of the Land Law*, 233: 'Since 1925 it has become an estate, and it may be that in the end English Law will evolve a Law of Property and not a law of Real Property and a Law of Personal Property.' *See also* Lawson, *Introduction to the Law of Property*, where the learned author treats the law of property as an integrated whole.

to say nothing of the High Court of Parliament[61] disagree with them also.

Challis may be described as the leader of the negative view. His arguments appear to rest on his assertion that 'in England the legal definition of a tenement has for centuries been by universal consent "whatever is intailable under the Statute *De Donis*"', from which he deduces with incontestible logic that leases are not tenements.[62] He fails to make clear where the definition springs from;[63] nor does he adduce much evidence of universal consent.[64] Even had eighteenth and nineteenth century conveyancing opinion been unanimous, it is not clear that a court would prefer this to the overwhelming weight of the old authorities. He is a bold counsel who will argue against the unanimous opinion of Bracton, Littleton and Coke.

Even before Littleton, Bracton had treated terms of years as being on exactly the same footing of tenure as other interests in land.[65] Littleton was (one would have thought) to put the matter beyond all doubt: 'Si un lease soit fait a un homme pur terme de ans,' he wrote, 'il est dit que le lessee ferra fealty a le lessor, pur ceo que il tient de luy, et ceo est prove bin per les parols de brief de wast . . . lequel briefe dira, que le lessee tient les tenements de le lessor, pur terme de ans, issint le briefe prova un tenure enter eux.'[66] In case anyone should still be in doubt, Coke repeats,[67] 'for there is also a

---

61 The Statute of Gloucester 1278 (6 Ed. I, c 5) speaks of '*home que tient a terme de vie, ou des ans, ou femm que tient en dower*'. This shows that the rigid line of cleavage between terms of years and life interests – tenure being admitted as to the latter – is of later development.

62 *The Law of Real Property*, 424. However, he frequently refers to copyhold *tenure* although copyholds were only ever (if at all) entailable under special custom and not under the statute (Challis, *The Law of Real Property*, 27). Also a life estate is a 'tenement (*ibid.*, 44) although not truly entailable as he admits (*ibid.*, 358; cf Bl. Comm., ii, 113). The person named as 'heir of the body' of a tenant *pur autre vie* takes not as heir, but by special occupancy: *Low v Burron* (1734) 3 P Wms 262.

63 Maybe he had in mind Coke's discussion of the term 'tenements' in connection with the statute *De Donis Conditionalibus* 1285 (Co. Litt. i. 20a). However, Coke does not mention leaseholds in that context.

64 He cites *Att.-Gen. of Ontario v Mercer* (1883) 8 App Cas 767 at 772, but Lord Selborne, L.C. only says 'the word "tenure" signified this relation of tenant to lord', which arises from the doctrine that all land is held of the king.

65 ii, f 80a.

66 *Tenures*, s 132. Challis relies on '*il est dit que*' to argue that Littleton uses 'very cautious language, redolent of doubt and bewilderment' (*Law of Real Property*, 425); but surely '*et ceo est prove bien*' and the categorist closing words are scarcely redolent of bewilderment, or of doubt.

67 Co. Litt., ii, 93a.

tenure between them,' adding, 'and Littleton's opinion in this case is holden good law at this day.'[68] Nor is this without Year Book support.[69]

It is therefore suggested that the evidence is very strong that the tenant for years has a tenement and that the relationship of lord and man which we commonly designate 'tenure' exists between landlord and tenant for years, even though leaseholds are not technically real property, in the sense of having long ago commanded the obsolete real actions. To discover the phenomenon of tenure, we look first for fealty or homage; secondly for certain services due from man to lord, of which few examples are as good as the paying of a rent; thirdly for the lord's power of distress in case there should be default in the payment of the services; and fourthly for a process of escheat, whether technically now called so or not,[70] by which the land goes to the lord if the tenant's interest comes to an end. Each of these is found in connection with the leasehold.[71]

Finally, to prove that the leasehold interest is not merely a tenement but is a distinct tenure known to English law, we need only to go to the Law of Property Act 1925 by which the term 'land' includes 'land of any tenure'.[72] Since all the undoubted tenures have been converted into socage[73] these words would be quite meaningless unless the Act conceives leasehold as a tenure distinct from socage.[74] Furthermore, the Crown Private Estates Act 1862 expressly mentions 'leasehold tenure'.[75] Thus while assertions can still be found in some books denying it the status of a tenure, leasehold 'was in fact a form of tenure before the Property Acts . . . and still

---

68   *See also Milmo v Carreras* [1946] KB 306 *per* Lord Greene MR at 310.
69   Y.B. 5 Hen. VII. Hil. pl. 2 *per* Fairfax, J.
70   'Escheat' and 'reversion' were originally synonyms (Holdsworth, *H.E.L.*, iii, 68).
71   Fealty is due, but not homage. (Littleton, *Tenures*, s 132, and Coke thereon). In the words of fealty as given by Littleton (*Tenures*, s 91), the tenant refers to '*les tenements que ieo claime a tener de vous*'. Service is usual, but not essential, as in other tenures. The term 'rent-service' properly includes rent due under a lease: Littleton, *Tenures*, s 213; Cheshire, 428–9; Megarry and Wade, 792–3. As to distress, *see* Littleton, *Tenures*, ss 58, 213, Megarry and Wade, 691.
72   Law of Property Act 1925, s 205 (1) (ix); *See* Megarry and Wade, 46.
73   Frankalmoign may possibly have survived through a legislative blunder (*see* p. 41 *supra*) but the Act cannot be referring to this.
74   *See* e.g. Stroud's *Judicial Dictionary*, title 'Tenure': 'the Chief tenures of present importance are freehold, copyhold, leasehold'.
75   S 3.

is'.[76] Perhaps the word 'tenant' and the phrase 'security of tenure' supply the best argument of all.

In Scotland, on the other hand, no one seems ever to have spoken seriously of the relationship between tacksman for years and landlord as being one of tenure.[77] The Scots view of a tack is that it is a purely contractual right, although by statute the tacksmen have been given special protection against eviction before the proper determination of the lease by the singular successors of the granter.[78]

TACK

To Scots eyes it seems well nigh impossible to discover tenure where the feudal signals of its existence, that is infeftment with the superior, sasine and its registration, are so notably lacking. It seems reasonable to affirm that the tack in Scotland does not, and never has, come within the orbit of the doctrine of tenure as understood in that country. Nonetheless 'tenant' and 'security of tenure' are part of the English language today and they are consequently used wherever that language is spoken. It is to be noted, however, that the older Scots authorities, before the influence of England became so strong in the language, invariably preferred the term 'tacksman' to that of 'tenant'.

For convenience probative leases of heritage for over thirty-one years could be recorded in the Register of Sasines under the Registration of Leases Act 1857 and securities could also be registered, burdening such registered leases. The Conveyancing (Scotland) Act 1924 assimilated the forms applicable to registered leases with those applicable to dispositions of feudal property and securities registered against them.

STATUTORY RIGHTS OF POSSESSION

This is not the place to discuss the details of modern statutes by which what might be called an artificial right to continue in posses-

---

76   Rivington, *Law of Property in Land*, 26.
77   Stair says 'as to the extension and effect of tacks, they are little less than infeftments' (II.9.9). He is however, there dealing with their practical effects, having already (II.9.1) analysed them as being in principle mere contractual rights.
78   *See* Chapter 14.

sion has been given to certain tenants. By the Crofters Acts 1886–1908 and other Acts following the Small Landholders (Scotland) Act 1911 a mass of complicated legislation covers this subject in Scotland.[79] The position created under the original Crofters Acts is, however, an interesting one, for under those Acts the crofter acquired what has been called a 'perpetual tenure'[80] subject to his fulfilling important conditions, for example that he should cultivate the holding in a proper manner and not obstruct the landlord in his rights: a sort of purpresture. But such a crofter had no right to alienate or sub-let, and if he attempted to do either, a quasi-recognition took place though bequest (or, in cases of physical infirmity, anticipated bequest) to a relative[81] was excepted from this rule. This croft holding was declared to be equivalent to a lease[82] and therefore presumably outside the scope of tenure; but in reality 'the right is one altogether *sui generis,* containing elements and conditions incompatible with the contracts of lease or feu'.[83] A special Land Court was set up to administer these Acts.[84]

In England and Scotland the Agricultural Holdings Acts have given farmers and market gardeners security of tenure and important ancillary rights.[85] In both countries the notoriously complex Rent Restriction Acts, starting as a temporary measure in 1915, protect many possessors of domestic premises against eviction when their terms of years run out, and control the raising of the rent.[86] Although he is often styled for convenience a 'statutory tenant' such a person who must necessarily rely entirely on the Acts, has a purely personal

79 *See* Green's *Encyclopaedia*, title 'Small Landholders' for a list of such legislation.
80 Green, *Encyclopaedia*, title 'Small Landholders', para. 327.
81 Crofters Act 1886, ss 1, 16; Small Landholders (Scotland) Act 1911, ss 7, 21. For the meaning of 'relative' *see McLean v McLean* (1891) 18 R 885; *Mackenzie v Cameron* (1894) 21 R 427.
82 Crofters Act 1886, s 19.
83 Green, *Encyclopaedia*, title 'Small Landholders', para. 337. *See also MacDonald v Dalgliesh* (1894) 21 R 900.
84 As to this court, see Lord St Vigeans (Chairman), 'Custom', *Sources* (Stair Society, Vol 1), 163 at 167. There is no real equivalent in England, but the Scottish Land Court is not unique: Ireland has had a counterpart for many years.
85 For details, *see* Halsbury's *Laws of England* (4th edn.), title 'Agriculture', paras. 1001–1200. The latest statute is the Agricultural Holdings Act 1948 modified by the Agriculture Act 1958 and the Agriculture (Miscellaneous Provisions) Acts 1963, 1972 and 1976. *See also* the Agricultural Holdings (Scotland) Act 1949 as amended by the Agriculture Act 1958 and the Succession (Scotland) Act 1964.
86 *See* Megarry, *The Rent Acts*, for a detailed account and Fraser, *Rent Acts in Scotland*. (The most recent statutes are the Rent Acts 1971 and 1974.)

right and cannot properly be viewed as coming within the relation-ship of tenure.[87] He has no power of assignment, even to his family.[88] His tenurial obligation of fealty to his landlord presumably comes to an end with his real, as opposed to his statutory, tenancy. But this point is so theoretical that it is unlikely ever to be judicially decided.

87   *Per* Bankes, LJ, *Remon v City of London Real Property Co* [1921] 1 KB 49, 54. *See also McKinty v Belfast Corporation* [1973] NI 1 and [1975] *Annual Survey of Commonwealth Law*, 233–5 as to the nature of a protected tenant's interest under the Rent Restriction Acts, and Megarry, *Rent Acts*, 196–8.
88   *Lovibond and Sons v Vincent* [1929] 1 KB 687 (Will); *Keeves v Dean* [1924] 1 KB 685 (*Inter vivos* sale). But devolution of the statutory tenancy is allowed in cer-tain circumstances.

9 General Conclusions as to Tenure

It has been remarked that the doctrine of derivative tenure is a subject which has never been fully investigated in England.[1] Why this is so may be appreciated by considering the only real attempt that has been made to do it.[2] The writer in question placed to the credit of the doctrine:

1 The evolution of the English doctrine of estates. This doctrine will be considered in detail in the chapters which follow, but it may be remarked in passing that it originated rather from the effect of *De Donis Conditionalibus* 1285 and other statutes than from the doctrine of tenure.

2 The possibility of separate ownership of different horizontal strata in the same geographical locality. Plucknett has remarked[3] that it is very difficult to see how this conclusion can be reached. In Scotland, separate ownership of flats built one above the other has never presented any difficulty in practice and has been greatly assisted by the existence of feudal tenure, which enabled the superior to impose positive conditions running with the land. On the other hand a glance at the modern law of France shows a system where the doctrine of tenure does not exist, but nonetheless the separate ownership of different strata is perfectly possible.

The truth is, of course, that the doctrine of tenure was spread over so wide an area of English law that it became exceedingly thin and theoretical.[4] This is not to say that it did not have important

1 Plucknett, *Concise History of the Common Law*, 543.
2 Hogg, 'Effects of Tenure on Real Property Law', (1909) 25 LQR 178 *et seq.*
3 Plucknett, *Concise History of the Common Law*, 186. Hogg relied on *Humphries v Brogden* (1850) 12 QB 739, which did not turn upon matters of tenure.
4 P. & M., i, 236.

effects, but they were all of an indirect character. Thus a number of vitally important legal institutions arose through the urgent desire of English landowners to escape from the unpleasant consequences of tenure. By far the most important of these is the trust, one of the most distinctive phenomena of English law. The high regard in England for the possessor as such has always militated against the full logical force of the doctrine of tenure, for it cannot be maintained that all land rights are derived from the Crown if one can acquire an indefeasible title merely by camping in a field for twelve years in clear violation of the rights of the king's indirect nominee.[5]

Scotland, as we have seen, was more cautious in not spreading the doctrine further than was absolutely necessary; and in Scotland the doctrine has clearly had very much more practical significance. There, the whole system of feudal conveyancing taught the holder of land that the land was not his absolutely, but that he was only a link in a chain derived from the Crown. Modern reforms have affected the practical importance of tenure in conveyancing; entry, for example, is now deemed to take place on registration without recourse to the superior,[6] but the theory has been scrupulously preserved. The warm tenurial relationship of feudal lord and man has in many cases now gone, but it certainly lasted several centuries longer in Scotland than in England, and the feudal organisation of society remained the basis of Scots life for a vastly longer period than of English.[7] The legal expression of this fact is shown most markedly in the very early decline into practical insignificance of the local feudal courts in England and their survival at the expense of the king's court in Scotland. A very lengthy work would be needed in order to discuss this adequately: here, therefore, it is proposed to indicate only the main points concerned, in outline.

Feudal jurisdiction, by which is meant the jurisdiction of a feudal superior as such over his vassals as such, undoubtedly obtained a footing in England in the years immediately following the Conquest,[8] but in England it was always overshadowed by the supreme jurisdiction, based on supreme power, of the king's courts at Westminster.

5   As to squatters' titles, *see* Chapter 23.
6   *See* Chapter 24.
7   *See* Grant, *S.E.D.S.*, 197 *et seq.* as to why this was so.
8   P. & M., i, 57 *et seq.*; Holdsworth, *H.E.L.*, i, 176 *et seq.*; Ault, *Private Jurisdictions in England.*

These royal courts soon began to interfere with the feudal lord's exercise of jurisdiction, even in the matter of the land rights of his tenants, which were then considered to be peculiarly his own affair. Despite the express words of Magna Carta,[9] supposedly a guarantee of the rights of the subject against the Crown, the king's courts usurped[10] the jurisdictional powers of the local seignorial courts. The power of the feudal courts in England had already been broken by Henry II's rule that no-one need answer for his free tenement without the king's writ, and by the time of Edward I the process was practically complete. Feudal jurisdiction survived the early Angevin period only at the extreme top and bottom of the feudal scale.

At the top the counties palatine of Chester, Durham and Lancaster enjoyed full powers of control over the land rights, as indeed all other legal business, within their respective territories. But Durham was the only one which survived long as a truly independent jurisdiction, since Chester and Lancaster became the *appanages* of various members of the royal family. Even over these palatinates, while they existed, the king's courts were able to insist on an ultimate appellate jurisdiction in error.

At the bottom, the courts of the lords of manors remained for many centuries the only courts having jurisdiction in matters of villein tenure, and even when this was recognised and protected by the royal courts as copyhold, these seignorial courts continued to exist – mainly for conveyancing purposes only – right up to 1925. The enfranchisement of all copyholds has now removed the last vestige of their power. The powers of the manor courts were almost always confined to civil matters, and even there they lost most of their effective jurisdiction to the king before the later Middle Ages.[11]

The history of feudal jurisdictions in Scotland presents a very different picture. Here the medieval kings notoriously lacked the supreme force which was the ultimate argument behind the English trend towards centralisation and nationalisation. Throughout the length and breadth of Scotland were to be found very large numbers of chiefs, nobles and religious houses who were the *de facto* rulers of their territories and the kings of Scots had to depend on these local

---

9 Magna Carta 1215, ss 34–9. Holdsworth, *H.E.L.*, i, 58.
10 The phrase is Potter's (*Historical Introduction to English Law*, 101).
11 P. & M., i, 602; Holdsworth, *H.E.L.*, i, 179 *et seq.*

magnates for the raising of the national armed forces. Similarly, they had to depend on them in practice for the administration of justice and the preservation of what was always so emphatically the king's peace in England.

Legal form was given to this economic necessity in one of two ways. In general it was a recognised rule of medieval Scots law that all landownership, or at least superiority, carried jurisdiction with it as an implied pertinent of the lands in question.[12] A grant of sac and soc later became common form in nearly every charter. These feudal jurisdictions were classified in later times as being of two kinds: regality and barony. A regality, the more important type, was a virtual investiture of the grantee in the sovereign rights of the Crown over the lands in question.[13] These grants therefore went even further than the English palatine grants, as is clearly demonstrated by the fact that the lord of regality could intervene before the royal court and stop the proceedings, if it had so much as dared to try one of his subjects for crime, let alone presumed to infringe his monopoly in matters concerning rights over land in his area. The lesser type, the barony, was usually of an area comparable to the average English manor, but enjoyed far more power than an English manor court ever had. Thus many lords of barony had a grant *cum forca et fossa*, which was the power to inflict the death penalty in criminal cases.[14] All of them seem to have exercised exclusive jurisdiction in the matter of claims of right to land within the barony. So strong was this that, shortly before the establishment of a regular Court of Session in the sixteenth century, Parliament expressly prohibited the royal courts from interfering in matters of title to heritage.[15]

Even where, in an exceptional case, the king had a recognised jurisdiction over a county or a royal estate, it became the practice to grant the office of sheriff or other royal official to the local nobility or other favourites on a hereditary basis.[16] Consequently there was

12   Craig, 3.7.2; Stair II.3.3; Lord Kames, *Historical Law Tracts*, 189.
13   Innes, *Scotch Legal Antiquities*, 40. Cf Erskine I.4.7. *et seq.* Lord Kames, *Historical Law Tracts*, 199, shows that even Baron courts had the right of repledging from the King's courts, as well as from each other.
14   Innes, *Scotch Legal Antiquities*, 58 *et seq.*
15   A.P.S., ii, 47 (ii) (Jurisdiction in Heritage Act 1457).
16   Lord Kames, *Historical Law Tracts*, 190.

little to choose between these 'royal' courts and those which were openly feudal. Even the most important office of the central judiciary, that of Justice-General of Scotland, was for centuries a subsidiary ornament among the titles of the Duke of Argyll. It was in that family from the reign of James I of Scots to that of Charles I, when it was resigned to the Crown, with important reservations, for example, of Argyll and the Isles. Another Duke of Argyll held the office for fifty-one years in the eighteenth century.[17]

All this was clearly bound up with the Celtic organisation of society. As Lord Kames says, 'The first barons were no doubt the chieftains of clans, and the right of jurisdiction specified in the charters of creation, must not be considered as an original jurisdiction flowing from the king, but as the jurisdiction which these chieftains enjoyed from the beginning over their own people.'[18] With the coming of a stronger central administration in the sixteenth century the Crown was placed in a position to assert its authority, as had been done five hundred years earlier in England, but it did not become really effective until after James VI succeeded to England. In the Highlands and Isles, however, these changes were not much felt until after the rising of 1745. The Heritable Jurisdictions Abolition Act 1747, swept away the whole heirarchy of feudal courts, whether openly such, or such *de facto* by the granting of hereditary judicial office under the Crown.

The English mesne lord, once the immediate post-Conquest period was over, came to have a purely nominal connection with the land of which in the eye of the feudalists he was the sole real owner. In Scotland, on the other hand, feudal doctrine was supported by hard fact. The subject-superior was the commander of his vassals in war, their judge and virtual legislator in time of peace, so no Scot could deny, as his English cousin could, the importance of the doctrine now under consideration. Even so the Scot, so conscious of tenure as between subjects, did not seem to have been so practically aware as the Englishman that in the last analysis the tenure of all the lands in the kingdom, by lords of regality or by cottars, is a derivative and dependent tenure from the Crown.

17 Burke, *Peerage*, title 'Argyll'.
18 Lord Kames, *Historical Law Tracts*, 199.

PART II

TRENDS OF DIVERGENCE

THE DOCTRINE OF ESTATES:
RIGHTS AND INTERESTS IN LAND

Chapters 10 to 16

CONFLICTING APPROACHES TO ALIENABILITY:
ENTAILS AND SETTLEMENTS

Chapters 17 to 22

CONVEYANCING METHODS:
SEISIN AND SASINE

Chapters 23 to 26

10 The Importance of Edward I. Scots and English Classifications

In an earlier chapter it was shown that the legal systems of Scotland and England were closely similar until the accession of Edward I. In Westminster Abbey his dust lies under a granite block inscribed *Malleus Scotorum*.[1] Nearby stands the so-called St Edward's chair, built around the sacred stone of Scone, the ancient crowning seat of Scotland, brought as plunder to the shrine of that earlier Edward by his first namesake after the Conquest. These things symbolise the initial point which it is desired to make in this chapter: that this one Plantagenet ruler did more to create the present divergence between Scots and English law, and especially land law, than any other influence.

It is well known that Edward I made important changes in the English law of land. Previous changes had made their way to Scotland, albeit somewhat slowly, without resentment or challenge. Why, then, were Edward's reforms never to penetrate north of the Tweed?

The answer lies not in legal but in political history. The death of the Maid of Norway[2] left the succession to the Scots throne in dispute among a number of Norman barons. What followed is a matter of general knowledge: Edward I of England was called in to judge the issue and his behaviour was in a sense responsible for the evolution of Scotland as a distinct nation. We may leave it to a Scot to assess this:

> The greatest of the Plantagenets . . . was not the cruel monster of early Scottish legend. But . . . his temper could be stirred into

1 'The Hammer of the Scots.'
2 Margaret, grandchild of Alexander III.

cruelty by opposition. He had in his nature, too, that thread of the attorney which ... Sir Walter Scott remarked in his own noble character. This element was undoubtedly present in Edward's dealings with Scotland. ... Not satisfied with suzerainty, he was determined to make Scotland his property, his very own. ... The result was that, far from winning Scotland, Edward converted that nation into a dangerous enemy ... Edward's end, to unite the whole island, was excellent. The end, however, did not justify the means, for the means were to press in a pettyfogging spirit, every legal advantage, to the extreme verge, or beyond the extreme verge, of the letter of the law.[3]

The political consequences of these blunders are not the concern of this study, but their effects on private law, and especially land law, were of fundamental importance. Until this period Scotland can scarcely be said to have had a legal system of her own, apart from the simple precepts of Celtic civilisation. Such law as she had, had been received almost undiluted from Westminster. Now all was changed. Scots legal thought, still too immature to have many conceptions of its own, shunned everything English as emanating from a polluted source. It turned instead to the continental law-giver, and especially to England's hereditary enemy, now therefore Scotland's friend. French legal thought was henceforth to have a profound effect on that of Scotland, not so much through direct imitation, as through the custom of sending potential judges and administrators to France for their legal training.[4]

Continental admiration for Roman law, which had always been specially strong in the universities, was to permeate the whole jurisprudence of Scotland.[5] When at last a king of Scots succeeded by an irony of fate to Edward's throne, it was too late for very much to be done to reunite the once common legal entity of the island.

In the field of land law, however, there was not very much scope for the absorption of Roman law ideas. Scotland's land law was feudal and feudal it had to remain, for the whole social and economic life of the Scots was irrevocably based on a feudal organisation of society. Barred from following English developments by new-found national pride, and yet unable to revolutionise itself on civilian lines,

3 Lang, *History of Scotland*, i, 175. Cf Plucknett, *Legislation of Edward I*, 1.
4 Gardner, 'French and Dutch Influences', *Sources* (Stair Society, Vol 1), 226 *et seq*.
5 Baird-Smith, 'Roman Law', *Sources* (Stair Society, Vol 1), 171 *et seq*.

Scots land law had little choice but to remain in its pre-Edwardian state. It borrowed at a later date much terminology and some conceptions from the old feudal laws of the Continent, but in the main it preserved the earlier structure of English land law, which in that country was undergoing, and was to undergo through the centuries, some very considerable changes. Had Edward's reforms once been firmly established in Scotland, no subsequent cleavage could have caused such a profound divergence as occurred in the land law.

The legislation of Edward I has been the subject of authoritative examination.[6] Therefore only its main features will be mentioned, in outline, so far as they relate to land law.

The Statute of Marlborough was enacted in 1267, before Edward's accession, but he, being then the dominant figure in England, was almost certainly the leading spirit behind its 'revolution'.[7] Maitland considered that the statute 'in many ways marks the end of feudalism'.[8] He was naturally concerned only with England. The Act's first chapter, to the effect that great and small should receive justice in the king's court, is in very vivid contrast to the feudal organisation of the Scots courts, noted in the last chapter. The English lord lost at this early stage, if indeed he ever had it, the power to repledge his subjects from the royal tribunals. This was still well known in Scotland many centuries later. The twenty-second chapter, which required a royal writ before the lord could distrain his free tenants to answer for their freeholds, was not new.[9] It reaffirmed a rule always more or less acknowledged in England, yet totally unknown, or at least totally disregarded in Scotland. Henceforward even the very limited judicial power of the English lord over his tenants could not be exercised without royal leave.

The Statute of Westminster I in 1275 dealt with many matters. It is remarkable for its assertion that the king's writ is to run even within 'liberties' and that where in exceptional places, such as the

---

6 Plucknett, *The Legislation of Edward I*; cf Holdsworth, *H.E.L.*, ii, 291 *et seq.*
7 Powicke, *Henry III and the Lord Edward.*
8 Maitland, *Equity*, 336; *Forms of Action at Common Law*, 42; Plucknett, *Legislation of Edward I*, 28.
9 Plucknett, *Legislation of Edward I*, 25-6.

March of Wales, the king's writ does not run, he is nonetheless 'soverein seyneur'. As such he may do justice to all who complain to him. These provisions serve to underline the contrast with Scotland. The Statute of Westminster II in 1285 and that named *Quo Warranto* in 1290 continued the same trend of weakening the feudal courts and strengthening the Crown.[10]

More important, however, for present purposes were those of Edward's reforms which directly related to the substantive law of land. The first of these Acts, directed against alienations in mortmain to the Church, has already been noticed as probably having no real equivalent in Scotland.[11] Its terms prohibited such grants altogether, but in practice the king granted licences of dispensation very freely. A remarkable point is that, in contrast to other feudal systems, for example in Scotland or France, the mesne lords, who stood to lose as much as the Crown by such alienations, apparently did not have to agree.[12] The practice under this Act was thus yet another sign of the overall power of the Crown.

THE STATUTE *QUIA EMPTORES* 1290

Better known and particularly interesting is the celebrated statute called *Quia Emptores Terrarum* (Statute of Westminster III) 1290[13] which more than anything else made the Tweed a division between two distinct systems of land law. This Act purported to be made in the interests of feudal lords, who by excessive subinfeudation on the part of their tenants lost effective control of the feudal incidents of service, wardship, reliefs and so on, through the removal of the actual tenant in possession too far away from them down the feudal hierarchical ladder. If *A* sub-feus to *B*, *A* can easily enforce his rights by distress against *B*; but if *B* has sub-feued to *C* and *C* to *D*, *A*'s rights, while theoretically still the same, are obviously harder to enforce in actual practice. And the profitable right to the wardship

---

10   Plucknett, *The Legislation of Edward I*, 45, 47.
11   Statute of Mortmain (*De Viris Religiosis*) 1279. *See* Chapter 4 *supra*.
12   The situation is not very clear. There is nothing in the Act requiring their consent. But *see* Y.B., 21 Ed. III, Hil., pl. 15, Plucknett, *Legislation of Edward I*, 101.
13   *See* P. & M., i, 337; Holdsworth, *H.E.L.*, ii, 348; iii, 80 *et seq.*; Megarry and Wade, 30–2.

if *B* dies leaving a child heir may also be wellnigh worthless. Instead of the whole profits of the ground, *A* will only get *B*'s service from *C*, which may be exactly what he would have got from *B* as rent, or conceivably even less, if *B* sub-feued for a nominal return. Similarly with escheat, because the lord whose immediate tenant in demesne suffers an escheat gets the land in that event, while other lords on the forfeiture or death without heirs of their immediate tenant, get only a seignory, of possibly nominal value.

The king stood to lose as much by all this as any other lord, but Maitland's view that *Quia Emptores* 1290 was solely in the Crown's interests has been doubted.[14] The Act benefited all lords, humble as well as great. Its provisions are straightforward enough: in future no alienation of land in fee simple[15] was to be by way of subinfeudation, but by way of substitution instead: or, as Scots legal language would put it, grants *de me* of the *dominium utile* became impossible: all must be *a me de superiore meo*. Substitution was not against the lord's interest, as he has the same degree of closeness of connection with the actual possessor of the land as before.[16]

The results of this statute 'were momentous and none the less so because they were unforeseen'.[17] No new tenure of any kind could be created in England after this, except by the king. This meant, among other things, that the rent-service owned by a free tenant to his lord, once compounded for its then value in money, could never be revalued in terms of contemporary values. As a result of the Act the seignory in England became of such little value that records of its ownership have long ceased to be kept. The inability to grant newly in frankalmoign was a useful check on those inordinate grants to the Church, which we have seen to have been a feature of medieval Scotland. Henceforward if the Church acquired land (under a Mortmain licence) it could only do so on the same conditions as the donor had it, for example in return for so-called military services.

14 P. & M., i, 337; Plucknett, *Legislation of Edward I*, 103.
15 *Quia Emptores* operated only to prohibit an alienation in fee simple. Any less grant, e.g. of a fee tail, was not barred (Y.B., 21 & 22 Ed. I. (R.S.), 641); nor did it apply to copyholds.
16 Substitutionary alienation was almost certainly possible before the Act (Bracton, f 81). The lord could apparently not even refuse a corporate vassal. This is remarkable considering the grave financial loss caused to the lord. In Scotland corporate vassals could be refused right up to 1874 (Bell, *Principles*, 722).
17 Plucknett, *Legislation of Edward I*, 106.

Since escheat might still reduce the number of steps in the feudal
ladder, the tendency was more and more for the tenure of land to be
in England a matter between the king and the tenant-in-chief,
rather than, as in Scotland, between subject and subject. Moreover,
as the direct substitution envisaged by *Quia Emptores* 1290 was a
matter solely between alienor and alienee, the mesne lord did not
survive even as a piece of conveyancing machinery, as he did right
up to 1874 in Scotland. Again, subinfeudation had been used on
occasions as a device to escape the rigours of tenure. With this
rendered impossible, English ingenuity had to have recourse to the
rather desperate extremity of the Use, with its very fundamental
implications, including the notion of an equitable estate in land.[18]
Megarry and Wade emphasise the profound effect of this medieval
statute which is still in force in English law today, and is indeed one
of the very pillars of the great edifice of the law of real property.

> It operates every time that a conveyance in fee simple is executed,
> automatically shifting the status of tenant from grantor to grantee
> and fulfilling the rule that all land held by a subject shall be held
> in tenure of the Crown either mediately or immediately. The lord
> of the fee is the successor in title to the person who was lord in
> 1290, for there can have been no change in the tenure since then.[19]
> But it is rare for records of a mesne lordship to have been pre-
> served for so long, except in the case of manors where mesne
> tenure remained of importance until 1925 and later.[20] Other
> cases are governed by the presumption that, if no mesne lord
> appears, the land is held immediately of the Crown.[21] Innumerable
> mesne lordships came to be forgotten as, with the passage of time
> and the inflation of the currency, the ancient services or commuta-
> tion rents ceased to be worth collecting. After 1290 the feudal
> pyramid began to crumble. The number of mesne lordships could
> not be increased, evidence of existing mesne lordships gradually
> disappeared with the passing of time, and so most land came to be
> held directly from the Crown.[22]

---

18 *See* Chapter 15.
19 But it is possible that a subinfeudation in fee simple can be brought about (since
    1881) by the enlargement of a long lease: *see* Megarry and Wade, 670.
20 Megarry and Wade, 34.
21 Williams, *Law of Real Property*, 58; Challis, *The Law of Real Property*, 33; and
    see Re Lowe's W.T. [1973] 1 WLR 882.
22 Megarry and Wade, 32.

'Feudalism' is a vague and unpopular phrase,[23] but if it signifies that king, intermediate subject-superior and vassal all have an interest in the same piece of land, *Quia Emptores* 1290 may be viewed as having almost destroyed it in England. In Scotland, on the other hand, in the absence of *Quia Emptores*, feudalism in this sense flourished until centuries later and still shows a remarkable vitality.

The whole system of Scots conveyancing rests on the fact that subinfeudation is possible, and a grant *de me* was a vital part of almost every Scots conveyance.[24] Craig however conjectured that an express prohibition of subfeuing in a charter might be effective,[25] while Stair suggested that the time had perhaps come when excessive subinfeudation should be checked by legislation.[26]

THE STATUTE *DE DONIS CONDITIONALIBUS* 1285

The other Act of Edward I which had important effects in land law is that known as *De Donis Conditionalibus* 1285.[27] From this not merely the English law of entails, but the vital doctrine of estates may be said to be eventually derived. The former will be subsequently the subject-matter of a detailed examination,[28] but it is necessary here to appreciate the effects of the statute in order to see why it resulted in the doctrine just mentioned. The terms of the Act fairly clearly state the principle that where land had been given as a conditional gift to an individual and the issue of a particular marriage, the parent-donee should not be capable of disposing of it even if such issue had been born alive. Children were thus given an indefeasible right to succeed their parent in the land:[29] but could the heir born of the marriage, having eventually received the land after the death of his parent, treat it as his own, or must he keep in intact for the remoter issue? If so, during how many generations

---

23   Cf Maitland (P. & M., i, 67) and Plucknett, *Legislation of Edward I*, 21–2). As to some of the most frequent current abuses of 'feudalism' *see*, Kolbert, 'Misuse of the Term "Feudalism"', FAO, *Land Reform*, 1975 No 1, 72 *et seq.*
24   For explanations *see* Chapter 24.
25   Craig, 1.15.23.
26   Stair, II.4.6.
27   Statute of Westminster II (13 Edw. I, c 1).
28   Chapter 19.
29   Simpson, 81–2.

was this to continue? The first question was answered in favour of the issue, the second at first by the traditional doctrine that such gifts became absolute in the fourth generation. For reasons which are not very apparent, this view was not followed, and it came to be the received doctrine of English law that the entailed land was to remain inalienable until all the descendants of the body of the original donee were extinct, when it reverted to the original donor, or his heirs, unless otherwise expressly disposed of by him.[30]

Until that event took place, or until, on the earlier interpretation, all hope of the land's reverting to the donor had been lost, there were in a quite real sense two simultaneous holders of the land. The holder in actual possession was not a full holder, for he could not alienate the land. But – and this was the vital result of the doctrine of estates – he could alienate his interest (that is, his estate) in it. The other holder did not possess at present, but had an interest in the land which was fully protected by the law and could not be alienated.[31] While the parent-donee was alive and had a living son, the number of holders could be said to have risen to three, for the son, too, had an interest protected by law.[32] These parallel and co-existent interests in land came to be called 'estates'.[33] Each holder does not own the land, but he owns and can dispose of, his interest or estate in it. To English lawyers this has seemed to flow from the fundamental doctrine of derivative tenure itself, for by that doctrine no subject can own land. The king alone owns land in England: the subject, though, has something, that is his holding from the king, which may for convenience be called an estate 'in' the land. This he may be said to 'own'. Even the tenant who holds land for the longest possible period known to English law, the fee simple, does not have an absolute interest in it, for in certain events escheat may bring his interest to an end and the land will then pass to his lord. His estate, called technically a fee simple, therefore differs from other subjects' interests in land of more limited duration purely in degree

30 Simpson, 64. *See also* Chapters 12 and 18 *infra*.
31 Action could be brought through the writ. Formedon (*forma doni*) in the reverter (Holdsworth, *H.E.L.*, ii, 350).
32 Here the writ was called Formedon in the descender (*ibid.*). There could also be a remainderman, with Formedon in the remainder to protect him (*see* Chapter 13 *infra*).
33 For the evolution of this phrase, *see* Holdsworth, *H.E.L.*, iii, 111. The term is found in its modern sense in Y.B., 20 & 21 Ed. I (R.S.) 12, 34, 38, 50.

and not in kind. All are estates, some of long, some of short, but all of limited duration.

SCOTS CLASSIFICATION OF LAND RIGHTS

Scots law traditionally approaches the classification of interests in land from a totally different standpoint. Craig has left such a profound impression behind him, especially on this very question, that Scots law is now irrevocably based on the doctrines of Roman law and continental feudalism as understood by Craig. Yet he was not decried at the time as a revolutionary introducer of foreign doctrines. The tendency of Scotland, already noted, to take its academic law teaching from France and the Netherlands, was centuries older than Craig; and whereas continental feudal systematic theories reached England only in the seventeenth century,[34] they were almost certainly well understood in Scotland by at least the later Middle Ages. The fact that Scotland's richest landholders were the clergy, trained in Rome-derived canon law, and that these landholders were also the judges of Scotland in matters of land may be significant. Finally it must be remembered that English law evolved its rival theory of estates only after, and largely, if not entirely, as a result of *De Donis Conditionalibus* 1285, which was presumably unknown in Scotland.[35]

The Scots classification has been explained as follows:

> In Scotland we distinguish . . . rights affecting land into two kinds, *viz* property, and a right burdening or limiting property. Property, in its nature unbounded, cannot otherwise be bounded, but by rights burdening it or narrowing it: and it is restored to its original unbounded state so soon as the burdening right is extinguished; but a burdening right, being in its nature bounded, becomes not more extensive by the extinction of other rights affecting the same subject.[36]

---

34 This is what Maitland meant when he asserted that the feudal system was introduced into England by Spelman (*see* Hogg, 'Effects of Tenure on Real Property Law', (1909) 25 LQR 178).
35 But *see* Chapter 18.
36 Lord Kames, *Historical Law Tracts*, 46; cf Lord Haldane's comparison in *Carnegy v Joseph* 1916 SC (HL) 39, 43.

This sharp distinction between ownership and all other rights is clearly in accordance with the best Civilian traditions,[37] yet there are obvious difficulties in applying 'the dead law of an alien people'[38] to a system of land rights based on a doctrine – that of derivative feudal tenure – scarcely known to that ancient law at all.

The following chapters examine more closely the principal rights and interests that may exist in land under the doctrine of derivative tenure to try to discover whether the English theory of estates or the Scots concept of property and charges on it, more effectively covers the large and varied collection of interests which may from time to time be created with regard to the same portion of the earth's surface. By natural law these may be many in number and multifarious in kind, for as Jenks reminds us:

> A piece of land cannot rise up and run away, or be carried off, or disappear[39] or die; while a horse or sheep can do all these things. A piece of land has therefore a permanency which enables successive interests (possibly extending over a long period) to be created and preserved in it.[40]

In addition to this quality of permanence land may be used in different ways by different people simultaneously. Rights of occupation, travel, shooting, fishing and so on may all be vested in separate individuals at the same time over a single plot of ground.[41]

37 Girard, *Droit Romain*, 264.
38 Lord Kames, *Historical Law Tracts*, 383.
39 Justinian, *Institutes*, 2.1.20.
40 Jenks, *The Book of English Law*, 251.
41 Diamond, *Primitive Law*, 269.

11   Rights of Feudal Lord and Vassal

The Scots classification of interests in land starts under a major difficulty. Having decided to make a sharp distinction between the *dominus* of any given piece of ground and all others having rights in relation to it, it is obviously quite imperative to discover which of the various persons connected with it is to be treated as the *dominus*. To the classical Roman lawyer this was not a problem. *Solum italicum* being a *res mancipi* was subject to full civil law ownership (*dominium ex jure quiritium*), that is allodial ownership.[1] Hence when Scots law is dealing with allodial property such as udal land, there is no difficulty. The allodial proprietor may easily be discovered and equated with the Roman *dominus*. All other rights, including presumably those of his family to hinder an alienation of the land, are treated as *jura in re aliena* and charges on the ownership of the *dominus*.

Unfortunately the overwhelming majority of Scots lands are held not by an allodial, but by a feudal title. In this scheme of land-holding, with its hierarchy of sovereign, superior and vassal (the last two being often many times repeated) it is by no means readily apparent in whom the *dominium* is vested.

English lawyers do not agree with the imposition of a civil law notion such as ownership on a feudal system of landholding; but when pressed by ardent feudalists have answered that the *dominium* of the lands in England is vested in the king, whose English subjects have mere *jura in re aliena* over (if one must use civilian terms) or estates in (as they prefer to say) the property of the Crown.[2] This

---

1   Gaius, *Institutes*, II.14a.
2   This is now received as the classical doctrine of English law. Hogg, 'Effects of Tenure on Real Property Law', (1909) 25 LQR, 178 *et seq.* shows that even Spelman hesitated to use the now standard language, as did Wright. The 'answer' referred

theory most conveniently answers the feudalists in their own language, while preserving intact the traditional English doctrine of estates.

For some reason which is rather obscure (but may be simply that Scots opinion had already hardened before the English evolved their theory) Scots law has not taken this easy way out of its self-imposed difficulty. Instead it has taken over, through the medium of Craig, the immense continental learning on this subject.[3]

Scots Law: the Problem of Dominium

Many of the continental writers start with the assumption that *dominium* is indivisible, which is the traditional view of the civilian. France's leading exponent of Roman law defined ownership as follows: 'C'est la domination complète et exclusive d'une personne sur une chose corporelle.'[4] Buckland, his English opposite number wrote, '*Dominium* is the ultimate right, that which has no right behind it. It may be a mere *nudum jus* with no practical content, but it is still *dominium ex jure quiritium*. It is a *signoria*.'[5] But what is not available is a quotation from the *Corpus Juris Civilis* to this effect.[6] However, that may be, the majority of medieval feudalists took this view of ownership: accordingly they could not conceive, as Craig was eventually to do, of a divided *dominium*, for ownership must be in one defined legal person. The only question which remained for them to solve was the basic one, namely, in which person, the superior or the vassal, is it to be found under the feudal arrangement of landholding?

The grand feature of the Scottish feudal system was that it invested the sovereign with the character of original and supreme proprietor of all land subject to his dominion. By him territories

---

to in the text appears to be that of Blackstone (Bl. Comm., ii, 105), and this has been regarded as incontrovertible by almost all writers; *see* e.g. Williams, *Real Property*, 7; Megarry and Wade, 13; Cheshire, 13; Coke, however, wrote 'though a subject has not properly *directum* yet he hath *utile dominium*' (Co. Litt. 1b).

3   The continental countries no longer know the meaning of this question, having abandoned a feudal for a registered system of land titles. Pothier was interested in this problem; *see* Piret, *La recontre chez Pothier des conceptions romaine et féodale de la propriété foncière*.

4   Girard, *Droit Romain*, 267.

5   Buckland, *Textbook of Roman Law*, 188.

6   Schultz, *Principles of Roman Law*, 152, 154.

were allotted to his more powerful subjects, who subdivided them among their dependants, and these in their turn made subordinate grants, which descended through successive grades to an extent commensurate with the exigencies of the military situation right down to the lowest rank.[7] The result is that a subject can be at once a vassal of his own superior and a superior of his own vassal, that is a mid-superior

The interest which is reserved to the superior is called the *dominium directum*, because it is in the feudal sense the more eminent right[8] which empowers the superior not only to collect his feuduty but to exact implement of the conditions of his grant. The interest of the mid-superior is to pay feuduty to his superior and to collect his feuduty from his own vassal and to exact implement of any additional conditions which he may impose and provide that his vassal relieves him of the conditions imposed upon by him by his superior other than the payment of his feuduty. The interest of the ultimate vassal carries with it exclusive possession and enjoyment of the land so long as the conditions of the grant are fulfilled.[9] Lord Kames wrote, 'The superior's right to the land is in its nature unlimited, extending over the whole. The vassal's right, on the contrary, is in its nature limited, being in effect a burden on the superiority.'[10] He points out that several rules of Scots law support his view. For example, a resignation *ad remanentiam* or even a simple renunciation is sufficient to extinguish the vassal's right and to restore the superiority to its original unlimited condition; but a renunciation by the superior in favour of the vassal avails nothing unless it is effected by the full machinery of a feudal sasine.

Since the time of Craig Scots law has been fully committed to the view put forward by that writer in his *Jus Feudale*, that of the division of the *dominium* into *directum* for the superior and *utile* for the vassal. All the institutional writers, even including Erskine, who was very apt on occasions to press feudal law into Roman forms have followed Craig in this.[11]

7 Menzies, *Lectures on Conveyancing*, 510.
8 Erskine, II.3.19.
9 Craigie, 4.
10 *Elucidations*, 76.
11 Stair, II.3.7. Erskine, II.3.1; Bell, *Principles*, 675–9; Green's *Encyclopaedia*, title 'Superior and Vassal'.

Craig's view is now the established doctrine of Scots law. At times it seems to come very near to the English conception of estates. Thus the Scots Property Law Commissioners reported in 1837 that 'to the vassal belongs the *dominium utile* or property – the Crown and all intermediate parties, if any such exist between him and the Crown, possessing mere estates of *dominium directum* or superiority'. Modern writers usually refer to both *dominia* as estates.[12] That the matter is still not free from controversy may be shown by comparing the above statement of the Property Law Commissioners with Lord Dunedin's view in *Heriot's Trust v Caledonian Railway*:[13] 'On a sound view of the feudal system as developed in Scotland the superior was truly the *dominus* of the land, subject to the *dominium utile* being in the vassal.' Yet even in the same case[14] he had to admit that for the purposes of the Act he was construing 'owner' in Scotland is the vassal and not the superior.

The double *dominium* theory leaves much to be desired. In particular it becomes strained when the land is sub-feued. The authorities vary between saying that all the superiors have *dominium directum*, which surely robs *directum* of its last shred of meaning (if not *dominium* also), and saying that a mid-superior has both *dominia*, in relation to his superior and his vassal respectively. This makes a *dominium* a mere relationship, not a right *in rem*, which was its very essence at Rome. One may wonder whether in such a connection the term ownership has any real meaning at all. The simplest solution is to recognise two estates in land, the superiority, or *dominium directum*, and the property or *dominium utile*, with the mid-superior in the middle with what amounts to a third estate. In theory all subject superiors are mid-superiors but immediate vassals of the Crown normally pay small feuduties and are burdened with few feudal conditions.

ENGLISH LAW: SEIGNORY

English law does not look on the superiority, which it calls the seignory, as being an estate in the land. It is not correct to say that

---

12   E.g. Green's *Encyclopaedia*, title 'Superior and Vassal'; Bell, *Principles*, 675.
13   [1915] AC 1046, 1075.
14   [1915] AC 1046, 1067.

the English treat all rights affecting land as estates: estates are certain interests in land viewed from the point of view of duration, and it is not only the land itself that may be thus treated. What English law calls an incorporeal hereditament is a right affecting land, but one not sufficiently extensive to carry full possession either now or in the future, but estates may also be created in interests such as this.[15] Thus one may have a right of way for life or for a term of years or for a fuller period equivalent to a fee simple. It is to this category of incorporeal hereditaments that English law has relegated the seignory of a feudal lord.[16] No more striking illustration of his insignificance in that system could be found.

THE DIFFERING STATUS OF SUPERIOR AND SEIGNEUR

The first application of the rival classifications of interests in land under the sister systems thus brings to light a fundamental difference of approach. Scotland's division of rights into *dominium* and rights *in re aliena* has found itself in an uncomfortable dilemma as to the whereabouts of that very *dominium* in the feudal system of land-holding, while England's doctrine of estates has denied the honourable title of an estate in the land to what is in feudal tradition the senior component right in a feu.

This is not a point of mere theoretical importance. The double *dominia* of Scots law find their expression in a number of rules which show that the superior as well as the vassal is treated by the law as 'owner' of the land. The complete absence of corresponding rules in England underlines the English lord's lack of any but a purely nominal connection with the land which in Scotland would be 'his'; and indeed the connection of a lord of a manor with his copyhold land was much greater, both from the conveyancing point of view and that of the feudal services. Nevertheless a manor is only an incorporeal hereditament, not an estate in the land.

In *Hay v Corporation of Aberdeen*,[17] Lord President Dunedin said:

15 *See* further Chapter 13.
16 Plucknett, *Concise History of the Common Law*, 543.
17 1909 SC 554, 559.

> It was long ago decided that a conveyance of superiorities was a
> good conveyance, but while the court decided that, they also laid
> down in the most strict terms that a conveyance in which the
> subject was described as a superiority was not a proper way to
> convey a superiority, but that the proper way . . . was by a convey-
> ance of the lands with the exception from the warrandice of the
> feu rights.

In England a conveyance of a seignory or a manor, the former
being extremely rare,[18] should correctly refer to the subject matter
conveyed as such seignory or manor and not as the land. In *Rooke v
Lord Kensington*[19] it was held that a conveyance of 'all the other
lands, tenements and hereditaments' in a county did not pass a
manor, even though a manor is clearly a hereditament.[20]

The direct interest of the Scots superior in the land has been
shown even more strikingly by the fact that he is deemed to have a
perfect title to its possession except as against the feuar and those
claiming through him. Consequently he can bring actions against
trespassers and squatters.[21] Since the English lord is not entitled
to possession (unless and until an escheat takes place) he cannot
interfere with those who abuse his tenant's right to possess, so that
even if a squatter obtains a title under the Statute of Limitations, the
lord cannot intervene or complain. The status of the Scots superior
as *dominus* was particularly well brought out in the case of superiorities held immediately of the Crown. The liability for taxation, as well
as the parliamentary francise, was for long vested in the superior-in-
chief, although his vassals, whether direct or remote, had the
practically exclusive use of the ground.[22] If a superior became
entitled to this *dominium utile* by any means, no new sasine need be
taken.[23] This last rule, unlike the others, has a parallel in England.
A mesne lord taking by escheat did not need any conveyance with
the livery of seisin. This seems at first inconsistent with the rule
that he has only an incorporeal hereditament, but such a livery of

---

18 Because its lack of practical value caused a lack of attention as to its whereabouts.
    See also, as to difficulties of theory, Holdsworth, *H.E.L.*, iii, 81–2.
19 (1856) 2 K & J 753, 772.
20 This seems a strong case, but it was an *eiusdum generis* point.
21 Stair, II.4.3. *Lagg v Tenants* (1624) M 13787. *Edmonstone v Jeffray* (1886) 13 R
    1038.
22 *Hamilton v Bogle* (1919) I Ross LC 22.
23 *Barstow v Black* (1870) 8 Macph 671.

seisin was not as absolute a necessity in England as in Scotland; an heir, for example, did not need it.[24]

The view that the English lord has no right or estate in the land but only in this incorporeal hereditament, the seignory, has so permeated English legal thought that it has been doubted whether even the king does have the *dominium* (as has been suggested) of England and not just a more practically important incorporeal hereditament or supreme seignory.[25]

24   *See* Chapter 24.
25   Hogg, 'Effects of Tenure on Real Property Law', (1909) 25 LQR, 178, 181; cf *Att.-Gen. of Ontario v Mercer* (1883) 8 App Cas 767, 772 *per* Lord Selborne, LC.

12 Fee Simple and Dominium Utile; Fee Tail, Remainder and Reversion[1]

Those interests which English law recognises as actual estates in the land or corporeal hereditaments can now be compared with their Scots equivalents, so far as these exist. The estates in question are the fee simple, fee tail, life estate, and estate *pur autre vie*, being freeholds. There are also the leasehold estates, which will be discussed later.[2] Each of these estates is an interest in land which endures or, rather, may endure, for a different period. But where there is more than one such interest existing in the same piece of land at the same time, it is obvious that only one of them can actually carry the right to possession.[3] Thus, if an English grantor gave land to *A* for life and then to *B* and the heirs of his body, and then to *C* and his heirs, *A* alone would be entitled to possession and have, therefore, an estate in possession. The others, for whose benefit the land will remain away from the grantor after the death of the life in being (*A*), are said to have in the meantime mere estates in remainder, or more shortly, remainders. If there had been no last grant in fee simple to *C* – for that is the effect of the words employed – there would have remained with the grantor a fee simple in reversion, or again more shortly, the reversion. As has been explained in considering the statute *De Donis Conditionalibus* 1290, these estates in remainder and reversion are present rights to the land, which may be alienated and protected, if necessary, by action.[4] So we shall consider not only

---

1 For the modern English law of estates *see* Megarry and Wade, 40–109.
2 *See* Chapter 14.
3 Possession is a dangerous word to employ as the holder of years may be entitled to actual possession of the land. If so, the first freehold estate still has the 'freehold possession' or, as it is technically called, the seisin. *See* Chapters 14 and 23.
4 *See* Chapter 25.

whether Scotland knows each of the 'estates' mentioned, but also how far she knows equivalents of them in reversion or remainder.

In contrast a Scottish grantor of a feu charter immediately creates two estates in land, the *dominium directum* or a right of superiority which he retains and which is burdened with the grantee's *dominium utile* or right of possession.[5] If a Scottish grantor grants a feu charter to *A* for life then to *B* in fee the grantor retains the *dominium directum* which is burdened with the *dominium utile* of *B* which in turn is burdened with the liferent interest of *A*.[6] *B* could immediately sell the *dominium utile* under burden of *A*'s liferent without the consent of *A*.

A grant 'to *B* and the heirs of his body' so as to create a new entail has been impossible since the Entail (Scotland) Act 1914.[7] Because *B* has an absolute right to dispose of his *dominium utile*, a destination over to *C* and his heirs gives only a *spes successionis* and is not necessary because *B* is in Scots law the owner of the *dominium utile* from the date of the grant.

FEE SIMPLE AND DOMINIUM UTILE

The fee simple absolute in possession is the largest estate known to English law and, as has often been remarked, is in almost every practical respect the equivalent of the ownership of goods. The holder of land in England for a fee simple interest may treat the land as subject to his use and pleasure. He may use it himself in any way he pleases,[8] subject to such public control provisions as the Town and Country Planning Acts and provided also that his enjoyment does not infringe the rights of other landholders.[9] He may let it, for the use of others and may dispose of his interest, but subject to the general rule that he must not subinfeudate it in fee simple.[10]

5   Erskine, II.3.7.
6   Craigie, 36.
7   S 2.
8   As to fee simple owner's rights of enjoyment, for details *see* Cheshire 155–62; cf the Scots position, Bell, *Principles*, 940 *et seq.*; Rankine, *Landownership, passim.*
9   *See* e.g. the rules of nuisance, Clerk and Lindsell on *Torts*, paras. 1391–1473.
10 *See* Chapter 10. The legislation of 1925 imposed certain other restrictions, e.g. a perpetually renewable lease cannot now be granted.

Formerly too he was actually subject, as he still is in theory, to the services arising from the fact that he holds the land by a feudal tenure. These have, however, been practically nominal for centuries. It therefore seems mere historical pedantry to deny him in law what he has long had in common speech: the status of a landowner.

Such is the attitude of the present day. But if we examine the position of the holder in fee simple in the past we may appreciate why he has been denied the status of an owner of the land. Apart from the subservience involved in the ceremony of homage and the other feudal services, the estate in fee simple differed radically from ownership in that it was limited in point of time. The traditional wording of the grant in England, 'to *A* and his heirs'[11] meant originally what it said, and *A*'s estate in the land would endure so long as he had heirs, that is blood relations whether lineal or collateral, in existence. If at any time the heirs became extinct, or if, by treason or felony, he or they became incapable of holding land, the estate came to an end.[12] Such was the original position. Unfortunately, however, for clarity of thinking on this matter, these estates – clearly of limited, though never of certain, duration[13] – became virtually everlasting through the acquisition by the tenant of the power to alienate by way of substitution, so imposing a new tenant with whom the heirs may claim relationship, and even more, through the possibility of creating additional 'heirs' by will, even including corporations which can never die, and eventually the abolition of forfeiture for crime.[14] Since they are thus wellnigh

---

11   Cf 'to *A* and the heirs of his body', which created an entailed interest. *See* Chapter 22.

12   Holdsworth, *H.E.L.*, III, 106 *et seq.* In Bracton's time land granted to a bastard in fee simple sent back to the lord on the bastard's death issueless, even if the bastard had alienated it to another man who had heirs: f 12b: P. & M., ii, 14 (21).

13   Of course, they might last for ever, if there was a due succession of heirs. For this reason it is sometimes erroneously stated that 'he who has a fee simple in land has a time in the land without end, or the land for a time without end'. *Walsingham's Case* (1573) 2 Plowd, 547, 555. This uncertainty of duration distinguished the freehold from leasehold which lasts for a predetermined period only. The fee simple is, therefore, an estate that may, will not, last for ever: but Scots grants are often expressly 'for ever' (Appendices III, IV, XV).

14   Holdsworth, *H.E.L.*, iii, 106 *et seq.*; Plucknett, *Concise History of the Common Law*, 540 *et seq.*; Digby, *History of Real Property*, *passim*. It is not possible to treat all the estates in detail here. The estate tail is considered at pp. 122–5 *infra*.

everlasting, it seems obvious now to speak of estates in fee simple as carrying the ownership, the essence of which was always that it lasted as long as the *res* itself. But English law derives its ideas and its terminology on this point from the early Middle Ages, when the fee simple was quite clearly a limited right. We should also remember that ownership is a civil law conception, to which the common law 'property' does not directly correspond.[15] Even less can seisin[16] be equated with it.

In medieval Scotland a feu was granted by proper investiture when the grantor went to the ground with at least two of his other vassals and handed over a sod of earth and a stone to his new vassal who thereupon took the oath of fidelity. For convenience the new vassal was also given a written document, a *breve testatum* as evidence of the investiture, which was the forerunner of the feu charter. Alternatively, to save the grantor the trouble of going out to the ground, he issued a *breve testatum* to his commissioner or bailie who went to the ground and handed over the earth and stone along with a declaration that the delivery had been carried out. This was called improper investiture[17] and the declaration was the forerunner of the instrument of sasine. Both proper and improper investiture were superseded in the fifteenth century by feu charters with a separate precept for infeftment: in time this was added as part of the feu charter. It is essential to understand that the granting of a feu charter did not of itself create the relationship of superior and vassal; the key document was the instrument of sasine, which was the document which was put on the Register of Sasines until 1858. The feu charter specified the amount of the feuduty and the conditions under which the land was held. These were repeated in the instrument of sasine which was recorded and was the public evidence of the ownership of land.

If the recipient of a feu charter wished to dispose of the whole or part of his property he could sub-feu by granting a feu charter usually with an increased feuduty and additional conditions. In such a case he remained the vassal of his own superior and was responsible for the payment of his own feuduty and for the fulfilment of the conditions

15   Pollock and Wright, *Possession in the Common Law.*
16   Chapter 23.
17   Erskine, II.3.17; Menzies *Lectures on Conveyancing*, 528; Craigie, 30.

contained in his own feu charter, but at the same time he in turn collected feuduty from his own vassal and could enforce the conditions which he had imposed. He thus became a mid-superior and had burdened his own *dominium utile* with the rights of his own vassal, making it a *dominium directum*.

Alternatively, he could grant a disposition which merely transferred his right to the whole or part of the *dominium utile* to the grantee. The disposition contains a precept of sasine which enabled the grantee to hold the land either under the grantor for payment of a penny together with an obligation to relieve him of the feuduty and obligations due to his superior (*de me*) or from him under his superior (*a me de superiore meo*).[18] The two methods of holding when combined in one disposition were called an alternative holding (*a me vel de me*). The disposition was followed by an instrument of sasine which was recorded in the Register of Sasines. The grantor remains liable to his superior until his vassal enters with that superior. If the grantor had himself entered with the superior and the grantee was prepared to pay a casualty, the grantee resigned his right to the *dominium utile* to the superior in return for a charter of resignation. Alternatively when the grantor was not entered with the superior a charter of confirmation was necessary to recognise the vassals who had not entered with the superior. Both the charter of resignation and the charter of confirmation contained precepts of sasine and the grantee obtained and recorded an instrument of sasine thereon in the Register of Sasines, with the result that he became the entered vassal and the grantor fell out of the feudal chain.

Whether he holds the *dominium utile* as an entered vassal or not, the owner thereof is the real owner of the land and his estate in land is the nearest equivalent to the English fee simple absolute in possession. It is possible that there may be a liferent interest which would rob him of possession during the life of the liferenter, but his right is absolute and he can dispose of it without regard to the liferenter's consent, though subject to his possessory rights. His position is thus practically the same as that of the owner of an English fee simple, differing in practical terms only in the right of the superior

18   Craigie, 319.

to a payment of feuduty and to enforce any conditions imposed by the feu charter.

The feudal system even influenced the form of wills. To dispose of land by will before 1868 it was necessary that the dispositive clause should contain the word 'dispone', describe the land at least in general terms, and contain a precept of sasine. This really meant that the will should contain a disposition under reservation of a liferent for the testator in case he decided to change his will. If the feudal clauses were omitted from the will it was sufficient to found an action by the beneficiary against the heir to denude and grant a disposition to him in terms of the will. The Titles to Land Consolidation Act 1868[19] abolished the necessity of framing bequests of land in the form of conveyances *inter vivos* and the use of the word 'dispone'.

A series of statutes in the nineteenth century, beginning with the Infeftment Act 1845, gathered together by the Titles to Land Consolidation Act 1868 and finished off by the Conveyancing (Scotland) Act 1874 (which provided that infeftment by recording a deed in the Register of Sasines implied entry with the superior), introduced shorthand methods of conveyancing but did not alter its essential feudal structure.

The owner of a fee simple absolute in possession in England and the owner of the *dominium utile* in Scotland are alike treated as the owners of the land in practical terms, for although the Scottish right is in theory a burden on the superior's *dominium directum*, the possession and enjoyment of the land remains with the owner of the *dominium utile*.

One last minor difference should be noted here, since it arises naturally from the difference of approach between the idea of an estate and the notion of *dominium*. When the English tenant died without successors of any kind, his estate had run its course and *ipso facto* perished. In Scotland in similar circumstances the fee did not perish, since *dominium* lasts as long as the *res* itself. The king merely took it as ultimate heir, like any other ownerless object, and donated it to be held of the same superior.[20] The English lord did not take

19 Ss 20, 21. Craigie, 624 *et seq.*
20 Bell, *Lectures*, i, 386; Menzies, *Lectures on Conveyancing*, 505; *Finnie v Lords of Treasury* (1836) 15 S 165.

the vassal's interest, because it was now ownerless: he took because the vassal's interest in it had come to its appointed end.[21]

CONDITIONAL AND DETERMINABLE FEES

The difference of theory has thus not had a very marked effect on the substantive law as to the fee simple and *dominium utile* in their simplest, absolute form. But in practice much more complicated interests may be created and it is in connection with such interests that differences between the two systems become more apparent. For example English law knows, in addition to the fee simple absolute, such estates as the fee simple on condition and the determinable fee simple. These have been the subject matter of some very abstruse learning,[22] but all that need be noted here is that they are treated in the classical English law as distinct estates, less than the fee simple. So long as they remain subject to the possibility of coming to an untimely end, a true fee simple in reversion is still in being in relation to the same land. Since this is the case, such grants are not regarded as within the prohibition of *Quia Emptores*.

It has always been accepted in Scots law that the superior was entitled to impose conditions on the *dominium utile*. In early feu charters attendance at the superior's courts was the only common condition, but in the middle of the eighteenth century when terraces and blocks of flats in towns began to be developed, feudal conditions were used to impose obligations to maintain common parts of the building and the common gardens, usually in proportion to the feuduty. In 1806 in Edinburgh George Heriot's Trust entered into a contract with the Corporation containing detailed conditions re-

---

21 Co. Litt. 13a; Bracton, ii, f 118.
22 A determinable interest lasts until some event occurs (time element): a conditional one provided some condition is not broken (condition element). This fine line is still important: Cheshire 314–26. For example, a simple fee upon condition merely gives the grantor (or whoever is entitled to his interest in the land, if the grantor is dead) a right to enter and determine the estate when the event occurs (Littleton, *Tenures*, s 331; Co. Litt. 214b; Challis, *Law of Real Property* 208, 261; Megarry and Wade, 77). Unless and until entry is made the fee simple continues: *Matthew Manning's Case* (1609) 8 Co Rep 94b at 95b; Challis, *Law of Real Property*, 219; *Re Evans' Contract* [1920] 2 Ch 469 at 472. The possibility of reverter after a determinable fee operates *automatically*. The right of entry arising on a breach of condition is exercisable *at the option* of the grantor or his successor (Megarry and Wade, 77).

garding the development of the Trust's lands which were incorporated in the feu charters of the various flats and houses. They limited the use of garden ground and the heights of buildings and provided that plans must be approved by the trustees. In 1822 the Earl of Moray introduced conditions not only for the design of the houses, which were to be those made by his architect, Mr Gillespie Graham, but also for the stables and pleasure grounds. He further provided that Mr Gillespie Graham should be paid £5 for the use of his plans of each house, and the feuars were to pay for all the sewers, streets, boundary walls, railings, and so on, so that none of the cost should fall upon the Earl.[23] The lead of the Earl has been followed ever since and the owners of feuing estates throughout Scotland have granted very detailed feu charters governing the design, layout and use of the ground developed. The conditions are both positive and negative, and are enforceable only by the superior, who alone can relax them. The immediate sanctions to enforce feudal conditions other than for payment of money against successive vassals are actions of interdict or specific implement, and the final sanction is irritancy (forfeiture) of the land and all that is built thereon. It was also possible to give a superior a right of pre-emption which could be exercised against successive vassals, but the Conveyancing Amendment (Scotland) Act 1938, s 9 provided that in the event of a sale by the proprietor of the feu any such right, together with any irritant clauses should become null and void unless the superior intimated his intention to exercise his right of pre-emption within forty days of receiving notice of the intended sale, or within any shorter period specified in the charter. The Conveyancing and Feudal Reform (Scotland) Act 1970, s 46 has further limited the right of the pre-emption, cutting the time for acceptance of an offer to twenty-one days, and in practical terms virtually ensuring that a right of pre-emption could only be exercised once. All conditions limiting the use of the land are viewed as restrictions on the natural rights of the owner of the *dominium utile* and are construed by the Courts very strictly against the superior.[24] However, Scottish feudal conditions can achieve

23 Youngson, *The Making of Classical Edinburgh*, 204–23.
24 *Aberdeen Tailors v Coutts* (1840) Rob App 296; *Aberdeen Varieties Ltd v James F. Donald (Aberdeen Cinemas) Ltd* 1940 SC (HL) 52.

much more than English restrictive covenants because they can be positive. Nevertheless it is broadly true that, apart from possible burdens of a liferent or fetters of an entail, the right of the owner of *dominium utile* is absolute in that he can dispose of it as he wishes and any restrictions on his use thereof must be specific and must appear on the Register of Sasines. Any restriction on his power of disposal can only operate according to established common law in the case of a liferent or statute in the case of an entail, as well as appearing on the Register of Sasines, otherwise it is void.

FEE TAIL AND TAILZIE

At one time, before the statute *De Donis Conditionalibus* 1285, the best example of a conditional fee in English law was the estate which *A* had when land was given to '*A* and the heirs of his body'.[25] The eventual effect of that Act was to make the estate tail a distinct estate in English law. This is clearly an estate less than the fee simple, for it will not endure so long as there are heirs of *A*, but only so long as there is a more restricted class of heirs, that is his actual descendants. Even more limited classes, such as male descendants, may be delimited if desired. Unlike the fee simple, the fee tail cannot properly be artificially prolonged by alienation or testament although through elaborate legal fictions and statutory interference such things have become possible in comparatively recent times.[26] These developments do scant justice to the principle that the tenant in tail has not the full fee, but only a much more limited estate. So long as the estate tail remains such, however, there must always be behind it, and as it were supporting it, a fee simple. If this was granted to someone else at the time when the fee fail was created, it is called a remainder; but if the grantor made no special arrangements as to the fee simple, he is said to have retained the reversion himself. Again, the grantor might have arranged for another fee tail to follow the one which now has the possession. If so, it too will be for the time being an estate in remainder.

In Scotland the estate tail does not exist; it eventually became possible to create a tailzied feu, but this was a grant of the fee

25   *See* Chapter 18.
26   The Fine and Common Recovery (*see* Chapter 19). As to testament only in 1925 (Law of Property Act, s 176 (1)).

(*dominium plenum*) subject to fetters against its alienation or charging. It in no sense created a limited estate carved out of the fee simple, as was the case in England. Lord Kames justly remarks that a tenant in tail in Scotland has the property of the estate completely vested in him.[27] This is well shown on a death. The heir of entail is served heir exactly as if he were succeeding in fee simple. There is no residuum which descends to another line of heirs. The Act of 1685 proceeds on this footing. It presupposes that the heir of entail can alienate the whole fee and permits certain fetters to be imposed on him in special circumstances.[28] Again, the form of a Scots entail makes it clear that it is an alienation of the whole of the settler's rights: similarly an English settlement makes clear the English doctrine of estates.

This, unlike some of the other, rather theoretical differences considered elsewhere in this chapter, has had important practical results. If the person who would in England be the tenant in tail is proprietor, he has by the very nature of his right all the powers of a proprietor, for example, of alienation or charging. To the Scot, or indeed any civilian-minded jurist, these are the basic inevitable consequences which spring from ownership.[29] Consequently any restrictions of such powers will have to be authorised by statute and are apt to be very rigorously construed. The Scots 'tenant in tail' is thus a full vassal with the *dominium utile* differing from his brother holding for the equivalent of a 'fee simple' only in certain statute-authorised restrictions affecting his alienation of the property. Apart from them he has automatically all the rights and powers of an ordinary *dominus*.

It follows that if the entire *dominium utile* is in the tenant in tail, this will not only affect his position in relation to the land, it will also very materially affect the status of the parties who in England would be described as the reversioner and the remaindermen. The position of the former in Scotland was that he had no inherent right to regain the land in the event of the last heir of the institute dying without heirs. He might be expressly given such a right by a

27 Lord Kames, *Elucidations*, 362; Sandford, *Entails*, 202.
28 Lord Kames, *Elucidations*, 345; *Historical Law Tracts*, 140.
29 It seems that to English legal minds there are no inevitable consequences of ownership, which may well be a mere *nudum ius*.

clause of return, but this was easily rendered nugatory. The persons delimited by the terms of the entail as successors to the institute, who may or may not be the equivalent of the English heirs of the body, are called substitutes. But they are only heirs whose right may, if certain very stringent conditions are fulfilled, be indefeasible; they do not in any sense whatever have a share or estate in the land. This is because (*a*) the *dominium* being in the fiar, there is nothing left for them to have; (*b*) they take purely as heirs, who can have no rights as such until the death of the present institute; nor in Scotland under the earlier law (following the Roman teaching), until they had actually made *aditio* by service; and (*c*) no real right in land can exist without sasine, which they will not receive until the institute is dead. Consequently they are limited to actions against the tenant in tail to ensure that he complies with the terms of the tailzie and cannot in any way act as estate-owners for example by alienating their interests (in remainder) as an English remainderman could do. Exactly the same rule as the Scots one prevailed at Rome, so as to prevent the alienation of a 'remainder':[30] this, of course, was a natural consequence of the Civilian attitude to *dominium*.

Pressed to its logical conclusion, the doctrine that the tenant in tail is the sole person having any proprietary right to the land leads to the unfortunate result that on a forfeiture for treason the whole fee is lost. Under the statute *De Donis Conditionalibus* 1285 the treasonable tenant in tail in England caused a forfeiture only for his lifetime.[31] His equivalent in Scotland, in an exactly similar factual position, lost the whole fee because of the different legal principles involved. Later by legislation in both countries the position has been altered, but the treasonable Scot is still at a disadvantage.

Thus, the grant of an entailed feu in Scotland does not leave in the grantor any residuary right of eventual succession corresponding to the English reversion. Nor, equally, can a remainder in fee simple be granted to take effect after the entail. But this is not to say that the settler may not, after prescribing the course of descent of the land to the various substitutes, end with a clause directing that when all the prescribed heirs are exhausted the land shall return to his own right heir or to a third party assignee.

30   Buckland and McNair, *Roman Law and Common Law*, 93.
31   Dalrymple, *An Essay towards a General History of Feudal Property*, 172.

Such a clause of retour (or return), as it is called, is of a very different character to the English reversion. The returnee, if such a phrase may be used, has no more than a *spes successionis* in the land, still less an actual estate. He has not even the protection of the statute of 1685 and his rights may easily be defeated by any of the heirs of tailzie making an assignment for value of the land.

None of these problems is likely to occur in future. It has not been possible to create new entails since 1914[32] and there can now be very few heirs of entail who were born before the beginning of the entail; and since 1848 anyone born after the date of the entail has been able to disentail without the need to obtain any consents.[33]

32 Entail (Scotland) Act 1914, s 2.
33 Entail Amendment Act 1848, s 1.

13 Life Interests, Servitudes and Comparable Rights

LIFE INTERESTS: SCOTS LAW

At first sight the feudal liferent and the Roman usufruct have very much in common. The land in either case is to be used by a man during his lifetime. He is also to enjoy the fruits, but after his death the land will again become free from his interest and available for the use and pleasure of the *dominus*. Here, it would seem, is an interest in land which triumphantly vindicates the civilian approach of Scots law. Nothing could be more clearly a personal servitude. In the *Corpus Juris Civilis* there is a mass of detailed rules, developed through centuries of experience and supported by the highest legal erudition, analysing this relationship and providing practical rules for its administration.[1] It is therefore not surprising that all writers on Scots law without traceable exception describe the liferent as a usufruct.[2] The simplicity and elegance of the Civil law theory naturally appealed to minds trained to Roman law in continental or continental-inspired universities. The liferenter, therefore, has neither estate in the land nor any share of the *dominium*, which remains throughout in the fiar. There seems no reason to introduce into this context the Craigian barbarity of a divided ownership. This approach is well brought out by Menzies, who wrote.[3]

> The life-rent of lands again is a right only to enjoy the produce, consisting either in the actual crops or in the rents; and life-rents

---

1 Justinian, *Digest*, 7, 1; *Institutes*, 2.4.pr.
2 E.g. Craig, 1.11.6; Stair, II.6, 1; Erskine, II.9.39; Bell, *Principles*, 1037; Green's *Encyclopaedia*, title 'Liferent and Fee'.
3 *Lectures on Conveyancing*, 662; *See also* Gloag and Henderson, 557–69 and Dobie, *Manual of the Law of Liferent and Fee in Scotland*.

must generally be exercised *rei salva substantia*, i.e. without encroaching upon the substance of the property of fee.

All this is plain Roman law sailing. It is therefore something of a shock to discover on closer examination that the liferent has become entangled in feudal technicality. If it is true that a life interest is a mere personal right in another's property, it ought surely to follow that the liferenter should escape the necessity of a feudal infeftment in his right, which does not, we are told, touch the *dominium*, whether *utile* or *directum*. This remains unaffected in the fiar and superior, with whom alone, we might well assume, the feudal law would therefore be concerned.[4] Such is, unfortunately, not the situation in the law of Scotland. A liferent, unlike any other servitude, is not constituted without sasine.[5] Erskine, perhaps the most civilian of the institutional writers, assures us that a usufruct of land does not become real, as praedial servitudes do, by the natural use or exercise of the right.[6] There follow some remarkable words: '. . . for a liferent of lands, though it be doubtless a burden upon the subject liferented, is truly a feudal right, much resembling property, which constitutes the liferenter *interim dominus* or proprietor for life.'[7]

This language seems to be an admission of failure. If the last sentence is true, why do Scots lawyers so consistently describe the liferent as a mere burden, servitude or usufruct? Would it not be better to postulate a triple subdivision of the *dominium* into *directum*, *utile* and *interim*? Perhaps the reason why this is not done is that it would come perilously near to the English doctrine of estates.

The feudal nature of a liferent is well illustrated by the fact that a proprietor of land can alienate his fee while retaining the liferent and that, if he does so, no new sasine need be taken. He is already seised of (infeft in) the liferent as an integral part of the fee.[8] This type of liferent, says Erskine, 'is considered a limited fee or property,

---

4 Just as that feudal law (in Scotland) refused to have any truck with tacks which it considered to be outside the tenurial relation. *See* Chapter 8. It is otherwise in England, in both cases.
5 Scots law seeks to ensure that all burdens on land appear in the Register of Sasines.
6 II.9.41.
7 *See also*, Lord Kames, *Elucidations*, 89. He does not explain how he reconciles this with his view that even the fiar has not the property, which remains in the superior of the fee.
8 Erskine, II.9.41.

rather than a liferent'. Its holder can even enter the heirs of vassals of the fiar, thereby becoming entitled to the casualties during his life.[9] Surely no more striking demonstration of his not being a mere encumbrancer could be imagined? He is here giving real rights to others which may well outlast his own interest. Again, the liferenter's place in the feudal hierarchy is demonstrated by the rule that it is the liferenter and not the fiar who is primarily liable to the superior for the payment of the feu-duties.[10] The casualty of non-entry was avoided by the infeftment of a liferenter.[11] This makes it look as if the liferenter had the *dominium utile*, at least for this purpose. A life-renter of regality lands has been held to have all the jurisdictional powers and privileges of the lord of the regality.[12] Similarly, the life-renter had the franchise, if any, attached to the lands.[13] Having the franchise was often cited as proof that the superior had *dominium*. If he, why not the liferenter? A liferenter by reservation was entitled to the custody of the title deeds.[14] Felony by the liferenter caused escheat for his lifetime to the superior of the fee.[15]

A liferent may be freely created in the superiority of lands as in the *dominium utile*. But the logic of the usufruct of the *dominium directum*, out of which the use has gone to form the *utile* of the feu, being subjected to a servitude carrying the right to use as well as fruits, is obscure. Although *usus* without *fructus* was well known at Rome, the contrary was not admitted.[16] The liferenter is entitled to the regular feu duties as long as he lives, but the occasional incidents (casualties) fell to the fiar, save in the case of a liferenter by reservation. The reason why the casualties are not considered to be

9 Erskine, II.9.42; *Lady Crawfordjohn v Laird of Glaspen* (1611) M 8252. Even a liferenter by constitution may be given this power by express words. If so, he can exercise it even after the death of the constituter of the right. (*Gibson-Craig v Cochran* (1838) 16 S 1332; affirmed (1841) 2 Rob (HL) 446.

10 Bell, *Principles*, 1061.

11 Erskine, II.5.44; *Bryce* (1566) M 9333. This was originally a conjunct fee, but the wife had renounced the fee, retaining only the liferent, Stair's assertion to the contrary (IV.8.7) must be read in the light of Erskine's criticism. It is significant that this case was before Stair had romanised Scots legal thought. A court after his time might have reached other conclusions.

12 *Marquess of Douglas v Countess of Sutherland* (1700) M 8245.

13 Bell, *Principles*, 1053.

14 *Wallace v Deas* (1831) 10 S 164.

15 Bell, *Principles*, 730.

16 Justinian, *Institutes*, 2.5.2.

fruits so as to go to the usufructuary, is obscure. Possibly it is because they are not the regular annual produce of the land, as the feu duties are deemed to be; but the Romans included as fruits the occasional offspring of animals.[17]

The Entail Amendment Act 1848[18] provides that when under any settlement a liferent in possession is provided for someone who was not born at the time of the creation of the settlement, he takes it as if it were the *dominium* or fee. He can obtain a declarator to this effect, by which he becomes the fiar for all purposes. Such an enlargement of the usufruct into ownership is clearly out of accord with Civilian ideas of the former as a mere burden on the latter.

It is therefore suggested that the view of the liferent as a mere burden or servitude is a not very successful attempt to impose on a long-existing institution – the feu for life – an analysis and a status borrowed at a later date from a Roman law institution which was by no means its exact equivalent. This is only part of a general tendency among Scots institutional writers to express feudal ideas and objects in Roman legal language which is sometimes simply inappropriate. Nevertheless a liferent is a burden on the *dominium*, whether it be a usufruct or not, and the right of the liferenter must be recorded in the Register of Sasines for all to see.

There is an important practical consequence of the Romanistic Scots attitude to the liferent: there is no need to have special statutory rules prohibiting waste, like those in England. A usufructuary by the very nature of his right was always bound to return the *res* in as fair a state as that in which he received it. But Parliament, either to make assurance doubly sure, or because it had not heard of the usufruct idea as applied to Scots law, passed such an Act in 1491.[19] Again, at Rome the alienation of a usufruct was impossible:[20] so, too, in Scotland,[21] and consequently Scots law has set its face against any direct equivalent of the English estate *pur autre vie*, which arises most often by the alienation of a life estate. It is possible to assign the profits and use of a liferent, but this does not convey the

17 Justinian, *Institutes*, 2.1.37.
18 Ss 47–48.
19 A.P.S., ii, 224 (6) (Liability for Waste).
20 Justinian, *Institutes*, 2.4.3.
21 Erskine, II.9.41.

real right and the assignee is not entitled to infeftment.[22] Stair refused to concede that this Roman principle might be circumvented by a subinfeudation for the liferenter's lifetime.[23] But this feudal escape from a Roman technicality does now seem to be possible,[24] which shows once more the unsuitability of applying civilian ideas to feudal institutions, and also incidentally the advantage of not having a *Quia Emptores*.

So far we have been concerned with the position of the liferenter himself, but what of the fiar? He may or may not be infeft in the lands as well as the liferenter.[25] If he is, he has all the rights and privileges of a holder of the *dominium utile* in so far as they are not inconsistent with the right of the liferenter to use and enjoy the land for the time being. He may sell or pledge his interest, subject to the 'usufruct', and generally stands in much the same factual position as an English reversioner or remainderman after a life interest. To this extent, therefore, remainders and reversions may be said to exist in Scots law, although of course the terminology employed to describe them is very different.

LIFE INTERESTS: ENGLISH LAW

The English approach to the status of the life interest[26] is the direct opposite to that of the Civilian Scots. The feu was, we are told, originally for life only.[27] The early history of the life interest in England certainly looks as if it were. In the earliest stage of all a man's lord might claim to make his heir redeem the land.[28] The reversionary rights of the kindred prevented an alienation for longer than a lifetime, if that.[29] Even when the position was changed so as

---

22 Justinian, *Institutes*, 2.5.1; Stair, II.6.7 (the opening sentence must be read subject to what follows); Erskine, II.9.41.
23 Stair, II.6.7.
24 Bell, *Principles*, 1056; *Redfearn v Maxwell* 7 March 1816, FC.
25 If not, he had a mere personal right (as to which, *see* Chapter 23).
26 For the modern English law *see* Cheshire, 263–71; Megarry and Wade, 42–3, 66, 100–3.
27 Craig, 1.4.5; 1.9.18. *Bredon's* Case (1597) 1 Co Rep 67b at 76b.
28 Holdsworth, *H.E.L.*, iii, 120. This stage lasted until 1874 in Scotland, but ended in 1100 in England (*see* Chapter 17, *infra*).
29 *See* Chapter 17.

to allow inheritance on payment of a fixed relief and freer alienation, many rules of English law survived as significant relics of the earlier state of affairs. Thus a gift of land to a man without words of limitation gave him only a life estate right down to 1925.[30] This seems to indicate that originally the normal grant was one for life alone. Still more important, the tenant for life was seised of the land (in the English sense), which meant that he was treated as its holder for many purposes – including those of public law and litigation. Being seised, he of course enjoyed the many and considerable advantages of seisin,[31] which left no room for the idea that the tenant for life was a mere usufructuary.[32] For one thing, he could alienate the land: the only question was for how long he could do it.[33] For another, he was not bound by any rule of law to preserve the *res*, until a deliberate and express change in the law was made to render him liable for waste.[34]

When English lawyers came to enunciate their doctrine of estates in land, they had no difficulty in fitting the tenant for life into it. He had seisin and he was protected by the real actions: indeed he differed from other freeholders only in that his estate would probably come to an end sooner than theirs would. He was 'tenaunt pur terme de vie',[35] which is by no means the same thing as usufructuary. His right differed only in degree and not in kind from that of the tenant in fee simple.

Nevertheless, the practical positions of the English tenant for life and the Scots liferenter are not nearly so unlike as these differences of classification might lead one to expect. The liferenter has sasine either alone or along with the fiar; he too represents the land for purposes of public law; he likewise was made liable for waste by statute. In the light of the original similarity of Scots and English land law, which was also the period of the tenant for life's greatest

30 *See* Chapter 22.
31 Holdsworth, *H.E.L.*, iii, 120; *see* Chapter 23, *infra*.
32 Bracton is probably the only English writer to use the term. He was very subject to Roman influences.
33 By a tortious feoffment he could alienate the land in fee simple (*see* Chapter 23). Only after the life tenant's death could the reversioner bring action to recover the land (Plucknett, *Concise History of the Common Law*, 570).
34 Bracton, ff 315–6 describes a writ against doweresses for waste, but other tenants for life could do what damage they liked until the Statute of Gloucester, 1278.
35 Littleton, *Tenures*, s 56.

prestige in England, it may perhaps be that he was not originally deemed a usufructuary but, like his counterpart south of the Border, a fiar for a limited period, being relegated to his present servitude-holding position by the new learning of Craig and his successors.

That the Scots usufruct-liferent and the English feudal estate for life were probably originally the same institutions can be seen if we turn from conventional to legal liferents (life interests arising by operation of law). The surviving widow's rights to dower-terce, and even more strikingly the widower's rights by the curtesy of Scotland and of England, are so exactly similar as to make comparison superfluous. They were almost exactly the same in the classical land laws of the two countries, but quite so in the days of Glanvil and the *Regiam Majestatem*.[36] That these two sets of rights, so exactly similar in practical effect, are so differently described in the two systems indicates that the language of one system must be incorrect. Since the English language is so much older (see, for example, the Statute of Gloucester 1278), we can draw only one conclusion.

The undoubted power of the English tenant for life to alienate, when properly exercised,[37] gave rise to the estate *pur autre vie*, as the assignee holds not for the period of his own life, but for that of the alienor's. This is on the principle *nemo dat quod non habet*, which had, however, been ignored in connection with the fee simple. This estate *pur autre vie* caused much trouble to the medieval lawyers. At one time it was treated as a mere chattel interest, like the term of years.[38] While it was so regarded, it could be devised by will, so that the death of the tenant during the '*autre vie*' did not necessarily cause any difficulty. If undisposed of by will, it reverted to the donor.[39] On the other hand, once it was recognised as a freehold estate carrying seisin, it fell under the ban of testamentary incapacity, which then attached to freeholds, and this created an obvious practical and logical difficulty. The estate was not at an end at the tenant's death, for it was to endure throughout the *autre vie*; yet it could not revert to the latter, for he had parted with all his interest in

---

36   *Regiam*, II.16, is taken almost *verbatim* from Glanvil, VI. Much of this law, lasted in Scotland until Balfour's day, but minor changes appear in the Institutional writers.
37   As to wrongful exercise, *see* note 33 *supra*.
38   Bracton, f 13; cf Littleton, *Tenures*, s 56.
39   P. & M., ii, 81.

the land. The freehold reversioner or remainderman was kept out by the still existing estate. It must be recorded to the discredit of English law that the estate was left to the mercy of the first comer, who might take by the natural law title of *occupatio*.[40] Such a person came to be called the 'general occupant' to distinguish him from the 'special occupant', a fancy name for the heir of the tenant *pur autre vie*, who only took if the words 'and his heirs' had been in the deed creating his ancestor's interest. He could not take as heir, for the estate was not an estate of inheritance. Entry as special occupant became possible only in the sixteenth century.[41] Modern statutes made the confusion, if anything, even worse.[42]

EASEMENTS AND SERVITUDES

This concludes the list of the English freehold estates and their approximate equivalents in Scotland; the Scots do not recognise the division between the last two of these 'estates' and other rights over land less than ownership. Consequently they consider alongside the personal servitude of liferent-usufruct the praedial servitudes which are termed in English law easments and profits. A profit is a servitude which carries the right to take away some of the land or its produce; an easement[43] is a servitude without such asportation rights.[44]

In connection with these interests the use of Roman law terminology seems not only permissible, but desirable and wellnigh irresistible. Even the English writers on this subject have made use of it.[45] The metaphor of the Romans by which they spoke of the land burdened with an unusual right attached to another parcel of land as being in slavery to its neighbor is also an apt analysis of the position. It must be apparent at once how conveniently this

40 Y.B., 38 Hen. VI, P. pl. 9; Holdsworth, *H.E.L.*, iii, 124. For *occupatio* in Roman law *see* Justinian, *Institutes*, 2.1.12 *et seq.*
41 Co. Litt. 41b; Farrer, 'Acceleration of Remainders', (1916) 32 LQR, 392, 399, showing that the special occupant was unknown to Littleton.
42 Potter, *Historical Introduction to English Law*, 522. General occupancy was abolished by the Statute of Frauds, 1677, s 12.
43 For the modern English Law, see Megarry and Wade, 805–84; Cheshire 513–91. For the modern Scots law of servitudes, *see* Gloag and Henderson, 547–56; Walker, 1376–88.
44 Gale, *Easements*, 1.
45 E.g., Bracton f 220; Digby, *An Introduction to the history of the Law of Real Property*, 127; Cheshire, 514.

language fits in with the Scots classification of rights into *dominium* and burdens thereon. No more cogent illustration of a *jus in re aliena* than a servitude such as a right of passage can be imagined. Here there are not the objections to the use of civilian terminology for what is essentially a feudal right, the liferent. The servitudes are burdens, it is true, on land which is held by feudal technicalities which concern, in the Scots view, only those rights to which investiture is necessary for the completion of their real status. Praedial servitudes become real merely by exercise and do not require sasine.[46] They thus form an exception to the usual requirement of registration.

To the English lawyer the situation was more complex. He might agree in theory that a right of way, for example, was a burden on the ownership of the servient tenement, but where was the ownership? His approach was complicated by the doctrine of estates. Servitudes were not estates in the land, for the essence of an estate is that it gives possession of the land for a time,[47] and servitudes do not carry the right to possess. Yet the person entitled to an easement could early enforce it by the same actions as he could his ordinary rights over land, for example, the remedy in nuisance and the real actions.[48] Consequently it came to be thought that he was 'seised' of an easement. Almost all rights of action then depended on seisin and because the servitude was protected by the same actions as the land itself, it came to be thought that the servitude must be a sort of abstract piece of land, an incorporeal hereditament.[49] In this, as in the land itself, estates might exist.[50] A servitude can obviously be looked at in two ways:

1 from the point of view of the dominant land it is a privilege, a right, a piece of intangible property;

2 from the point of view of the servient land it is a burden, a restriction.

Scots law concentrated on the latter; English law on the former.

46 Bell, *Principles*, 979; Erskine, II.9.41.
47 *Walsingham's Case*, 2 Pl. Com. 549, 555.
48 Holdsworth, *H.E.L.*, iii, 153 *et seq.*
49 Similarly at Rome it had been called a *res incorporalis* (Justinian, *Institutes*, 2.2.2).
50 Co. Litt. 1a, 1b, 6a.

These ideas may well have been derived from an analogy with the incorporeal hereditament which was discussed earlier, the seignory.[51] Since the lord's right to the feudal services, or the patron's right to present to a benefice, were fully protected by law, although not carrying a right to possession, it was not difficult to compare the right to enter and draw water with the right to enter and present a clerk. Both came to be regarded as hereditaments, because they passed to the heir, not to the executor. Both were incorporeal because they implied no right to the physical enjoyment of the property and accordingly they became rights in, rather than burdens over, land; and therefore real property. They were different from estates in the land (corporeal hereditaments) only in not carrying possession, rather than in their radical nature. Littleton's phrase '*terres ou tenements*' illustrated the English approach: though not actually land, servitudes are tenements held by feudal tenure.

All this is very heavy learning. It is unfortunate that the English lawyers forgot the Roman language in which they had been instructed by Bracton, for he had been largely responsible for the content of the English law of servitudes.[52] It seems so much easier to regard what is in fact a burdening right as a burden, rather than to invent such a droll spectacle as a physically non-existent tenement. This in turn had the odd result of making the lawyers conjure up a livery of seisin of such things as a right of way. In their view a man was not seised until he had made a successful journey over the servient land, or, in the case of an advowson, actually presented an incumbent.[53] If in relation to the liferent Scots law was too prone to adopt civilian language and apply it to a feudal institution, English law went to the other extreme and applied feudal conceptions to a branch of law where they were not very suitable or convenient. This, too, was the one branch of land law the content of which the English had borrowed directly from Rome.[54]

Questions of analysis apart, the substantive law of servitudes in

---

51 *See* pp. 110–11, *supra*.
52 Digby, *An Introduction to the History of the Law of Real Property*, 127.
53 P. & M., ii, 123 *et seq.*; Pike, 'Feoffment and Livery of Incorporeal Hereditaments', (1890) 5 LQR 29; Holdsworth, *H.E.L.*, iii, 97.
54 Gale, *Easements*, Preface; Digby, *An Introduction to the History of Real Property*, 127.

Scotland and England is very similar.[55] In both, these rights may be acquired either by express grant or by prescription, the latter rather remarkably in Scotland, as feudal rights to land cannot there be so acquired.[56] Indeed the main differences seem to be only that English law abandons Roman principle in admitting the possibility of a profit in gross (vested in the grantee and his heir irrespective of landholding) and that it creates estates (time-limited interests), in servitudes. Scotland, following Rome, will not allow these. Again, non-user is not of itself enough to extinguish a servitude in English law, but it is in Scotland.[57] More interesting, perhaps, is the refusal of English law to admit the servitude of prospect, that is of retaining an uninterrupted view,[58] though it does allow the easement of light, which is almost equally difficult to define and administer.[59] But negative servitudes such as light or view can be acquired in Scotland only by express grant and not by prescription.[60]

Thirlage, a quasi-monopoly attached to a mill,[61] was a common Scots law right in the nature of a servitude, which had no parallel in England.

RENTCHARGE

An English incorporeal hereditament with a direct equivalent in Scotland is the rentcharge,[62] which arises where a periodical payment of a definite sum of money is secured on land without any tenurial relationship existing between the parties. The Scots call it a real burden. The real burden is secured by an actual feudal infeftment and sasine, which prompted the civilian-minded Lord Kames to the *cri de coeur*, 'Nothing in my apprehension could be more absurd'.[63] The difficulty arises because the law is designed for convenience

---

55   So much so that an English writer (Gale) actually cites Stair as an authority, e.g. at p 28.
56   Cf Cheshire, 530–54; Megarry and Wade, 828–65; Bell, *Principles*, 979 *et seq*. Minor differences are that Scots law distinguishes between rustic and urban servitudes, English law between easements and profits.
57   Twenty years non-user (Prescription and Limitation (Scotland) Act 1973, s 3).
58   *Aldred's case* (1611) 9 Co Rep 58b.
59   *Bryant v Lefever* (1879) 4 CPD 172; *Bury v Pope* (1588) Cro Eliz 118.
60   Bell, *Principles*, 944.
61   Stair, II.7.15; Erskine, II.9.19; Bell, *Principles*, 1016. As to the English suit of mill, which died out very early, *see* P. & M., i, 368.
62   As to which see Megarry and Wade, 792–9; Cheshire 624–35.
63   Lord Kames, *Historical Law Tracts*, 162.

rather than logical satisfaction and without infeftment the annual payment would not be sufficiently protected. But admittedly this is yet another sacrifice of principle to expediency: a phenomenon common in England, but rare enough to invite comment in Scotland. For the same practical reason, the rentcharge continues to be recognised as a legal interest in England after 1925.[64]

Historically, the real burden for money seems to have developed out of the post-reformation legislation of the Stuarts, by which the right to receive the feu-duties remained with the lords of erection after their superiorities in the former kirk lands had been taken back to the Crown.[65] The right to receive the feu duties having thus been separated from the feudal superiority, what was in effect an incorporeal feudal right in heritage (incorporeal hereditament) was evolved; and it can be used nowadays to achieve much the same objects as the English rentcharge.

GROUND ANNUAL

A special type of real burden for many was the contract of ground annual which was used most commonly when lands could not be sub-feued, for example, lands held burgage or where there was before 1874 a prohibition against subinfeudation. In form the seller granted the purchaser a disposition with a declaration creating a ground annual for a specific sum; the purchaser granted a personal obligation to pay the ground annual followed by a disposition of the lands to the seller in security of the payment of the ground annual. The contract was recorded in the Register of Sasines and the obligation to pay the ground annual ran with the land. The device was often used by builders who preferred not to subfeu, even where subinfeudation was not prohibited.

SECURITIES OVER LAND

Various rights in the nature of incorporeal hereditaments have long been used in the two countries to create real securities over land.[66] In

64 Law of Property Act, s 1 (2).
65 Bell, *Principles*, 884–6; *See* pp. 43, *supra.*
66 The Scots law of heritable securities and the English law of mortgages are considered in Chapter 29.

Scots law they were many and diverse with technical differences of great complexity.[67] The English developments were less involved at common law, but equity had its own complications to add. These included the conception of the equitable right to redeem after the legal term for repayment had gone by. This is now treated as if it was an equitable estate in the land.[68] Formerly both countries knew also the possibility of parting with the property itself on a redeemable basis. This is now impossible in England,[69] and obsolete in Scotland, where it had been known as the wadset. Scots law has long allowed an *ex facie* absolute disposition to be used to secure repayment of future advances of money, a type of mortgage used extensively by building societies. In such an arrangement the right of the borrower to the reversion was a personal and not a real right. The *dominium utile* was held by the lender who was liable to the superior for payment of feuduty and the observation of the feudal conditions. This type of mortgage was abolished in 1970,[70] but existing *ex facie* absolute dispositions continue until they are discharged.[71]

REVERSIONS

The existence of a reversionary right is not incompatible with the general doctrine of Scots law that ownership is in the person feudally infeft in the land and in no one else. A superior has a reversionary right to any part of the *dominium utile* which is not possessed by the vassal for the period of long negative prescription and he needs no infeftment because he is already infeft in the land, subject only to the rights of the vassal who has lost it wholly or partially by long negative prescription. Not only was a right apparently akin to a reversion thus created by such mortgage arrangement: it was indeed actually so called.[72] But the Scots reversion is not an estate in the land. It is a mere personal obligation, to which

---

67   Bell, *Principles*, 896 *et seq. et seq.*; Dalrymple, *An Essay towards a General History of Feudal Property*, 106–42.
68   Plucknett, *Concise History of the Common Law*, 603 *et seq.*, gives a short account.
69   Law of Property Act 1925, s 85 (1).
70   Conveyancing and Feudal Reform (Scotland) Act 1970, s 9.
71   *Ibid.*, s 40.
72   Bell, *Principles*, 902.

Parliament gave a real status in 1469,[73] provided the obligation is recorded in the Register of Sasines.

73 A.P.S., ii, 943. This is the earliest registration statute in Scotland (*see also* Chapter 26 *infra*).

14 Leases and Tacks

The main interests in or over land which English law regarded as being within its technically distinct category of real property[1] have now been briefly considered. The principal criterion applied to them once the epoch of the real actions (from which the name is derived), was gone, has been the fact that these interests descended traditionally to the eldest son of the person who died seised of them, while all other property (personal property) descended to the next of kin as a whole. Real property, too, alone gave rise to the relict's right of curtesy and dower mentioned in the last chapter.

There is one important interest in land to which these technical privileges did not attach and which has always been reckoned personal property: the lease or term of years.[2] Scotland, much more logically, has treated all real rights of whatever kind connected with land (including the tack, or lease) as being heritage, subject to succession customs akin to those of the English realty. English law, on the other hand, admits the tenure of leaseholds, which Scots law denies. English law also admits that the termor has an estate in the land while Scots law, knowing nothing of estates other than as between feudal superior and vassal, traditionally treats him on an almost purely contractual basis. Thus the system that might well have treated the term as realty, treated it as personalty; while the one which might well have done the opposite, reserving the word 'heritage' for those rights completed by sasine, allowed leases to have the status of heritable rights. The latter must be considered the more logically defensible, for the Scots preserved only the

---

1 So called because it was the subject of the real actions, as to which *see* Holdsworth, *H.E.L.*, iii, 3 *et seq.*
2 For the modern English law *see* Megarry and Wade, 613–719, and is covenants in leases, 720–42; Cheshire, 381–412 and 449–61, respectively.

sensible Roman division between moveable and immoveable. Moreover, on their classification of rights in land, the tack was as much a *jus in re aliena* as the praedial servitudes. English law, on the other hand, drew a logically indefensible, though convenient, distinction between one tenurial estate in land and all the others, from which it differed only in degree and not in kind.

Why this was so can only be explained historically. Scots lawyers approached the lease from the point of view of the Romans, which was also that of the earliest English law. Consequently Scots legal writers define the lease as 'no more than a personal contract of location, whereby land, or any other thing, having profit or fruit, is set to the tacksman, for enjoying the fruit or profit thereof, for a hire which is called the tack-duty'.[3] Being a mere personal right, the tack was not originally enforceable against the singular successors of the granter. There was no room here for any feudal machinery, such as infeftment, which was designed to make a potentially real right enforceable against all who might thereafter obtain the land, or for any feudal theories such as those of tenure and estates.[4]

In practice, however, the tacksmen, who in medieval Scotland were always poor country folk, had as much need for security in their holdings as the feudal vassals; indeed, since they did the actual agricultural work, the whole country had an interest in their not being dispossessed, for without their uninterrupted labours the harvest would fail. It is hardly surprising, therefore, that the Parliament of Scotland intervened on their behalf and provided as follows by an Act of 1449:

> . . . it is ordanit for the sauftie and favour of the puir pepil that labouris the grunde, that thai, and al utheris that hes takyn or sal tak lands in tyme to come fra lords and has termes and zers thereof, that suppos the lords sel or analy thai lands that the takers sall remayn with their tacks on to the ische of thare termes, quhais hands at ever thai lands cum to for sic male as thai tuk thaim of befor.[5]

---

3 Stair, II.9.1.
4 Admittedly Sandford says (*Entails*, 253) 'Where a tenant is vested by the proprietor with the power of assigning, he has transferred to him in part the character of *dominus*'; but it was this share of *dominium* that Scots law refused the tacksman. Sandford is, of course, writing of the practical position rather than the legal theory.
5 A.P.S., ii, 35 (Tacks Act)
   It is ordained for the safety and favour of the poor people that labour the ground

This great social legislation created problems for the lawyers of later days who sought to apply it and to classify and define the new status of tacks in proper legal terminology. The first problem was whether the Act protected all who have terms of years, even though they are not poor nor engaged in labouring the ground? This was answered in the affirmative.[6] The next problem was to decide who was bound. Did it, for example, bind the superior of the landlord, who came into possession of the fee by the casualties of ward or non-entry? This would have been too much of a stretching of the Act's very clear language, so it was reluctantly admitted that tacks 'sleep' during ward.[7] But the Act was extended to all singular successors, not just buyers. Even the superior was bound to respect tacks during liferent escheat, 'which is a casualty falling, not by the nature of fees, but by statute or custom'.[8] To obtain the protection of the Act the essentials were writing (if the tack is to be for more than a year), a fixed rent, an ish or term of expiry; and the tenant must remain in possession.

These practical questions solved, it remained to discuss the nature of the tacksman's right after the Act. It was clearly more than a mere contractual obligation now that it was enforceable against the landlord's successors. Yet it was not feu, whose very essence was the act of feudal investiture and sasine. This was never contemplated in tacks. Stair gives an answer well in accord with the general theory of land rights in Scots law. He tells us that tacks owe their status as real rights entirely to the Act.[9] Hence they do not rank as proprietary rights. Being real rights *in re aliena* they are servitudes, not praedial but personal servitudes; for just as a usufruct gives a personal servitude for life, so a tack gives such a right for a time.[10] Unlike the liferent, however, there is no need for sasine to constitute a tack.

---

that they, and all others that have taken or shall take lands in time to come from landlords and have terms of years thereof, that suppose the landlords sell or alienate the lands, that the tacksmen shall remain with their tacks on to the end of their terms in whose hands soever the lands come to for such rent as they took them for before.

6   Stair, II.9.2. The Act refers to 'and utheris' as well as the 'puir pepil that labouris the grunde'.
7   Stair, II.9.25.
8   *Ibid.*
9   Stair, II.9.2.
10   *Ibid.*

Like the praedial servitudes, it becomes effective by the tenant's entering into possession. The Act of 1449, unlike that relating to reversions of twenty years later (which was noted at the end of the last chapter) does not make registration a pre-requisite of heritage. It could not have done so, having regard to the social circumstances of the tacksmen; and furthermore the tacksman's possession makes registration unnecessary, because all comers are bound to have notice of his existence.

The Registration of Leases (Scotland) Act 1857 provided an alternative to possession by allowing leases exceeding thirty-one years[11] or containing a clause binding the lessors to renew (so that the lease will extend for over that period)[12] to be recorded in the Register of Sasines, so that the right of the tacksman was brought to the notice of the public by registration instead of by physical possession. The period for a lease to qualify for registration was reduced in 1974 to twenty years or more[13] and at the same time long leases were not to be used for leases of private dwelling-houses.[14] The reason for this provision is to prevent long leases from being used to circumvent the future abolition of feuduties and ground annuals by granting long leases for an annual rent instead of a feu.[15] Long leases are now acceptable in the case of commercial, industrial or agricultural property and minerals, but 'unacceptable' in the case of private dwelling-houses.[16]

The English leasehold differs from the tack in that it is the subject of tenure and an estate in the land;[17] but even more strikingly in the opposite direction by not being recognised as real property (heritage). The reason lies in the peculiar history of the 'term of years'. This phrase indicates the main peculiarity of the interest: that, as opposed to the estates so far considered, it endures for a fixed and definite time.[18]

11   Registration of leases (Scotland) Act 1857, s 17.
12   *Ibid.*, s 1.
13   Land Tenure Reform (Scotland) Act 1974, s 18, Schedule 6.
14   *Ibid.*, s 8.
15   *Ibid.*, s 1.
16   *See* Halliday, *Land Tenure Reform (Scotland) Act* 1974, 27 (General Note), Current Law Statutes 1974, c 38, General Note, Part II.
17   *Walsingham's Case*, 2 Plowden 555; Preston, *An Elementary Treatise on Estates*, i, 7.
18   *Lace v Chantler* [1944] KB 368.

Originally, however, English lawyers would have denied that the termor, as he was generally called, had an estate in the land. Their first approach to him was similar to that of the Scots lawyers. The two parties concerned had entered into a contract, such as the modern licence, which would give the termor a mere *jus in personam*, actionable, if at all, in covenant. He could not use the assise of novel disseisin, by which one dispossessed of freehold land might recover it through royal intervention, for he was not seised. The whole concept of seisin is a difficult one. But for the present[19] we can take it as being possession of land recognised by the courts and normally arising out of an actual delivery. As the assise of novel disseisin was only the *actio spolii* of the Canon law in a different guise, it seemed natural to follow the Roman law, under which those who had the use of land by reason of a contract of *locatio conductio* (hire) had not *possessio* of it. Seisin was treated as the equivalent of *possessio*,[20] and so the termor did not have seisin. No doubt this reasoning had also influenced Scots lawyers in reaching a similar conclusion. This 'youthful flirtation with Romanism'[21] has been laid at Glanvil's door.[22] Hence it reached Scotland probably through the *Regiam Majestatem*. Here, yet again, we find Scots law keeping the earlier view of English law, which had become modified in the latter country.

The beginning of the change is shown in Bracton.[23] By then the termor has a possession of some sort, although it is not the same possession as that of the feudal tenant, the freeholder. It is not seisin. Nor was the termor's possession unprotected in Bracton's day. Formerly the only remedy was that of covenant, which was far from satisfactory, because it lay only against the original grantor and not always then; but the royal council provided a new writ available against anyone who interfered with the termor's possession.[24] This was obviously developed by analogy with novel disseisin.[25] If the termor was ejected by the landlord or his assignees, he might

19 *See also* Chapter 23.
20 Holdsworth, *H.E.L.*, ii, 205.
21 P. & M., ii, 115.
22 Holdsworth, *H.E.L.*, ii, 205.
23 F 27.
24 F 220. Holdsworth, *H.E.L.*, iii, 214.
25 Bracton, f 220.

recover the land itself by this action, which came to be called ' *Quare ejecit infra terminum*', while, Bracton thought, against strangers both he and the landlord could sue; but it was held that the action lay only against the landlord and his assignees and others deriving their title through him. By Edward II's reign, however, termors were protected against third parties through a variant of trespass called *ejectione firmae*.[26] The action lay only for damages until 1468 when the right to recover the land itself was allowed. The nearness of this to the Scots Act is not mere coincidence. The Black Death caused an economic crisis which resulted in the protection of the leasehold *in specie*.[27] As so often, the change came in Scotland through legislation, in England through the medium of the courts.

The action of ejectment in England was so efficient that the freeholder envied it. At length by a generous use of highly absurd fictions, even involving an imaginary ejectment of one imaginary termor by another imaginary termor, he got it,[28] so that the archaic real actions passed away through sheer disuse. Since this was so, it may be asked, why was the leaseholder not treated as one seised of real property? The estate *pur autre vie* was thus promoted to the rank of real property. The answer lies partly in the result which followed such promotion: it removed the power to alienate by will. Medieval man was prohibited from investing money on usury, but long terms of years were used to circumvent this rule. The investor, unlike the hereditary landowner, wants complete freedom to treat the land as mere invested capital. He does not necessarily want it to go to his heir-at-law. For these and other economic reasons the leasehold was not promoted to the category of real property. There was also a theoretical difficulty (not that these have troubled the English lawyer a great deal). How could the termor have seisin and at the same time his landlord also have seisin? By treating the term as a chattel they avoided the problem. The landlord was seised of the land, the tenant was possessed of the term.

On the whole this approach has not worked out so badly for English law.[29] Although the English leasehold began as a usurer's

26 For details, see Holdsworth, *H.E.L.*, ii, 214 *et seq.*
27 Plucknett, *Concise History of the Common Law*, 574.
28 *See* e.g. Plucknett, *Concise History of the Common Law*, 374. (Scots law did not indulge in fictions in this manner.)
29 Holdsworth, *H.E.L.*, iii, 217.

trick, and progressed as the holding of the yeoman farmer, it has never been restricted to any special purpose. It ranges from the letting of a small flat for a week to the leasing of vast tracts for a thousand years or more. It has also been used for fictional purposes.[30]

Without the leashold, English land law could hardly have survived. The Scots tack, on the other hand, has played a more limited part, for its essence is a comparatively short term. Much of what its English brother, bereaved of feu at an early date, has had to perform, it has been able to leave to that transaction.

30   E.g. the lease and release: *see* Chapter 24.

15 Equitable Interests in Land

An outline has now been sketched of the main types of interest in land that may be created under Scots law and English law: but in the expression 'English law' there is a latent dichotomy, namely the historical distinction between the rules of the Common Law and the rules of Equity, both of which are included within the term 'English law'. A whole range of rights and interests in land has developed out of what the English call Equity which cannot be omitted from any consideration of English rights in land. These, and analogous or similar institutions in Scotland, will therefore be examined.

ORIGINS OF EQUITY

In about 1224 the Franciscans arrived in England.[1] As a result there developed, in the view of Maitland,[2] the use, the first equitable interest in land. The proprietary incapacity of professed religious was well known. Monks and nuns, however, all had a 'sovereign', who could hold property for the community as a whole. The other friars such as the Dominicans had also priors who could hold for them. The Franciscans, however, had neither abbot nor prior, being all equal in absolute incapacity to hold property, so new arrangements were necessary to meet the practical needs of the brethren. Donors therefore asked local councillors or other citizens to act as owners of the friars' humble shelters. No-one at that time would have suggested that the friars had any sort of proprietary interest in the shelters; indeed the whole system was devised just because they could not

1   Mitchell and Leys, *History of the English People*, 69; Maitland, *Equity*, 25; Sandars, *Uses*, i, 12; 'in the early years of the thirteenth century', P. & M., ii, 229.
2   'The Origin of Uses', *Collected Papers*, ii, 403 *et seq.*

own. In the eyes of the law the owners were the city fathers, but had they used the buildings as their own, there would have been a public outcry. The king's chief minister, the chancellor, would have had to intervene, particularly as he was a prelate as well and therefore concerned with matters of conscience.[3]

Once the friars became an accepted part of English town life, others saw in their special arrangements an opportunity too good to miss. If they were going on a crusade, why should they not make over their land to the council or some other group of responsible men for their own use when they returned and, if they did not, for that of their infant sons? In this way the lands would be cared for in the absence of the owner and, although this may not have been realised at once, the dreaded incidents of wardship and marriage would be avoided, as the adult feoffees, not the infant heir, would be the feudal tenant. Scots vassals could avoid them only by financial bargains with their superiors, converting the holding to feu or taxed ward. Such a change of tenure has been impossible in England since *Quia Emptores*. Men could evade the mortmain restrictions by a conveyance to laymen to the use of the Church. They could make an indirect will of lands by directing that the feoffees should hold to the uses to be told them in the feoffor's will. They could convey the benefits of landholding without the embarrassing necessity of a livery of seisin. They might even escape the dread possibility of an escheat by setting their lands to uses before embarking on a doubtful enterprise.

The early settlors probably did not stop to consider what would happen if the feoffees made use of the lands for their own purposes, for they would invariably be 'trustworthy' friends: but as the practice became more common, the inevitable occurred. Some of the new owners of land under these arrangements proved unworthy of the trust and took advantage of the fact that the land was theirs in the eyes of the law: after all they were seised, so they could do as they liked with the land. Their obligations to their feoffors were purely moral ones, binding only in conscience.[4]

Such was the view of the Common Law. However, this strict, legal

3 As to the development of equitable jurisdiction and interests, *see* Megarry and Wade, 110–72; Cheshire 41–83.
4 As to the effects of religious feeling on legal development in the Middle Ages, *see* Holdsworth, *H.E.L.*, ii, 4 *et seq.*, 137 *et seq.*

view was not the only possible one and happily there were other forces in the land as well as the common lawyers. Some saw that the king might be petitioned to uphold his coronation oath to provide his lieges not only with justice but with *aequitatem et misericordiam.*[5] Such petitions seem to have become frequent. They were dealt with not by the king in person, except perhaps in the first few cases, but by his chief administrative officer, the chancellor, who was also the king's confessor and as such keeper of his conscience. By this process the beneficiary of the use came to be protected not by course of law, but by executive order, enforced if necessary by the chancellor's undoubted power of imprisonment. Hence the beneficiary, while still not recognised by the Common Law, came to have an enforceable 'right' to the subject matter of the use.

The later history of the trust must be told very briefly. In time the use came to cause a serious loss of those feudal incidents, wardships, marriages and reliefs in particular, which the medieval king had relied on for his revenue. Henry VIII sought a way out of this difficulty in the Statute of Uses, 1535, by which an 'ordinary'[6] *cestui que use* (or beneficiary) was to be treated for all purposes as the legal owner of the property. The feoffee to uses became a mere conducting agency through whom the seisin reached the beneficiary. There was no difference in result between a grant to *A* for the use of *B,* and one to *B* directly.

This should have been the end of the use and the equitable interest (as it had come to be called) in English land, but the Act of 1535 was very unpopular. Landowners found themselves subject once more to all the rigours of tenure (as their Scots opposite numbers had been throughout). They could not escape wardship, marriage and so on as they had been able to do so easily, and they lost their ability to make wills of land. It says much for their feeling on the last point that they prevailed on Henry to assent to the Statute of Wills only five years later. The lawyers, too, and especially those who had found their living by assisting parties who sought the aid

---

5 Trevelyan, 'The Coronation Oath', *Crown and Empire* (1937).

6 The term 'ordinary' is used here as the Statute caught most normal arrangements but those where there was an active duty to perform, or where there were public or charitable purposes, survived. (Plucknett, *Concise History of the Common Law,* 586). Those that survived were important in keeping the idea of the use alive until passive uses were able to reappear later under the name of trusts.

of Equity, were threatened with grave loss of funds. Hence they set to to think of a way round the statute. How they did this is very complex. The usual story is that in the days before the Act it had been held that a 'use upon a use', by which is meant a grant to *A* to the use of *B* to the use of *C*, was void so far as the latter was concerned, for, it was argued, the use having been declared for *B*, it cannot also be declared for *C*.[7] But after the Act *B* got the legal estate (that is the ownership so far as the law is concerned). If such a form of words was found after the Act, must it not be presumed that the grantor intend *C* to get something? It was eventually ruled that it would be unconscionable for *B* to act as if the property was his: he must respect the wishes of the donor that *C* was to have the use of the property or, as it was now called, the trust. This seems to have come about roughly a century after the Act of 1535, where the justice of the case required it. *Sambach v Dalston* (or *Daston*)[8] was usually cited as the first case decided on this point, but the Court in that poor and fragmented report decreed that the land concerned should be conveyed and not held in trust. It is clear however that second uses were enforced by the chancellor and that this became a general practice in the second half of the seventeenth century.[9] This is a more probable time for such a development, after the passing of the Tenures Abolition Act 1660, than the troubled days of 1634 when the financially hard-pressed king would surely not have suffered, on moral grounds only of conscience, a potential diminution of a source of income.

Thus the Statute of Uses was undone. The English landowner might still, provided the proper conveyancing terms[10] were employed, create two interests in the same property, one of which was recognised by the ordinary courts of law, the other by the equitable jurisdiction of the Chancery, which had been gradually transforming

---

7 *Tyrrel's Case* (1557) 2 Dy 155a; Holdsworth, *H.E.L.*, iv, 469–73; Ames, *Lectures on Legal History*, 242–7.

8 (1635) Tot 188. The case is better reported as *Morris v Darston* (1635) Nels 30. *See* the discussion of this point in [1957] CLJ 72, 78 (D. E. C. Yale); (1958) 74 LQR 550 (J. E. Strathdene); and (1966) 82 LQR 215 (J. L. Barton).

9 *See Grubb v Gwillim* (1676) Lord Nottingham's Chancery Cases, (Selden Society, Vol 73), 347.

10 I.e. 'to *A* to the use of *B* to the use of (or in trust for) *C*'. Later this was shortened to 'unto and to the use of *B* in trust for *C*'. *See* Megarry and Wade, 169, and *Hopkins v Hopkins* (1738) 1 Atk 581 *per* Lord Hardwicke, L.C. at 591.

itself from a purely religious and political institution into something which was becoming more and more like a court. The system which it administered, too, was becoming more and more like law in subject matter and treatment, and the suitor in the court of equity was now less the humble petitioner begging favours from the mighty and more the seeker after 'rights'.

What was the nature of these new equitable interests in land ? To the medieval canon lawyer the answer was easy: the friars had the usufruct or *usus* of the land.[11] But if this were so, where was the *dominium* without which no servitude could exist ? That was more difficult. Some at least thought that it was in their holy mother, the Church; but as the use developed into a more general institution, men came to say that while the feoffee (trustee) had the land so far as the Common Law was concerned, the beneficiary had it so far as the chancellor and his Equity were concerned. Since they described any interest carrying possession as an estate in the land, this could be put more shortly by saying that one had the legal estate the other the equitable interest. This is the language of modern English law.

So long as the chancellor was acting in an administrative and religious capacity, these equitable 'estates' were, no doubt, rather vague and uncertain; but in time as the system called 'equity' began to become analogous to law, he insisted on a certain amount of order in accordance with the maxim: 'Equity follows the law.' By this is meant that equity recognised roughly the same sort of interests in land as were recognised by the traditional law. Thus we can speak of an equitable fee simple, fee tail, life interest and so on. Even an equitable right of way or other incorporeal hereditament may exist. All these equitable estates and interests have one feature in common: they are enforceable against anyone whose conscience has been affected by knowledge of them, but they do not affect a *bona fide* purchaser of the legal estate,[12] whose conscience has not been affected with knowledge or presumed knowledge of the equity in question. This rule runs right through the law of property[13] and has been called 'the polar star of equity'.[14]

11 Thomas of Ecclestone, *Monumenta Franciscana*, 1; cf Maitland, 'The Origin of the Use', *Collected Papers*, ii, 415.
12 *Pilcher v Rawlins* (1872) 7 Ch App 259; *Wilkes v Spooner* [1911] 2 KB 473.
13 Maitland, *Equity*, 114–26; Cheshire, 59–71; Megarry and Wade, 115–26.
14 *Stanhope v Earl Verney* (1761) 2 Eden 81, *per* Lord Henley, L. C. at 85.

Attempts to classify these interests in terms of Roman law are bound to fail, for the English equitable estate is an invention of English legal history and, if not unique, is at least something which the Roman law did not have and which the civilian-minded lawyers of the Continent or Scotland cannot confine within any 'known' category of rights.

SCOTS LAW

The Scots seem to have agreed with Pope John XXII that the distinction between ownership and use was unreal and that the Franciscan vow could not be literally enforced. Innes tells us that the friars in Scotland could not acquire or hold land 'except their church and place of dwelling'.[15] The latter, however, often included spacious gardens. The Franciscans in Scotland seem to have had sovereigns called *custodes* or wardens, so there was no need for a development such as the English one. Moreover the more general practice of putting land to uses was possible there for two main reasons. First, the Scots superior was not bound to receive assignees and certainly would not have done so if he thereby lost the lucrative right to casualties such as ward. Besides, if he did receive them, he took a substantial relief. Secondly, although medieval Scotland had a chancellor, he never had powers at all comparable with those of the English officer. This was mainly due to the comparative weakness of the central government in Scotland. The English chancellor's jurisdiction rested ultimately on his physical power to compel obedience to his decrees. This the Scots one, and his master, lamentably lacked.

When eventually the Court of Session was founded on a regular basis and arrogated to itself the power to try land questions, it was modelled more on Continental than on English institutions.[16] French law knew no separate institution such as Equity. The Court of Session is a court of Equity as well as of Law. It therefore ought to proceed by the rules of conscience in abating the rigour of the Law, and

---

15   Innes, *Scotch Legal Antiquities*, 171.
16   But *contra*, see H. McK[echnie], *Common Errors in Scottish History*, Historical Association Pamphlet, G.32, 11.

to give aid in the actions brought before it to those who can have no remedy in a court of pure law.[17] This is 'the *nobile officium* of the Court of Session, so much talked of, and so little understood'.[18] It should be observed, however, that this *nobile officium* is by no means the whole of Equity in Scotland, but only the extraordinary equitable power. The 'ordinary' powers have been largely absorbed into the normal fabric of the common law.[19]

Although the language used in connection with mitigating the regions of the 'strict' law is very similar to that employed in relation to the chancellor's jurisdiction in England, this *nobile officium* should not be identified at all closely with the English Equity. Just as similar institutions in two systems may seem to be different because referred to in different language,[20] so an artificial semblance of similarity may be engendered by the same language being employed to describe two radically different institutions.[21] To Scots, as to most continental lawyers, Equity and *jus naturale* are synonymous.[22] The Court of Session's comparatively rare excursions into the field of *nobile officium* are intended to supplement the defects of the law and to soften its inflexibilities, but this is done only where the application of the letter of the law would lead to an unfair (inequitable) result. In so far as the *nobile officium* is used, the law is reformed along sounder lines. English lawyers may suppose Lord Mansfield, C.J., to have had exactly this conception in mind in some of his attempts – many of them successful – to bring the English Common Law into line with Equity (fairness) as he saw it.[23] But the English Equity is not *jus naturale* and it does not exist somehow inside the Common Law, to reform it: it exists outside that Law as an entirely separate system. Equity does not say that *A* has no legal right because it would be unfair to admit that he had it that a right contrary to natural justice cannot exist. What it says is that *A* has an undoubted right by the Common Law of England, but that

17   Stair, IV.3.1. Erskine, I.3.22.
18   Lord Kames, *Historical Law Tracts*, 214; *Gibson's Trustees* 1933 SC 190, 198.
19   Walker, 'Equity in Scots Law', (1954) 66 Jur. Rev., 103.
20   E.g. usufruct and life estate. *See* Chapter 13.
21   E.g. seisin and sasine. *See* Chapters 23 and 24.
22   *See* e.g. Lord Wark, 'Law of Nature', *Sources* (Stair Society, Vol 1), 249, where the *nobile officium* is discussed at pp. 254–6. *See also* Wilson and Duncan, *Trusts, Trustees and Executors*, 201–24.
23   For a detailed consideration, *see* Fifoot, *Lord Mansfield*.

because of the particular facts of this particular case and the conduct
or guilty conscience of this particular individual (*A*), he cannot be
allowed to exercise his undisputed right; but must instead do what
is just and fair and in accord with Equity and good faith. In 1873,
the old courts of Common Law and Equity were abolished and a
new Supreme Court established administering both; but the
substantive rules of both remain unchanged. Section 25 (11) of the
Judicature Act 1873 provided that:

> Generally in all matters not herein before particularly mentioned
> in which there is any conflict on variance between the rules of
> equity and the rules of the common law with reference to the
> same matter, the rules of equity shall prevail.

Maitland seeing equity as a gloss on the law observed that for that
reason the possible occasions for conflict would be few anyway.[24]

In dealing with the trust, then, the Scots system does not have the
machinery of separate courts which so naturally gave rise to the
English double nomenclature of the legal and equitable estates.
Indeed the trust, in so far as it is known in Scotland, is not parti-
cularly referred to the *nobile officium* of the Court of Session, or to
Equity.[25]

Scots law has long known something which bears the name of a
trust. Craig mentions the possibility of a trust feu the validity of
which, he says, cannot be doubted.[26] He treats it as a *fideicommissum*.
It is not established whether or not trusts had existed for very long
before his time. Nowadays they are used when a settler wants to
benefit some individual or group, but there is a practical bar to
their being infeft themselves, for example, because they are not yet
born. This most often occurs in connection with marriage and
testamentary settlements. Hence, although its field is more limited,
the Scots trust seems to be comparable in function with that of

---

24 Maitland, *Equity*, 16–20: *see* however *Job v Job* (1877) 6 Ch D 562 (liability of
    executors); *Walsh v Lonsdale* (1882) 21 Ch D 9 (enforceability of an agreement for
    a lease); *Berry v Berry* [1929] 2 KB 316 (variation of a deed by parole evidence) and
    Hill v C. A. Parsons and Co Ltd [1972] Ch 305 *per* Lord Denning MR at 313–316.
25 *See* the list of the fields of the *nobile officium* in Lord Wark, 'Law of Nature',
    Sources (Stair Society, Vol 1), 249 at 254 *et seq*. Since most Scots regard the
    trust as a form of contract there is no need to have recourse to equity. *See* Candlish-
    Henderson, 'Trusts in Scottish Law' (1949) 31 *Journal of the Society of Compara-*
    tive Legislation (3rd series), 36 *et seq*.
26 Craig, 2.5.9.

England. As is so often the case, these basic functional similarities are obscured by different conceptions of the nature of the rights involved and even more by differences of technical language.

However, it seems that although England and Scotland alike know the trust, Scotland treats them as part of the law and does not have to look to the *nobile officium* to sustain them.

THE NATURE OF THE TRUST

Much obscurity still surrounds the legal nature of the rights just mentioned. Thus one authority states that 'the most distinctive characteristic of the office of trustee is ownership',[27] while other authorities say that 'the title of the trustee is nothing but a burden or security',[28] or even that the trustee 'is not materially different from a factor holding a power of attorney'.[29] Similar difficulties obscure the nature of the beneficiary's and truster's rights. All this due to mistaken attempts to define the trust relationship in Roman law terms. Thus Lord President Inglis, following Stair,[30] defined a trust as 'a contract made up of two nominate contracts of deposit and mandate. The trust funds are deposited for safe custody, and the trustees receive a mandate for their administration.'[31] As Menzies points out,[32] a fatal objection to this definition is the physical impossibility of depositing immoveable property. Bell's attempt[33] to circumvent the difficulty by saying that it is the right to the heritage, not the heritage itself, which is deposited, fails on the ground that it is as impossible to deposit an incorporeal right as an immoveable territory. Nor is the mandate element of the definition any happier. A contract of *mandatum* may be terminated by the mandant at will, as indeed might the contract of *depositum* by the depositor. Nor were *post mortem* mandates ever possible at Rome.

27 Menzies, *Trustees*, 3.
28 Bell, *Lectures on Conveyancing*, ii, 751. Forsyth, *Law of Trusts*, 12.
29 McLaren, *Law of Wills and Succession*, s 1768.
30 Stair, I.12.17; I.13.7.
31 *Croskery v Gilmour's Trustees* (1890) 17 R 697, 700.
32 Menzies, *Trustees*, 21 *et seq.* (Menzies' 2nd edition was published in 1913). For the modern law of trusts in Scotland *see* Walker, 1773–1884; Gloag and Henderson, 630–48.
33 Bell, *Commentaries*, i, 32.

In spite of his refutation of these definitions, Menzies by no means adopts the English position: to him the relationship is essentially one of contract. After telling us that the conception of trust as a contract has been unnecessarily complicated by talk[34] of a three-fold relationship of truster, trustee and beneficiary, Menzies continues;

> There is only the two-fold relation of contract, the contractee – who in this case is the truster – on the one side, and the contractor – the trustee – on the other. The beneficial interest created is an assignation of the truster's right against the trustee under the contract. ... The beneficiary has accordingly a personal claim – a *jus in personam*, it may be a *jus ad rem* – against the trustee to perform his contract.[35]

While this view of the relationship has been generally accepted in Scotland,[36] it has by no means passed unchallenged. Thus Lord Kincairney[37] said:

> When a trustee undertakes a trust containing an explicit direction he does not enter into a contract that he will fulfill that direction, and he will not be liable for breach of contract if he fails to do so. His obligation is that of a trustee, not that of a contractor, and in the obligation of a trustee there is an element of discretion which is not present in a contractual obligation.

Again, in *Allen v McCombie*,[38] all three lords expressly declined to regard the trustee – beneficiary relation as one of contract. Lord President Dunedin took the view that under the surface talk about contracts, the same ideas 'as have made the obligation of the trustee only enforceable in the Chancery have run through our jurisprudence'.

It is therefore not surprising to find the Scots writer Mackenzie Stuart using language which an Englishman would not feel to be strange in his own mouth:

> A trust may be defined as the legal relationship which arises when an estate is owned by two persons at the same time, the one being

34   E.g. by Forsyth, *Law of Trusts*, 12.
35   Menzies, *Trustees*, 25–6.
36   *See* e.g. McLaren, *Law of Wills and Succession*, s 826.
37   *Carruthers v Carruthers* (1895) 22 R 775, 790. Reversed on other grounds [1896] AC 659; 1896 23 R (HL) 55.
38   1909 SC 710, 717–8; cf *Buchanan v Angus* (1862) 4 Macqu 374 *per* Lord Westbury, L.C.

under an obligation to use his ownership for the benefit of the other. . . . The owner who is under an obligation . . . is a trustee; and his ownership is trust ownership. The person for whose benefit this ownership is used is the beneficiary: he has the beneficial ownership.[39]

This duality of trust ownership and beneficial ownership is on all fours with the English legal and equitable estates theory, but one can sympathise with the logical difficulty of Lord Advocate Jeffrey: 'How can it be held that the entire right of property subsists in two distinct persons at one and the same time?'[40] The English answer that one has the ownership so far as the Law courts are concerned, the other having it so far as the Equity courts are concerned, is not available in Scotland. But ever since Craig Scots law has known a division of ownership into *directum* and *utile*, so that a subdivision on other grounds has a clear precedent, however much it deprives the term 'ownership' of its traditional significance.

Turning from these general points to details of machinery, it may be noted that Scots law has long recognised two methods of creating express trusts.[41] These are:

1 a deed of absolute disposition to the trustee, qualified by a separate back-bond or back-letter declaring the trust;
2 a deed bearing *in gremio* the trust purposes, or at least expressly declaring that the property is held on trust and referring to another document where the detailed provisions of the trust are set out.

There are important differences between these two forms of deed. The former necessarily operates to vest the property in the trustee, who becomes the feudal owner, responsible *inter alia* for the payment of the feu duties.[42] Like the trustee in English law he can transfer a

---

39 Mackenzie Stuart, *Law of Trusts*, 1. The Trusts (Scotland) Acts 1921 and 1961 make statutory provisions as to trusts and trustees in Scotland. There had been earlier Acts since the seventeenth century.
40 *McMillan v Campbell* (1834) 7 W & S 441 at 447–8.
41 For rules as to implied and constructive trusts which are similar to those of English Law, *see* Green's *Encyclopaedia*, title 'Trust', paras. 347–407.
42 'The party having the right and procuratory ex facie absolute, and getting resignation and sasine in the same terms, is held and taken to be vested in the radical and original right of the granter and becomes the proper vassal . . .' (*Gardyne v Royal Bank of Scotland* (1851) 13 D 912 *per* Lord Justice-Clerk Hope at 918) cf *McLelland v Royal Bank of Scotland* (1857) 19 D 574 *per* Lord Ivory at 582 and *City of Glasgow Bank v Nicolson's Trustees* (1882) 9 R 689.

good title to a *bona fide* purchaser for value without notice of the trust.[43] The Scots, however, stole a march on the English by the rule that if the back-bond is registered or produced in legal proceedings, this is notice to all the world of its existence.

Originally the law allowed trusts to be established by verbal evidence but this was altered by the Act 1696 c 25 which enacts that 'no action of declarator of trust shall be sustained as to any deed of trust made hereafter except upon a declaration or back-bond of trust lawfully subscribed by the person alleged to be the trustee and against whom or his heirs or assignees the declarator shall be intended, or unless the same be referred to the oath of the party simpliciter'. The statute only applies when one man alleges that he has trusted another to take the title in his own name.[44]

The other type of deed, which is that more commonly adopted for family settlements, is an interesting foretaste of the vesting deed and trust instrument required in England by the Settled Land Act 1925.[45] In an arrangement of this kind, it will depend on circumstances whether the truster retains or disposes of the 'radical' right to the property. If the trustee is to hold after discharging the more limited trusts, for the truster himself, the truster remains in a sense owner.[46] If there is what the English would call an equitable fee simple in remainder, the 'radical right' is in the beneficiary entitled to this.[47] This radical right is the heritable proprietorship of the estate:[48] its holder can sell it,[49] mortgage it,[50] or have it attached by his creditors.[51] Even where the disposition is *ex facie* absolute, the

43   Stair, IV.6, 5. *Redfarn v Somervail*, (1813) 1 Dow 50; *Heritable Reversionary Co v Millar* (1892) 19 R (HL) 43 *per* Lord Watson at 47; *Union Bank v National Bank* (1886) 14 R (HL) 1; Wilson & Duncan, *Trusts, Trustees and Executors*, 3 *et seq.*
44   *Horne v Morrison* (1877) 4 R 977.
45   Settled Land Act 1925, ss 4 (1), 6, 8 (1). Megarry and Wade, 299; Cheshire, 170 *et seq.*
46   *Campbell v Edderline's Creditors* (1801) 1 Ross LC (Land Rights), 458; *McMillan v Campbell* (1831) 7 W & S 441; *Gilmour v Gilmour* (1873) 11 M 853, where Lord Justice-Clerk Moncrieff said 'in *Donaldson*, 11th March, 1786, Lord Braxfield said: "as long as the estate is not sold it is my property. And I may, if I please, denude the trustees by paying off the debt."'
47   *Smitton v Smitton's Trustees* (1837) 2 D 225; *Turnbull v Tawse* (1825) 1 W & S 80.
48   *Gilmour v Gilmour* (1873) 11 M 853 *per* Lord Justice-Clerk Moncrieff.
49   *Brisbane v Crawford* (1826) 4 S 427.
50   *Lindsay v Giles* (1844) 6 D 771.
51   *Campbell v Edderline's Creditors* (1801) 1 Ross LC (Land Rights), 458; *Globe Insurance v Murray* (1854) 17 D 216.

truster can sue for example a railway company for damage done to the property,[52] or exercise a franchise attached to the lands.[53]

It can thus be appreciated that the 'radical right' of a Scots truster is for almost all practical purposes as good as the English equitable ownership. Nor do these points leave it really possible to describe it as merely of a contractual, rather than a proprietory nature. It will be seen later that Scots law was forced in another connection to admit the existence of a 'fiduciary fee' to preserve an important feudal principle.[54] The gradual confluence of the language used to describe these interests is a token of the gradual translation of Scots lawyers from being almost pure Civilians, if not to pure Common lawyers at least to a position where it can be claimed that they represent the best of both systems.[55] The trust and the equitable estate are among the most important legal conceptions that English law has evolved. Scotland has come to recognise that fact and no longer seeks to take advantage of the practical convenience of the trust while pretending that it is really only some Roman *obligatio*.

During the nineteenth century trusts were greatly developed in Scotland in a manner which shows clearly the influence of English law. Between 1861 and 1910 a series of statutes dealt with the rules for the administration of trusts: these acts were consolidated and added to by the Trusts (Scotland) Act 1921 which remains the main basis of the rules applicable to the administration of trusts, read together with the Trusts (Scotland) Act 1961 and the Trustee Investments Act 1961.

52 *McBride v Caledonian Railway Co* (1894) 21 R 620.
53 *Skeete v Duncan* (1873) 1 R 18; *Monteith v Scott* (1868) 7 M 300.
54 *See* Chapter 25.
55 T. M. (Lord President) Cooper, *The Common and the Civil Law – a Scot's view.* (1950) 63 Harvard LR 468.

16 The English Legislation of 1925

ESTATES AND OTHER INTERESTS: GENERAL CONCLUSIONS

The subjects dealt with in Part II are of a more technical character than those considered in Part I, and it is difficult to come to any clear general conclusions as to the respective merits of the two theories of land rights which have been here described and applied to the various relationships in question.

The English doctrine of estates, so far as it goes, may claim to be clear, straightforward and consistent; but in practice it was abandoned from time to time under pressure from the counter-attractions of the doctrine of seisin. In medieval times in particular it was straightforward and therefore tempting to view the tenant who was actually seised of the land, for whatever estate, as being *de facto* owner.[1] By applying its general theory of estates to all interests in land carrying possession now or in the future English law has been able to give effect to the wishes of settlors and testators in ways not deemed possible in Scotland, for example, by allowing an automatically determinable fee simple and an estate *pur autre vie*.

The incorporeal hereditament is not such a happy offshoot of the English law of land, although it must be admitted that no great harm seems to have been done by adopting this curious notion. Here there was a marked contrast with the position in Scotland. The refusal of English law to treat the term of years as real property is not only contrary to its basic idea of treating all estates as being essentially the same and varying only in degree, but is equally inconsistent with the term's standing as a tenement or tenure. This is why some modern writers decline to recognise it as a tenure, though some of the older authorities are quite categoric.[2]

1 *See* Chapter 23.
2 *See* Chapter 8.

The notion of the equitable estate in land has obviously had enormous effects. English law may be said not only to have invented the whole conception, but to have used it to immense advantage in many branches of land law. Thus under the name of the equity of redemption, it has played a vital part in the development of mortgage law in England.[3] Another novel achievement of equity was the avoidance of most of the unpleasant results of the dependent tenure of land on a feudal basis by means of the use. Even more freedom was given to settlors by this invention, for feudally impossible interests such as springing and shifting ones became possible in equity through the employment of the use and subsequently even at law after the Statute of Uses.[4] But the part played by the equitable estate in the development of land law in England is too vast a topic to be dealt with here, and through the 1925 legislation it has become even more important and vital than ever before.

Scotland started, so far as the available sources are concerned, from a basis which was admittedly that of a very different system of land law. Sometimes the employment of Roman law terms has been successful and helpful more particularly in showing that the term 'landowner' has a legal basis in Scotland which it lacks in England. The view of servitudes as burdens on the land rather than as separate incorporeal hereditaments seems eminently sensible, though in the case of the personal servitude of usufruct, Roman theory had to be distorted in the effort to apply it to feudal fact.[5] The distinction between lease and feu is in theory vast, far wider than the actual difference between them (largely mere duration) would appear to warrant. The agonised attempts to force the English equitable estate into a civil law strait-jacket were doomed to failure and seem now at last to have been abandoned. All this raises the question as to whether it is necessary or desirable to retain as much Roman terminology as still exists. More especially, the division of *dominium* into *directum* and *utile* in order to agree with feudal actualities (which it would only do well if all held in chief of the Crown) is a matter of regret. But it is scarcely the function of a historical and comparative

---

3 After the legal date of repayment has passed, the mortgager has a right of redemption in the eyes of equity. This right was treated as an estate, which puzzled Stair (II.10.3). *See* Chapter 28 *infra*.
4 *See* Megarry and Wade, 160–7; and Chapter 29.
5 *See* Chapter 13.

work to criticise existing terminology, still less institutions. Lord Kames, whose classification of rights in land has been the basis of this discussion was only too well aware of this problem:

> The Roman law, illustrious for its equitable maxims, deserves justly the highest regard. But the bulk of its institutions, however well adapted to the civil polity of Rome, and the nature of the government, make a very motley figure when grafted upon the laws of other nations.[6]

English Property Legislation, 1925

This Part opened with a brief consideration of the land legislation of the reign of Edward I; but no historical survey could be allowed to end without some reference, albeit brief, to the other comparable legislation of the reign of George V.

The Acts of 1925 made such drastic changes in the details of the English land law that many thought that continuity with the past had been completely broken. On closer examination, however, it was seen that the fundamental principles remained unchanged. All land was still held by feudal tenure of the king, although no troublesome factual evidences of that theory were allowed to survive. More drastic reforms were made in relation to the doctrine of estates which has been the subject of this Part. For seven or eight centuries the possible legal estates that might be created had been the same: the fee simple, the fee tail, the life estate, the estate *pur autre vie* and the term of years. But by the very first section of the Law of Property Act 1925 all this was fundamentally changed. Only the fee simple was allowed to survive *at law* among the freeholds, and that only when absolute and vested in not more than four adults who must hold in possession, not in remainder or reversion.[7] The term of years absolute, formerly not even a part of the law of real property now paradoxically has come 'full circle', and exists as one of the only two possible estates.[8]

The effect of these provisions must be carefully noted. They do

---

6 *Historical Law Tracts*, 367.
7 Law of Property Act 1925 s 1 (1) (a); s 1 (6); s 34 (2).
8 *Ibid.*, s 1 (1) (b).

not mean that a settlor who wishes to do so cannot create a life interest, or that an entail can no longer exist. They may: indeed all the interests which could formerly be created (except a perpetually renewable lease[9] may still be created but they take effect only as equitable estates and have no recognition as far as the legal estate is concerned. The purpose of these changes is to make conveyancing easier. A prospective purchaser, through the system of making settlements by two deeds,[10] only one of which he is allowed to see, is kept in the blissful state of being 'Equity's darling' – a *bona fide* purchaser for value without notice of the equities relating to the land. These appear in the other deed which he is not allowed to read. They cannot therefore affect the land in the hands of the purchaser, but instead affect the purchase money in the hands of the trustees.[11] This idea had a counterpart in Scotland, but it seems improbable that there was conscious imitation either way.

The effect of these changes in English law is to drive a stout wedge between the fee simple absolute in possession (which Scotland's *dominium utile* must almost always be) and all other freehold interests in the land, which are reduced to a subordinate status. There must, after all, be something in Scotland's view that the *dominium utile* is radically different from all lesser interests in land, since England has come to a not dissimilar conclusion by a different and very roundabout route after so many centuries. Even the English-invented bogey of the incorporeal hereditament appears to have been exorcised by the wording of the Law of Property Act 1925 which calls them 'interests or charges in or over land'.[12]

Another effect of the English changes of 1925 was to create a gulf between English land law and that of Ireland, North and South, which had until then been very similar to it. They also made some new divergencies from Scots law, for example, by the abolition of primogeniture.[13]

---

9   Converted into a term of 2000 years (Law of Property Act 1922, s 145 and 15th Schedule). Megarry and Wade, 643–5.
10   Settled Land Act 1925, s 4 (1). Megarry and Wade, 300–1.
11   *See* Megarry and Wade, 306–8 as to the 'curtain' principle and *ibid.*, 371–83 as to the overreaching effect of dispositions under the Settled Land Act 1925 and Law of Property Act 1925.
12   Law of Property Act 1925, s 1 (2).
13   As to which, *see* Chapter 22.

17 Family Restraints on Alienation

The old native customary methods of landholding (folk-land in England, Celtic and Norse (udal) landholding in Scotland) shared the feature of being family rather than individualist systems of holding land.[1] In this context the term 'family landholding' must not be misunderstood as suggesting that the family was recognised as owner for all purposes by a developed legal system. All that it means here is that there was a strong customary belief that a man should not alienate his land to the disappointment of his family. In early times, such as those under discussion, the most potent source of behaviour patterns and therefore of law is traditional popular belief: custom. However, even before the Conquest this principle had been considerably broken into in England by the spread of the Rome-inspired book-land tenure,[2] which reflected a new conception: that of the free alienation of land by its holder for the time being without regard to the interests or wishes of his family, born or unborn. There is no direct evidence that book-land was ever known in Scotland. Certainly over a great part of Scotland the traditional family methods of landholding continued for many centuries and feudalism percolated northwards into Scotland only very slowly.

It is often assumed that the feudal system of landholding with its relationship of feudal lord and vassal was itself a matter of concern to individuals only and that as the feudal doctrine of derivative tenure advanced family landholding retreated; but this is far from being the case. The idea that land belongs to the family, born or

---

1 *See* Chapter 1.
2 *See* Plucknett, 'Book-land and Folk-land', 6 *Economic History Review* 64; *Concise History of the Common Law*, 518; Denman, *Origins of Ownership* 66–8; John, *Land Tenure in Early England*, 1–63; Jolliffe, 'English Book Right', 50 E.H.R. 1.

unborn, rather than to any individual absolutely, was too innate in human psychology to be thus easily eradicated. Although it was forced by the pressure of events to dress itself in feudal forms, that sentiment had an important part to play in the evolution of the land laws of both kingdoms.

In the earliest stage of the feudal arrangement, when fees were granted only for life, there could naturally be no element of family landholding, but this stage was already passing away in France when the Normans invaded England,[3] and it is not very clear how far, if at all, it was ever known in that country.[4] At least as early as 1100 it was undeniably established there, not merely that fees were hereditary, but that the lord of the fee was bound to recognise the deceased tenant's heir as his new vassal on payment of his relief without any formal act of entry or investiture such as Scotland and other feudal nations were long to consider necessary. Even more striking is the fact that he must keep the fee empty for the infant heir of his tenant to come in to on attaining full age. Since the feudal system entered Scotland from England after 1100, it seems extremely probable that it was already a hereditary system before its introduction there.

The original purpose of the military tenures was to provide active and efficient soldiers and counsellors for the feudal superior. The development by which fees became available to the heir (even a babe in arms or a girl, irrespective of physical or mental condition) can then be seen in its true light: a recognition, in violation of the whole purpose of these tenures, of the great strength of the tradition that land belongs to the family, not just to the individual. Furthermore, in early feudal grants in both countries other members of the grantor's family frequently joined in the conveyance. Maitland quotes many instances where all the known relatives, including tiny children, not merely consent to a charter by the head of the family, but are actually paid for doing so.[5] In the oldest genuine Scots grant extant Duncan II says that he had made his brothers concur.[6] It has been asserted that this practice was employed by the Church only, out of an

3   Esmein, *Histoire*, 186.
4   Plucknett, *Concise History of the Common Law*, 523.
5   P. & M., ii, 308 *et seq.*
6   *See* Appendix II.

abundance of caution and to secure its titles beyond any possibility of challenge.[7] But the *Libri Feudorum* suggest that the practice was evidence of a general principle very well known to the feudal law of continental Europe. They state in categoric terms:

> Alienation of an ancestral feu is invalid even with the consent of the superior, unless the vassal's agnates also consent, the agnates being those upon whom the feu sooner or later must devolve.[8]

It is suggested that the evidence is best explained on the basis that the whole kindred had a definite right as expectant heirs and that if they did not join in a conveyance they might subsequently challenge its validity before the courts. To the straight-forward mind of medieval man it must have seemed obvious that a grant to a man and his heirs should give those heirs something. The maxim *nemo est heres viventis*[9] is a Roman subtlety that was lost on the twelfth century Englishman. Even further away was the hyper-technicality that a grant to a man for life with a remainder to his heirs gives all to the apparent life tenant and nothing to the heirs.[10] If additional evidence of the family's right to challenge an alienation is required, it can be found in the fact that such a right survived in the burgh customs of both England and Scotland.[11] It is notorious that these burgage customs frequently preserved legal rules which had become obsolete in the country as a whole.

But the influences which had introduced book-land were still at work after the introduction of the feudal system. Roman law exercised a growing influence in favour of free alienation, primarily to the Church, which did not become any weaker with the Conquest, as can be seen from the relevant portions of Glanvil and the *Regiam Majestatem*, which on this point follows Glanvil word for word:

> For every free man who owns land may give a certain part of his lands and a tocher for his daughter or any other woman, and that

7　E.g. by Plucknett, *Concise History of the Common Law*, 526.
8　*Libri Feudorum*, 2.39. pr. (Lord Clyde's Translation, 1132).
9　'No-one is the heir of a living person.'
10　*Shelley's Case* (1581) 1 Co Rep 88b. Megarry and Wade, 60–5; Cheshire, 252–4; *See also* Chapter 25.
11　Borough Customs, ii (Selden Society, Vol 21), 61–3; *Leges Quatuor Burgorum* c 106. *See* Chapter 7 *supra*.

whether he has an heir or not. And if he has an heir, any man may – whether his heir assents or not – give a part of his free holding to any person as remuneration for services or to any religious institution in name of free alms.[12]

Thus by Glanvil's time in England, and by that of the *Regiam Majestatem* in Scotland, so far as feudal law at that time extended there, it was open to the holder of land to part with a reasonable amount of it for a purpose recognised as justifying alienation. Indeed if he had both conquest and heritage he could alienate the whole of the former.[13] All such alienations must, however, be performed while in *liege poustie* and above all not on one's deathbed. It is noteworthy that at this date English law knew the distinction between conquest and heritage and the prohibition of deathbed deeds. These were to pass away very quickly in England, but were preserved in Scotland right down to the second half of the last century.[14] This is further evidence of a general tendency of Scotland to share English rules down to Edward I's reforms and thereafter to retain the pre-Edwardian law.

In the pages of Glanvil traces of the older restrictions on alienation in the interests of the family are still clearly apparent. If a man has an heir – by which is now understood the single son or other person selected by the rules of primogeniture – he may not disinherit that heir by granting the whole of his land to a favourite younger son or to a stranger.[15] There is, however, no mention of the agnates as a whole, for probably their position has been greatly affected by the new succession system based on primogeniture which had come in following the Conquest.

The necessity for the primogenitary heir's consent to an alienation (save in the exceptional cases already mentioned) remained in force a little longer. It has been asserted that it was abolished in Scotland by a statute of William the Lion (1165–1214),[16] but it seems probable that this is a later ascription to legislation of a change brought about by the skill of conveyancers and the decisions of the courts,

12   Glanvil, VII, 1; *Regiam*, II.18.2–3.
13   Glanvil, VII, 1; *Regiam*, II.20.5.
14   Titles to Land Consolidation (Scotland) Act 1868, s 20; Conveyancing (Scotland) Act 1874, s 37.
15   Glanvil, VII, 1. *Regiam*, II.19–20.
16   Sandford, *Entails*, 24.

for this is too early for revolutionary changes by legislation to be at all likely. Moreover, modern historians do not accept the authenticity of such early Scots 'statutes'. Developments in England, on the other hand, strongly suggest the actual course of events. A simple conveyancing device was invented whereby the heir's powers of objection could be rendered harmless. The warranty which was an essential part of every feudal conveyance (and is still in use in Scotland[17]) could be phrased so as to bind not only the grantor but also his heirs. If this were done, the heirs could not succeed to the land without also succeeding to, and becoming bound by, the warranty. This was held to be the case in 1225.[18] It is significant that this was a decision of Bracton, J., who was a champion of the individualist as against the dynastic view of landholding. Thus at length the law came to recognise a landowner in the modern sense: one who can alienate the land at his own pleasure without consulting any member of his family.

Such a power of free alienation seems to amount to a complete denial of family landholding in the sense in which we have hitherto used that term. The first round of the battle had gone to the individualists. Yet the paradox is that the landowners who thus acquired freedom of disposal used it in very many cases to tie up the land in a particular family according to their own design. They thus sought to deprive future generations of the liberty which they themselves had won. This appears to be yet another proof of the strength of the traditional idea that land should belong to the family rather than to the individual. But always henceforward this idea had to contend with the opposite tendency of the owner, for the time being, wishing to sell.

17   *See* Appendix XI.
18   Bracton, *Note Book*, pl. 1054.

18 Maritagia and The Statute
De Donis Conditionalibus 1285

MARITAGIA

The quotation from Glanvil and the *Regiam* cited in the previous chapter makes a reference to the *maritagium*. Modern historians are agreed that it is to this institution that the eventual evolution of the English estate tail may best be traced.[1] Since the text referred to is also Scottish, it is likely that medieval Scotland also knew this institution. In view of the general trend of events it is extremely probable that it went through much the same stages of development there as in England down to the legislation of Edward I.

What then was this *maritagium*? As the passage from Glanvil suggests, it was at first a provision by the father of the bride for the new family: a dowry or tocher of land. Accordingly it could not really evolve until the rule already discussed was recognised that a man might alienate land for this purpose with or without the consent of his heir. It probably developed out of the fact that the new Norman succession system of primogeniture left the younger sons of a landed family without support. Some of them were no doubt bought heiresses endowed with land, but if the means or opportunity for this was lacking, the next best thing would be to look for a wife whose father was wealthy enough to provide her with a *maritagium*. Failing that, the man's father might provide one.

These marriage endowments came in very soon after the Conquest.[2] In the course of time their incidents and effects would have

---

1 Holdsworth, *H.E.L.*, iii, 111; Simpson, *Introduction to the History of Land Law*, 60–4.
2 P. & M., ii, 16.

been gradually regularised, and apparently this had come about in England by the time of Glanvil and, presumably, by that of the *Regiam Majestatem* in Scotland. Glanvil points out that there were two types of *maritagia*, one subject to homage and feudal services, the other, *liberum maritagium*, free of these burdens. He was mainly concerned with the *liberum maritagium*. His language clearly envisages the gift as one by way of subinfeudation (*de me*), to be held of the grantor. The arrangement was intended to give the new branch of the family about a century (three generations) in which to become established, during which time the donor required no feudal services from the donees. Indeed he would himself perform them to the superior-lord of the fee. In return for this exemption there was a clear understanding that if the cadet branch failed to become established and died out before the third heir (that is the fourth generation) had entered, the *maritagium* would return to source. Thus the family stock of land would not have been depleted without a good reason in the firm establishment of a new house. It is in order to secure this possible return that the homage, which would have bound the grantor and his heirs to warrant the grant, was omitted for the time being; but once the third heir had entered, the new branch was deemed to be fully established and capable of discharging the feudal obligations of homage and service.[3]

It is obvious that during the three 'test' generations the *maritagium* should not have been alienable for that would have defeated the whole scheme; but unfortunately there appears to have been no express ruling that this was the case. It was also vital that the husband-donee should only have a lasting right to the lands if issue were born of the marriage. Both these points had their part to play later. The *maritagium* provided English law with a new phenomenon, that of the reversion, for during the test period the donor retained an interest in the land, which might come back to him or his heirs on failure of the donee's issue.

Men soon saw what a useful method of dealing with land this grant-cum-reversion arrangement was. They began to use it with variants, for example as a limitation to the male descendants only or to males in preference to females. Sometimes the grant might

3 Glanvil VII, 18; *Regiam*, II. 57.

not be made in connection with a marriage at all: if the reversion were useful in that one field, might it not be employed in other spheres too, for example to ensure that an ordinary fee should descend only to males or to males in preference to females? This development had clearly come about before 1285,[4] and thereafter a marriage consideration was not a necessary prerequisite for the creation of a reversion.

The juristic nature of this new reversion and of the *maritagium* itself caused much discussion among the lawyers of Henry III's time when their use was becoming increasingly popular. English legal theory was at this period still in a formative stage and the doctrine of estates still lay in the future. Scotland was as yet mainly content to receive her legal theory as well as most of her substantive land law from England. The parting of the ways was to come about in the next reign.

Bracton, who was much influenced by Roman law, came to a conclusion by no means unlike that which we shall see was the answer of Scots law, that is that the whole fee (*dominium plenum*) is in the donee. A grant of land to a man and his heirs, gave him the whole seisin (medieval English lawyers thought rather in terms of seisin than of ownership) and gave the heirs nothing, since by the warranty device they could not prevent their ancestor from alienating.[5] If the grant were not just to '*A* and his heirs', but to '*A* and the heirs born of a particular marriage', or to '*A* and the heirs of his body', Bracton considered that this made no difference to the general effect. The heirs still got nothing and the donee the whole fee, though in this case not at once – first he had to beget heirs of the appropriate class, since that was the necessary condition of the grant. Until then his interest was deemed to be a conditional one, which would endure only if such children were born. The grant was thus in Bracton's view an example of the conditional gift so well known to Roman law. Fulfilment of the condition completed the gift and the donee thereupon acquired an indefeasible title to the land; indefeasible, that is, by the extinction of the issue, whether that occurred in five minutes or in fifty years. Consequently the grantee, having once begotten the appropriate type of issue, could sell or otherwise

4   *See* the Preamble to Statute of Westminster II, 1285 (*De Donis Conditionalibus*).
5   *See* Chapter 17.

alienate the land. Neither the heirs described in what was in effect the gift's condition, nor the grantor could make any effective objection.[6] The latter's reversion was viewed as a mere *spes*, lost once the condition was fulfilled.

English and Scots law advanced thus far together – we may assume. There is a scribal interpolation in some MSS of the *Regiam Majestatem*[7] which shows that Bracton's text probably circulated in Scotland; but even if it did not, the ideas put forward by Bracton would be those of all civilians, which the early Scots judges, being mostly churchmen, tended to be. Certainly Bracton's view that the donee in tail acquired an indefeasible interest as soon as the condition is fulfilled closely corresponded with the conclusions of the classical Scots law.[8] There is thus a direct chain of continuity between the views of Bracton and those of modern Scotland, but Bracton's view is very far removed from that of the developed English law on this subject. This is yet another instance of the tendency for Scotland to preserve the pre-Edward I English law.

ENGLAND: *DE DONIS CONDITIONALIBUS* 1285

The practical difficulty in England was that the view of the *maritagium* as a conditional fee and the consequent right of the donee to alienate as soon as the condition was fulfilled ran quite counter to the intention of the fathers and fathers-in-law who made these gifts. They intended the land to serve as an endowment for a new family and to be returnable if that family should fail to become established according to plan. The idea of such an endowment's being alienated as soon as a baby capable of enjoying the land provided for it was born was not merely unjust, it was unthinkable. Nor was the sale in question any more defensible if the baby in question died soon after birth: in such a case the land should clearly revert to the donor. Consequently there was considerable public disquiet when the practical results of Bracton's theorising became apparent to the

6 Bracton, f 17.
7 Lord Cooper, *Regiam Majestatem* (Stair Society, Vol 11), 44.
8 *See* Chapter 12.

fathers and fathers-in-law. The Petition of the Barons in 1258 asked for a remedy against such alienations in breach of the whole spirit of the gift.[9]

Since the landowners were then the dominant interest in Parliament, it is not surprising that they eventually obtained a remedy. This was the cause of the passing of the famous Act *De Donis Conditionalibus* in 1285, as the preamble sets out at great length. The enacting clauses are not so well drafted as the preamble and show signs of inexpert amendment:[10]

> Rex . . . statuit quod voluntas donatoris secundum formam in carta doni sui manifeste expressam de caetero observetur, ita quod non habeant illi, quibus tenementum sic fuit datum sub conditione, potestatem alienandi tenementum sic datum, quo minus ad exitum illorum quibus tenementum sic fuerit datum remaneat post eorum obitum, vel ad donatorem, vel ad eius haeredem.

The rest of the Act is mainly concerned with remedies and affords no answer to the essential question which is left open (presumably by mistake), namely, does it bind the donee alone not to alienate, as its wording suggests, or does it also bind his heirs, and if the latter, for how many generations ?

This point came up for decision in 1311[11] when Bereford, C. J. decreed in effect that the Act did not mean what it said, but that the draftsman (Hengham) intended the heirs to be bound for the traditional period of the *maritagium,* that is until the third heir entered. This would presumably be in accordance with the donor's wishes (following the opening words of the Act) since, as Glanvil explained, it was a customary condition of such gifts that they became absolute after the fourth generation had entered and hence fees simple. Modern rules for the interpretation of statutes were very far away.

If the development of the English law of entails had stayed there, it would not have constituted anything very remarkable, nor would the land have been preserved in the family for ever: but a most

9 Stubbs, *Charters,* 386 (27).
10 Plucknett, *Legislation of Edward I,* 132 *et seq.*
11 Y.B. 5 Ed. II (S.S.), i, 177; ii, 226.

daring step was taken by an obscure judgment in 1344[12] which changed the whole status of the entail in English law. It was held that after the third generation had entered the land still remained subject to the terms of the gift and might not be alienated so as to defeat the wishes of the grantor and the possibility of reversion to himself and his heirs. The reversioners could enforce their right to it by a writ of formedon in the reverter at any time in the future, no matter how remote, if the heirs of the donee's body became extinct. Thus the vituperations so often showered on *De Donis Conditionalibus* – not least by some Scottish writers[13] – are not justified by the wording of the Act. They should be directed against the judges, long supposed to have defeated the wicked ends of the statute by their predilection for freedom of alienation. So bold a piece of judicial legislation as that of Bereford, C. J. and his successors can scarcely be paralleled. The classical English law of entails thus owes its origin not to the statute itself, but to the very remarkable construction put on it by the courts. In the Scots law we shall see the opposite tendency has been at work: a clear statute allowing entails was construed in a hostile spirit by the (predominantly English) House of Lords.[14]

The first break in the tradition of family landownership was made by Bracton's attempt to relegate the entail to the status of a conditional gift, a view which has obvious Roman law roots. However, this Roman influence towards individualism was alien to the dynastically minded feudal English baronage, to which Bereford, C. J. and his brethren belonged. *De Donis Conditionalibus* as eventually interpreted was clear evidence of the great strength still attaching to the tradition that land belonged to, and must be preserved for, the family in all its succeeding generations.

The judges were only giving legal effect to a popular sentiment of their day. They were, it would seem, enabled to do this the more easily because of the flaws caused by the inexpert amendment of Hengham's draft. If the third heir had been expressly mentioned the extending interpretation could not conceivably have been made. It was thus the lacuna in the Act which gave the champions of family

---

12 Y.B. 20 Ed. III (R.S.), ii, 202.
13 E.g. Lord Kames, *Elucidations*, 341; Sandford, *Entails*, 361.
14 *See* Chapter 21.

landholding their opportunity. The defective amendment may have been the work of some prelate wishing to have only the original donee bound: he would naturally favour the Roman view. It cannot be without significance that the medieval Scots judges were very frequently Civilian prelates. Hence the retention there of Bracton's Roman conceptions. Nonetheless *De Donis Conditionalibus* was to have important repercussions on Scots law, as will be shown shortly.

Theoretical difficulties were raised as well as the practical question of the duration of inalienability created by the Act. Bracton's view could not be sustained now that the donor and his heirs clearly had some sort of continuing right. The donee obviously could not have the whole fee for another reason, too: his issue could now preserve their right to succeed him by the writ of formedon in the descender. For a time opinion wavered and some thought that the fee was in the heirs of entail, the donee having only an estate for life, but this left the reversioner's interest uncertain and shadowy. Finally the lawyers of Littleton's day fixed the classical English doctrine that 'le reversion del fee simple est en le donor'.[15] The other parties have lesser estates in the land, interests of more limited duration. Scots law knew nothing of these niceties, but adhered to the Roman simplicity of the *dominium plenum* in a single hand.

By various methods English law thus arrived at the conclusion which was reached in Scotland by a single comprehensive statute, that land might be kept in perpetuity in a particular family, the apparent owner for the time being having no power to alienate to the prejudice of succeeding generations. Thus by the first half of the fourteenth century English law had reached what must have seemed quite a satisfactory conclusion to the fight between family and individualist traditions in landholding. The ordinary landowner had been freed from the customary restraints on alienation in favour of the agnates, but if any particular landowner wanted to keep land in the same family for as long as it lasted, he could arrange this effectively by adopting the simple machinery of a grant in tail. The only difference from an ordinary grant lay in the words of limitation employed. The second round of the contest in England had therefore gone to the champions of family landholding.

15 Littleton, *Tenures*, s 19.

SCOTS ATTITUDES TO INALIENABILITY

The struggle between heritability and alienability in Scotland must be viewed in the correct historical perspective. The whole of England was subject to the feudal doctrine of tenure and to the effective control of parliament and the royal courts at Westminster. Scotland, on the other hand, was throughout the Middle Ages a country in which the king, and the royal courts had only a limited authority. Large portions of it remained subject to the Celtic customs of family landholding. Even in the notionally feudalised but far from orderly Lowlands, the strength of the idea that land belonged to the family rather than to the individual remained very much greater than in England. Only with the coming of a stronger central government under James VI, and the consequent breaking down of the traditional pattern of Scots patriarchal society, was there any serious attempt to interfere with the prevailing dynastic view of landholding.

The judges of Scotland tended to take their legal thinking from England until Edward I's time, so it is likely that the developments already noticed in England in connection with the *maritagium* also applied to Scotland, though probably with some time-lag. With the passing and interpretation of *De Donis Conditionalibus* however, the situation altered, and while it is not clear exactly what that situation was – beyond the fact that the statute never found its way onto the Scots statute book – some account of it probably did find its way to Scotland, at least in the view of Craig:

> It was determined and enacted by all the estates assembled in Parliament at Westminster that the owner of any feu (ancestral or novel) in which he was duly vested, should be allowed to name the heirs, both institute and substitute, to whom the feu should transmit at his death, and attach to their rights of succession both conditions and limitations – both as to the order of succession and the persons who should succeed – as he chose, provided always that the heirs named were sound in body and in mind and the superior had given his consent. Prior to this, tailzies were unknown, as can be proved from any family charter-chest. They began with the Act of the English Parliament to which I have referred – an act which, as I shall have occasion to show, was not inconsistent with the spirit of feudal institutions. The Civil Law contains no mention

of tailzies, and neither does the Feudal Law – which is not remarkable, for after all, a tailzie consists in nothing but a condition qualifying the feudal grant.[16]

Many Scots lawyers thereafter misunderstood the effect of the English Act in several fundamental points:

1   Most important, there never was the complete freedom of selection of heirs which Craig describes: they had in England always to be descendants of the body of the donee and it was only from this narrow field that the English entailer could select the heirs. An unbarrable entail extending to and binding collateral relatives of the donee could not be envisaged, for to give land to a man and his heirs was to give him the fee simple. The institution of remainders over, whereby after the extinction of the issue of the donee the land did not revert to the donor but went under a separate limitation to the donee's next brother or other relative and the heirs of *his* body, went some way to meet the difficulty. But it is inaccurate to regard these remaindermen as the equivalent of the Scots substitutes, since the remainderman is not regarded as an heir taking under the original entail, but as another donee, having a quite distinct estate in the land coexistent from the time of the creation of the estate tail, even if not yet in possession.

2   Equally, there was not complete freedom as to the conditions and limitations to be imposed on the heirs. Such restrictions were in England a matter for the general law rather than for the whim of a particular settlor. Thus only certain rigid varieties of estate tail were permitted, as is still the case. A limitation in tail general (the norm) descends to all the issue of the donee according to primogenitary succession: a tail special restricts the descent to the issue of a particular marriage and an interest in tail male, or tail male special, further confines the line of descent to those who can trace their claim through the male line only. Apart from the theoretical possibility of a similar tail female, these are the only arrangements allowed. Scots law would allow each of these types of entail to be created, although a destination to heirs female of the body does not mean that the claimants must be females claiming through females.[17]

16   Craig, 2.16.3 (Lord Clyde's Translation, Vol 1, 699).
17   *See* Chapter 22.

The Scots settler was free to make his own arrangements without being restricted to the four stock types just mentioned. He was not even bound to choose the heirs from among the donee's issue.

3   The consent of the lord-superior was not necessary to the grant of an estate tail in England, or indeed any other alienation.

4   After *De Donis Conditionalibus* 1285 (as interpreted later) the fee was not wholly in the disponee, but the grantor retained the fee simple reversion in his own person; or alternatively, he might grant it to a third party as a remainder. He could not, however, give it to the grantee in tail without automatically ending the entail.

It is possible that no authoritative text of *De Donis Conditionalibus* found its way to Edinburgh. At all events, Scots authorities make no mention of the lacuna in the Act by which only the original donee was bound. It was not filled in by the English judges until the 1340s, and by then wars had caused a long break in ordinary relations between the two countries. These wars raged on and off from about 1292 to 1346. During that time Scotland had no time to think of law, but when peace came the Scots may well have wished to catch up with the times. It is significant that the wars covered the period between the passing of *De Donis Conditionalibus* and the final fixing of its meaning by the English courts.

Even if the Scots got the original idea of the entail from the period before *De Donis Conditionalibus*[18] there were to be very important differences between the two systems. In part these may be due to the text's not being available in Scotland, but undoubtedly some of them are traceable to the fact that Scotland's judges, as already mentioned, tended to be prelates and therefore civilians. For example, in Scotland an entail need not be confined to a named person and the heirs of his body, as it had to be in England. The tailzing of a fee might occur in a disposition to any heirs 'which are not according to the line or course of law'.[19] They may thus be collaterals or even strangers in blood: indeed Stair tells us that in his time the term 'heir of tailzie' was usually understood to mean heirs other than descendants, who were described as 'heirs male' or 'heirs female'.[20]

18   Sandford, *Entails*, 36.
19   Stair, III.4.33.
20   *Ibid.*

Since Scots law does not regard the tailzied fee as an estate tail carved out of a continuing fee simple, there is no reason why its destination should not extend to collaterals.

Yet there is one restriction on the choice of heirs. It is uncertain when it came in (though that it was before Stair's day), but it has a curiously English ring about it. If 'heirs whatsoever', that is the ordinary intestate heirs, were nominated, the effect was to pass the fee (simple) free from all restraints.[21] Now if one is thinking in terms of a grant of *dominium plenum*, there seems no special reason why prohibitions against alienation should not be attached to it merely because the substitutes happen to be the normal heirs of line. This rule is not due to any special magic in the words of limitation. The phrase 'heirs whatsoever' was not necessarily used to pass the fee in Scotland, which never had the rigid English attitude to words of limitation.[22]

It follows from the principle just mentioned that if at any time an estate subject to the fetters of an entail stands limited finally to an individual and his heirs whatsoever, this is held to close the entail. The last substitute under the previous part of the destination takes for the equivalent of a fee simple.[23] There is thus no reversion to the granter such as English lawyers would expect on the extinction of heirs of the body.

The slightest deviation from the normal order of succession was sufficient, however, to permit the creation of an entail. Stair cites as an example of a slight variation being enough the case where the succession was limited to the heirs whatsoever, female heir-portionment excepted.[24] However doubt was cast on this example by the decision in *Primrose v Primrose*,[25] where exactly this limitation was held not to be enough to create an entail and the institute was treated as unlimited fiar. This case was heard in 1854 and shows that by then the English policy of avoiding entails had been established in Scots law too by the policy of the House of Lords,[26] but Stair's remark was probably true of the classical law.

21 *Mowbray's Trustees v Mowbray* (1895) 22 R 801 *per* Lord Rutherford Clark at 808.
22 *See* Chapter 22.
23 *Gordon v Gordon's Trustees* (1881) 7 App Cas 713.
24 Stair, III.4.33.
25 (1854) 16 D 498.
26 *See* Chapter 21.

The purpose of the tailzie in Scotland was to maintain the dignity and prestige of the old landed families. It was therefore employed there from its earliest introduction, according to Craig,[27] to exclude females from the succession in favour of males, even remote collaterals. In final default of heirs male, however, it was quite common to find a destination to heirs female and the heirs male of their bodies. This was often coupled with a name and arms clause requiring the holders of the estate to use the surname and armorial bearings of the granter's family. There may possibly be a link between this preference for the heir male and the fact that in Celtic succession females were entirely barred.

It is clear that if entails were thus used to prevent the lands from falling into female hands, an economic motive as well as feudal theory lay behind the requirement that the superior of the granter must consent to the tailzing of a fee. The marriages of female wards, as Craig points out,[28] tended to be worth quite a lot more than those of males. Feudal principle also required this consent because it involved a change in the conditions on which the superior originally granted the fee, that is that it should be held by the donee and his ordinary heirs. The normal process, therefore, for the creation of a tailzie was by a resignation of the fee to the superior followed by a regrant of it to the surrendering fiar (or to someone whom he wished to benefit) and to the specified categories of heirs.

There seems, on the other hand, no inherent difficulty in the alternative which Craig himself suggests – that of subinfeudation. *A*, a vassal duly infeft, could subinfeudate to his son *B* and the heirs male of *B* and so on. If *A* wished to do so, he could reserve a liferent to himself. The superior could make no objection, apart from the special casualty of recognition in ward fees,[29] as all this takes place under the canopy of *A*'s vassalage, which will naturally pass to his heirs general.

It would be incorrect to suppose that any such thing as a legally recognised unbarrable entail (like the English one) existed in the medieval period in Scotland. Paradoxically enough this may be due to the strength of the family idea there, which made it unnecessary

27　Craig, 2.16.12.
28　Craig, 2.16.13.
29　Craig, 2.16.20.

to prohibit what no reasonable person thought of doing. The legal battle in Scotland between the principles of dynastic and individual landholding did not open in earnest until the seventeenth century; this was after the main stages of the English contest, which is the subject of the next chapter.

19 Developments in England after 1285

The interpretation put by the English courts on *De Donis Condi-tionalibus* 1285 enabled land to be preserved in a family through succeeding generations.[1] But this defeat of the forces of free alienability was not a final victory. Those forces soon returned to the attack, but not through legislators repealing *De Donis Conditionalibus* or confining it within its original limits: the landholding element in Parliament would have been strong enough to stop that. More craftily they chose the courts as their battleground and the technicalities of medieval procedure as their chief weapons.

It is important to realise the immense prestige and importance which English medieval lawyers attached to seisin, that is actual possession of land on a freehold basis.[2] Its importance was such that it was at one time thought that even a tenant for life could make an effective, albeit tortious, feoffment. The rule as to warranty referred to in Chapter 17 could be used to bar the remainderman's objections, assuming that he was the heir of the tenant for life, as he would be in many cases, although, of course, not always. The evil in question was dealt with by the Statute of Gloucester 1278, under which the heir was not bound by the warranty unless 'sufficient assets' came to him from that ancestor to recompense him for his loss.

A tenant in tail after *De Donis Conditionalibus* was also seised of land and so there arose a presumption in English legal minds that he should be able to make an effective feoffment, but against this had to be set the Act itself as interpreted by the judges. It was clear that no feoffment would bar the remaindermen, far less the

1 *See* Chapter 18.
2 The Scots term 'sasine' had a different meaning. See pp. 231–7 and Chapter 24.

reversioner. Moreover the courts, still in a mood to help the family or dynastic side, soon extended the Statute of Gloucester to protect the heirs of entail being actual descendents of the donee in tail.[3] The champions of free alienability therefore embarked on a typically tortuous course of action. Reduced to essentials, the idea was that a collateral warrantor, that is someone other than the tenant in tail, should not be caught by the Act, so that the heir would be bound without any question as to sufficiency of assets arising. Littleton explains how it worked in his day:

> If land be given to a man and to the heirs of his body begotten, who taketh wife, and have issue a son between them, and the husband discontinues the tail in fee and dieth, and after the wife releaseth to the discontinuance in fee at the warranty and dieth, and the warranty descends to the son, this is a collateral warranty.[4]

The heir would be bound by the warranty because he inherited it from his mother. The Statute of Gloucester 1278 was inapplicable because he inherited the lands from a different person, his father. Furthermore the English law denied to the heir any opportunity of declining this *damnosa hereditas*, as he could have done in Scotland or at Rome.

The heirs of entail might thus be barred by a collateral warranty, but it was an unsatisfactory device, as it depended on the various relatives dying in the right order. Moreover, it could not be relied on to bar the remaindermen or the reversioners, so it was necessary to invent some more efficient machinery. Accordingly the procedure known as the fine was employed as a device to bar the entail. The term 'fine' is a short anglicisation of *finalis concordia*, which gives a better idea of the nature of the transaction. It was a fictitious lawsuit-turned-conveyance akin to the *in jure cessio*[5] of Roman law. A writ was issued in the usual way, but the parties then agreed to a compromise and the court gave its formal sanction to this. Finally the whole transaction was recorded in triplicate, the third copy (the 'foot') being entered on the rolls of the court. This fine was generally used as an ordinary method of conveyancing, but also on occasions

3   Y.B. 20 & 21 Ed. I (R.S.), 302.
4   Littleton, *Tenures*, s 713 (Cary's Translation, 650).
5   *See* Buckland, *Textbook of Roman Law*, 233–5.

in an attempt to bar entails. It did not become effective, however, until late in the fifteenth century, when the feudal nobility had been decimated in the Wars of the Roses and lost its old power. The Fines Act of Richard III (1484)[6] re-enacted by Henry VII,[7] made a fine fully effective to bar the entail as against the descendants of the body of the conusor (that is the alienor). Even against remaindermen and reversioners it became effective if certain proclamations were made and five years elapsed without their entering a formal protest to preserve their rights. In practice, of course, they generally did so, and the result was to create an estate in the conusee which would last only as long as issue of the conusor remained alive. This curious estate is what English law knows as a base fee. That term has a very different significance in Scotland, where it indicates a subinfeudation not confirmed by the superior.[8]

Another device tried out in the later Middle Ages, the common recovery, was even better from the point of view of those who favoured freedom of alienation at the expense of family landholding. It was hoped that by a court's giving judgment for the land against the tenant in tail the latter would be able to pass it effectively to an alienee, dressed up for the occasion as a judgment creditor. After various false starts, rendered ineffective by successive statutes,[9] it seemed impossible for a tenant in tail in possession, still less a tenant for life, to pass the fee simple effectively, for the remaindermen were certain to intervene. If they did not, the alienee at best got a base fee. Eventually a master edifice of fiction was constructed whereby the tenant in tail was enabled to part with the land without technically suffering any loss to which the remaindermen could object. The tenant in tail was sued by the alienee-to-be. Instead of defending the action, he vouched to warranty some casual stranger, often the usher of the court, who defaulted, being a man of straw. Two judgments were then given, one for the alienee against the tenant in tail, the other against the vouchee to warranty in favour of the tenant in tail, who was thus deemed to be recompensed for his loss through the vouchee's neglect. The remaindermen must

6   1 Ric. III, c 7.
7   Fines Act 1490.
8   *See* Chapter 24.
9   E.g. Recoveries Acts 1540 and 1572.

attack the wholly imaginary land thus owed by the vouchee to the tenant in tail. Their actions of formedon would naturally be fruitless.

Unless he is so impressed by the virtues of land being made free from family restrictions that he considers any method, however underhand, legitimate to gain that end, every English lawyer must blush to acknowledge that the courts of his country gave their sanction to this 'bare-faced fraud'.[10] These arrangements are a startling change from the days when Hengham and his brethren were the chief champions of family landholding and were no doubt due to economic causes, but the methods by which the courts – now deserters from the cause of family landholding – gained their end cannot be described as anything less than grossly dishonest. When the Scots judges were faced with a statute permitting unbarrable entails, some of them may have disliked them as much as the English judges had come to, but they never descended to such expedients as these.

The invention of the common recovery has traditionally been attributed to *Taltarum's Case* (1472),[11] but there is reason to think that they only became at all frequent in the highly commercial Elizabethan era.[12] Pressure of riches flooding in from the New World sent the value of property soaring. The English landowner and his lawyers were not to be deterred from such a high opportunity by the regulations of an ancient statute as interpreted by their long-dead predecessors; even less by considerations of legal principle. The tenant in tail, although throughout he has only had a limited estate, the fee tail, thus became able by a masterpiece of illogicality to convey an estate (the fee simple) which he never had. Coke had to deny the whole doctrine of estates when he said that a gift in tail maketh the donee . . . chief owner of the land.[13] If the theory had been, as it was in Scotland, that the tenant in tail was *dominus* subject to mere fetters against alienation, the common recovery might have been justifiable and the Court could have claimed to be releasing a captive from his chains. But where he did not have *dominium* he

---

10   Plucknett, *Concise History of Common Law*, 621.
11   Y.B. 12 Ed. IV, 19.
12   *See* Holdsworth, *H.E.L.*, iii, 119–20.
13   *Mildmay's Case* (1606) 6 Co Rep 40a.

could certainly not in logic, common sense or justice convey it to another.

Thus, not without very considerable suspicions of foul play, the third and decisive round in the battle between inheritability and alienability in England went to the latter's adherents. Never again would the entail be a safe method of keeping land in the family.

ATTEMPTS TO RESTORE FAMILY LANDHOLDING

But there was still spirit left in the champions of family landholding. It was their next task to try to frame a provision which, while giving the tenant in tail for the time being possession of the land, would prevent his taking advantage of this new learning about the common recovery. They found one which was destined to fail in England but to achieve indirectly a brilliant success in Scotland, becoming indeed the bulwark of family landholding there. The inventor of this device was an Irishman:[14] Rickhill, J., in the reign of Richard II. He created a settlement under which each of his sons successively was given an estate tail, with a condition that if he did anything to break the entail he should forfeit his estate.[15]

In the sixteenth century there were several attempts to test this scheme against the newly born common recovery. A simple condition of forfeiture on suffering a common recovery was clearly useless, for by then the damage would be done. Hence the draftsmen tried to catch the land at an earlier stage. This device was tested in *Corbet's Case*,[16] of which Holt, C.J., said:

> Ay, Corbet's Case (which) was only a preparative for Mildmay's Case (which was the real one) but I have heard my Lord Chancellor Finch say (when at the Bar) that it was not known to be so till too

14 Co. Litt. 377b.
>   *This invention devised by justice Richel in the reigne of King Richard the second, who was an Irishman borne and the like by Thiring, Chief-Justice in the reigne of Henry the fourth, were both full of imperfections; for* Nihil simul inventum est et perfectum, *and* Saepe viatorem nova non vetus orbita fallit: *and therefore new inventions in assurances are dangerous. And hereby it may appeare, that it is not safe for any man (be he never so learned) to be of counsell with himselfe in his own case, but to the advice of other great and learned men.*

15 Littleton, *Tenures*, s 720.
16 (1599) 1 Co Rep 83b.

late, and then Anderson was very angry: they should bring a proper action.[17]

In *Mildmay's Case*[18] the matter was argued all over again on substantially the same facts. The forfeiture clause was very lengthy, containing over a thousand words. In brief it went as follows: if at any time Anthony (the first tenant in tail) should finally decide to enter into any negotiations leading up to a possible common recovery or other disentailing device, or begin or attempt to begin, any such negotiations, and so on, he was immediately after such deciding, attempting and so on, to forfeit his estate and the entail would pass on to and bind the next person entitled with a similar condition. Scots readers will recognise this as the prototype of their own entails, which will be discussed in the next chapter.

The English courts, having now come down on the side of free alienability, treated the whole of the proviso as void, primarily on the ground that English law will not allow estates to depend on such vague and uncertain things as 'attempting' and 'going about'. Coke wondered where the line was to be drawn. Should there be a forfeiture if the tenant in tail asked his lawyer whether he could burden the land with his debts or allot some of it to his daughter as a dowry? It was also resolved that it was impossible and repugnant that an estate tail should cease as if the tenant in tail was dead (had he issue or no), for an estate cannot cease so long as it continues.[19] Surely, however, in the common recovery the estate tail does so cease while it still continues, for it ceases in the sense that it ceases to be a fee tail, but continues in the sense that it still keeps out the remainderman. Better than these nonsenses was Coke's frank admission that he could not abide 'perpetuities' at any price. In his view they were against the common law, for at common law all inheritances were fees simple: but the common law position (that is Bracton's) had already been set aside by statute and precedents of great authority for centuries.

This decision did not deter the plaintiff in *Mary Portington's Case*[20] from trying again. This action was entered in the Common

17 *Brewster v Kitchen* (1702) Comb 425.
18 (1606) 6 Co Rep 40a.
19 (1606) 6 Co Rep at 40b.
20 (1614) 10 Co Rep 35b.

Pleas in 1610 and had lasted fourteen terms and been argued more than seven times before it was eventually decided in 1614. The fame of this protracted litigation probably reached Edinburgh.[21] The settlor in this case gave the land in tail to his third daughter, who purported to bar the entail with remainder to his first (Mary), second, fourth and other daughters, subject to a proviso like that in *Mildmay's Case*, but even more carefully drawn. The forfeiture was to fall when the daughter entered into a binding agreement to bar or did any act whereby the estate would be lost or the entail barred, thus avoiding the vagueness of the earlier settlement. Similarly, the repugnancy argument was met by a statement that the forfeiture was to take effect notwithstanding any act, matter or thing contained elsewhere in the will. On the forfeiture the land was to pass as if the defaulting tenant in tail had died without issue. In spite of all this care Mary Portington was unsuccessful. The Court took the general point that the power to disentail by a common recovery was an inherent incident of an estate tail, of which it could be deprived only by the express words of a statute. A mere private donor could not thus give an estate and yet deny it one of its natural attributes. So far as criticism of the common recovery was concerned, Coke said that they were 'one of the main pillars which supports the estates and inheritances of the kingdom', adding that 'there was never anything by the wisdom of man so well devised or so surely established upon law and reason which the wit and craft of those who are subtle and wicked has not abused'.[22] He also quoted from the 'great case betwixt T. Vernon and Sir Edward Herbert, which was argued by learned counsel before the Lords in Parliament' in which:

> Hoord, an utter-barrister, of counsel with Vernon (who was barred by a common recovery) rashly and with great ill will inveighed against common recoveries, not knowing the reason and foundation of them; who was with great gravity and some sharpness reproved by Sir James Dyer, then Chief Justice of the Common Pleas, who said, he was not worthy to be of the profession of the law who durst speak against common recoveries, which were the sinews of assurances of inheritances and founded upon great reason and authority.[23]

21 *See* Chapter 20.
22 *Mary Portington's Case* (1614) 10 Co Rep 35b at 39a.
23 *Ibid.*, 40a.

One has great sympathy for Mr Hoord! Saint Germain entitled Chapter 26 of the first Dialogue in *Doctor and Student*, 'A question made by the Doctor, how certain recoveries that be used in the king's courts to defeat tailed land may stand with conscience', and seriously doubted the morality of the common recovery.

After *Mary Portington's Case* it became clear that the entailed interest would no longer serve the purpose of those wishing to keep land within the family in England. The fourth round had gone to the alienability school. As soon as there was a tenant of full age in possession, the continuance of the land in the family now depended solely on the pleasure of that heir and he could bar if he chose by submitting to the expensive jiggery-pokery of a common recovery. In view of the financial advantage to himself, there was a very real danger that he would do so. It therefore became the aim of the draftsmen of English settlements to postpone the tenant in tail's coming into possession for as long as they possibly could. They arranged this by the creation of prior life interests and in any other way that seemed reasonably likely to succeed.

At common law the estate tail could be postponed for only a very short time. Every legal estate had to be so arranged that it would begin immediately the prior interests ended. Nor could any interest be limited to an unborn person,[24] a rule that was to find an echo in the modern statutory law of Scotland.[25] But through the medium of the use these tiresome rules could be circumvented and such things as a springing interest, to arise at a future date, arranged. After the Statute of Uses it was eventually decided that such things as springing and shifting interests could be created at law if the machinery of a grant to use was employed.[26]

The champions of family landholding now had a new weapon, enabling the settlors to create all kinds of executory (that is future) interests. The only necessity was to avoid creating something which the common law judges could construe as a contingent remainder and therefore destructible.[27] An obvious expedient was to limit the land to an endless series of tenants for life, each the heir of the

---

24   Y.B. 10 Ed. III, de Termino Michaelis, note 8.
25   As to which, *see* Chapter 25.
26   Plucknett, *Concise History of the Common Law*, 588 *et seq.*
27   As to contingent remainders *see* pp. 258–64, *infra.*

previous one. This was ruled void as a disguised attempt to give an unbarrable estate tail and also as creating a 'possibility on a possibility'.[28] Nor was the attempt of the great Duke of Marlborough any more successful. He devised lands in trust for several persons for life, with remainders to their first and other sons in tail male successively and provided that at the birth of every such son his tutors were to revoke the uses to him in tail male, and to limit the lands afresh to him for life and *his* sons in tail male, a similar re-settlement being carried out at their birth and so on. This was held to be illegal and void by the courts.[29]

The Duke of Norfolk's Case[30] involved a less ambitious scheme. The head of the Howards settled a long lease in trust for his second son but if his eldest son died without issue in his father's lifetime, so that the family honours and lands came to that second son, the lease was to go to the third son and so on down to all the six sons if necessary. The eldest son did die in his father's lifetime; but the second son (the duke) had purported to suffer a common recovery. Faced with this problem, the common lawyers fled to their traditional technicalities, saying that the third son's interest was void as a perpetuity. Lord Nottingham, L.C., was not satisfied with this view, for although he agreed with them that perpetuities were 'against the reason and policy of the law', he added, 'that must be strange and monstrous perpetuity that must determine within the short space of a life'.[31] He therefore upheld the settlement. It thus became clear that land might properly be kept in the family for a lifetime, but he would not be drawn on the question of how long a settlement might thus tie up land before it became void as a perpetuity. It was obvious that a line had to be drawn somewhere between the *Marlborough*

---

28   Co. Inst. 25b; 184a; Fearne, *Contingent Remainders*, 250; 502. *Re Nash* [1910] 1 Ch 1. Cf Shaw Fletcher *An Historical Essay on Contingent and Executory Interests in Land in English Law*, 76:

> *There is in truth, no maxim or rule against double possibilities, and its statement by Cole was the result of an unfounded apprehension in the minds of the judges in the Sixteenth Century that the device of contingent remainders, which were unknown to the Common Law, might be misused for the purpose of creating inalienable interests in land.*

See also *The Rector of Chedington's Case* (1598) 1 Co Rep 153a *per* Popham C. J. at 156b.
29   *The Duke of Marlborough's Case* (1759) 1 Eden 404.
30   *The Duke of Norfolk's Case* (1681) 3 Ch Ca 1.
31   (1681) 3 Ch Ca at 46.

and *Norfolk* types of settlements. Through a line of decisions starting in 1661[32] and culminating in 1890[33] it became established that any estate limited to the unborn child of an unborn child was void. Thus the settlor might keep the land in the family during the whole lifetime of his unborn son and heir, but he could not prevent his son's unborn son from barring the entail as soon as he was of age. This is known as the Old Rule Against Perpetuities.

Emboldened by their success in the *Norfolk* case, but cautious through long and bitter experience, the adherents of keeping land in the family edged their way forward. The *Norfolk* decision had allowed land to be inalienable during a single life. In *Stephens v Stephens*[34] it was held that a devise to an unborn person, the child of a living person, to become vested on that child's attaining his majority, was valid. *Thelluson v Woodford*[35] decided that any life in being, not necessarily that of a beneficiary, might be chosen. *In re Villar*[36] shows what this means in the hands of a determined draftsman. Here the settlement was during the lives of all the descendants of Queen Victoria living at the testator's death – some one hundred and twenty persons in all. It was just possible to follow the duration of those lives, but a similar provision today would very probably be held void for uncertainty.[37] A smaller class should therefore be chosen, such as the descendants of King George V.[38] *Cadell v Palmer*[39] provided the finishing touch to the Modern Rule Against Perpetuities by allowing any period of twenty-one years to be chosen after such lives in being without reference to any minority. Thus the Rule emerged, by which land may be settled in the same family for a period not exceeding any life in being and twenty-one years plus, where relevant, the period of gestation, for a child en ventre sa mere is treated as if it had been born.[40]

32   *Grig v Hopkins* (1661) 1 Sid 37.
33   *Whitby v Mitchell* (1890) 44 Ch D 85.
34   (1736) Cas t Talbot 228.
35   (1798) 4 Ves 227; (1805) 11 Ves 112.
36   [1929] 1 Ch 243.
37   Megarry and Wade, 220. Compare the clear case of uncertainty where a testatrix chose the period 'until 21 years from the death of the last survivor of all persons who shall be living at my death'. (*Re Moore* [1901] 1 Ch 936).
38   *Re Leverhulme* (*No. 2*) [1943] 2 All ER 274.
39   (1833) 1 Cl & F 372.
40   *Thelluson v Woodford* (1805) 11 Ves 112 at 141.

When the so-called 'Old Rule' was abolished for instruments taking effect after 1925[41] the Modern Rule became the only rule. The Perpetuities and Accumulations Act 1964 has since provided one alternative, intended to be much more straightforward than 'Royal lives' clauses: this is a fixed period of years, not exceeding eighty, and specified as being chosen as the perpetuity period for the limitation.[42]

The Act made one other vital change. Before 15 July 1964 limitations were judged looking forward from the moment when the instrument creating them became effective; and if the gift could possibly vest outside the period of a life or lives in being plus twenty-one years it was void, even though in fact it might prove to vest in time. After 15 July 1964 one may 'wait and see' whether the gift does vest in time; if so, it is valid.[43] Any interest under a settlement must be arranged so as to vest within that period so as to become capable of alienation.

Such are the English rules as to the confining of land in a family. Its permanent achievement was seen to be impossible ·once an unbarrable entail was held to be illegal. Since then the English settlor has sought to do it for a limited period. As is so often the case in England, the rule eventually adopted rests on convenience rather than on logic. There is no special significance in the period of eighty years or of a life and twenty-one years once their connection with the settlement and a beneficiary's minority has gone. It was simply thought that the rule of the dead over the living should not be allowed to endure indefinitely. But one cannot help feeling that some more logical criterion might have been chosen.

The family landholding party had one more idea which was to prove more successful than its predecessors. Under the traditional English marriage settlement the husband is given a life interest with remainder in tail to his eldest and other sons. If this was all, the son could clearly bar the entail and take the land out of the family at his father's death. But he can also bar with his father's consent in his lifetime. This he is encouraged – by any legitimate means – to do, soon after attaining his majority, in order to execute forthwith a

41　Law of Property Act 1925, s 161.
42　Perpetuities and Accumulations Act 1964, s 1.
43　*Ibid.*, s 3 (1).

resettlement on his father for life, then himself for life, and then the heirs of his body in tail and so on. The land is thus made safe for another generation. This resettlement process is an echo of the scheme in the *Duke of Marlborough's Case*,[44] but with the very important difference that an adult beneficiary's free consent is interposed in every generation. This frees it from the stigma of a perpetuity. Consequently the practice of resettlement has proved the best weapon for those who would keep the land in the family in England. Even that cannot be guaranteed success nowadays, for the Settled Land Acts gave a power of sale to every tenant for life in possession under a settlement.[45] Since, however, he obtains no financial benefit by such a sale, the money being automatically settled, it seems probable that such sales will take place only in the interests of good estate management.

Furthermore, since the common law rules were evolved, various taxes adopted for specific political motives have added their weighty influence against tying up land within the family by the threat of confiscation of inherited wealth or by taking a large slice on transfer. In Scotland (though now subject to the same destructive taxes) the family party previously had much greater prospects of success.

44　(1759) 1 Eden 404.
45　Settled Land Act 1882, s 3 (i); Settled Land Act 1925, s 38 (i).

20 Developments in Scotland: The Entail Act of 1685

There is ground for supposing that the tradition by which land is looked on as inalienable out of the family was even stronger in Scotland than in medieval England. In England after *De Donis Conditionalibus* 1295, the *maritagium* was enlarged to be a perpetual entail.[1] In the similar development in Scotland this was nearly always a male entail. The difficulty is that to create such interests as an entail one must presuppose a right in the head of the family at least to arrange which members of his family shall enjoy which parts of the estates. Disputes in connection with Scots entails more often lay between different members of the same family than between the family and some stranger-alienee. It often happened that the family head, while not wishing to alienate the lands, wished desperately to control the succession to them after his death. He would want especially to prevent their coming to female heirs (let into the succession by a feudal novelty), with the consequence of portionment.

When Scotland became a sufficiently peaceful country to allow orderly legal development (which scarcely occurred before the sixteenth century), the contest between family and individual interests in land began in earnest. The judges of the Court of Session until the Reformation were chiefly canonists and afterwards tended to be Civilians by training and thus approached a feudal institution such as the entail with suspicion. The Roman tradition has tended to favour the idea of free alienability. The law of a country which favoured the dynastic view was accordingly administered by judges who favoured the opposite view.

It is important to appreciate the principles from which the Scots

---

1 *See* Chapter 19.

courts started when dealing with entails. They amounted to something very like Bracton's view of the *maritagium*. The person who would in England be the tenant in tail was viewed by them as *dominus*, whose right to alienate would be recognised except where it had been effectively taken away. The earlier Scots cases are therefore mainly concerned with examining the clauses of the charter to see if the right of alienation had been taken away.

The intention of the granter was least effective where there was a simple substitution, for example 'to *A* and his heirs male' or 'to *A* and the heirs male of his body'. In these cases *A* and each of the successive heirs as they came into possession were fiars (*domini*) and, as such, in the absence of prohibitory clauses in the charter, had the full right of all fiars to alienate or otherwise treat the land as their own. The destination merely had the effect that the order of succession which it laid down would continue unless and until any fiar chose to alter it. As there were no prohibitions against alteration, any succeeding fiar could sell the land, or charge it with his debts, or alter the succession scheme arranged by his ancestor.[2] Nor was there any change if the original granter reserved a power to alter the entail, as was shown by *Dalgarno v Durham*,[3] which was a case after the Act of 1685, but which did not come within its terms and therefore had to be decided on 'common law' lines. The settler disponed the estate to one of his grandsons and the heirs of his body; whom failing, to another grandson and his like heirs; whom failing, to the granter's own heirs and assignees. The institute (the elder grandson) disponed the lands gratuitously to his half-sister for life and her son in fee. The other grandson in this action sought to annul this disposition as being in breach of the tailzie. The Court of Session held that, this not being an entail within the 1685 Act, the elder grandson was 'a simple fiar under no restraint or prohibition, and that a substitution was no impediment nor bar on the institute to dispone (even) gratuitously'.[4]

The position then of the holder under a simple destination at common law in Scotland was comparable with that of an English tenant in tail in possession at the present day. He can bar at any

2 Erskine, III.8.22.
3 (1705) M 4319
4 (1705) M 4319 at 4321.

time, even gratuitously, but if he does not do so, the scheme of succession established in the settlement will continue in force for the time being.

PROHIBITION AND INHIBITION

The result of the first skirmish was thus in favour of the adherents of alienability, but the Scots settler was not to be easily discouraged. The second step historically seems to have been the introduction of prohibitory clauses into the charter, that is prohibiting any action by the institute or substitutes which would result in changing the succession. Sometimes there were express prohibitions dealing with sale, charging and so on; sometimes prohibitions in more general terms. An instance of such a prohibitory clause has been found in a deed of 1489, but that is exceptional and most of the sixteenth century deeds are simple destinations.[5]

The effect of prohibitory clauses of this kind was considered in a hostile spirit by the courts as they were regarded as being inconsistent restraints on the *dominium* already given. This is the English judges' repugnancy point expressed in more logical language. The whole point in England was that the tenant in tail had not got *dominium*, the fee simple remaining with the reversioner or remainderman. In spite of this hostile spirit the court held in *Earl of Callander v Hamilton*[6] that such a prohibition would prevent a valid gratuitous alienation in breach of its terms. The substitutes might pursue to reduce (that is annul) such a gift. Almost certainly incorrectly, this decision was based on an Act 'against unlawful alienations made by bankrupts' of 1621. As Sandford shows,[7] there seems little connection between this Act and the *Callander* case. Nor was it relied on in later cases,[8] which make it clear that the right of the heirs to reduce is not in any way dependent on the presence of bankruptcy.

While a prohibitory clause may thus be effective among the heirs

5 Sandford, *Entails*, 34.
6 (1686) M 15476.
7 Sandford, *Entails*, 102; Bell, *Principles* 1718 also ascribes the decision to that Act.
8 E.g. *Wallace of Ingliston v Lord Forrester* (1692–3) 4 BS 64; *Ure v Earl of Crawfurd* (1756) M 4315.

themselves, the position is not the same as regards onerous alienations or chargings, because the prohibition creates a mere personal obligation and cannot affect creditors and purchasers. This was held in *Young v Bothwells*,[9] even though the tailzie had been created for a marriage consideration. English readers should note that the presence or absence of notice on the part of the purchaser for value is immaterial.

It was suggested[10] that the heirs of entail might as creditors, even though only personal, make use of the process known as inhibition. By this a debtor might be rendered incapable of alienating land or other property in defraud of creditors. If this view was correct, once inhibition had been used, even onerous deeds might have been reduced. But it is impossible to argue this after cases like *Bryson v Chapman*.[11] There appears also to have been an attempt to use the special process of interdiction 'which strikes at deeds granted without the consent of the judicial advisers of the interdicted'.[12] This was equally fruitless.[13]

In these opening rounds, then, the courts were on the whole successful in maintaining their view that the tenant in tail is *dominus* and as free as any other owner to treat the land as his own without regard to the claims of the living substitutes or future generations. But in the major battle which followed they were less successful.

The device next employed by the adherents of family landholding took the form of the insertion into the charter of two clauses said to have been invented by Hope, the Lord Advocate of Charles I, though he may very well have learned of them during some official visit to London, where the name of Mary Portington would have been current at the bar.[14] 'There is a new form found out,' Hope says,[15] 'which has these two branches, *viz* either to make the party

9   (1705) M 15482.
10 E.g. by Hope, *Minor Practicks* ss 304, 305; *see also* Mackenzie, *Institutions of the Law of Scotland*, III.8.16.
11 (1760) M 15511; 5 BS 940.
12 Duff, *Deeds of Entail*, 1.
13 Bell, *Principles*, 1716 citing *Cranston v Cranston* (1586) M 7125.
14 This accords with Sandford's view (*Entails*, 36):
    > It is not surprising that, after this device had been attempted in the testamentary deeds of that country in the reign of Queen Elizabeth, the same form should be adopted here. It met, however, with a different reception when its effect was tried.
15 *Minor Practicks*, 143.

contractor of the debt to incur the loss and tinsel of his right in favour of the next in tailzie, or to declare all deeds done in prejudice of the tailzie, by bond, contract, infeftment or compromising, to be null of the law.' He seems to put the two clauses forward as alternatives, but in fact he and later draftsmen thought it as well to use both. From Hope's day onwards every properly drafted Scots entail contained these resolutive and irritancy clauses. The former causes an automatic forfeiture of the interest of any holder under the entail who purports to grant a deed in breach of the prohibitions of the entail; the latter *ipso facto* annuls the deed itself.

Stair discusses these clauses at length. He says that most feudal writers were inclined to regard them as void, being inconsistent with the fee already given, although they would allow their effectiveness where the prohibitions were not absolute, but only not to alienate without the consent of the superior of the fee or other persons. In his view these limited restrictions could be the subject matter of the interdiction process already mentioned, but this must be read cautiously in the light of the decisions just cited on that point. Finally Stair says that although these two clauses had been inserted many times in tailzies, their legal effect had only once been fought out in the courts.[16] The occasion was the great case of *Viscount of Stormont v Creditors of Annandale*[17] in which Stair himself sat. This was the main battle in Scotland between the rival principles of alienation and inheritability. In it and the Act which followed it, the Scots covered much of the ground which in England had been the subject of the prolonged battle recounted in the previous chapter.[18]

David, Viscount of Stormont by a tailzie resigned the lordship and lands of Scone in favour of himself and the heirs male of his body; which failing, to Sir Mungo Murray and the heirs male of his body; then to Sir John Murray and then to Andrew, Lord Balvaird with similar limitations, and remainders over. These destinations were to take effect subject to the proviso:

> ... that it should not be lawful to the said Mungo, nor any other person contained in the tailzie, or their heirs male, to violate or dissolve the said tailzie, or dispose or wadset the estate or any

16 Stair, II.3.58.
17 (1662) M 13994, 15475.
18 *See* Chapter 19.

part thereof, or do any deed whereby the same may be evicted or comprised from them, without the special consent of all the persons in the tailzie, or their heirs, being of full age; and if any of the said persons, or their heirs, should contravene the said provision, that they should lose their right and title to the said infeftment, and of all the lands and others therein contained *ipso facto*; and the said charter and infeftment, with all right and title thereof, should be null and expire and their right thereof should accresce and belong to the next heir of tailzie who is immediately provided to succeed failing the contravener.[19]

The close anology between this and the clauses in the English deeds in *Mildmay's Case*[20] and *Mary Portington's Case*[21] is apparent. It should, however, be observed that here the prohibitions were not absolute: the heir could alienate if all those entitled under the entail who are of full age consented. This brought the settlement within the class which Stair suggested that the feudal writers would have allowed. It also recalled vividly the days when the consent of a man's whole agnates was necessary before he could alienate land. That stage was, of course, not nearly so far away in Scotland as it was in England, for Celtic landholding still continued in much of Scotland even in Stair's day.

Sir Mungo Murray was duly infeft in the lands, but died childless. He was succeeded by James, Earl of Annandale, only son of Sir John Murray, deceased. The earl, contrary to the prohibitions, allowed his creditors to obtain bonds and comprisings against the tailzied lands; and then died without issue. The action was brought by Viscount Stormont (son of Andrew, Lord Balvaird, deceased) to be served heir of tailzie free from the claims of the earl's creditors. Their bonds were in his submission null as a result of the irritancy clause.

For the creditors it was argued that clauses prohibiting alienation and securing debts on the tailzied lands were 'noways sustainable in law and justice' so as to prejudice creditors for onerous causes; that the irritancy clause annulled only the rights of the infringing party and not those of the creditors; and thirdly, that, since the viscount

---

19   *Viscount of Stormont v Creditors of Annandale* (1662) M 13994, 13995.
20   (1606) 6 Co Rep 40a.
21   (1614) 10 Co Rep 35b.

took the lands as the earl's heir, he must take them subject to his ancestor's debt, like any other heir.

None of these pleas prevailed. Clauses prohibiting alienation are not contrary to law, being commonly found in ordinary feudal grants and indeed implied in ward holdings. Since the clause was repeated in the sasine by which the late earl was infeft and that sasine had been properly registered, there had been sufficient notice to his creditors not to deal with him as an absolute fiar. If the third contention was true, the whole point of the clauses would be lost as there would be no check on the substitutes burdening the land. Some other arguments appear from Stair's report of the case,[22] including the interesting one that clauses prohibiting alienation should never be understood to extend to necessary alienations, for example those made for the maintenance of the fiar's wife and children. 'The matter being at great length debated from law, practique and reason,' the lords gave judgment for the pursuer, Viscount Stormont. Stair explains[23] that the judgment 'did pass with great difficulty, the Lords being near equally divided.' He takes the insertion of the clauses in the various sasines to be the determining factor. Had this not been done, he says, it would have been improper to decide against onerous creditors. They would obviously have stood in a position akin to that of the *bona fide* purchaser for value without notice in England. He also attached some importance to the fact that the whole of the family's lands were not included in the entail.[24] Perhaps he had in mind the fact that a peerage had been granted to go with the lands.[25]

Stair was therefore in favour of the dynastic view of landholding, under proper safeguards. He voted with the majority in the *Stormont* case and summed up his views of the devices employed in England to defeat entails and of the *Stormont* decision as follows:

> The perpetuities of estates, where they have been long accustomed, have sufficiently manifested their inconveniency; and therefore, devices have been found out, to render them ineffectual; only the Majoratus of Spain hath been most reasonable and stable, that the King nobilitating a person of merit and fortune, either by the

22 M 13996.
23 Stair, II.3.58.
24 *Ibid.*
25 Burke, *Peerage*, title 'Mansfield'.

King's gift, or his own right, that estate can neither be alienated
or burdened, but remains alimentary for preservation of the dignity
of that family. But these perpetuities in England are now easily
evacuated; first, by warrants to sell, purchased in Parliament,
which pass without much difficulty; and if they become frequent
with us, it is like we will find the same remedy. They are also
evacuated by a simulate action of fine and recovery, whereby the
purchaser pretends, that he is unwarrantably dispossessed of such
lands by the present fiar, who colludes and is silent, having
received a price or other consideration, so that these sentences,
though collusive, must be irrevocable. In tailzies the heirs male,
or heirs of line of every branch, being the issue of the first person of
that branch, do succeed (*but failing these the estate often goes to
remote branches*); and therefore there is a good caution by the law
of England, that after the possibility of issue is extinct, the present
fiar can do no more as to the fee, but what a liferenter could do;
for the next branch being ordinarily altogether strangers to that
fiar, little care will be taken to preserve the fee.

In the tailzie of Stormount, the whole estate was not comprehended; and it was distinctly provided, that in case any of the heirs
of tailzie for the time should contravene, that the right should
be devolved on that person who would succeed, if the contravener
were dead: but in such tailzies, formerly it was not so clearly
ordered, being only provided that the contravener should lose his
right, and the next heir of tailzie should have place; whereby it
remained dubious, whether the next branch of the tailzie were
meant, so that the contravener lost his own interest, and all
descending of him; or whether he lost the interest of all descending of that branch; or whether he lost only his own personal
interest; wherein the design of the constituter of the tailzie might
be dubious enough.[26]

In later times, when the English anti-entail policy had been forced
on Scotland, there were to be many Scots judges who viewed the
decision in *Viscount of Stormont v Creditors of Annandale*[27] with
disfavour. Lord Meadowbank remarked in *Hamilton v Macdowal*[28]
that it had been the unanimous view of the court in *Agnew of
Scheughan*[29] that the Stormont case was wrongly decided and that
entails had not a foot to stand on but the Act of 1685, of which they

26   Stair, II.3.58.
27   (1662) M 13994.
28   3rd March, 1815 F.C. 302 at 327.
29   I.e. *Stewart v Vans-Agnew* (1784) M 15435.

were the creatures. Lord Kames likewise thought that the case was affected 'by a prevailing attachment to entails, which were not then seen in their proper light'.[30]

THE ENTAIL ACT OF 1685

Perhaps Mackenzie, the successful counsel for Viscount Stormont, foresaw the possibility of this about-turn by the judges, for he used his official position as King's Advocate to bring in the famous Entail Act of 1685, which was to put the matter beyond the reach of even the House of Lords. That the bill was passed at such a late date (measured by English developments) surely demonstrates that the Scots landowners were far more deeply imbued with reverence for the tradition of family landholding than were their English peers. They were prepared to pass a bill much stronger than *De Donis Conditionalibus* 1285 no less than four hundred years later. During that period England had seen the struggle between that tradition and the new principle of free alienability end with the virtual triumph of the latter. But in Scotland the dynastic view of land-holding not only gained a narrow win in the courts, but so far consolidated its hold by legislation that all the efforts of the English House of Lords to destroy it proved ineffective for a century and a half.[31]

The first part of the Act of 1685 provides:

> It shall be Lawfull to His Majesties Subjects to Tailize their Lands and Estates and to Substitut aires in their Tailzies with such Provisions and Conditions as they shall think fitt and to affect the saids Tailzies with Irritant and Resolutive clauses whereby it shall not be lawfull to the Airs of Tailzie to sell, annalyze, or Dispone the said Lands or any part thereof or Contract Debt or Doe any other Deeds whereby the samen may be apprised, adjudged or evicted from the others Substitute in the Tailize or the Succession ffrustrate or interupted Declaring all such deeds to be in themselves null and Void and that the next Air of tailzie may immediatly upon the contravention pursue declarators Thereof and Serve himself air to him who died last

30 Lord Kames, *Historical Law Tracts*, 158.
31 *See* Chapter 21.

infeft in the fee and did not contraveen, without necessity anyways to represent the Contraveener.[32]

The remainder of the Act was devoted to requirements designed to prevent the inalienability thus allowed from operating unfairly against *bona fide* creditors or alienees. The irritant and resolutive clauses had to be set out in all charters, sasines, and other documents relating to the land, so that it was obvious to all that the seeming owner had no power to sell or charge. Moreover, the original tailzie had to be produced before the Court of Session for its 'authority' and had then to be registered in an official register. The first point was interpreted very strictly: each successive sasine had to set out all the clauses at length and a mere general reference to them was not enough.[33] The authority of the Court, on the other hand, came to be given as a matter of course,[34] which shows that the judges cannot have been as antagonistic to unbarrable entails as English ones would have been. They could have used this requirement to prevent 'perpetuities' had they wished to do so, with much less logical farcity than that of the common recovery. Instead, the only impediment to the creation of an entail, apart from ensuring that the necessary clauses were properly drafted was the requirement for a double registration under the Act of 1685:

1   a special entry in the Register of Tailzies, and

2   the ordinary entry in the Register of Sasines.[35]

Even a brief comparison of the Act of 1685 and the Statute *De Donis Conditionalibus* 1285 makes it plain how greatly they differ. They were passed with the same object, the preservation of land in the family; but the Scots Act represents this aim pursued in a more developed legal system than that of England in 1285. The requirement of registration is itself evidence of a more cautious approach; that of the repetition of the penal clauses in every document relating to the tailzied lands, an attempt to safeguard the interests of outsiders. There are additional clauses designed to preserve the rights of the

32   A.P.S., viii, 477 (26). Cf the enacting clauses of *De Donis Conditionalibus* 1285 (p. 174 *supra*).
33   *Garnock v Heirs of Entail* (1725) M 15596.
34   Sandford, *Entails*, 178.
35   *Douglas v Stevens* (1765) M 15616; *Russel* (1792) M 10300.

king and other superiors which show that the drafters were unwilling to put the heirs of entail in a privileged position, for example as regards forfeiture, comparable with that in England. Other differences arose from the different traditions of the Scots land law. While English entails are all of certain fixed types, Scotland has always allowed the settler a great deal of latitude both as to the heirs whom he calls to the succession and as to conditions and fetters imposed on such heirs. The Act did not restrict this freedom, for if prohibitions against sale and charging were contained in the charter and if the requirements of the Act were strictly complied with, those prohibitions could be effective in preserving the land for the family. It still remained for the individual settler to decide how far, if at all, he would avail himself of the machinery of the Act and many entails were created after 1685 which did not comply with its terms. They accordingly fell to be regulated by the common law principles discussed earlier in this chapter.

A small point overlooked by the Act was the position of entails already in being at the time it was made. On the authority of the decision in *Viscount of Stormont v Creditors of Annandale*[36] many such had been created.[37] In *Garnock v Heirs of Entail*[38] it was held that the requirement that the prohibitions should be set out in all feudal documents applied equally to these. As to registration, the cases at first favoured the exemption of pre-1685 entails, but later, when judicial policy had changed, this was reversed.[39]

Those who care for the law of Scotland as a distinct national institution must be grateful that this great statute was passed before the merger of the legislatures It is clear from what follows that the Parliament of Great Britain would not have passed it. In its judicial capacity it was to try its best to sabotage it.

36 (1662) M 13994.
37 Lord Kames, *Elucidations*, 342.
38 (1725) M 15596.
39 *Lord Kinnard v Hunter* (1761) M 15611; *Douglas v Stewarts* (1765) M 15616.

21   Modern Developments: the House of Lords and Scots Entails

Once the 1685 Act was passed a spate of litigation as to its effects arose which was to continue for a century and a half. The contests ranged over many topics, but essentially they all represent the ancient struggle between the principles of family and individual land-holding. Here the battle was between those who sought to carry out the intention of the Act, that land might be entailed and so preserved for a particular family (subject to certain safeguards), and those to whom unbarrable entails were anathema, to be very grudgingly admitted only if the most meticulous strict interpretation could not find a missing word on which to pounce as an excuse for ignoring the plain words of what was, in spite of all the abuse heaped upon it, a most unambiguous statute. With the latter party the (English) House of Lords allied itself without hesitation: indeed, it led it.

Modern Scots pronouncements on the subject[1] might lead one to think that Scots lawyers have also always been antagonistic to the Act and to the entail. This extract from a letter from Lord Hardwicke L.C., to Lord Kames shows that such was by no means the case. He writes as if Kames was an exception among the Scots judges in disliking the Act, which he probably was. It also shows the frame of mind in which the English lords sat to hear appeals about Scots entails:

> As to the general mischief of your strict entails, and the evil consequences of locking up the land of a country *extra commercium*, I have long been convinced of them, and rejoice to find a person of your knowledge and experience in the law and constitution of

---

1   E.g. Sandford, *Entails*, 361; Duff, *Deeds of Entails*, 2.

Scotland in the same way of thinking. It gives me the better hopes that it will not be long before some proper remedy is applied.[2]

INTERPRETATION OF SCOTS ENTAILS BY THE (ENGLISH) HOUSE OF LORDS

A detailed examination of all the cases on the interpretation of the Act would be out of place here, but a glance at one or two of the main ones may show the route by which the House of Lords in the absence of legislation sought to apply 'some proper remedy.' It is significant that the Lords in the two cases now to be examined overruled the decision of the Court of Session – in one of them unanimous – in favour of the entail. It must be borne in mind that there was no Scots representation in the judicial House of Lords at this time and that it was judges trained in a system which had come to abominate entails who were setting out to wreck another system of law which for its own national reasons was particularly favourable to entails. In the long run the Scots lawyers were 'converted' to the English view, but only after more than a century of struggle to uphold the older principles of inheritance and inalienability out of the family.

In *Edmonstone of Duntreath v Edmonstone*[3] Archibald Edmonstone executed a strict entail of his Scots estates. He disponed them to his eldest son, Archibald, and the heirs male of his body; whom failing to his second and third sons and their like heirs and so on. He then reserved his own liferent with power to alter the entail even on his deathbed. Several clauses followed in which reference was made to 'Archibald E. and the other heirs of tailzie' but the vital prohibitory clauses only said that 'it shall not be lawful to, nor in the power of any of the heirs of tailzie and provision above named' to alter the succession, alienate or charge the lands. On the death of the entailer the younger Archibald brought an action of declarator against the substitutes to have it declared that he held as fiar free from any prohibitions. The Court of Session found for the defenders on the grounds that the whole tenor of the deed clearly showed that the

2 Lord Kames, *Elucidations*, 388.
3 (Court of Session 1769) (House of Lords 1771) M 4409.

entailer intended Archibald to be bound. The destinations to him and his brothers are made 'always with and under the burdens of the provisions [and] conditions . . . after expressed', and the form of words 'Archibald E. and the other heirs of tailzie', so often repeated, makes it clear that the pursuer was considered in no other light than as the first heir of tailzie. The House of Lords overruled this finding on the grounds that the Act authorised fetters to be imposed only on the heirs of tailzie and not on the institute, who must be deemed to be free of all restrictions unless expressly restrained. Any words of restraint should be very strictly interpreted as interferences with the freedom of the fiar, it being undesirable that land should be kept *extra commercium*. As the pursuer had argued:

> The intention of the donor must not only be indubitable, but the restriction will be of no avail unless that meaning is expressed in the proper place (not gathered from particular expressions, nor from the general scope of the deed) and in legal technical language.[4]

Lord Eldon, L.C., reviewing this case in 1813, said that 'in the Duntreath case it had been decided that fetters were not to be implied; though, perhaps then the English policy weighed a little in the judgment.'[5] An even more striking illustration of this phenomenon is to be found in *Sharpe v Sharpe*.[6] In that case Mathew Sharpe of Hoddom executed a deed of entail in 1765, which was not registered. In 1768 another deed was made in almost identical terms and duly registered, but on this occasion, unfortunately, certain words were left out of the irritant clause by what was obviously a clerical error:

> And upon every contravention which may happen, by and through any of my said heirs failing to perform all and each of the said conditions and provisions, and acting contrary to any or all of the restrictions and limitations before written, it is hereby expressly provided and declared, that not only my said lands and estates shall not be burdened with or liable to the debts, deeds, crimes and acts *of the heirs of tailzie as before provided, but also all debts, deeds and acts* contracted, granted, done or committed, contrary to these conditions and provisions, or restrictions and limitations, or to the true intent and meaning of these presents, shall be of no

4   (1769) M 4409, 4410.
5   *Duke of Roxburghe v Bellenden Kerr* (1813) 2 Dow HL at 210.
6   (1835) 1 S & M 594.

force, strength nor effect and ineffectual and unavailable against the other heirs of tailzie, and who, as well as the said estate, shall be noways burdened therewith, but free therefrom in the same manner as if such debts or deeds had not been contracted or granted, or such acts, omissions or commissions had never been done or happened.

The words in italics were omitted in 1768. General M. Sharpe, one of the heirs of entail, brought this action for declarator that he had an absolute right to the estate as fiar, with freedom to sell or burden it at pleasure.

Lord Corehouse, the trial judge (a great feudal authority), held that, as this was a mere clerical omission he was at liberty to supply the appropriate words. He said:[7]

> To supply omissions in a deed, by conjectures however plausible, or deductions however clear, with regard to the intentions of the maker, is very different from restoring the syntax of the deed, defective in consequence of a clerical error, by means of a reference to the context itself; the first is at variance with the principles of construction applied to all deeds *stricti juris*, and with peculiar rigour to entails; but the second is consistent with these principles, and was admitted by the House of Lords in the case of *Munro of Fowlis*.[8]

His judgment was upheld by a unanimous decision of the Inner House, but the House of Lords was not impressed by this and found for the appellant. Lord Brougham, L.C., was able to distinguish *Munro of Fowlis*[9] on the ground that in that case there was only one possible omission while here there were several; and moreover, the strict interpretation of Scots entails had to be upheld at all cost. His reasons for rejecting the contrary principle of the reasonable amendment of clerical errors are instructive:

> If it is a sound one, this principle must be applicable to the construction of all instruments; nay, more so in every other case than that of tailzies, which are well known to be, of all conveyances, those which the law regards with the most rigorous strictness; nor is there in the question itself, considered in some points of view, anything peculiar to the Law of Scotland; and the authority of this

7 *Ibid.*, at 602.
8 *Munro v Munro* (1826) 4 S 472.
9 *Ibid.*

> decision could, if sanctioned by your Lordships, never be confined
> nor its influence restricted to Scotch cases. Indeed, as I know of no
> English instrument whatever, the construction of which is so
> confined within strict technical rules, I can fancy no parallel case
> arising in this country in which the present decision of your
> Lordships might not to be applied *a fortiori*. If we allow a provision
> so essential as an irritant clause in a Scotch tailzie, where construc-
> tive intention goes for nothing, to be supplied by conjectural
> criticism (I can give it no other name), with what boundless
> licence should we not be armed in dealing with an English will,
> where nothing but the intention of the testator is to be regarded ?[10]

It may be wondered whether the decision in an English appeal was
ever influenced by fears as to its effects on Scots law!

Many other cases could be cited in support of the contention that
it was the English House of Lords which forced the Scots law into a
quasi-English mould by insisting on a rigid adherence to the
doctrine of very strict interpretation invented by the House itself in
Edmonstone of Duntreath v Edmonstone.[11] However, *Willison v
Callender*[12] provided a yet more striking instance of the House of
Lords overruling the native tribunals in matters of entail law. This
was not a question of the interpretation of the Act of 1685, but one
as to the law applicable to those entails which for one reason or
another did not come within its terms and therefore depended for
their validity on the Scots common law alone. The Court of Session
had held without much hesitation that the Act only provided a new
protection against creditors or onerous conveyances dependent on
registration and that in the case of entails not registered or otherwise
defective under the Act the old rule remained, that a prohibition,
while not effective against onerous third parties, was binding on the
heirs of entail.

There could be no possible objection to this reasoning, but in a
trilogy of eighteenth century cases[13] the substitutes succeeded in
establishing the more questionable principle that the heir of entail,
after an onerous conveyance, must reinvest the proceeds of sale in

10 *Sharpe v Sharpe* (1835) 1 594, 612.
11 (1771) M 4409.
12 (1724) M 15369.
13 *Lord Strathnaver v Duke of Douglas* (1728) M 15373; *Gordon-Cuming v Gordon*
    (1761) M 15513; *Young v Young* (1761) 5 BS 884.

other lands to be held on the same limitations as those which he had sold. As Sandford explained,[14] these cases were founded on the idea that an unregistered entail, while not sufficient to give the heirs a *jus vindicandi* over the property itself, could and did give rise to a personal right *inter haeredes* whereby the heir in possession was obliged to fulfil the intention of the settler by spending the money on other lands to be settled on the same basis. He had an undeniable power to alienate for onerous causes, but he had no right to do so as against the other heirs and so defeat their claims.

None of the three cases referred to went up to the House of Lords. Consequently their principle of the heir's personal liability to reinvest – so strikingly reminiscent of a later English arrangement – remained the established and undoubted law of Scotland until 1811, a space of nearly a century. In that year a hint of trouble was given in *Lockhart v Stewart*,[15] which reached the Lords. Lord Eldon, L.C., expressed grave concern as to the whole conception on which the Court of Session had based these decisions. He referred the case back to it for a solemn consideration by the whole court. At this stage the parties, unfortunately for the development of the law, decided that they had had enough and compromised.

Lord Eldon's words were not wasted, however, as the same point arose in *Stewart v Fullarton*[16] and *Bruce v Bruce*.[17] The hearing of these two cases was consolidated, as they involved the same points of law. It is some indication of their importance that Sugden appeared for the appellants and Brougham for the respondents. It is a strong thing for the House of Lords to overrule the decisions of the English courts, especially in conveyancing matters, when they have stood unchallenged for over a century and many settlements have been drafted in reliance on them. It is far stronger for an alien tribunal, however august, to overrule such decisions on the part of the highest national courts of another legal system, but on this occasion they did so.

John Stewart of Blackbarony executed a tailzie of his lands at Ascog and elsewhere in 1763. Although it was drafted in terms which

14 Sandford, *Entails*, 168.
15 (1811) 11th June, F.C.
16 (1830) 4 W & S 196.
17 *Ibid.*, at 240.

show that the Act of 1685 was in contemplation, the prohibition against sale, unlike the other prohibitions, was not fenced with irritant and resolutive clauses. The substitutes could not therefore rely on the Act to restrain a sale, but claimed that the purchase money should be reinvested on the same destinations. Eleven Lords of Session upheld this contention. Four dissented.

In the House of Lords, Lord Eldon[18] found it impossible to deny that a simple prohibition was still as effective against volunteers as at common law, the Act having said nothing to alter that position. He refused, however, to follow the line of cases just mentioned and hold that the heir who sold the entailed lands was bound to reinvest the proceeds in other land. Even if such a right existed in theory, it must be quite unenforceable, for the heir could immediately sell the newly purchased lands and so on *ad infinitum*. Lord Lyndhurst, L.C., based his decision on the fact that, as the entailer plainly meant the entail to take effect under the Act of 1685, he cannot have meant a common law obligation to arise and this could not be implied because of the strict interpretation rule.[19] It may be noted that the entails in the three Scots cases mentioned earlier were all intended to take effect under the Act.

Lord Wynford's judgment is the most interesting. He compared the English and Scots laws of entails as follows:

> By the law of England an estate can only be entailed for the lives of people who are in being, and until someone that is at the time of the making of the entail unborn shall attain the age of twenty-one. This rule of our law would easily be defeated, if the settlor of an estate might impose a condition that, if the person on whom the estate was settled sell the estate, that he shall be trustee of the proceeds of sale of such estate for those to whom the estate would have descended if the entail of it had not been barred. Our courts held that such a condition was against the policy of our law and on that account void; and although a tenant in tail took an estate with such a condition annexed to the grant of it, he might bar the entail, sell the estate, and do what he pleased with all the proceeds of the sale, without being in any manner accountable to those who would have succeeded to that estate. By the law of Scotland an estate may be continued in the line or lines designated

18   *Ibid.*, at 211.
19   *Ibid.*, at 238.

by the settlor, so long as any of these lines are in existence, if the deed of entail be in conformity with the statute of 1685. . . .[20]

No real objection to the speech can be made down to this point. But, perhaps realising that he was advancing onto less certain ground, Lord Wynford paused here to assess his qualifications to speak on matters of Scots law.

I doubted whether, considering the difference between the laws of England and Scotland, although void in England, it might not in Scotland create such a moral obligation, that the person who accepted the estate on that condition, would be obliged to reinvest the money for which it was sold in the purchase of other lands, to be held for the benefit of those who were the objects of the settler's bounty. An apprehension that the habits of an English lawyer might lead me into a train of reasoning not warranted by Scotch law, according to which your Lordships are to decide the question submitted to your judgment by this appeal, occasioned this doubt. Your Lordships will not be surprised, that I should pause in a case in which there has been so great a difference of opinion in the Court below; but I protest against what has been said in another place, namely, that English lawyers are not competent to advise your Lordships on a question of Scotch law. As well might they say, that one who had studied logic in Edinburgh would not be able to reason on any question of morality or policy that arose in England, although in possession of all the circumstances connected with the case to be discussed. One who is acquainted with the general principles of jurisprudence, and has been in the habit of investigating legal questions, of interpreting written laws, and weighing the authorities on which unwritten laws depend, will be fully competent to decide points arising under the laws of any country. Such a person would make up for his want of familiarity with the subject brought before him, by the additional caution and attention which the novelty of the case would naturally excite. If he has not so much knowledge of the subject as Scotch lawyers may have, before he has heard and considered the arguments and authorities, he will decide on such as are adduced without any preconceived prejudice. If I am wrong in this, our Government withholds from our colonies the greatest advantage that those colonies have to expect from their dependence on it, namely a just administration of the laws of each colony; for a single English lawyer decides, at the Privy Council, cases arising under almost

20   *Ibid.*, at 232.

every system of law that prevails in the world. I have devoted much of my time and attention to this case, and, in the consideration of it, I have forgotten that I was ever connected with English judicature. I have formed my opinion on Scotch authorities only.

I have no doubt that the printed Cases, and the arguments at the bar, have furnished us with all the authorities that bear on the point to be decided. Since I have had the honour of assisting in Scotch appeals, I have always found that the talents, the learning, and industry of the Scotch bar, have given, in the best and clearest manner, all the information that this House can require for the decision of any question submitted to its judgment. My opinion is formed on grounds taken by a learned Judge in the Court below.[21]

He then cited with approval the speech of one of the dissenting judges, whose party had stood in a minority of four to eleven in the court:

Lord Cringletie[22] in his excellent judgment says, 'a prohibition is a mere restraint, and does not constitute any obligation whatever in law or equity. . . . There is no legal means of securing this supposed right to have the purchase money reinvested, or in any manner used for the benefit of those who, according to the order of succession, would have been entitled to the estate if it had not been sold.'

Such machinery has been invented by modern legislation.[23] Lord Wynford continued:

Now according to the statute – 1685 – an estate and every thing belonging to it, is at the disposal of its owner, unless the person who has conveyed it to him has restrained his power of disposal of it in the manner prescribed by it.

The Act says no such thing[24] and evidently his lordship felt some anxiety on the point for he falls back immediately afterwards on

---

21 *Ibid.*, at 232–3.
22 *Ibid.*, at 233–4. Prof. Candlish Henderson quoted to the late Dr Farran the following couplet once current in Scots legal circles:
    Necessity and Cringletie agree to a little,
    The ane kens nae law, the other as little.
23 I.e. the Entails (Scotland) Act 1882 (cf the analogous provisions in the English Settled Land Act 1925).
24 *See* the provisions set out *supra* (the remainder of the Act (*see* A.P.S., viii, 447 (26)) does not bear on this point).

broad considerations of policy obviously derived from his English background:

> It is not unreasonable that a man should be permitted to preserve his estate for the benefit of persons for whose benefit he may feel an interest, as, for instance, for the unborn children of the settlor's children, or of those who are the immediate objects of his bounty: but there are few countries in which property is allowed to be continued in particular families, for the vain purpose of preserving a name; and Lord Cringletie tell us that in Scotland an entail is *strictissimi juris* tolerated by the law on certain conditions. Property, therefore, is free from the fetters of entails, unless the law imposing such fetters is fully complied with. Where the words of a statute are clear and intelligible, a series of decisions from the time of its becoming law down to the present hour, would not authorize your Lordships, sitting judicially, to give a judgment inconsistent with it. Where a law is doubtful, decided cases may assist your Lordships in putting a construction upon it; but where there is no ambiguity in a statute, your Lordships will take the law from the Legislature and not from the Courts of Justice.

The text of the Act has no words at all in the sense which Lord Wynford suggests, so they can scarcely be 'clear and intelligible'. But the whole point was that the Act of 1685 had no application and that therefore the decision depended on the common law alone. As to this, there was a series of decided cases which had stood unchallenged for over a century.

LATER LEGISLATION ON SCOTS ENTAILS

The truth seems to be that the English judges in the House of Lords started with such a violent prejudice against entails that they were not prepared to admit even that the law of another jurisdiction could possibly countenance them. But even the adherents of family landholding could not be defeated so long as the 1685 Act remained unrepealed. The judicial attempts to whittle down its effect undoubtedly freed one or two settlements from the provisions of the Act, but it is plain that the only real answer to the evils, if evils they were, which it created, lay in its eventual repeal or modification by the legislature. It must be left to the political historian to explain why no such action was taken over so long a period. The English lords of judicial standing spared no pains in reducing the effect of the Act as far as they could when sitting as judges; yet none of them was moved in his legislative capacity to present a bill to remove the Act from the statute book, or even to amend it. It seems most unlikely that this was due to scruples that they as Englishmen ought not to interfere with a Scots national institution. Nor is it likely that the sixteen Scots representative peers could have outvoted such a measure. More probably it was due to the general legislative inertia of eighteenth century Parliaments.

The Entails Act of 1770[25] gave the holders of entailed property power to carry out certain very limited improvements and to charge three-quarters of the cost on the land, as against later substitutes. It also allowed a power of leasing for short terms, the longest being ninety-nine years for a building lease and it permitted excambions (exchanges) of small amounts of entailed land. The nineteenth century era of reform brought more important changes. The 'Aberdeen Act' of 1824[26] allowed the land to be burdened with fixed provisions for the holder's surviving spouse and children. The 'Rosebery' Act of 1836[27] extended the powers given by the earlier Acts and allowed a restricted power of sale over such part of the lands as might be necessary to pay off the original entailer's debts. It is true that the Act of 1685 did not free the entailed lands from them, but a clause had become very common whereby the heir of tailzie was made to pay them off out of unentailed property.

The Entails Act of 1848 ('Rutherford Act')[28] was much more revolutionary. It allowed any heir born after the passing of the Act to disentail without any consents, provided he was of full age and in possession. He was thus approximated to the English tenant in tail. The powers of then living heirs were more restricted. They had to have certain consents, normally those of all the other living substitutes, possibly a survival of the old idea of agnatic consents. Other powers less drastic than a complete bar, such as feuing and leasing, were also given. Permission was further granted to the heir of

25   10 Geo III c 51.
26   5 Geo IV c 87.
27   6 & 7 Will IV c 42.
28   11 & 12 Vict c 36.

tailzie's creditors to force a disentailment in certain cases of insolvency. Once these rules were in operation, the whole status of the Scots entail was completely changed. Consequently the old rules of very strict interpretation were abrogated, the Act declaring that if the deed of entail directed registration the presence of proper irritant and resolutive clauses was to be implied. Furthermore, the legal position of entails not within the Act of 1685, as being binding on the heirs of entail had never been satisfactory (at least to the English) and they were made totally ineffective unless registered. Finally, being aware of the immense resources of cunning which the dynastic school had shown in England, the draftsman proceeded to frustrate them in advance by a rule that estates settled by way of trusts or a series of liferents could only be subject to the settlement so long as no person unborn at the time of the settlement's creation became entitled to possession. When he or she did, they were to take as fiar free from all fetters and limitations. This marks the introduction into Scots law of what the English had long known as a rule against perpetuities. But the Scots variety is more logical in sticking to lives in being directly concerned in the settlement. *Re Villar*[29] would have been decided the other way in Scotland.

Other Acts between 1848 and 1882[30] extended these reforms, mostly on matters of detail. The Entails (Scotland) Act 1882 continued the work by improving the position of heirs born before 1848. These points may be ignored as having been only of transitional importance, but the heir in possession, whenever born, gained a power of sale over the land less drastic than a complete bar, by which the court could order that the clauses of entail should attach to the purchase money, which must be invested as required by the Act. This Act was contemporaneous with the English Settled Land Act, 1882, which created comparable machinery in the case of the English tenant for life. Owing to the process of resettlement[31] he was then in a position comparable with that of the Scots tailzied fiar, though he now has all the powers conferred on him by the Settled

---

29   [1929] 1 Ch 243.
30   E.g. the Entail Amendment Act 1853; and the Titles to Land Consolidation Act 1868, which enacted (s 14) that the cardinal prohibitions were in future to be implied if registration were provided for.
31   *See* Chapter 19.

Land Act 1925. Finally, the Entails (Scotland) Act 1914 prohibited the creation of new entails after 10 August 1914.[32]

The English explain the power of selling the land coupled with the settlement's continuing to bind the purchase money as an application of the equitable doctrine of conversion, based on the maxim: 'Equity regards that as done which ought to have been done.' Since there ought logically to be no sale of the fee simple by a mere tenant for life, the parties must be treated as if it had not taken place. But the Scots Act of 1882 need not be regarded as imposing this doctrine on Scots law. The statutory procedure is rather a restatement, with modifications, of the Scots principle upset by the unsatisfactory *Stewart v Fullarton*[33] appeal. Here, as is so often the case, we find two legal systems starting with totally different conceptions and terminology, and yet arriving at an almost identical practical result.

One difference remains. While in England a tenant in tail of full age in possession can now bar the entail by a simple deed (the hocus-pocus of the common recovery having gone in 1833,[34] or even by will after 1925,[35] his peer in Scotland (a dying race because no new entails have been made there since 1914) must still apply to the court for formal permission to disbar. When this is given, his deed becomes finally effective by being inserted in the Register of Tailzies. The land is then held for the equivalent of a fee simple, but on the destinations contained in the tailzie until by deed or will he declares his intention to the contrary.

Thus in both England and Scotland the school of thought which sought to prevent the alienation of land out of a particular family has eventually lost the day. Its opponents' methods of winning may be considered questionable, and, in the case of Scotland, largely alien interference. But the constant invention of new ideas by the defeated party shows the great strength of the dynastic view of landholding which it represents. Taxation, the new threat to keeping land in the

---

32 Entails (Scotland) Act 1914, s 2.
33 (1830) 4 W & S 196.
34 Fines and Recoveries Act 1833, ss 15, 40. This act was 'recognised as a master-piece of Parliamentary draftsmanship', the draftsman being Brodie, who was also one of the Real Property Commissioners. But the Act was not wholly without blemish: see *Re Wainwright* (1843) 1 Ph 258 at 261, 262. (Megarry and Wade, 90). For the process of disentailing under the Act, see Megarry and Wade, 90–2; Cheshire, 256–61.
35 Law of Property Act 1925, s 176 (1).

family is tending to emphasise the dynastic view again. Perhaps the future of family landholding lies in a gift of the principal mansion house to the National Trust in return for the hereditary office of resident caretaker.

22 Succession and Words of Limitation

The rules as to words of limitation (destination) in documents relating to land, and those as to the intestate succession are closely linked to the whole subject of inheritance and the canons of construction applied to words of limitation have had an important part to play in the history of the struggle between the supporters of family landholding and the protagonists of free alienability.

WORDS OF LIMITATION

The English attitude to words of limitation[1] is traditionally a very strict one. Thus even now the special and ancient formula 'to *A* and the heirs of his body' are necessary in a deed or will to create an entailed interest,[2] though the one possible alternative 'to *A* in tail' was introduced for deeds executed after 31 December 1881.[3] Right up to 1925 the presumption was that the words 'to *A* and his heirs' were necessary in a deed to pass the fee simple. Such phrases as 'to *A* and his issue and assigns for ever' if used in a deed operated to pass a mere life interest to *A*. Worst of all, worse even than the notorious rule in *Shelley's Case*,[4] for which there is a technical explanation,[5] was the rule which survived till 1882[6] that a grant 'to *A* in fee simple' gave *A*, not the fee simple, but again a mere life estate. This was presumed to be given wherever the right technical phrase for an

---

1 As to which see Megarry and Wade, 50–66; Cheshire, 152–4; 247–55.
2 Law of Property Act 1925, s 130 (1).
3 Conveyancing Act 1881, s 51.
4 (1581) 1 Co Rep 88b. For a detailed account, see Challis, *The Law of Real Property*, 154 *et seq. See also* Megarry and Wade 60–5; Cheshire, 252–5.
5 *See* Chapter 25.
6 Conveyancing Act 1881, s 51.

estate of inheritance was not used. Some relaxation had been made for wills in 1837,[7] as many testators found themselves without the necessary legal 'reason' to appreciate these fine distinctions. Finally, the necessity for technical wording was abolished by a reform centuries overdue in 1925, by which a grant without special words of limitation passes the fee simple or other the whole interest of the grantor, unless the context indicates an intention to create more limited estates.[8] Because a will 'speaks' only from death the law was more accommodating to testators and sought to discover their intentions rather than ride roughshod over their errors in dealing with over-technical rules. For the creation of entails, however, as already mentioned, the technical wording is still a necessity. Although special words are thus necessary to create the entail, it can be barred by the most loose phraseology. In a will the property must be expressly referred to, or the instrument under which it was acquired or entailed property mentioned generally, but otherwise no formal words are required; for example, 'Blackacre to *X*' or, 'all the property to which I succeeded under Uncle Harry's will'[9] would be enough. In *Acheson v Russell*[10] 'all my other estate and interest' in the property was held to be sufficiently specific. Even after it has rendered it perfectly harmless English law thus retains its traditional 'down' on the entail.

The Scots system, though it had its own share of rigid technicalities (for example, the actual word 'dispone' was essential in every conveyance of heritage until 1874[11]) did not insist on such complete verbal exactitude in this matter. Even to constitute the unbarrable entail under the terms of the Act of 1685 required no special or magic words.[12] Thus 'to *A* and his descendants' would be as effective as 'to *A* and the heirs of his body'.[13] But if technical phrases such as 'heirs male of the body' are employed, they are given their technical meaning and no ambiguous phrases, for

---

7   Wills Act 1837, s 28.
8   Law of Property Act 1925, s 60 (1).
9   Megarry and Wade, 96.
10 [1951] Ch 67.
11 *Kirkpatrick's Trustees v Kirkpatrick* (1874) 1 R (HL) 37. The word 'dispone' was rendered unnecessary by the Conveyancing (Scotland) Act 1874, s 27.
12 *Munro v Munro* (1826) 3 W & S 344.
13 Sandford, *Entails*, 49.

example in the procuratory of resignation, will affect this.[14] Thus
'nearest lawful heir male of line' could not be construed narrowly to
mean only heirs male of the body.[15] The Scots approach to words of
limitation is well shown by Sandford's comment on this point: 'the
general rule is that a destination to "heirs male" is a destination to
heirs male general; although in certain cases, this legal meaning may
be explained into "heirs male of the body" from the intention of the
maker being plainly indicated in other parts of the deed.'[16]

Destinations to 'heirs female', so rare in England, are found fairly
frequently in Scots settlements as a form of disposition over after the
failure of the male heirs. The heir female is the heir of the original
grantee in the direct line and not that of the last male heir. Thus an
elder son's daughter is preferred to a younger son's, even though the
latter died infeft in the property, and both are preferred to the
grantee's own daughter. This construction was finally established in
the interesting case of *Hope and Buchan v Dalrymple*.[17] John, Lord
Bargany, executed a tailzie in favour of his eldest son, John, Master
of Bargany, and the heirs male to be procreate of the said master's
body; whom failing to William, the second son of the settler and the
heirs male of the settler's body; whom failing to the eldest heir
female of the body of the settler and the descendants of her body
without division. The Master died in his father's lifetime, leaving
issue Joanna, the mother of Sir Hew Dalrymple, the respondent in
the House of Lords. His father then died, leaving issue William and
one daughter, the mother of Sir Alexander Hope, the first appellant.
William, the new Lord Bargany, made up his titles and then died
leaving issue James and Grizel, the mother of Mary Buchan, the
other appellant. James, Lord Bargany, was duly infeft but died
without issue. Thus the male issue of the settler became extinct and
the succession opened to 'the heir female of the body.' The question
was, who was described by these words? Dalrymple, Hope and
Mary Buchan all claimed. The Court of Session decided in favour
of Hope on what it called 'the conception of the tailzie.' The case
then went up to the House of Lords.

14   *Forrester v Hutchinson* (1826) 4 S 831; *Grahame v Grahame* (1825) 1 W & S 353.
15   *Sinclair v Earl and Countess of Fife* (1766) M 14944.
16   Sandford, *Entails*, 59. See *Campbell v Campbell* (1770) M 14949; *Hay v Hay* (1788)
     M 2315; (1789) 3 Pat (HL) 123.
17   (1739) 1 Pat (HL) 237.

The arguments for Mary Buchan are interesting.[18] She did not rely on the simple point that she was the sole female claimant, but claimed first, on the ground that the first heir of the settler had been served heir to him. Any later claimant could not therefore, she asserted, claim this position, but must serve himself heir to the person last infeft (James). Secondly, feus, being masculine only open to females as a last resort and then to the nearest heir of the male last infeft (James again). This view did not gain acceptance from the House; nor did they approve Hope's claim, backed though it was by the Court of Session's decision in his favour. They found in favour of Dalrymple, so that in Scotland the term 'heir female' is equivalent to 'heir of line,' that is the issue of the first son has precedence.

In English law a limitation to '*A* and the heirs female of her body' represents a feminist's dream, descending only to the female issue of *A*, that is those who, being females, claim exclusively through females.[19] Thus the daughters of the grantee would be preferred to the female issue of sons, who would have no claim at all. Thus if *Hope v Dalrymple*[20] had been an English case, none of the parties could have claimed. If Sir Alexander Hope had had a sister, she and her daughters would have had the only possible claim. This is not to say that a Scots feminist could not create a tailzie descending *de femelles en femelles*: the Scots settler had a much greater freedom of choice as to the heirs he chose than the English one. The sole restriction was that he might not, if he wished the entail to be valid, point out merely the ordinary heirs whatsoever recognised by the law.

Heirs

Who then are these ordinary heirs in Scotland and England? Not all land in England passed by the same canons of descent. Gavelkind and Borough English[21] for example, had special customs of succession, recalling Saxon arrangements. Leasehold, not being real

18 (1739) 1 Pat (HL) 237 at 239.
19 Co. Litt. 25a.
20 (1739) 1 C & S 237.
21 *See* Chapter 7. Gavelkind shows many evidences of the idea that land belonged to the family. It went to all the sons, and, by the rule 'the sire to the bough, the son to the plough', was not liable to forfeiture from them even in a case of treason.

property, passed on to the same relatives who took the goods and chattels and in the same proportions. A surviving husband, for example, took his wife's leaseholds absolutely.

In the simplest succession situations the rules for finding the heir were the same in both countries. The eldest son had the best claim; if he was dead, his issue had a prior claim; next came the younger sons in turn and their issue; finally the daughters of the deceased (who, like all females in the same relationship to him, took as co-heiresses and not by primogeniture), and their issue. Where the dead man left no descendants, the fief passed to his brothers. In England, however, the father was given in 1833 a priority over the brothers and sisters.[22] In Scotland the father only took if there were no brothers or sisters, or their lines were extinct.

It is between the brothers that the first major difference is seen. In English law the primogeniture rule applied and the eldest brother invariably succeeded. In Scotland until 1874 a distinction was made between conquest and heritage,[23] which had important results on the death of a middle brother.

Conquest was property acquired by sasine which had come to the deceased by purchase, gift or other singular title from a stranger or from one to whom he would not by law have succeeded. Heritage is that to which he has succeeded as heir-at law to his father or other relation. When a person died intestate and without issue, but leaving both older and younger brothers the next elder brother (not necessarily the eldest) and his line took the conquest, the next younger the heritage.

The distinction was abolished and all land was made to go as heritage in 1874.[24] From the next younger brother the estate went (in the absence of his issue) to the next younger one and so down to the youngest. Failing these, it mounted to the next eldest brother and so gradually up to the eldest. Finally it went to the sisters, if necessary. All this only applies to brothers and sisters german. Consanguinean brothers succeeded next after full sisters, but this rule, long known in Scotland, came in in England only in 1833,[25]

---

22   Inheritance Act 1833, s 6.
23   Bell, *Principles*, 1670.
24   Conveyancing (Scotland) Act 1874, s 37.
25   By the Inheritance Act 1833.

where at common law the half-blood on either side was excluded.[26] Uterine relatives could not take at all until that year in either country, but England allowed them and the mother to succeed (eventually) then, the Scots preferring to retain the old rule, as usual.

The same rules of precedence as between father and brothers and sisters, and among brothers and sisters *inter se*, applied equally to the paternal grandfather and uncles and aunts, great-grandfather and great-uncles and aunts and so on *ad infinitum*. Deceased members of these classes were represented by their issue in the same order. This marked the end of all possible claims in Scotland, the mother and all other maternal relatives being barred absolutely from intestate succession to heritage. This rule could clearly produce some very unfair results, especially where the lands had come from the maternal side of the family.[27] This may be one of the factors tending to favour the making of entails in Scotland. English law allowed the mother to succeed in theory by the Act mentioned, but this can rarely have occurred as the maternal relatives of the remotest paternal ancestor came first, then those of the next less remote, and so on down to the father's mother's family and then at last to the mother and her issue, the half-brothers and sisters of the intestate.

The above rules apply only to land. Moveable or personal property in both Scotland and England passed to the next-of-kin equally on intestacy.

In 1925 English law abolished the traditional scheme of primogeniture in favour of a uniform system for all types of property, akin to that which formerly applied to personal property, including leases.[28] The only exception of importance is where the intestate died possessed of an unbarred entailed interest, when the old rules applied to a limited extent.

Scotland, as in many other matters, preferred to retain the older feudal law, but the Succession (Scotland) Act 1964 provided that the whole of the intestate estate of a person dying after 10 September 1964 shall devolve without distinction between heritable and

---

26 Bl. Comm., ii, 224.
27 *Lennox v Linton* (1663) M 14867. As to moveables the rule was abolished by the Intestacy (Scotland) Act 1854.
28 Administration of Estates Act 1925, ss 33, 34. A table in Paterson's *Compendium* shows graphically the differences between the two primogeniture systems. *See also* the table in McLaren, *Wills*, Vol 1.

moveable property in accordance with the Act which, in general, divides the estate between the deceased's next-of-kin. The parents (or either of them) are given a right to half the estate along with surviving brothers and sisters, and to the whole estate if there are no brothers and sisters, and thereafter the surviving spouse is preferred to uncles and aunts and remoter relations. The rights of surviving spouses to courtesy and terce are abolished, but the surviving spouse is entitled to a prior right to the matrimonial home up to a value of £30 000. The special and general service of heirs is abolished and the confirmation of the executors is the link in title between the deceased and his heirs on intestacy.

In testate succession the confirmation of the executors is also the link in titles to land between the deceased and the beneficiaries, although the will itself can be used as the link if it contains words capable of conveying heritage.

23   The Importance of Seisin
in Medieval Law

Modern notions of ownership and even of 'lawful possession' of interests in land are of very late development compared with that of mere occupation.[1] Even today one often speaks of so-and-so's house when referring to that which he occupies whether he holds it as the owner or as tenant for years or merely in the capacity of a servant to its owner or even as a squatter without right. As often happens, common speech has here preserved an ancient simplicity which the analytical approach of lawyers is apt to obscure. He who occupies land in whatever capacity appears to the unsophisticated to have a more real connection with that land than anyone else can possibly have, even the owner of it or the man who ought to occupy it. This view has had effects of considerable importance in the development of land law in England and Scotland, especially in the former, if theory be looked at; especially in the latter, if practice is considered. Respect for occupation as such has been a characteristic of English law throughout the centuries. Scotland also well knew the strength of possession as a hard fact and by the strength of a man's right arm, but when order was established and law followed, Scots were too imbued with the sense of legal principle to recognise occupation as such, although an extremely important survival of the older view was that which required a symbolical delivery of possession (sasine) to complete a real right to lands.[2]

It is these two approaches, by no means unconnected, that it is proposed to discuss in this part of the work, concerned with conveyancing methods. Materials for the medieval history of Scots land

1   Diamond, *Primitive Law*, 260–1.
2   *See* Gloag and Henderson, 527–8.

law being scanty, much of what we now say of medieval England may be presumed to have been also true of early Scotland,[3] since the two systems were so close up to the time of Edward I and his reign brought less change in this matter than elsewhere in the English land law. Lord Kames thought that Scotland once knew the English respect for possession as such. He tells us that 'in the original conception of property, possession was an essential circumstance, and . . . when the latter was lost, the former could not longer subsist.'[4]

SEISIN AND POSSESSION

English law's extreme regard for possession or, as it is more usually called in this connection, seisin,[5] has been said to have had three important results in the English law of land:[6]

1   that ownership of an estate virtually depended on seisin;
2   that every transfer of a freehold estate had to be effected by an open and public livery of seisin;
3   that there could never be an abeyance of seisin.

Of these three rules Scots law appears to have known the first, but gave a very different meaning to 'sasine' from that which English law gave to 'seisin', at least in post-medieval times. Both knew the second rule but English law circumvented it, while Scots law made it the great pillar of its land system. Both knew the third rule but in Scotland it was the *dominium*, not the sasine, which could not be in abeyance.

The first of these results flowing from the importance of seisin in English law meant that a non-owner in possession was treated for many purposes as if he were the owner. Alternatively, we may say that for many purposes medieval English law did not recognise ownership but only seisin; and *vice versa* a true owner who was not seised was treated for many purposes as if he were not owner. This is

3   *See* Chapter I.
4   Lord Kames, *Historical Law Tracts*, 83.
5   The English word 'seisin' and the Scots word 'sasine' are derived from the same origin, the Latin word *sasina*, but they are not to be equated.
6   Cheshire, 42.

clearly contrary to principle. One who has not the right to possess should not be treated as anything but an unauthorised trespasser. A true owner should not forfeit any of his rights because he has had the misfortune to lose the *de facto* control of the land which is still his *de jure*. As Scotland has long known that respect for principle which is one of her chief legal features at the present time, Scots lawyers may be inclined to regard what follows as a sharp warning of what happens when a legal system is guided not by the clear light of logical principles, but by the mundane demands of day-to-day convenience. Yet they should bear in mind that much of what follows was probably also true of their system in the Middle Ages. For example, in 1454 Carruthers, who had been appointed Keeper of Lochmaben Castle, was ejected by Johnstone, a private enemy. The king allowed Johnstone to keep it and even paid him the Keeper's fees.[7] What is remarkable is not that medieval English law had a healthy respect for *de facto* possession, but that the effects of this respect should have lingered for so long, and even now are by no means dead.

The modern English distinction between seisin and possession as technical terms was unknown to the medieval lawyers.[8] The former is confined by a tradition of comparatively modern origin to the possession of land for a freehold interest, i.e. of real property. This includes incorporeal hereditaments, such as an advowson or right of way, but not a term of years: of that one is said to be possessed, like any other chattel, and not seised. This distinction was unknown to Bracton,[9] but became necessary once it was established, as he tells us that it was, that both the freeholder and the tenant for years have possession of the land. In order to keep these rights distinct 'seisin' was reserved for the former, 'possession' for the latter, so creating a division of possession comparable with that of *dominium* in Scotland.

If the freehold feudal tenant of land in medieval England was seised of the land he was in a very strong position: much stronger *vis-à-vis* the superior-lord of the land than was the case in Scotland. He could for instance – and this is a fundamental difference between

7 Grant, *S.E.D.S.*, 191.
8 Maitland, 'The Mystery of Seisin,' *Collected Papers*, i, 359.
9 Bracton, f 13b.

the two systems – alienate without the lord's consent being necessary. So, too, his heir could enter at his death without any renewed investiture, on the mere payment of a relief. This is quite contrary to Scots practice. But once deprive this English freeholder of seisin, through his wrongful dispossession by a stranger, and his rights are very drastically reduced, so that even until the nineteenth century he could not alienate his interest, which was no longer his estate, but merely his right of entry.[10] He might himself bring his action of novel disseisin – if he acted speedily enough – but he could not pass to another the right to bring it, for that is all that his 'ownership' now consisted of. Two reasons for this incapacity have been put forward. The first is that to allow a right of action to be alienated would lead to maintenance and champerty,[11] of which English law has always been very jealous. Probably of much greater significance to the medieval mind would be the practical difficulty that the only proper way of transferring title to land known to the common law was by a public delivery of the seisin on the land itself, which obviously a disseised owner cannot do.

Another rule of critical importance to the disseised landowner was that *seisina facit stirpitem*, that is that a person who is not seised has nothing which he can pass to his heir. This rule was in force in Coke's day,[12] for he tells us that 'a man, that claimeth as heire in fee simple to anie man by descent, must make himselfe heire to him that was last seised of the actuall freehold and inheritance.' He could not make himself heir to an ousted owner or one who had never entered. This is an extraordinary rule to which neither of the explanations just considered is applicable. Maitland's comment on it is interesting: 'a fear of maintenance very obviously fails us, and as it seems to me feudalism must fail us also, unless we are to suppose a time when seisin meant not mere possession but possession given, or at least recognised, by the lord of the fee.'[13] He concluded that there was no evidence of such a time in England. Had he glanced northwards,

---

10   Holdsworth, *H.E.L.*, iii, 92 *et seq*. The rule was abolished by the Real Property Act 1845, s 6.
11   Illicit arrangements whereby someone with no interest in a suit buys the right of action or agrees to pay the costs in return for a proportion of the proceeds.
12   Co. Litt. 11b.
13   Maitland, 'The Mystery of Seisin,' *Collected Papers*, i, 365.

however, he would have seen just such a view of seisin in actual operation. English law required the ancestor to have entered on the land before the heir could claim to succeed him. In later law what was called a 'seisin in law' was allowed, whereby the heir, on the death of his ancestor was deemed to have a seisin for the purpose of preventing the fee's being in abeyance; but to become the stock of descent the heir must make a seisin in deed, that is actual entry by himself or his tenants, through the attorning of the latter to him as freeholder.[14]

Other disabilities of the disseised landowner were those which prohibited his wife from having dower out of the land in question (though by Littleton's time a mere 'seisin in law' was enough to give dower[15]) or a husband from having curtesy, and that which prohibited his leaving it by will. This rule applied whether the testamentary power was the general one given to those who 'have' lands by the Wills Act 1540 or an older customary power in the case of certain burgage tenements. From all this it readily appears that at common law in England the position of one who claimed title to land but was not actually seised of it was far from satisfactory. Seisin, i.e. the taking of actual possession of the land, was essential to complete a proper title. Without it the 'owner' had a mere *nudum jus*: a right to sue, a right – as it was called – of entry. Landholding in the Middle Ages was a matter of *factum* as well as of *jus*: if the former were absent the latter would be very weak and not a real right of ownership at all. So far as this the Scots lawyers were in complete agreement. 'No real right to the property, and no real burden on land, can be created without a feudal grant completed by sasine.'[16] But sasine, unlike seisin, has not for a very long time been a mere question of factual possession of the land, if it ever was, for there always was about it an important element of right.

Where the two systems differ is not in the proposition that seisin is necessary for the completion of title but in the conclusions which English law drew from this. The first of these has just been explained – that if the owner were disseised he lost his full right to the land and was incapable of doing some important acts which he

14 Challis, *Law of Real Property*, 232 *et seq.*
15 Littleton, *Tenures*, s 448.
16 Bell, *Principles*, 756. Cf Lord Kames, *Historical Law Tracts*, 98.

could do only if he were still seised. Scots law does not agree with this conclusion, for in its eyes a real right, once completed by sasine, does not depend on *de facto* possession for its efficacy.[17] The second conclusion is one which Scots lawyers would certainly not have conceded for the last four centuries at least, namely that a disseisor (wrongful possessor) should be treated for many purposes as if he were the lawful owner of the land. Strong as this rule was in the Middle Ages, it is in a sense as strong or stronger in modern English law. By squatting in a field or house for twelve years without the least excuse to be there, the Englishman can deprive the true owner of it absolutely.[18] All he need do is to possess without acknowledging title in someone else and the land will for all practical purposes become his. By contrast his cousin in Scotland may sit there till Kingdom come, but he will not bar the real owner by negative prescription, which is unknown as a means of acquiring heritage. Consequently the heirs of the true owner may appear centuries later and eject him.[19] It is true that he may acquire a title to the lands by positive prescription, but this is by having a charter or disposition and registered sasine, albeit from a non-owner, in his favour. It can never come about by mere possession alone without written and registered titles of some kind.[20] Scots legal theory adheres to the doctrine that all titles flow from the Crown, while English law pays lip service to that proposition by saying that no one can acquire a positive title to land by lapse of time, yet allows this *de facto* by effecting a complete bar to the true owner and everyone else from interfering with the squatter's continued possession.[21]

The advantages of being a squatter (disseisor) in the Middle Ages

---

17 Bell, *Principles*, 769.
18 There is no 'positive prescription' vesting the title in the squatter, but the rights of the true owner are, in effect, completely destroyed. So fundamental is this strange respect of English law for the adverse possessor that even in areas where title is registered, a squatter acquires the equitable estate and on proof of his occupancy may obtain rectification of the register in his favour. (Limitation Act 1939, s 16).
19 As in *Young v Gordon's Trustees* (1847) 9 D 932; *Edmonstone v Jeffray* (1886) 13 R 1038.
20 Erskine, II.1.11; II.3.34. This is an application of the maxim *nulla sasina nulla terra*. Stair, II.3.16; Bell, *Principles*, 2009. *Duke of Buccleuch v Cunynghame* (1826) 5 S 57; *Edmonstone v Jeffray* (1886) 13 R 1038.
21 As to the nature of the title acquired by a squatter, *see* Megarry and Wade, 900–4; Cheshire, 901–4.

were not confined to the fact that if the true owner did not bring his actions with due diligence, he would be barred from bringing them for ever. The person who was actually seised of land, even as a squatter, was treated by the law for almost all purposes as if he were the actual owner. Thus it was *his* heir's infancy and not that of the true owner's heir which gave the lord of a military tenement the right to wardship and marriage; *his* wife received dower out of the lands; if *he* died a bastard without issue, the lord got the lands by escheat.[22] Most important of all, his feoffments gave quite an effective title to alienees. This also applied to those seised for a limited interest. Thus a tenant for life and a tenant in tail could pass the land to another by a tortious feoffment and that other would hold in fee simple. The disseisor himself could also do so. The medieval English lawyers did not see this as in any way absurd and indeed, unworried by such a technicality as *nemo dat quod non habet*, they allowed even the termor, who had not even got seisin, to give it to another.[23] The theory is that the landlord was formerly seised through the tenant's holding of him, but by the tenant's overt act inconsistent with his so holding, the landlord is disseised. In this context such things as the common recovery cease to cause surprise.

The alienee in such circumstances does not normally acquire a perfect title, for the true owner may still bring his cumbersome actions against him. However, until he does so, English law will presume that the man who is seised has a right to be seised. Therefore, as against all but one with an older and therefore better seisin,[24] he is entitled to the land and all the usual consequences will flow from that. Moreover, as time goes by the opportunities of action by the person formerly seised will grow less and less until they expire altogether, giving the disseisor's heir or alienee a title which is *de facto* perfect.

Why was it that the English common law was so favourable to the possessor of land as such? The great possessory assises, the actions by which possessors as such were protected, were introduced by positive legislative acts of early English kings, the assise of novel

22 Maitland, 'The Mystery of Seisin,' *Collected Papers*, i, 369–70.
23 Littleton, *Tenures*, s 611 (and Coke thereon).
24 Ancientry is practically the sole test of right in questions of seisin. In *Taylor v Horde* (1757) 1 Burr 60, Lord Mansfield, C.J. tried, but failed, to introduce an element of right based upon the Scots conception of seisin as feudal investiture.

disseisin having begun with an ordinance of Henry II in 1166. The protection of possession as such in English law is therefore not just a relic of barbaric traditions that might is right: these had already gone in Saxon days, but in medieval Scotland, the power of the sword often asserted itself in support of the holding of land acquired one knew not how. In less lawless England the protection of possessors seems to have been an act of deliberate policy, possibly for the following reason. The Royal courts had been supposed not to interfere with questions of title to land, which were left, or supposed to be left, as they actually were in Scotland, to the local feudal tribunals. But the Royal courts, thus debarred from questions of title, could protect possession on the ground of maintaining the king's peace. The Angevin kings therefore obtained power, popularity and public peace, to say nothing of handsome litigation fees, by protecting the possessor as such. These possessory actions were popular for a number of reasons, but especially because being more modern and backed by Royal authority they were far more expeditious and less chancy than the older highly formalistic and stylised writs of right.

Actions to deal with disseisin assume that the fact of disseisin was clear. This was not always as simple as it sounds and eventually a rule of thumb had to be settled. If A entered on B's land, could B gather his friends together at once and turn him out, or must he beg the king's help by the assise? The answer seems to have been that he was allowed to eject A within four days, but if A managed to remain in for more than four days, the practical remedy of physical ejection was lost and B must resort to the law, for otherwise B himself would be guilty of a disseisin. The unfortunate B at this stage came into the unenviable position of a disseised owner already described. How and why this particular period of four days was decided on as effecting a disseisin is one of those medieval problems – such as how many sheep make a flock, how many stones a pile? Presumably a few hours trespassing will not amount to a disseisin, for example while the owner is away at the market; presumably a week in adverse possession is ample to constitute it. Accordingly, a more or less random line had to be drawn.[25] Scotland escaped many

25 Maitland, 'The Beatitude of Seisin,' *Collected Papers*, i, 417–18.

difficulties by denying that anyone was seised who did not obtain the land by a public livery of sasine from the appropriate superior. Sasine thus implies an element of right which is not at all necessary to seisin.

SASINE

Regiam Majestatem tells us that the assise of novel dissasine was known in Scotland.[26] This certainly seems to indicate a protection of the seised as such, but it is not clear how far this was carried in practice. The close affinity between Scots and English land law at the time of the *Regiam Majestatem* suggests that the English law as just set forth then applied also in Scotland. However it was here Scots law which struck out on a new course by requiring formalities and eventually registration to attend the giving of sasine, thereby largely preventing those illegal sasines, which were recognised to such a surprising extent in England. One who occupied land without sasine in the developed law of Scotland was accounted a mere trespasser or tenant at will who could be ejected by the true owners.

But what of the Scot who has obtained a right to have lands, for example as purchaser or heir, but has not yet obtained official sasine? He cannot be brushed aside as a mere trespasser without right. Yet his interest in the land, even that of the heir, is not complete without the ceremony of sasine. Until that takes place his right is not a right *in rem*, a real right, but a mere personal obligation; a right ineffective against others deriving title, albeit later, from the same source, if they complete their rights by sasine. Thus suppose *A* grants a charter to *B* and *B* is not infeft by sasine, and then *A* fraudulently grants another charter to *C*, an innocent [27] purchaser, who is quickly infeft. Here *C* is preferred, as *B* had not a real but only a personal right to the lands. He should have taken care to obtain sasine, and now is left to his remedy in damages against *A*, if he can find him. As in England *sasina facit stirpitem* and an heir

---

26 *Regiam*, III.36.
27 Notice sufficient to put *C* on enquiry is sufficient to forfeit this status, without proof of fraud: *Petrie v Forsyth* (1873) 2 R 214.

must be served, as heir to the person last infeft and not to one who had a mere personal right,[28] and followed his service with an instrument of sasine.

There is a clear parallel here with the English rule already mentioned. But this was not carried to the extremes met with in England. Thus one who had only a personal right to lands, being not yet infeft by sasine, could alienate the benefit of the precept of sasine in the charter to him and so, though not seised himself, pass to another a right which by being completed by sasine in due course would become a fully real right.[29] There is not the theoretical objection mentioned to the English disseised owner's making a livery of seisin, for here the sasine proceeds not from the non-infeft owner but from the superior of the fee or alienor, the proper person to make sasine over to him if he had chosen to take advantage of the precept himself.

The Titles to Land Consolidation (Scotland) Act 1868[30] provided for the registration of notarial instrument in the Register of Sasines to enable a person to become infeft by specifying the details of the last infeftment recorded in the Register and narrating the deeds which gave personal rights which connected the person seeking to be infeft to the person last infeft. The notary inspected the connecting deeds (midcouples) and the last infeftment and signed the notarial instrument which was then recorded in the Register. A simpler deed, a notice of title, was introduced in 1924[31] as equivalent to a notarial instrument and also provided as an alternative that a notice of title could be dispensed with and a clause of deduction of title could be inserted in a disposition of land narrating the midcouples, and infeftment became complete when the disposition was recorded in the Register. These shorthand methods made assignations of unrecorded conveyances unnecessary and such assignations were abolished by the Conveyancing and Feudal Reform (Scotland) Act 1970.[32]

The first result of the importance attached to sasine (seisin) in

28   Stair, II.3.16.
29   Bell, *Principles*, 852.
30   S 19.
31   Conveyancing (Scotland) Act 1924, s 6.
32   S 48.

making the person seised *de facto* owner and the person not seised *de facto* non-owner is thus seen to have meant rather different things in the two legal systems of Great Britain. This is even truer of the second result, that all conveyances should be by way of a symbolical delivery of seisin. This is discussed in the next chapter.

24 Conveyances: Seisin and Sasine

CONVEYANCING: WRITING AND DELIVERY

Written documents for the conveyance of land and the creation of interests in it were known in pre-Norman England,[1] but it is not established whether a symbolical or actual delivery of possession was also necessary,[2] nor do we know the exact method by which folk-land was transferred, if it ever was.[3]

With the coming of the Normans, however, it became quite clear that a document alone, however hedged about with warranties and anathemas, could not transfer land from one person to another.[4] There had to be a livery of seisin or public handing over of the land to the new landholder, a requirement which almost certainly came over with the Conqueror from France, the essence of which was not ceremony or symbolism but the actual physical delivery up of the land. Only later did attention become diverted to the symbolic delivery which was but the outward and visible sign of the actual handing over of the seisin itself: the possession. Later still, attention was diverted still more to the document which discretion alone directed should be drawn up as evidence of the physical delivery's having taken place.

For many centuries, however, the physical delivery of possession did come to be evidenced by and expressed in the ceremony known to later times as the livery of seisin. A very important trace of its

---

1 *See* e.g. Appendix I.
2 Vinogradoff, *Folkland*, Collected Papers, i, 9; Plucknett, *Concise History of the Common Law*, 610; Maitland, 'The Mystery of Seisin,' *Collected Papers*, i, 383; P. & M., ii, 87.
3 It is probable that it could not be transferred at all without royal intervention which made it book-land.
4 P. & M., ii, 83.

original status as mere evidence to impress on bystanders what was taking place in their presence is found in the rule, also known to Scotland, that the ceremony must take place on the site of the land itself. This is probably connected with the open-field system of cultivation, which meant that an estate might be made up of numerous selions scattered about in the fields, very difficult to define in the charter in the absence of modern detailed plans; but no doubt well known and recognised by the local inhabitants, whose attendance as bystanders was a vital part of the ceremony. English law, however, was to evolve in Bracton's time what the Romans called a *traditio longa manu*.[5] Scotland did not share in this development, branching off before Bracton's idea on this point had penetrated into her system.

The ceremonies were originally very varied,[6] but eventually came to be standardised in more or less the following form, which is of special interest as showing that as late as the seventeenth century writing was not necessary for the creation of even so extensive a right as the fee simple in English land:

> The Feoffor and Feoffee (if they be present) or in their absence, their Attorneys (sufficiently authorised in Writing) do come to the House or Place whereof such Seisin is to be Delivered, and there in the Presence of Sundry good Witnesses, declareth the Cause of their meeting there; and then openly reads, or causeth to be read the Deed of Feoffment, (and Letter of Attorney, if by Attorney) or to declare the very effect thereof before them in *English*; which being so done, the Feoffer or his Attorney taketh a Clot of Earth, or a Bough or a Twig of a Tree thereupon growing, the Ring or the Hasp of the Door of an House, and delivers the same with the said Deed unto the Feoffee, or his Attorney, saying, I deliver these unto you in the name of Possession & Seisin of all the Lands, Tenements, &c., contained in this Deed, to have and to hold, according to the form and effect of the same Deed: And if the Feoffment be without Deed (as it may well be) then at the time of the Delivery of Seisin, the party must declare by word of mouth before Witnesses, the very State which the Feoffee must have thereby; and then delivereth Seisin & Possession in manner

---

5 Justinian, *Digest*, 41.2.1.21. Buckland, *Textbook of Roman Law*, 227.
6 Holdsworth, *H.E.L.*, iii, 221.

aforesaid; and then the date and manner of Seisin must be Endorsed.[7]

The Scots reader will at once be struck by the close resemblance of this description to the ceremony of sasine in his own system, which will be examined later.[8] The presence at the site, the recital of the documents, the attendant witnesses, the use of symbols, all have equivalents further north; but there is fundamental distinction. In this case the parties concerned were the feoffor (alienor) and feoffee; and the lord of the fee took no part. In England from immediately after the Conquest, it seems, the conveyancing of freehold interests in land is found to be a matter between outgoing and incoming feudal tenant. Before *Quia Emptores* 1290 no doubt, conveyances were often by way of subinfeudation *de me*, where the consent of the lord would not be necessary. What is more remarkable is that when the transfers became as a result of that Act necessarily *a me de superiore meo* the lord could not enforce an application to him for the reinvestiture of the fee.[9] Only in copyhold lands for rather different reasons was the practice of surrender and admission known and only centuries after *Quia Emptores* 1290. This absence of all recourse to the feudal lord on an alienation, as on a succession, was the greatest of all differences between the conveyancing systems of England and Scotland for eight hundred years. This speaks volumes for the strength of the feudal idea in Scotland and its early atrophy in England. Indeed, to describe English land law as 'feudal' when the very essence of feudalism – investiture – was lacking, can be little more than a verbal piety.

The history of conveyancing methods in English law, once the necessity for a public livery of seisin had been established, was largely that of various attempts to avoid this unpleasant and often embarrassing necessity. Ross points out that in connection with the same necessity in his own system, 'A person who has signed a disposition to his lands with little emotion, has been seen to burst

---

7 *The Young Clerk's Tutor, Enlarged,* 57. For a typical deed of endorsement *see* Appendix 6 *infra.*
8 *See* pp. 246–9 *infra.*
9   *It is only occasionally and in the century following the Conquest that we see anything of forms which illustrate the lord's rights in the land by requiring his participation in a conveyance, such as we see in France.*
     (Holdsworth, *H.E.L.,* iii, 225).

into tears at delivery of the earth and stone.'[10] The Scots, unlike the English, did not for a very long time avoid this psychological unpleasantness.

Some of the English developments took the form of adapting court proceedings to conveyancing. Others were formed, again through a fiction, out of proceedings *inter partes* designed for some other purpose than that of conveying the title to land.

The first type of improper conveyance (by which is meant any conveyance without the ceremony of livery of seisin) the fine, has already been mentioned in connection with the entail.[11] It was a tripartite record of the compromise of a bogus proceeding, which offered great security to the alienee because the third part (the foot) was entered among the official records of the court. So popular was the fine by the end of the twelfth century that special procedural rules were introduced in 1194. It says much for the continuity of English legal traditions that the same procedure lasted unchanged until 1833.[12] After a very short period of limitation fines were binding on all persons who might possibly have claimed to set them aside. But it is important to notice that the levying of the fine by itself was not enough to give the conusee seisin of the land. It was necessary for the sheriff[13] acting under the court's direction to put the conusee solemnly into possession of the premises transferred by the fine. It was thus not a complete answer to the problem of effecting a conveyance without the undue publicity of a livery of seisin.

The other method of forensic conveyance (the recovery) has also been mentioned,[14] but only in its developed form of the common recovery which proved so illogically effective as a method of barring entails. Collusive recoveries were also used as a method of conveying land, but until the sixteenth century they were regarded with grave suspicion by the courts and the legislature. In any case, they were no better than fines from the point of view of the publicity of the

---

10   Ross, *Lectures*, ii, 309.
11   *See* Chapter 19.
12   The Fines and Recoveries Act 1833, ss 15, 40 substituted a simple deed enrolled.
13   I.e. the English sheriff, who has been from the earliest times the executive officer of the royal courts within his country and not, as in Scotland, a judicial officer.
14   *See* Chapter 19.

proceedings. The sheriff had to appear at the site and bestow seisin on the recoverer, as the alienee was technically called.

So far as the common law was concerned, then, a livery of seisin was not to be avoided by the employment of either of these procedures: but English law was coming to have another institution, the use, which was to prove most advantageous in this as in many other connections. If the legal estate were once conveyed in due form with livery of seisin to the feoffees to uses, any effects desired could be carried out by dispositions (which could be arranged by word of mouth alone,[15]) of the uses on which those feoffees held the land. To these uses the legal requirements of a livery of seisin could have no application, for in the eyes of the law there was a tenant properly infeft in the land and what he did with the use of it was hidden from the critical examination of the courts by the screen of the legal estate. However, this screen was suddenly folded away by the Statute of Uses 1535 and what had been going on behind it stood revealed in the harsh light of legal day. This had usually been the procedure known as the bargain and sale, that is a simple contract to sell the land, but since equity was primarily concerned with conscience, it treated the parties from the moment of payment of the purchase price as if the whole contract had been carried out. 'Equity looks on that as done which ought to be done.' Accordingly the bargainee was treated as having an equitable right to the land from the moment of sale (what would now be called an equitable estate in it), by virtue of which he could compel the vendor to transfer to him the legal estate on demand. Alternatively he could continue to hold merely in Equity and so escape all the technical snags which were the consequences of holding the legal estate.

The impact of the Statute of Uses 1535 on these arrangements meant that by the parol bargain and sale a legal estate could now be passed, for the statute enacted that where land was held to uses, the legal estate should pass to the *cestui que use*. Consequently, anyone wishing to convey the legal estate in land could raise a use in favour of the purchaser and so save the publicity and expense of a feoffment with livery of seisin. However, this happy state of affairs was not to be for long, for the Statute of Enrolments, 1536 introduced a remedy

15 Plucknett, *Concise History of the Common Law*, 580.

for such alarming informality of conveyances. No lands or tenements were thereafter to pass from one person to another for any estate of freehold or any use thereof to be made by reason only of any bargain and sale thereof, except the same bargain and sale be made by writing, indented, sealed and enrolled (that is registered) as provided by the Act.

This provision is an extremely interesting one, especially that part of it relating to registration.[16] But the statute had another interesting effect. By it for the first time in English history, the legal estate in land for a freehold interest might pass from vendor to purchaser without any feoffment with livery of seisin, for the effect of the two statutes of 1535 and 1536 was to make a man seised to all intents and purposes who need never have entered on nor even seen the land.

This was in a sense exactly what had been desired for a considerable period, but the application to the Court for enrolment meant heavy fees and arduous formalities, so the ever-ingenious English property lawyers therefore began to look about for some device whereby they might retain the benefit of the Statute of Uses and yet escape the awkward registration rule of the Statute of Inrolments. They found what they were looking for in the latter statute's omission to deal with estates less than freehold: A bargain and sale for a term of years was not within its provisions and so it need not be enrolled, nor need the termor go into possession.[17] Having thus got the parties into the positions of landlord and tenant for years respectively all that remained necessary was for the landlord (reversioner) to release his reversion to the tenant. This could be done by a mere deed without livery of seisin, as the tenant was by statute already deemed to have possession. As a result of this deed the termor acquired the fee simple, the whole transaction having taken place without either livery of seisin or an enrolment.

The efficacy of this device (yet another important development in English law achieved by fiction) having been pronounced complete in *Lutwidge v Milton*,[18] it became the standard form of conveyance

16 *See also* Chapter 27.
17 Possession was normally necessary to give the lessee a real right to the land. (*interesse termini*). The Statute of Uses, however, was clear and no entry was needed in the case of grants to uses for years. The whole doctrine was abolished by the Law of Property Act 1925, s 149 (1).
18 (1621) Cro Jac 604.

in England. The usual practice was to make the bargain and sale for a term of one year at a nominal sum and then to date the deed of release from the day after the bargain-money was going to be paid.[19]

Unlike its predecessors the nineteenth century was not prepared to put up for ever with solemn farces of this kind and statutory changes then swept away most of the more curious institutions of English land law. Among them was the lease and release, and in 1845[20] a deed of grant was substituted for these documents. Corporeal hereditaments were thus said to lie in grant as well as in livery. This language was derived from the law as to incorporeal hereditaments – seignories, advowsons, rents and so on. After an initial period of confusion, during which it was thought that these, too, must be capable of seisin,[21] the rule had come to be for centuries that incorporeal hereditaments lie in grant. Finally, by the Law of Property Act 1925,[22] even the theoretical possibility of a livery of seisin was abolished together with feoffment and bargain and sale. All interests in land in England are now created or transferred by means of a simple deed.[23] Even this formality may be avoided in some cases by the application of the beneficent doctrines of equity.

This concludes a very brief survey of the development of methods of conveyancing in English law.[24] Before passing to the story in Scotland, it must be noted that after the Statute of Wills 1540 a will might operate to confer a legal estate on the devisee. As on the intestate succession of the heir however, to perfect his title the devisee had actually to enter on the land and so become seised.[25] The Statute of Frauds 1677 first required witnesses to a testament, and the Wills Act, 1837, completed the modern law on this subject, 'provided always that any soldier being in actual military service, or

---

19 Potter, *Historical Introduction to English Law*, 507–8.
20 Real Property Act 1845, s 2.
21 Cf Littleton, *Tenures*, s 618, and Coke thereon.
22 S 51 (1).
23 For an example of such a deed *see* Appendix X.
24 For a general account of modern English conveyancing practice, *see* Barnsley, *Conveyancing Law and Practice*; Farrand, *Contract and Conveyance*; Gibson, *Conveyancing*.
25 Maitland, 'The Mystery of Seisin,' *Collected Papers*, i, 365.

any mariner or seaman being at sea,[26] may dispose of his personal estate as he might have done before the making of this Act.'[27]

COPYHOLD CONVEYANCING

None of this conveyancing law applied to copyholds, for lands held by that tenure had always differed in this respect from those held by the free tenures. The differences centred mainly round the greater importance of the lord of a manor in connection with copyhold than that of the mesne lord in other tenures. In the case of copyholds it was necessary to apply to the lord on every conveyancing step as well as on a death. The appropriate method of transfer was by the vendor surrendering the holding to the lord's steward by means of a baton. This was usually done in the lord's court leet or court baron in the presence of the jury, who appeared at first sight to represent the ancient *pares curiae*. The purchaser had then to be formally admitted. Even an heir had thus to be admitted.

Every Scottish reader will at once recognise the close parallel between the methods just described and his own traditional conveyancing machinery. England by a paradox only recognised these 'feudal' methods of conveyancing in connection with this one tenure which developed long after feudalism as an active force in freeholds had spent its force.

However, great caution is necessary in drawing too close an analogy. The jury probably represent the neighbours who would in olden days have expounded the custom of the manor and supported the heir or vendor's claim to be entitled to it. Furthermore, the copyholder was admitted by the court proceedings; there was no need for a livery of seisin as well. It thus resembles booking rather than the ordinary Scots procedure. Undoubtedly both the Scots system of conveyancing and the English copyhold system developed from the same cause, that is that the lord-superior had originally a free choice of whether or not the new tenant should have the land. Conveyancing moves slowly and in both cases the procedure long survived his actual right to refuse an admittance.

26 This term has been held to include a female typist employed on a liner (*In b. Hale* [1915] 2 IR 362).
27 Wills Act 1837, s 11. *See* Megarry and Wade, 486–9.

FEUDAL CONVEYANCING IN SCOTLAND

Scots conveyancing demonstrates very clearly the reality of feudalism in that country.[28] The Scots Property Law Commission of 1837 was able to report with pride that 'the whole system of our land rights, whether the primary and radical rights of property, or the accessory and super-induced rights of security, continue to be strictly regulated by the principles of the feudal system, as it obtained in this country.'[29]

The feudal nature of the Scots system is very well brought out by the constant necessity for an application to the feudal lord (superior of the fee) on any change in the ownership of the fee, whether by way of alienation, when that was permitted, or succession. This is in sharp contrast with the complete absence of any necessity for the same in England, except in the special case of copyhold just mentioned. Since the relationship of lord and vassal is the keystone of the feudal arrangement, depending for its creation on the close personal bond of homage or fealty, it seems only to be expected that a renewal of the relationship by a new oath of loyalty should be required from the vassal's heir or alienee, for otherwise the feudal relationship would not be truly complete.

When the new vassal has done homage, the feudal lord renews the grant of the fee to him. This is technically called the investiture. Without it there can be no feudal right properly so called. The Books of the Feus state this very categorically, 'It must be kept in mind that feus can be constituted by no method other than investiture.'[30]

Once the fee had thus been constituted by the investiture or the ceremonial delivery of the land to the vassal, it could not be taken from him except for certain specific disloyalties; but this did not mean in Scotland that the vassal's heir or singular successor could succeed him in his rights without a further investiture. This is closely linked with the superior's right to refuse to accept singular successors. Whether such a stage ever existed in England is a controversial point,[31] but the stage was a very long one in Scotland.

28 *See* generally, Burns, *Conveyancing Practice*; Burns, *Conveyancing Handbook*.
29 Third Report, v.
30 *Books of the Feus*, i, 25 (Lord Clyde's Translation).
31 *See* Chapter 5.

A vassal of ward lands might incur the terrible casualty of recognition if he alienated more than half of them to another without his superior's permission, and even in the case of lands held by other tenures the superior could not be compelled to receive singular successors (alienees, adjudgers for debt) at least after the time of Robert III.[32] The first breach of this *retrait féodal* was made, like so many other important changes in Scotland, by legislation – in this case the Apprisors Act of James III in 1469,[33] by which apprisers, that is the execution creditors of the vassal, could compel the superior to receive them in place of the debtor vassal. Once this was admitted, the next step was obvious. The Scots lawyers took a leaf out of the English counterparts' book and pretended that a purchaser was a creditor. If necessary the vendor would enter into a bond to pay some large sum of money to the purchaser, which he would naturally fail to pay. The purchaser would then obtain judgment against the lands of the vendor for this non-payment and *qua* execution creditor (appriser) could insist by the statute on the superior's entering him. Later the fictitious bond was dispensed with and judgment on the obligation to transfer the land directly was enough to force the superior to grant a charter to the adjudger, of course on payment of a proper casualty.

In Stair's day this unsatisfactory situation continued, whereby the superior could, by refusing to receive the assignee as such, force him to the expense of obtaining a judgment, whereby the superior must infeft him as adjudger. Although he bewailed this stupidity,[34] it was not until a century later that superiors were by statute compelled to receive singular successors without the formality of a judgment against the assignor.[35] Even then, however, this situation was not wholly dealt with, for so long as the traditional methods of Scots conveyancing remained in force the superior was entitled to refuse to receive a corporate vassal, because it would produce no fruitful casualties.

---

32 Ross, *Lectures*, ii, 258 refers the power of the superior to refuse an alienation to an Act of 1400 (A.P.S., i, 213) which provided that 'if a tenant anaillied his land without licence of the overlord, in that case the overlord might recognosce them.' This Act, however, was probably passed in the interests of the tenants and restricted hitherto capricious recognition to this one case.
33 A.P.S., ii, 96,12.
34 Stair, II.4.6.
35 Abolition of Wardholding Act 1747.

Even the heir in Scotland did not succeed his ancestor in the fee by the mere fact of survivorship. It was just as logically necessary to have a renewal of the investiture to the heir as to a singular successor. Although there is some ground for supposing that in origin fees were granted only for life, the requirement that the heir must be infeft may not represent a right in the superior to refuse to admit heirs. Probably at a very early date he could not do that. But the heir's investiture in Scots law has got inextricably entangled with Roman law notions of the *heres* making *aditio*.[36] Until he accepted the inheritance and entered it by infeftment, he was not treated as heir but only as an apparent heir, with a mere personal right to the lands. The lands meanwhile are said to lie *in haereditate jacente* and the superior enjoys them by the casualty of non-entry.[37]

The heir who wished to accept the inheritance had first to 'make up his titles.' The significance of this term depended on whether the land in question was held immediately of the Crown or of a subject superior. The latter was deemed to know his vassals, so the heir in such cases was not required to make any formal proof of his relationship; the superior merely directed his infeftment by a writ or mandate beginning '*Quia mihi clare constat.*' The king on the other hand, could scarcely be expected to have formal knowledge of all his immediate vassals' family circumstances. Their heirs, therefore, had to make formal proof of relationship in a public manner. This was done up to the time of James VI by a sheriff's inquisition; thereafter by process in the Chancery. In either case, a writ was subsequently issued to the sheriff commanding him to infeft the now proven heir.

Yet the difficulties of a Scottish heir seeking to be infeft in place of his ancestors were by no means over once he had made up his titles by general or special service. The service does not transfer the heritage to the heir, nor does it subject the heir to the debts of the ancestor. It is the infeftment which completes both the active and the passive titles.[38] In other words it was necessary for the person to whom the mandate was addressed (who would be the sheriff in the case of a tenancy-in-chief, the superior's bailie in other cases)

36   As to which *see* Buckland, *Textbook of Roman Law* 312 *et seq.*, and Lord Kames, *Historical Law Tracts*, 361.
37   *See* Chapter 5.
38   Lord Kames, *Elucidations*, 101.

actually to conduct the ceremony of infeftment, which took a form closely akin to the similar livery of seisin in England. This will be dealt with in detail shortly.

Service of heirs was abolished by the Succession (Scotland) Act 1964. The confirmation of executors which is issued by the sheriff of the county in which the deceased died is now the link in title, but it cannot be recorded in the Register of Sasines: it must be followed by a notice of title or a disposition by the executors to the beneficiary, using the confirmation as a link to complete a title registrable in the Register of Sasines.

SUBINFEUDATION

Faced with the requirement of constantly going to the superior of the fee for a renewal of the investiture, it was only to be expected that Scots clients should seek and their legal advisers find, a way out of the difficulty, for every application to the superior involved considerable expense. They took the same course as had been taken in England before *Quia Emptores* 1290 and alienated the land not by way of substitution but, as they were entitled to do in the absence of that statute, by way of subinfeudation, so that the alienee held not immediately of the superior of the fee but mediately, by holding of the alienor who continued to hold of the superior as before. These were generally known as base holdings [39] as opposed to public ones.

In the disposition the seller obliged himself to infeft the purchaser by two manners of holding, one thereof to be holden of me (*de me*) in fee blench for payment of a penny Scots in name of blench farm at Whitsunday yearly if asked only and relieving the seller of all feuduties and services exigible out of the said lands by the seller's superior. He also granted another holding 'from me and my successors of and under my superior' (*a me de superiore meo*).

Until the seventeenth century two separate deeds were granted to the purchaser, one *de me* and the other *a me*. The infeftment *de me* gave the purchaser a title to the land against the seller and his

---

39   Not to be confused with the English base fee which resulted from an imperfectly barred entail; as to which *see* pp. 184–5 *supra*.

subsequent disponees as well as his creditors, but created a mid-superiority in favour of the seller. The title of the purchaser was a base fee until the purchaser obtained a charter of confirmation or of resignation from the seller's superior, when a casualty became payable. Thereupon the seller fell out of the feudal chain and was replaced by the purchaser, and the infeftment under the *de me* holding was ignored.

In the seventeenth century only one deed was granted with an alternative manner of holding, *a me vel de me*, and a precept of sasine applicable to either holding.[40] Infeftment on such a disposition gave the purchaser a valid title to the lands, but it remained a base fee held under the *de me* holding until he entered with the seller's superior. There could be a series of base fees, each creating a mid-superiority, until the superior claimed a casualty of non-entry. Then the holder of the last base fee obtained a charter of confirmation or a charter of resignation and confirmation from the superior on payment of his casualty, the mid-superiors fell out of the feudal chain and the last purchaser (now using the *a me* holding) became the public vassal of the superior.[41]

There is no objection to one person having a double infeftment in the same land; two instruments of sasine can appear on the register and the grantee can use either of them, or both.

However, in this procedure by way of subinfeudation there were certain snags, the biggest of which was that in ward lands sub-infeudation might be treated as a sufficient alienation to incur recognition.[42] Again, the sub-vassal did not enjoy a complete security. He was seised of the land as against his immediate superior (the disponer) but if the chief superior of the fee had not consented to the alienation he was not bound by it, until in 1747 the Abolition of Wardholding Act[42] made it competent for an heir or disponee to obtain a procuratory of resignation to compel the superior to receive the heir or grant new infeftment to the disponee, provided that the heir or disponee paid the casualty due to the superior.[43]

40   *See* Appendix VII.
41   Craigie, 319 *et seq. See also* Chapter 11.
42   *See* Chapter 5.
43   20 Geo II c 50, s 12.

It might well be that the proceedings before the superior[44] would be dilatory. Very lengthy documents had to be engrossed, and consequently the purchaser was well advised to take sasine under the *de me* part of the grant, which would give him a measure of protection in the meantime. But it was much more satisfactory to obtain the superior's assent to the transfer. This could be done in one of two ways. The simpler was that the superior should issue a charter of confirmation to the sub-vassal, approving and confirming the deed of the disponer, his vassal, and taking the sub-vassal as his own immediate vassal. The alternative method of obtaining the superior's consent was by the resignation of the fee into the hands of the superior *in favorem*, that is for the express purpose of its regrant to the disponee as a new vassal (but only the heir or disponee of an entered vassal could resign the fee into the hands of the superior). This was done by means of a full feudal charter corresponding to the original one by which the fee was first created and made for a great simplicity in the title and a greater security for the vassal than was possible by any other method. He had the fee now as well and as truly as the first grantee had had it.

The charter might be arranged in any way that the disponee might desire, for example to himself and his heirs male or even to himself for life and in remainder to heirs of entail. Opportunity could also be taken to alter the feuing conditions in the charter of resignation or of confirmation and resignation granted by the superior.

When the disponer was not an entered vassal a combined charter of resignation and confirmation was often granted, which was a charter of resignation containing a confirming clause which detailed any intermediate base infeftments. After obtaining a charter of resignation or a combined charter of resignation and confirmation the disponee or heir took entry under it in virtue of the precept of sasine in exactly the same manner as he took infeftment in virtue of the precept of sasine contained in a feu charter or a special service.

Apart altogether from using subinfeudation to create base fees

---

44 The Heritable Jurisdictions Act 1747 abolished the superior's courts, in the same year in which wardholding was abolished by the Abolition of Wardholding Act.

which would eventually be abolished by entry with the superior, any vassal could decide to subfeu as a permanent arrangement. He remained the vassal of his own superior and in turn granted a feu charter or feu charters of his own lands in which he imposed a larger feuduty than he himself was paying, imposed his own conditions and was careful to incorporate all conditions which appeared in his own feu charter so that his vassal would satisfy the requirements of his superior. An obvious example was a landowner who was tenant-in-chief of the Crown who feued part of his land to a farmer who in time was fortunate enough to find his farm adjacent to an expanding town. The farmer then subfeued an area of land to a builder for an increased feuduty or a grassum (capital payment) and imposed conditions suitable to the development of a residential estate. In turn, the builder subfeued single plots, again for an increased feuduty or grassum, by feu charters which incorporate additional conditions regulating garden fences, outhouses, maintenance of sewers, pavements and roads and other additional matters not covered by the builder's own feu charter. In a short space of time a chain of four feu rights has been created, landowner, farmer, builder and house owner.[45]

A method of reducing the length of the feudal chain was for the vassal to dispone his *dominium utile* to the superior, the disposition containing a procuratory of resignation *ad remanentiam*, and within sixty days (later on any time during the grantor's lifetime) the superior recorded an instrument of resignation *ad remanentiam* in the Register of Sasines. The *dominium utile* thereupon disappeared.[46] This procedure is still followed if there is a defect in the vassal's title which can be cured by the grant of a new feu charter by the superior. The same effect could be achieved by the superior granting a disposition of the superiority to the vassal. The form is exactly the same as that of a disposition of the *dominium utile,* except that the superior assigns the rents and feuduties and excepts the feu rights from the warrandice; in other words it is a disposition of the lands under burden of the *dominium utile*. If the *dominium utile* and the superiority are owned by one person and the

---

45   The Community Land Act 1976, if it comes into full operation, may put an end to the development of such profitable feudal chains.

46   Craigie, 406.

two interests are consolidated it is the *dominium utile* which disappears, and thereafter the former vassal holds on the prescriptive progress of titles of the former superior.

STATUTORY REFORM OF SCOTS CONVEYANCING

In the nineteenth century a series of Acts of Parliament simplified the mechanics of conveyancing without altering its principles.[47] Before 1845 the five deeds set out in Appendix VII were necessary to complete the title of one disponee, and the following clauses had to be included in a disposition of land:

1   narrative
2   dispositive containing words of conveyance, destination, description of subjects reservations, conditions, provisions, and burdens
3   obligation to infeft *a me vel de me*
4   procuratory of resignation
5   clause of warrandice
6   assignation of writs and rents from a certain time
7   clause of warrandice of that assignation
8   obligation to free the subjects of public burdens etc.
9   clause of delivery of titles
10   clause of registration
11   precept of sasine
12   testing clause

By the Infeftment in Heritable Property Act 1845 short forms of precept of sasine and instrument of sasine were introduced, and the ceremony of handing over earth, stone and so on, was abolished.

The Lands Transference Act 1847 introduced short statutory forms of the following clauses:

1   declaring date of entry
2   obligation to infeft
3   clause of resignation
4   assignation of rents

47   Craigie, 307 *et seq.*

5   obligation of relief from feuduties, casualties, and public burdens
6   warrandice
7   registration for preservation or preservation and execution
8   precept of sasine.

These forms reduce the length of a disposition to about a third of that of a pre-1845 disposition, and introduced reference to real burdens set forth in a recorded deed (usually an instrument of sasine or a feu charter).

The Titles to Land Act 1858 provided that (1) a clause of direction could specify the parts of the deed which the grantor wished to be recorded in the Register of Sasines[48] (2) the obligation to infeft and precept of sasine were no longer necessary (3) a clause of resignation would be presumed to be resignation *in favorem* unless expressly stated to be a resignation *ad remanentiam* (4) if lands were particularly described in any prior writ recorded in the Register of Sasines they could be referred to as such in any subsequent conveyance (5) if several lands were comprehended in one conveyance in favour of the same person they could be conveyed in future under a general name which could be referred to in future conveyances (6) all deeds, having a testing clause could be partly written and partly printed.

The forms of feu charters were similarly shortened, but in addition to reducing the number and length of the clauses of a disposition the Act introduced two fundamental improvements without prejudice to the older forms. Firstly, it provided that an instrument of sasine was no longer necessary and a feu charter or disposition could itself be recorded in the Register of Sasines, with a warrant of resignation signed by a solicitor. Secondly, it introduced a notarial instrument which could disclose on the Register of Sasines a series of links in title showing the existence of deeds of trust, settlements, changes in trustees, and other deeds affecting titles to lands. A notarial instrument was really only a certificate by a notary public that he had seen and examined the deeds mentioned and could be recorded in the Register of Sasines directly.

The Titles to Land Consolidation (Scotland) Act 1868 repealed the 1845, 1847 and 1858 Acts, but re-enacted them with some

48   This is no longer necessary because deeds are now photographed for the record volumes.

variations[49] and provided shortened forms for the formal clauses in dispositions.

The Conveyancing Act 1874 had taken the important steps of making infeftment by recording a feu charter or a disposition in the Register of Sasines imply entry with the superior (which removed the necessity for the clauses of manner of holding and resignation and made unnecessary charters of confirmation, charters of resignation and charters of resignation and confirmation which were streamlined by the 1847 and 1858 Acts) and replaced the whole solemn procedure of entry with the superior with a short notice of change of ownership sent by post by the vassal's solicitor with a fee of 25p.

The Conveyancing (Scotland) Act 1924 did not introduce any reform in principle. It abolished the notarial instrument and introduced the shorter notice of title; abolished and simplified the necessity for addresses of parties mentioned in statutory references to deeds on the Register of Sasines and referred to for descriptions and burdens; introduced a clause of deduction of title which made a separate notice of title unnecessary; and generally tidied up and simplified conveyancing practice.

Casualties have gradually faded away. The Conveyancing (Scotland) Act 1874 had provided that casualties must be converted into money and could only be collected at fixed times, such as every twenty years, and no longer on the entry of an heir or a singualr successor. They thus became regular rather than casual, and could be redeemed on a formula laid down in the Act. Finally they were abolished by the Feudal Casualties (Scotland) Act 1914, and all had to be redeemed by 1930. It was possible under this Act to stipulate for a permanent increase or reduction of feuduty, certain both as to time and amount.[50] The Act of 1874 also provided a formula for converting obligations for carriage or service into money, and the Conveyancing (Scotland) Act 1924 provided that if this was not done before 1935 the right was lost.[51] The Land Tenure Reform (Scotland) Act 1974 has now removed even the penny if asked for

---

49 For example, under the 1858 the use of notarial instruments was limited, but under the 1868 they were allowed in any case but needed a warrant of registration.
50 Feuduties themselves had to be expressed in money terms. The Feudal Casualties (Scotland) Act 1914 applied also to ground annuals (as to which *see* p. 137 *supra*).
51 S 12 (7).

only, though some Scottish lairds can on occasion be seen beside a roadside ready to present the Queen with a rose,[52] a pair of gloves or a pair of spurs, while others might yet wait elsewhere in the hope that they might be needed to hold her stirrup when she mounts her horse.

None of these reforms has however altered any fundamental principle of feudal conveyancing, though they have simplified and shortened the deeds, and virtually removed entry with the superior by reducing it to a short letter from the departing vassal's solicitor.

It is remarkable that in the period of twenty-nine years between 1845 and 1874 the number of deeds necessary for a disposition to take full effect was reduced from five to one, and descriptions by reference to a deed on the Register of Sasines (and reference to burdens by the same method) were introduced, thereby greatly shortening dispositions and saving unnecessary repetition. The forms of deeds settled in 1874 have merely been further shortened by the Conveyancing (Scotland) Act 1924 and the principles of conveyancing completed in 1874 have remained basically unchanged for a hundred years. Examples of a modern feu charter and a disposition are shown in Appendices VIII and XI.

52   *See* Frontispiece.

25 Rules against an Abeyance of Seisin

The sanctity accorded by the law to possession, or seisin in the case of freehold land, was said by Cheshire to have had three main results in English law of land:

1 that ownership of an estate depended on seisin;
2 that every transfer of a freehold estate had to be by open and public livery of seisin;
3 that there must never be an abeyance of seisin.[1]

The consequences of the first two results have now been considered, but the third is of a different character and developed into a rule, namely that interests in land must be so arranged as to ensure that there shall always be somebody effectively seised of the land, or, as the Scots would put it, that the ownership shall never be suspended.

English medieval law started with none of those occasions such as a non-entry where Scots law knew what looks to English eyes very like an abeyance of the seisin. Indeed the whole English doctrine of escheat was based on the principle that if at any time the lord of the fee was left without a tenant, or one capable of holding land, the fee ceased to exist and the land belonged to the lord. The same principle was known in Scotland in theory. 'The superior is entitled at all times to have a vassal.'[2] But because of the different rules as to escheat, the same consequences did not flow from it.[3]

---

1 *See* Chapter 23.
2 Bell, *Principles*, 679.
3 The rules on escheat are discussed in Chapter 5.

ENGLISH LAW

The first point where the difficulty arose in England was in connection with a grant to *A* for life and his children yet to be born in fee. This was also to cause trouble in Scotland. Bracton, writing at a time when the English law on this topic was not yet hardened into its traditional pattern, saw no difficulty in allowing the validity of such a disposition.[4] But later lawyers were not so confident.

The question often arose, what was the effect of a disposition to *A* and his heirs ? Did the heirs get anything and, if so, what ? To this the answer was negative at an early period,[5] because to have allowed anything else would have deprived the lord of the fee of his relief.[6] The donee (*A*) therefore got an ordinary fee simple. From this it was only a step forward to the notorious rule now known as that in *Shelley's Case*.[7] This was to the effect that the principle just enunciated would apply even when the grantor had attempted to evade it by giving the land expressly to *A* for life, remainder to his heirs in fee. Under the feudal principle that there must always be someone seised to perform the service due to the lord, as well as to prevent an evasion of the relief by dressing up the heir as a purchaser, this was clearly the correct solution. Only later when these feudal technicalities served to defeat the honest intentions of a grantor or testator did the rule become harsh and unconscionable.[8]

But by evolving such rules, English law did not evade the problem already mentioned in connection with Bracton. Could a settlor by words sufficiently clear to avoid the trap of *Shelley's Case*[9] so arrange his disposition that what came to be called a contingent remainder would be created, for example by granting land to *A* for life, remainder to the first of his sons to attain full age ? A remainder

---

4 F 13.
5 Holdsworth, *H.E.L.*, iii, 106.
6 Unlike the Scots superior, the English lord only had a relief from an heir, not from a purchaser; but in copyholds a fine was payable on each admission.
7 (1581) 1 Co Rep 88b. Megarry and Wade 60–5; Holdsworth, *H.E.L.*, iii, 107–11 observes that the rule was known in the fourteenth century (at 107).
8 Hence Lord Mansfield's strenuous but fruitless attempt to reduce the rule to a rule of construction (which is what it was in Scots Law): see *Van Grutten v Foxwell* [1897] AC 658 *per* Lord Macnaghten at 668–77. It undoubtedly remained a rule of law: Megarry and Wade, 62.
9 (1581) 1 Co Rep 88b.

in English law was created where the land was given for an estate less than fee simple and was settled so as to remain away from the grantor even after the ending of the particular estate. If the remainderman who was thus given an estate was a named person alive at the date of the grant there could be no difficulty. He took a present estate even though the possession and actual enjoyment of it may be postponed for the duration of the prior estate. This was known for obvious reasons as a vested remainder. Much more troublesome is the position where the person to whom the remainder is given is not alive, or not capable of taking because he has yet to fulfil some condition, at the time of the grant. He is said in this case to have a contingent, that is uncertain, remainder. Some of the most complex rules of English law deal with these remainders.[10]

Later lawyers did not share Bracton's confidence that a grant to *A* for life, remainder to his unborn children, was valid. To them it seemed an insuperable difficulty that there was no living person in whom the fee was meanwhile vested. Hence it was ruled that a person not in being at the time of the grant could not take, so the disposition to him was invalid.[11] In the reign of Edward II it was observed that in the case of a grant to the heirs of a living person there was no one who could perform the feudal ceremonies of homage until the heir was ascertained by the death of that living person, for *nemo est heres viventis*.[12] The rule in *Shelley's Case*[13] prevented this arising where the living person whose heirs were thus pointed out was the tenant for life, but it was not applicable where the heirs were those of some third party living at the time of the grant, that is, the grant was to *A* for life, remainder to the right heirs of *B* (a living person). Eventually in 1451 it was admitted that such a remainder would be valid, provided that *B* died in *A*'s lifetime.[14] Presumably the tenant for life's seisin was regarded as enough in the interval.

This was the only breach in the doctrine that was allowed in that century: the next saw the admission of a number of other possible

---

10 The authoritative work on this subject is Fearne, *Contingent Remainders*.
11 Y.B. 10 Ed. III. Mich. pl. 8. Holdsworth, *H.E.L.*, iii, 134.
12 'No-one is the heir of a living person.' Y.B. 2 & 3 Ed. II (S.S.) 4, *per* Bereford, J.
13 (1581) 1 Co Rep 88b.
14 Fitzherbert, *Abridgement*, Title *Feffements*, pl. 99.

contingencies and the formulation of stricter and more coherent rules as to how far these remainders were to be allowed in cases other than the death of a living person. Thus in *Colthirst v Bejushin*[15] the remainder was contingent on the son's dying in the lifetime of his parents. With some misgivings, this was held valid. In fact, it came to be recognised that any contingency might be selected provided that the now hardening rules as to the conditions in which remainders could be created were observed. These rules have been analysed as follows[16], the first three being applied to all remainders, vested as well as contingent:

1   The remainder must await the regular ending of the particular estate. No remainder which took effect by cutting down the prior estate could be valid. Scots law saw no objection to this.

2   No freehold estate could be limited so as to arise *in futuro*. To have allowed this would have been to admit an abeyance of the seisin contrary to the general feudal principle already enunciated. Hence the remainder must be so arranged that it will vest, if at all, at latest immediately on the determination of the particular estate. Hence a grant to *A* for life, remainder to his eldest son to attain the age of twenty-one, might be invalid if in the event the son had not attained that age at *A*'s death.[17]

3   The remainder must pass out of the grantor at the time of the original grant. There must, in other words, be an immediate livery of seisin to the holder of the particular estate, even though it be only for years.[18] This seisin so given to the particular tenant would enure for the benefit of the remaindermen.

The other two rules applied only to a contingent remainder:

4   It must be limited after an estate of freehold less than a fee simple. A term of years was good enough to support a vested, but not a contingent remainder, for in the latter case, there is no one seised of the land.

15   (1550) 1 Plowd 21.
16   Summarised from Holdsworth, *H.E.L.*, vii, 84 *et seq.*
17   Unlike the rules as to perpetuities (*see* Chapter 19), the contingent remainder rules only regard what actually occurs, not mere possibilities.
18   Littleton, *Tenures*, s 721.

5   The fee simple during a grant to *A* for life, remainder to the
heir of *B*, a living person, may be in abeyance,[19] for what English
law abhors is a vacuum in the seisin, not in the fee simple, and
the tenant for life is sufficiently seised. Scots law takes the
opposite view, for it is the *dominium utile* which must not be in
abeyance. There is quite often no one infeft in, that is seised of,
the land.

These, then, were the somewhat complicated rules by which the
validity of a contingent remainder was tested at common law. The
sixteenth century Statutes of Uses (1535) and Wills (1540) had their
special complexities to add, but before discussing them it is proposed to consider the nature of the interest of one awaiting the
vesting of a contingent remainder, for this has a considerable bearing
on what follows.

It is quite clear that such a person had no estate in the land. If the
person who may eventually take is as yet unascertained, as in the
case of a limitation to the heir of a living person (the oldest type
of contingent remainder in English law) there is nothing but an
'absolute bare possibility'. This cannot be an estate or be alienated
or otherwise treated as properly for obvious reasons. The point is
not quite so clear, however, where the remainderman is ascertained,
but it is not yet certain whether he will take – as in a grant to *A* if he
attains the age of twenty-one years. Here the remainderman might
seem to have something, even if only a *spes*. Still, the common law
courts in the sixteenth and seventeenth centuries were so terrified
of these remainders being used to effect a 'perpetuity';[20] that the
rule became established that they, too, could not be alienated.
Indeed like the other contingent remainders they gave such a shadowy
interest in the land that they could very easily be destroyed. Eventually they became virtually assignable in the eighteenth century,[21] when

---

19   *Ibid.*, ss 645, 646. *Colthirst v Bejushin* (1550) 1 Plowd 21 *per* Montagu C.J. at 35.
Co. Litt., 342b. But Fearne, *Contingent Remainders* 360 *et seq* argues that the fee
simple remains in the grantor. The older view, however, is to be preferred.

20   After *Stormont v Annandale's Creditors* (1662) M 13994 Scots law did allow such a
'perpetuity' and so did not have to distort other branches of the land law in
order to avoid it.

21   As to wills, see *Roe v Jones* (1788) 1 Bl H 30; (1789) 3 TR (HL) 88 Assignments
inter vivos were left to the Chancery, which undertook to enforce specifically assignments for valuable consideration: *see* e.g. *Hobson v Trevor* (1723) 2 P Wms 191.

this unreasoning fear of perpetuities was assuaged, and this was confirmed by statute later.[22]

But this is to anticipate. Before the Statutes of Uses 1535 and Wills 1540 contingent remainders were recognised in English law provided that they fulfilled the stringent conditions already mentioned. They might, however, be prematurely destroyed, that is before they became vested, even though initially valid and allowable. The methods of destruction were a matter of very technical learning. An apparently valid remainder might become invalid and fail, for example because the prior life estate by which it was (as it must be) preceded, came to an end too soon by the death of the tenant for life. At other times the contingent remainder might be artificially destroyed by the use of a tortious feoffment,[23] that is a conveyance by which a tenant for life or in tail conveyed a fee simple. It was possible to do this by the three most ancient modes of conveyance (feoffment, fine and recovery[24]) for they operated in such cases as if the grantor had formally repudiated his limited interest, claimed a fee simple as disseisor, and then alienated it.[25] Again, the doctrine of merger (consolidation) might be employed to destroy the remainder by a process of squeezing out, since the effect of a surrender by the tenant for life to the eventual remainderman or reversioner in fee was to destroy not merely the estate surrendered, but also the contingent remainder. It might also operate in reverse by the reversioner releasing the reversion to the tenant for life, as occurred in *Purefoy v Rogers*.[26] The English law produced a characteristic remedy for this unsatisfactory destructibility of contingent remainders, through the means of a grant of an estate *pur autre vie* during the tenant's life to trustees with the express and only purpose that they should intervene if necessary to preserve the contingent remainders. This was probably invented by Bridgman in the Civil War years.[27]

The effect of the Statute of Uses 1535 on this question was

22   Wills Act 1837, s 3; Real Property Act 1845, s 6.
23   For the classic account of tortious conveyances, *see* Co Litt 330b, n 1, by Butler.
24   Challis, *The Law of Real Property*, 138. See e.g., *Noel v Bewley* (1829) 3 Sim 103.
25   Megarry and Wade, 193.
26   (1671) 2 Wms Saund 380.
27   Holdsworth, *H.E.L.*, vii, 112; *Dormer v Parkhurst* (1740) 6 Br PC 351.

fundamental. Before that Act, persons who wished to avoid the harsh technicalities of the law of contingent remainders could do so through the device of a conveyance to uses. Behind the screen of the tenants of the legal estate, who would be duly and continuously seised of the land throughout, almost any desired arrangements might be made. Thus there could be gaps in the uses, for example while awaiting the birth of a child or his attaining full age ('springing uses'), or there could be a system of uses whereby the enjoyment of the land might be taken away from the particular tenant before the natural determination of his interest and vested in someone else ('shifting uses'). Neither of these was possible at common law, because of the threat of an abeyance of seisin.

The Statute of Uses 1535 laid down that the legal estate was not to remain in the feoffee to uses (trustees) but to pass, as it were, through them to the beneficiaries.[28] In ordinary circumstances this was straightforward enough, but it was far more doubtful what took place where the uses in question were of a kind not allowed at common law, that is springing and shifting ones. Were these now to affect the legal estate, so that it would spring and shift about with an agility formerly impossible, or was the law to remain soberly the same and any such attempt to do the legally improper to be treated as a nullity? The same problem arose under the Statute of Wills 1540 which, in conjunction with the Statute of Uses 1535 meant that executory arrangements and settlements contained in a will henceforth affected not merely the use but the legal estate in the land devised.

Most of the common law judges would clearly have preferred the latter alternative,[29] but convenience triumphed over tradition. It was eventually held that, provided that the machinery of a conveyance or devise to uses was employed, executory interests, including springing and shifting interests, might be made to affect the legal estate.[30] But an awkward question of theory remainded: did any right or *scintilla juris*, as it came to be called, remain in the feoffees to uses during the interval before a springing use came into being as a legal estate? This controversy raged for centuries, the prevailing common law view

28 *See* Chapter 15.
29 *See* e.g. Coke's remarks in *Chudleigh's Case* (1595) 1 Co Rep 113b.
30 *Brent's Case* (1583) Dyer 339b.

being that it did; but as late as 1860 we have the unprecedented spectacle of Parliament intervening in a question of archaic theory and deciding against the *scintilla*.[31] Yet this involves the consequence that no one is seised of the land until the remainder vests, unless we are to suppose with Fearne[32] that the grantor is still seised – a view contrary to traditional authority.

A relic of the older view survived in the rule that if the disposition were capable of being treated as a contingent remainder, it was to be so treated, with the consequent result of invalidity or destructibility.[33] Moreover, even those executory interests which did not fall into this trap were for a time during the sixteenth century considered as being as destructible as contingent remainders, but though *Manning's Case*[34] and *Pells v Brown*[35] checked this trend, it was only when Lord Nottingham's saner approach had prevailed and attention been fixed on rules as to remoteness of vesting as a better precaution against perpetuities, that English law became more rational in its approach to future interests. Even the theoretical destructibility of contingent remainders (long generally obsolete, thanks to Bridgman's device) was cut down by the Real Property Act, 1845,[36] and the Contingent Remainders Act, 1877. Finally, following its general policy of reducing the number of possible legal estates to the minimum, the Law of Property Act, 1925, enacted that in future all such interests should be equitable.[37] After 1860 the theory that there must always be someone seised of the land had virtually gone,[38] but the 1925 legislation in effect restored it, for the legal estate must thereby always be vested in an 'estate owner' and limited or springing interests affect only the equitable estate.

Blackstone summed up his account of this branch of the law with the comment that 'the doctrine of estates in expectancy contains some of the nicest and most abstruse learning of the English law.'[39]

31 Law of Property Amendment Act 1860, s 7.
32 *See* note 19, *supra*.
33 *See* Parker, J., in *White v Summer* [1908] 2 Ch 263.
34 (1609) 8 Co Rep 94b.
35 (1620) Cro Jac 590.
36 S 8.
37 S 1 (3).
38 Law of Property Amendment Act, 1860.
39 Bl. Comm., ii, 163.

SCOTS LAW

Scotland escaped in the main the growth of the complex technicalities which thus entangled the English law as to there being no abeyance of the seisin. Scots law generally adhered to the free and easy attitude of Bracton, that any type of conditions might be inserted in a feudal grant; and this included any destinations within reason that the granter thought fit to establish. Thus Scots settlements show a variety of arrangement not possible in England, especially at common law. Although Scotland did not have a court of Chancery, she scarcely needed one, for much of her 'Law' was the equivalent of the English Equity. Springing and shifting interests could be created without the difficulties just discussed.

Nonetheless, Scots lawyers were aware of the existence of the feudal maxim that 'the superior is entitled at all times to have a vassal'[40] and 'the Law of Scotland does not recognise a fee in a pendant state.'[41] It should be noted at once that in the Scots view the rule has nothing particularly to do with sasine. Many occasions exist when there is no one with sasine of the land: for example on every death in Scotland there was no one seised of the land (in the Scots sense) until the heir had made up his titles and received formal sasine from the superior, which might not occur for many years.[42] Moreover the feudal casualty of non-entry only gave the superior a temporary right to enter on the lands in the interregnum, but he came in just because there was an abeyance of his vassal's sasine. What is not allowed to be in abeyance, in Scotland, is not the sasine but the *dominium*. Although the language employed is not always perfectly consistent, it seems clear that a proprietor with a mere personal right to the fee is sufficient. The point is that there should never be a *res* without a *dominus* rather than that land should not lie without someone's being seised of it.

English readers who are inclined to regard the rule in *Shelley's Case*[43] as a special peculiarity of English law, may be surprised to

---

40 Bell, *Principles*, 679.
41 *Ibid.*, 1710.
42 As, for example in *Young v Gordon's Trustees* (1847) 9 D 932.
43 (1581) 1 Co Rep 88b.

learn that Scotland, too, knows this venerable examination chestnut. Of course, Scotland never knew the rigid canons of English law as to the exact significance of particular phrases of limitation.[44] But where land is destined to a man in liferent and to his children in fee, or to *A* in liferent and the heirs of his marriage in fee, or to *A* for life and to his heirs in fee (this one being the exact equivalent of that in *Shelley's Case*[45]) the result is to give the fee to the nominal liferenter and nothing to the issue or heirs.[46] But it is otherwise (as it would be in England) if the children are alive and the fee is given to them *nominatim*.[47] In Scotland, however, as opposed to England, this rule is only a rule of construction and not one of law. Consequently, by the use of appropriate words very clearly demonstrating the granter's intention, for example to *A* in liferent allenarly (that is only) and to the heirs in fee, the rule in question could be defeated.[48] Probably the origin of it was not so much a confusion between fee and liferent, as Bell suggested,[49] as a desire to prevent an abeyance of the holding by recognising that the fee was in unascertained persons. Certainly the rule cannot have arisen in Scotland to prevent an heir's being dressed up as a purchaser to cheat the lord out of his relief, for the superior was entitled to a relief as much from the latter as the former. Now, the Scots rule, like the English, has been abolished by statute.[50]

Although the feudal rule necessitating continuity of holding was very generally accepted,[51] Lord Dirleton, a seventeenth century writer, expressed his doubts as to its correctness[52] and surprisingly, Erskine flatly denied the existence of any such rule. He acknowledged the adherence to it of the great mass of authority, but continued:

> It appears to have no foundation either in nature or in law. Many things are, *ex sua natura*, fit subjects of property, which nevertheless have no proprietor; those, for example, which the proprietor abandons with a design to be no longer owner of them, or waste

44 *See* Chapter 22.
45 (1581) 1 Co Rep 88b.
46 *Frog's Creditors* (1735) M 4262. Cf *Cumstie's Trustees* (1876) 3 R 921 *per* Lord Dunedin at 941–2; *Colville's Trustees v Marindin*, 1908 SC 911.
47 Bell, *Principles*, 1712.
48 *Gerran v Alexander* (1781) M 4402.
49 Bell, *Principles*, 1712.
50 Trusts (Scotland) Act 1921, s 8 (1).
51 Stair, III.5.50; Bell, *Principles*, 1712; *Newlands v Newlands' Ceditors* (1794) M 4289.
52 *Doubts and Questions in the Law, especially of Scotland*, title 'Fiar', No 9–10.

lands of which no person hath as yet seised the possession. In like manner where the fee or property of any subject is granted to children yet to be procreated, and bare liferent to the father and mother, the property of that subject must of necessity be pendent till the existence of a child.[53]

Erskine continues by referring to the *haereditas jacens* and the influence of Roman law is at once apparent in this passage, but in so far as he is writing of Scots land law this is rather unsatisfactory, for Civil law principles prove inept when employed to describe a feudal situation.[54] However, Erskine does not rely on civilian theory alone: he cites Scots cases in support of his view: *Douglas v Douglas and Drummond*[55] and *Gibson v Arbuthnot*.[56]

In *Douglas v Douglas and Drummond*[57] Robert Douglas by contract of marriage with Helen Gourley became bound to infeft himself in certain lands by a precise date and being so infeft immediately thereafter to resign the same for new infeftment to his future spouse in liferent and the heirs of the marriage in fee; which failing, to his own nearest lawful heirs and assignees whatsoever, with reservation of his own liferent. His son brought this action against him to denude, that is to divest, himself of the fee and to vest it in his children as heirs of the marriage. But the father alleged that he had assigned the fee to a third party (Drummond) for onerous causes. If the fee had been vested in the father, then such an assignment could not be upset. The Court held that the father was bound to infeft the children as soon as they came into existence. It also found that the assignment to Drummond was gratuitous, so that it did not prevail over this obligation. There is no direct statement as to the whereabouts of the fee.

Gibson v Arbuthnot[58] is an interesting case because here the settlement was after the liferents on the husband and wife 'for the use and behoof of the children to be procreated betwixt them in fee'. The Lords found that the husband had obliged himself to provide half of the conquest to himself for the use and behoof of the

---

53 Erskine, II.1.4.
54 This has also been noted in his discussion of usufruct and liferent: *see* Chapter 13.
55 (1724) M 12910.
56 (1726) M 11481.
57 (1724) M 12910.
58 (1726) M 11481.

children of the marriage, whereby he became a trustee for the behoof of the children of the marriage in fee. To an English lawyer this approximates very closely to the familiar English institution of an equitable estate. How novel a conception this was to Scotland is well shown by Erskine's citation of the case as an example of the fee's being *in pendente* and even more so by the speech of the dissenting judges in *Newlands v Newlands' Creditors*.[59]

Here the settlement was on Lieutenant Newlands 'during all the days of his lifetime, for his liferent-use allenarly, and to the heirs lawfully to be procreated of his body in fee'. The question was whether under this arrangement the fee was in the Lieutenant so as to be available to be taken in execution by his creditors. His eldest son brought the action to preserve the settled land from this fate. In the Court of Session counsel for the creditors put forward all the usual arguments. The Court could not find the father to be a mere liferenter because then the fee must either have been *in pendente* till the existence of the children or must have remainded with the disponer, which was clearly contrary to his intention. But counsel for the son, boldly in view of the multiplicity of authority against him, pleaded that Scots law would admit of exceptions to the feudal principle and leave the fee in abeyance, for example between the death of the vassal and the entry of the heir. Erskine was quoted in support for saying that the rule 'has no foundation in law or in nature',[60] and so was *McKenzie v Lord Mountstewart*.[61] Even if this view were rejected and the fee held to be in the father, it would be so 'for the behoof of the son'. He adds, 'Such trust fees were very common in the Law of Rome. They are often resorted to in our practice and still more frequently in that of England.'[62]

The Lords of Session were unanimous in upholding in principle the rule that a fee cannot be pendent: there is no subject without a proprietor. An estate descending from ancestor to heir or conveyed by family deeds can never be *res nullius*, though it may remain for a time *in haereditate jacente*, and by the Law of Scotland, if it can find no other owner, it will belong to the king. A majority of the court

59 (1794) M 4289
60 Erskine, II.1.4.
61 (1707) M 14903. In that case the heir was *in utero*.
62 (1794) M 4289 at 4292.

thought that in spite of this, effect must be given to the intention of old Newlands, that his son should not enjoy the fee. The maxim that a fee can never be *in pendente* never produces the result that someone should become entitled to the fee, whom the donor did not intend to have it. In the present case, it was held by a legal fiction that a fiduciary fee was vested in Lieutenant Newlands, but which substantially is no more than a liferent as it excludes the power of disposal, either onerously or gratuitously.'[63]

As in England, the fear of a 'perpetuity' moved in the minds of these judges when considering the separate question of whether the fee might be pendent. But it is not clear what is the answer to their difficulty. There was then no rule in Scotland that unborn persons thus given a future fee must be in the first generation from the life-renter and fiduciary fiar. Could not a remote heir, for example the grandson of a great-grandson, have been selected? The fee would have been inalienable until he came into being but since 1848 there has been a statutory rule in Scotland that a person unborn at the date when a settlement comes into force can claim the fee without payment of any compensation to anybody, whatever else may appear in the settlement.[64]

In view of this danger of a perpetuity, the House of Lords might have been expected to carry out their usual technique of upholding the minority view, but they did not do so. Lord Loughborough, L.C. (a Scot), expressed great doubt as to the grounds on which the decision had been given. 'Though I feel no conviction, though my mind inclines to doubt exceedingly that the judgment proceeded on safe grounds, yet I have not the courage to venture a reversal.'[65] This was because he had been assured by a Scots judge of great experience that marriage settlements had long been drafted on the footing that the majority view was correct. He deliberately invited the Session to reconsider the matter in a future case, but when the opportunity occurred,[66] they declined to do so, regarding themselves as bound by the House of Lords in *Newlands v Newlands' Creditors*.[67]

---

63 *Ibid.*, at 4293.
64 Entail Amendment Act 1848, ss 47, 48.
65 M 4289 at 4295.
66 *Watherstone v Renton* (1801) M 4297.
67 (1794) M 4289.

Subsequent decisions followed this lead,[68] but statute has now modified the position.[69]

This case provides the usual answer to the question put earlier as to the whereabouts of the fee if the liferent be granted with restrictive words such as 'allenarly.' But in case of difficulty Scots law sees no objection to the fee's remaining, again on a fiduciary basis, in the original granter, by reservation: many settlements contain a reservation of power 'to alter the trusts.' Or again, if desired, the fee may be vested in trustees to hold and protect it during the continuity of the settlement and this ownership by the trustees will be sufficient to satisfy the feudal maxim.[70]

One conclusion must be, therefore, that Scots law has adhered strictly to the rule prohibiting an abeyance of *dominium*. But this adherence was obtained only at the expense of admitting a fiduciary fee, which seems to involve a distinct legal and equitable estate or something very close to it, contrary to the older traditions of Scots lawyers.[71]

Although the existence of springing interests thus caused some theoretical difficulties in Scotland, that other bugbear of English settlors, the shifting interest, does not appear to have caused any great problems. Craig believed that the English settlor was given by the statute *De Donis Conditionalibus* 1285 the right to choose *successionis tempus*.[72] This was not true of England, but was of Scotland, so that an interest given, such as a liferent, may be cut down by the occurrence of some later event or the breach of some condition, if the settler desires it.[73] One example of this is the Scots entail, which in its classical form provided a tailzied feu which came to an end before the death of the fiar in certain events, for example on an attempt to alienate. Such a limitation was void in

68 *Dewar v McKinnon* (1825) 1 W & S 161 (HL); Bell, *Principles*, 1712.
69 Trusts (Scotland) Act 1921 s 8 (1), makes it unnecessary to use the word 'allenarly' section 8 (2) allows court-approved trustees to be appointed in place of the fiduciary fiar.
70 *Fisher v Dixon* (1833) 6 W & S 431; *Gifford's Trustees* (1903) 5 F 723; Bell, *Principles*, 1715.
71 *See* the discussion in Chapter 15; cf Trusts (Scotland) Act 1921.
72 Craig, 2.16.4.
73 This is not impossible in England, if on the occurrence of the determining event, the land is merely to revert to the settlor: *Wainwright v Millar* [1897] 2 Ch 255. But a remainder might have been void under the Rule Against Perpetuities.

English law, although allowed in certain cases under the operation of the Statutes of Wills 1540 and Uses 1535 subject to the rules against perpetuities.[74] Another common Scots instance is a liferent to a widow to cease on her remarriage.

74 *See* Chapter 19.

26 General Conclusions as to Seisin and Sasine

The rules in both systems which are said by English lawyers to be derived from the basic importance of seisin (that is possession) in medieval land law and its three main results have now been examined. Whereas the general tendency has been to find similar institutions disguised behind different technical descriptions and different classification, with this topic the opposite has occurred. Two substantially similar words of common derivation disguise a fundamental difference of conceptions, and although some of the rules as to sasine and seisin have appeared at first sight to be the same, they have turned out on a closer examination to be radically different.

Thus the first result, that a person who is not seised is treated for many purposes as non-owner, may be acceptable to both systems, but this language hides the very fundamental difference between them that in England mere adverse possession alone, if continued for the appropriate period, will in effect give title, by destroying the old owner's title, while in Scotland this is not the case. Sasine does not mean mere possession of the freehold, which is the meaning of seisin; but feudal investiture proceeding directly or indirectly from the chief lord of the feu. This is a striking distinction and clearly results from the ultra-practical approach of English lawyers on the one hand, and the strict adherence to feudal principle of Scots lawyers on the other. It re-emphasises the early decline of feudalism in England and its long survival in Scotland.

Again, the casual observer watching a livery of seisin in England and sasine in Scotland would not be able to see much difference between them: no doubt they were the same in origin. But their effect while they lasted (both having now been abolished) was very different. In England this might be the only formality necessary for a conveyance: in Scotland however a charter was *de rigeur* as well as the elaborate ceremonies of resignation and regrant. They and the sasine itself were quite worthless unless properly attested by the written instrument of a notary public (an official much less known to English practice[1]) and its registration, virtually unheard of in England.[2] These differences of conveyancing technique mark a deep cleavage between the developed land systems of the two countries, although their original feudal land laws had much in common. Scots conveyancing practice probably stood in greater need of reform up to the nineteenth century, the amount of paper, time and money involved in an ordinary transfer of land being enormous; while English conveyancing stands more in need of it at the present day, as its lack of any uniform system of registration, even of assurances, makes it archaic and expensive, with its 'investigation of title' (which could be done in a minute under a system of registered titles), to say nothing of its being incomprehensible to the lay public and even to most foreign lawyers. It has been seen, however, that progress is being made.

Finally, the extreme technicality of the English rules designed to guard against an abeyance of seisin are quite unrivalled in Scotland, which has never got into that high state of alarm about perpetuities, which was once a mania of the English legal profession. Scotland has had, however, to let in the English notion of an equitable estate in the form of a fiduciary fee in order to calm those who took their civilian principles over seriously.[3]

The term 'seisin' as used in England has brought together in this chapter and in English legal tradition three topics, at least one of which has no particular connection with the term 'sasine' as understood in Scotland.

---

1   They were anciently appointed by ecclesiastical authorities, and a 'duly certified notary public' is still required by the Solicitors Act 1974, s 87 to have in force a practising certificate as a solicitor under that Act, duly entered in the court of faculties of the Archbishop of Canterbury in accordance with rules made by the Master of Faculties, or a practising certificate as a notary public issued by the court of faculties in accordance with such rules. *See* generally 28 Halsbury's *Laws of England* (3rd edn) paras 121–51; and as to notaries in Scotland, Bell's *Encyclopaedia of the Laws of Scotland*, 744, 745.

2   Except in Yorkshire (*see* Chapter 27).

3   *See* Chapter 25.

Two other minor results flow in English law from the rules as to seisin. One of these is the peculiar nature of the English joint tenancy, where two, three or four[4] persons hold an estate in land by the same seisin. If this is the case, they have a type of interest not known (save in the case of trustees[5]) in Scotland, where the conjunct interest resembles closely the English tenancy in common. This exists where two or more persons hold land[6] in common at the same time, but without the unity of title and seisin which is the characteristic of joint tenants, each having a distinct and separate, if as yet undivided, share in the land. The main result which flows from the single seisin of joint tenants is that among them what is called the benefit of survivorship applies. This means that if *A*, *B* and *C* are joint tenants, and *A* dies, his heirs get nothing, unless in his lifetime he has taken steps to 'sever' the joint tenancy and convert it into a tenancy in common: *B* and *C* remain joint tenants of the whole. If *B* dies, again without having severed, *C* takes the whole and his heirs succeed him, to the exclusion of those of his colleagues.[7] The rule works obvious injustice, for *A* and *B* may have been minors or lunatics unable to sever, or merely ignorant of the necessity for doing so. It seems a pity that the legislators of 1925 did not abolish the equitable joint tenancy at the same time as they abolished the legal tenancy in common. This would have produced a situation like that in Scotland. The unfairness of the English rule is shown by the fact that co-heiresses, who should logically have been the supreme example of joint tenants, are not dealt with exactly on the basis of joint tenancy. The rule as to survivorship is not enforced between them where they leave heirs other than their sisters.[8] Another conjunct estate is that known as a tenancy by the entireties,

---

4 Not more than four can hold a legal estate as joint tenants on trust for sale after 1925, but there is no such restriction upon beneficiaries of the equitable interest (Law of Property Act 1925, ss 34, 36; Trustee Act 1925, s 34 (2); Megarry and Wade, 417–18).

5 Trustees in Scotland hold on the same basis as English joint tenants: *Gordon v Eglinton* (1851) 13 D 1381; *Gillespie v City of Glasgow Bank* (1877) 6 R (HL) 104, *per* Lord Blackburn at 111; *Magistrates of Banff v Ruthin Castle Ltd* 1944 SC 36. Menzies, *Trustees*, 81; Wilson & Duncan, *Trusts Trustees and Executors*, 19.

6 In equity only, after 1925. Law of Property Act 1925, ss 1 (6), 34 (1), 36 (2); Settled Land Act 1925, s 36 (4). Megarry and Wade, 408.

7 For a more detailed discussion *see* Cheshire, 221–36.

8 As to co-parceners, *see* Megarry and Wade, 429–32.

which applied in English law only where the parties were husband and wife, but no new tenancies by entireties could be created after 1882[9] and any surviving at the end of 1925 were converted into joint tenancies.[10] Scotland did not have any special tenancy of this kind, her conjunct fee serving the purpose of these three English tenancies.

The other rule is the peculiar one known in English law as *possessio fratris*. The old common law rule already noted[11] made a seisin in deed, that is actual entry into possession of the land, the determining factor in deciding who was the stock from whom a descent should be traced to find the heir. Traditionally, relations of the half-blood of the person last seised could not take, so that a brother who took possession and then died leaving a sister german and a consanguinean brother, was succeeded by his sister, who was said to come into the succession by the *possessio fratris*. If her brother had not been seised, the father would have been the *Stammvater* and so her half-brother would have got the lands. This anomaly[12] has now been abolished, but it may serve to remind us of the high regard of English lawyers for possession.

---

9   Married Women's Property Act 1882, ss 1, 5. *Thornley v Thornley* [1893] 2 Ch 229.
10 Law of Property Act 1925, 1st Schedule, Part VI; *See* Megarry and Wade, 432–4 and Wolstenholme and Cherry, *Conveyancing Statutes*, i, 372.
11 *See* Chapter 23.
12 Challis, *The Law of Real Property*, 238.

PART III

THE BEGINNINGS OF
RECONVERGENCE

SOME MODERN DEVELOPMENTS

Chapters 27 to 32

27 Land Registration in Scotland and England

DEVELOPMENT OF THE SYSTEM IN SCOTLAND

In such a system as the Scots, which places tremendous importance on the question whether investiture has or has not taken place, it is not surprising to find that much thought is given to the rules of evidence by which the fact of investiture may be proved.[1] Thus as early as the Books of the Feus, proof must be by the testimony of the new vassal's peers of his superior's court and no other evidence would suffice.[2]

> When a superior who already has a number of vassals gives investiture in this way, the grant should be ceremoniously performed before at least two of those vassals; otherwise, even though the investitutre may be witnessed by other persons, it is invalid. If, while the superior is still in possession of the lands, a question should arise as to whether investiture has been truly granted or not, the investiture should not be held proved except by the evidence of the peers of the superior's court, or by a public instrument confirmed by two or three of such compeers.[2]

The mention of a 'public instrument' in this context is interesting, as it foreshadows the Scots custom that the ceremony of investiture should be recorded by a notary public. It is difficult to say when this first became general[3] but it was clearly regarded as imperative in the

---

1 Like 'sasine', the term 'investiture' originally signified possession rather than its ceremonial delivery (*Libri Feudorum*, 2.2).
2 Books of the Feus (*Libri Feudorum*), 2.2. (Lord Clyde's Translation).
3 Craig, 2.2.18; 2.7.1., suggests that the practice was introduced from England by James I of Scots, long a prisoner there. Stair, II.3.16 quotes this with approval, citing (*Town of Stirling v Lord Urthill* (1625) M 6621, where a sasine without writing was upheld because it took place in an earlier reign. Ross, *Lectures*, ii, 136

later Middle Ages, as the notarial instrument of sasine was then the sole permissible evidence which could be brought to show that the ceremony of investiture had taken place. Even if the superior subscribed in person with a thousand witnesses, this would not avail in the absence of a notary.[4] Once this was established, it is not unnatural to find the State, through the legislature, interfering to make certain safeguards against forged or incorrect sasines. This was attempted in a series of registration statutes in the sixteenth and early seventeenth centuries. It has been remarked that no circumstance distinguishes the jurisprudence of Scotland from the other European nations more than her early invention of public registers and the perfection to which the use of them was eventually carried.[5] England has never attempted to compete with Scotland in this regard: indeed it might be fair to say that it is not the early establishment of registration in Scotland which is remarkable, but rather its continued absence as a general institution in England.

It is obvious that the Scots system of registration was not introduced by a single measure in that state of comparative perfection to which it has subsequently attained. The matter was the subject of a steady flow of legislation extending over two centuries. Moreover, some vitally important questions of the construction of these statutes were not judicially determined until as recently as the last century.[6]

The first Registration Acts, those of 1503[7] and 1540,[8] related merely to sasines given to crown vassals, which were ordered to be entered in a book and presented in the Exchequer 'that the king's grace may know his tenantis, and all utheris haifand interes may haif "recourse thereto".'[9]

The next two Acts, those of 1555[10] and 1587[11] were more ambitious as they extended to all 'sessings upone preceptis that passis not

---

shows that the practice was much older. Such instruments were never common in England, however, and the practice may well have been brought into Scotland from France.
4   Stair, II.3.16.
5   Ross, i, 92.
6   E.g. *Young v Gordon's Trustees* (1847) 9 D 932.
7   A.P.S., ii, 252 (35).
8   A.P.S., ii, 360 (14).
9   *Ibid.*
10   A.P.S., ii, 497 (21).
11   A.P.S., iii, 455 (40).

furth of the Chancellarie'[12] bringing them into line with those which did, that is they became registrable in the books of the sheriff. But these Acts contain no sanction for non-performance of their requirements, whether by nullity or otherwise, and so cannot have been very effective in their operation.

This is clearly demonstrated by the fact that it was considered necessary to pass another Registration Act as soon as 1599.[13] This was an improvement on any of its predecessors, both in what it enacted and in the sanctions by which it attempted to secure obedience. Its main object was not the security of purchasers or third parties, but rather the protection of true owners from forged infeftments and other feudal documents, as is at once apparent from the words of the preamble:

> Considering the greit hurt his majesties subjectis sustenis and the innumerable falsetties daylie inventit by forging of divers privat writtis the same being keipit obscure quill the moyane of the tryell of the falset of thame to be takin away Speciallie instrumentis of seasingis, reversionis. . . [14]

By the operative part of the Act all such documents were to be null and 'to mak na faith in judgment' unless they were registered within forty days of their making in certain local registries established by the Act.

Developments in law are apt to be in the nature of experiments and this new conception of the penalty of nullity for non-registration was found to be a mixed blessing, simply because it enabled the unscrupulous granter of a disposition to deny it and to rely on its statutory nullity, even if he were clearly in the wrong and could be proved by other means to have granted it.[15] Moreover the inde-

---

12 A.P.S., ii, 497 (21).

13 A.P.S., iv, 184.

14   *Considering the great hurt his Majesty's subjects sustain and the innumerable falsities daily invented by forging divers private writs, the same being kept hidden while the means of the trial of the falsity of them be taken away, especially instruments of sasine, reversions . . .*

15 This is the sort of point on which the English court of Chancery proved so useful: 'In cases of fraud, equity should relieve, even against the words of the statute' [of Frauds]. *Viscountess Montacute v Maxwell* (1720) 1 P Wms 618 *per* Lord Parker, L.C. at 620. *See also Mundy v Joliffe* (1839) 4 My & Cr 167 at 177; *Whitbread v Brockhurst* (1784) 1 Bro CC 404 at 413; *Maddison v Alderson* (1883) 8 App Cas 467, *per* Lord Selborne L.C. at 475 and *per* Lord Blackburn at 489; Megarry and Wade, 561–2.

pendent and economical Scots revolted at this new and expensive
'tyranny.' The Act repealing it, the Abolition of Register Act
1609[16] is such a remarkable document that it warrants quotation:

> Forasmekle as the estaitis presentlie conveyned undirstanding the
> just grief and miscontent which the subjectis of this kingdome of
> all degreis and rankis has consavit upoun the [e]rectioun of that
> unnecessair register callit the register of the secretarie. . . . The
> same register serveing for little or na uther use then to acquire
> gayne and commoditie to the clerkis keiparis thairof and to draw
> his majesties good subjectis to neidles extraordinaire trouble
> tormoyle fascherie and expenss . . . the saidis estatis acknowlegeing
> and considering that faderlie cair qlk the kingis most sacred
> majestie has evir had to avoid the overchargeing of his heynes
> subjectis with only unnecessairie burdyngis and how that his
> majestie has evir abhored and detested the introductionn of ony
> new Innovationis qlkis howsoevir by private men for thair particu-
> lair gayne were pretendit for the good and benefite of the estaite
> do nevirtheless oftymes prove nothing but ane cullor for ane
> extraordinarie intentit extortioun of his majesties subjectis. . . .
> THAIRFORE the saidis estaitis . . . freethis exoneris and relevis
> all his majesties subjectis of that neidles and extraordiner bur-
> dyne.[17]

This language evidently proceeds from a health mistrust for lawyers
and their innovations, but the need for a systematic registration of
sasines was so keenly felt by the profession and others that only
eight years later we find the 'unnecessair register' reintroduced by
an Act of 1617.[18] It is obvious from the preamble, however, that it

16   A.P.S., iv, 407.

17   *Forasmuch as the estates presently convened understanding the just grief and*
        discontent which the subjects of this Kingdom of all degrees and ranks have
        conceived upon the erection of that unnecessary register called the register of
        the secretary . . . the same register serving for little or no other use than to
        acquire gain and commodity to the clerks and keepers thereof and to draw His
        Majesty's good subjects to needless extraordinary trouble turmoil bother and
        expense . . . the said estates acknowledging and considering the fatherly care
        which the King's most sacred Majesty has always had to avoid the overcharging
        of His Highness' subjects with any unnecessary burden and how that His
        Majesty has always abhorred and detested the introduction of any new
        innovations whatsoever by private men for their own gain which were pretended
        to be for the good and benefit of the estates do nevertheless often prove nothing
        but an excuse for an extraordinary intended extortion from His Majesty's
        subjects . . . THEREFORE the said estates . . . frees exoners and relieves all
        His Majesty's subjects of the needless and extraordinary burden.

18   A.P.S., iv, 545 (16) (Register Restored).

was the protection of purchasers from undisclosed third party rights and similar injustices which the re-establishment of the register was intended to achieve. After reciting the ills caused by such frauds, it tells us that they cannot be avoided unless 'the saidis privat rightis be maid publict and patent to his hienes lieges'. The Act proceeds to enact that there shall be a public register, in which all reversions, regresses '. . . and siclyke all instruments of seasing salbe registrat within thriescore dayes efter the date of the same.' The sanction for non-registration within the appointed time is that the documents not registered 'sall make no faithe in Judgement by way of actioun or exceptionn in prejudice of a third partie who hathe acquyred ane perfyit and lauchfull right to the saidis landis and heretages, but prejudice alwayis to thame to use the saidis writtis agains the pairtye maker thairof his heiris and successoures.'

The 1617 Act was not, however, the last enactment even of that century on the registration of sasines and other documents of title to land. A Registration Act of 1669,[19] which included resignations *ad remanentiam* within the necessity of registration, is of interest because it uses the simple phrase 'to be null' as its penalty in case of non-compliance.' A further Registration Act of 1693[20] is more important, however, for by it all infeftments, whether of property or of annual-rent or other real rights on which sasines should thereafter be taken, are to rank according to the priority of the date of registration, without regard to the distinction between base and public holdings, or between those clad with possession and those without it. This statute, by making the date of registration all-important in deciding between claims under different sasines, established clearly the result that an unregistered sasine could never compete with a registered one. Unregistered sasines compete *inter se* not according to date but according to the principles applicable to personal rights.[21]

The last Act needing consideration in the present context is the Evidence Act 1696[22] by which it is declared that 'no seasine or other writt or diligence appointed to be Registrat shall be of any force or

---

19 A.P.S., vii, 556 (4).
20 A.P.S., ix, 271 (22).
21 *Young v Gordon's Trustees* (1847) 9 D 932 at 941.
22 A.P.S., x, 60 (18).

effect against any but the granters and their heirs unless it be duely booked and inserted in the Register.' To be 'duly booked' a deed had to be presented and entered in the Minute Book within sixty days, although it was not necessarily engrossed in the Register within that period.[23]

The most interesting feature of a system of registration such as that of Scotland lies in the fact that it had to be applied to some very difficult cases. *Young v Gordon's Trustees*[24] is particularly interesting both because it went up to the House of Lords and because of the curious fact that it seems to have been the first major case in which it was emphatically decided that an unregistered sasine is absolutely void. Moreover, it affords an interesting subject for comparison, as it is probable that an English appeal to the House of Lords on comparable facts would have achieved a very different result.

The case related to the estate of General Thomas Gordon of the Greek army. He had inherited large estates in Aberdeenshire under the terms of a settlement made in 1745 by which the lands came after several generations in 1775 to the general's father, who had obtained an instrument of sasine, but did not have it registered until some nine months later (that is beyond the statutory time limit then in force). It was on his father's death in 1796 that the general succeeded. He was served heir of provision to his father under the destination and took out a precept from the Chancery, on which he was infeft. But this infeftment was never recorded. In 1810 General Gordon granted a fee-simple disposition to himself and his heirs and assignees whomsoever, on which a charter of resignation and infeftment followed. This barring should have been perfectly valid, because the settlement was not properly fenced and recorded under the Act of 1685. Finally in 1839 he executed a *mortis causa* disposition or trust settlement of all his property, heritable and moveable. After his death the heirs of provision under the original settlement of 1745 (and another of 1753, by which the superiority of the lands in question was settled on similar terms) raised a reduction of the deeds of 1810 and 1839, that is sought to have them set aside on the ground of nullity.

23 *Maclaine v Maclaine* (1855) 18 D (HL) 44.
24 (1847) 9 D 932.

The pursuers claimed on two grounds:

1 that the deeds were in violation of a clause of return contained in the two settlements of 1745 and 1753;[25]
2 that General Gordon was never validly infeft in the lands subject to the settlement, as an unregistered infeftment must be regarded as absolutely void.

The second argument was accepted by the Lord Ordinary, Lord Cuninghame. The lands therefore remained, and had remained throughout the general's lifetime, in the *haereditas jacens* of his great-uncle who died in 1775, that is the holder next before his father, who like the general himself had never had a sufficient title to the lands to take them out of the *haereditas*, which can only be done by a valid, that is properly registered, sasine. Consequently the deeds of 1810 and 1839 must be void, for *nemo dat quod non habet*.

On the appeal to the Inner House, four lords concurred in upholding the decision of Lord Cuninghame. They considered themselves bound by *Kibbles v Stevenson*.[26] The case having gone up to the House of Lords, that House remitted this difficult question of Scots law for the decision of the whole Court of Session. After a prolonged hearing, a majority of their lordships (ten in number) decided to uphold the judgment and to advise that the appeal should be dismissed. Two lords dissented. Said Lord Fullerton, who drew up the majority judgment:

> In case of an original conveyance the seisin of the disponee, if unregistered, does not divest the granter; for it leaves in him the heritable right, which may be validly acquired from him by a second disponee completing his title by a registered seisin. Again, in the case of seisins taken on succession, which are more analogous to that under consideration here, the seisin taken by an heir on the superior's precept could not, if unregistered, take the right out of the *haereditas jacens* of the ancestor. On the death of such heir, the successor must have been entitled and bound, if he wished to have a secure title, to take the right out of the *haereditas* of the party last infeft by a registered seisin, by serving to him and not to the party holding by the unregistered seisin.[27]

25 For the effects of such clauses, *see* Chapter 12.
26 (1831) 9 S 233.
27 (1847) 9 D 932 at 937.

This decision apparently ignores the literal words of the Act of 1696, that an unregistered sasine was to be void 'against any but the granter and his heirs'. The pursuers were claiming as heirs called in the destination of the deed of 1745. The Court of Session seems to have preferred to sacrifice literal accuracy to the preservation of its logical analysis of feudal principles. Their lordships must have felt certain qualms at this boldness, as their judgment closes with a defence:

> It may be said that this is a mere subtlety, undeserving of regard; and that the supposed anomaly of the contrary view is one but in theory, from which no practical inference ought to be drawn. It is sufficient to answer, that this is a question of title, of which the whole form and structure is built on theory. What is the whole doctrine of our real rights, as completed by constructive and symbolical delivery, but a combination of subtleties? But they are subtleties in which the strict adherence to theory is indispensable, for the best of all practical reasons, that the theory affords the only means of solving with certainty and consistency, those numerous questions, which would otherwise become the subject of loose and arbitrary adjudication. It is the theory and that theory rightly adhered to, which in this, as in other departments of law, unites the undigested series of separate cases into one consistent system of jurisprudence.[28]

This passage admirably sums up the gulf between the philosophical approach to law which prevails to the North of the Tweed and that to be found to the South. Such language is rarely, if ever, found in English reports. The English courts, holding to their maxims that 'Equity looks to the intent rather than to the form' and 'Equity regards as done that which ought to be done' would almost certainly have found against the pursuers, whereas the (supposed) absence of any conception of separate legal and equitable rights in the same land makes it difficult for Scots law to give effect to them. It is perhaps surprising that the English House of Lords did not use their undoubted power of interfering with Scots law on these appeals to achieve a more equitable result.

---

28 *Ibid.*, at 950.

THE RECORDING OF DOCUMENTS

The Act of 1617[29] provided that each writ presented for recording in the Register of Sasines had to be engrossed in the register within sixty days. This caused difficulty because it was often impossible to complete the engrossment in time, but the Evidence Act 1696[30] cured this difficulty by providing that no sasine or other writ appointed to be registered should be of any effect against any but the granters and their heirs unless it was duly booked and inserted in the register. The word 'booked' meant that it had to be entered in the Minute Book, within sixty days: it could be engrossed in the Record volume after the sixty days had passed. The Keeper added a certificate bearing the date of presentment and specified the book and folio of the record volume in which it was engrossed, and the principal instrument of sasine was returned to the person who presented it. The Titles to Land Consolidation (Scotland) Act 1868[31] provided that all conveyances with warrants of registration and all notarial instruments could be recorded in the general Register of Sasines during the lifetime of the grantee, and the date of entry in the Minute Book would be the date of registration.

The Land Registers (Scotland) Act 1868[32], provided that all writs should be recorded in the General Register of Sasines and that the Particular Registers of Sasine would be abolished before the end of 1871 except for burgage land which was recorded in the appropriate Burgh Register. It also provided that writs should be registered separately for each county.[33] Burgh Registers were discontinued by the Burgh Registers Act 1926[34] and incorporated in the appropriate division of the general Register of Sasines.

PRESENT PRACTICE IN SCOTLAND

The general Register of Sasines is the national land register of Scotland and forms the chief security of title to land in that every

29 A.P.S., iv, 545 (16) (Register Restored).
30 A.P.S., x, 60 (18).
31 S 15.
32 S 8.
33 The general Register of Sasines is divided into thirty-three Divisions applicable to the counties (including the County of the Barony and Regalty of Glasgow). The Divisions are grouped into eight Districts.
34 S 1.

writ affecting land must be registered, priority of title depending on priority of registration; and the register is open to the public. The method of registration is as follows:

1   The writ is posted to or presented at the Register House in Edinburgh and entered into the Presentment Book, which shows the priority of registration.
2   A draft Minute (which is an abstract of the writ based on the last Minute applicable to the land) is prepared, typed, revised, and checked against the writ. Any amendments can be made at this stage, and if an error has been made in the writ it can be uplifted, corrected and presented at a later date. If so, it then takes its priority from the later date.
3   The Minute is printed.
4   The Minute Book pages are assembled, checked, signed and bound, and copies are printed for future use.
5   The writ is photocopied and the Certificate of Registration endorsed on the original writ. The Register House seal is then impressed on each page and plan and the writ is returned to the solicitor who prepared it.
6   The photocopies for the Record Volume are assembled and bound. The bound volume is examined in the District and compared with the Minute Book.
7   The Minute Books and the Record Volumes are transmitted periodically to the Scottish Record Office for permanent custody.

The Keeper of the Registers makes up and maintains an index of names and an index of places showing in the Minute Books, which in turn give the book and folio number in the Record Volume. There is no index of the Record Volumes.

In the last decade mechanical methods have been widely used to produce the Minute Books, the Indexes and the Record Volumes, and have saved an immense amount of typing and time which was formerly spent in checking index slips.

The Minute Book provides members of the public with a simple and accurate method of obtaining information about all registered writs relating to property, and the whole process of registration depends upon the accuracy, completeness and clearness of the Minute. In 1871 the Register House introduced search sheets to enable searches into the titles to land to be made quickly and accurately without having to search laboriously through the Minute Books and Indexes. Whenever a separate piece of land is conveyed a new search sheet is made for it, with a print from the Minute showing the description of the ground conveyed.

By way of example, if say a tenant-in-chief of the Crown sells part of his land to a farmer, the transaction is shown on the tenant-in-chief's search sheet, and a new search sheet is opened showing the farm as a separate entity. In due course the farmer finds that his farm lies at the edge of an expanding town so he feus, say, thirty acres to a builder with a feu charter providing suitable conditions dealing with roads, footpaths, fences, drains, and so on, and a new search sheet is opened showing the thirty acres. The builder erects 240 houses on the thirty acres and grants a feu charter to each purchaser with additional conditions controlling drainage, fences between house plots, erection of garages and outhouses and so on. As each feu charter is recorded a new search sheet is opened for each house plot, which will show the history of the ownership of that plot and of all heritable securities, recorded servitudes, improvement grants, and so on, affecting it. The result is that the one search sheet opened on the sale of the farm has multiplied into 241 search sheets, and that number could well increase even more in the event of the provision of electricity sub-stations, or road widening schemes. However, the system is easy to use, it is very accurate and it has the side-effect of re-checking the titles of the property whenever a new search is asked for. The search is guaranteed by the government, although the search sheets themselves do not depend upon any statute for their existence.

There are professional searchers who issue a search guaranteed by an insurance company. Such guaranteed searches are made up from an examination of all the yearly volumes and Indexes of Minute Books. The method is laborious but extremely accurate.

The Books of Council and Session are another register of deeds affecting titles to land, and are particularly important when the land is held by trustees whose appointments and resignations are not recorded in the Register of Sasines. This Register begins in 1554 and is a safe deposit for important documents which might be lost. It is no longer necessary to have any consent to register a writ for preservation. The original is retained in the Register House and a certified copy or Extract is issued, which, by the Registered Writs Execution (Scotland) Act 1877,[35] is the equivalent of the writ itself.

If the writ contains an obligation to pay a sum of money (for instance a Bond and Disposition in Security or a Standard Security) the consent of the debtor to registration for preservation and execution is included in the deed. If the sums due remain unpaid the extract has added to it a warrant for all necessary action to enforce payment which has the effect of the decree of the Court of Session.

The Register of Services of Heirs was kept by the Chancery Office, which issued Extracts. Although the Succession (Scotland) Act 1964 abolished the procedure of service of heirs it is still possible to obtain service as heir to an ancestor who died before 10th September 1964.

The Register of Entails was established by the Entails Act 1685[36] (but since the Entail (Scotland) Act 1914 it has diminished greatly in importance) and since 1857[37] long Leases could be recorded in the Register of Sasines.

Searches in the Register of Inhibitions and Adjudications are regularly made. An inhibition is a writ which prohibits a debtor from selling or burdening his property and an adjudication is a transfer of property to a creditor in satisfaction of a debt. The Register also discloses sequestrations. In any transaction concerning land it is necessary to search in this Register against anyone who had an interest in the property during the five years preceding the transaction.

It seems that by 1874 Scotland had reached the conclusion which England had reached several centuries before, namely that a single deed could be sufficient to transmit the title to lands; but a really vital difference remains, for in order to be effective such a deed must be registered in the appropriate register in the manner prescribed by the Acts. Until so registered it effects merely a change in the personal rights of the parties as no sasine is given.

Scotland has thus a full system of registration for most documents

35   S 5.
36   *See* Chapter 20.
37   Registration of Leases (Scotland) Act 1857.

affecting the title to land. But she has not yet achieved the full-scale system of title registration known to most countries overseas.

DEVELOPMENT OF THE SYSTEM IN ENGLAND

England still lags far behind Scotland in the matter of land registration, though English landowners in the Middle Ages clearly saw the value of some incontrovertible official records being kept of their dealings with land. This accounts for the great popularity of the fine throughout that period, a third copy as already noted being enrolled in the archives of the court.[38] But the English lawyers never advanced from that point to a universal, compulsory register of deeds, still less that complete system of registration of title just mentioned. That revolutionary monarch Henry VIII was in favour of such a register of deeds and at the time of the Statute of Enrolments 1536 a bill was prepared to set it up, but this never passed into law.[39] It has, however, been suggested that the Scots statutes on the subject were derived from this idea.[40] Since the earliest Scots Act dates from 1503 may it not just possibly be the case that the opposite is true?

The system established by the Statute of Enrolments 1536 broke down largely because it was not applicable to all dispositions by way of bargain and sale. The cunning of the English lawyers was thus directed against registration from the very outset. One may suspect that it had been the opposition of the conveyancers which had broken down the proposal for a wider register, for although there was a considerable desire among merchants in the seventeenth century for an efficient system of recorded titles, such as that then known in the Netherlands, whereby they might be more secure in lending money on the security of landed property,[41] nothing further was done on the subject of land registration in England as a whole until 1925.

There were, however, established in the early eighteenth century two experimental local systems of deeds registries applying to the

38 *See* Chapter 24.
39 Potter, *Historical Introduction to English Law*, 512.
40 Ross, *Lectures*, ii, 205.
41 Dr Farran expressed his indebtedness for this point to Professor G. P. Jones, Sheffield.

most populous and largest counties in England: Middlesex and York-shire.[42] These registers were not registers of title: any documents purporting to deal with the legal estate in land in these two counties had to be entered in them, as it still must be in Yorkshire. The would-be purchaser must still carry out that cumbersome and expensive investigation of title which has for so long been the bug-bear of English land purchasers and the bread and butter of English conveyancers. He is protected only by the existence of the register from the possibility of non-registered deeds affecting the legal estate being valid. If he gets a disposition to himself registered, it will prevail over all unregistered deeds whether prior or subsequent to it in time of creation. Registration constitutes notice to all the world of the deed, so that it is necessary to search the register before dealing with any land subject to it. But none of this has any application to the enforceability of equitable estates and interests which may exist in the land. Memorials of documents exclusively connected with these do not have to be entered in the local registry; if the purchaser has notice of them, he will be bound by them whether or not the disposition to him is properly registered.[43]

The effect of all this is not so very different from the situation in Scotland, even to the extent that there a period on the register unchallenged may operate by way of positive prescription to give validity to a disposition which would otherwise be invalid.[44] Para-doxes seem to abound in this subject, but it may be noted again that it was in England that land could be conveyed simply by documents alone[45] while in Scotland elaborate ceremonies were necessary until the middle of the nineteenth century. Yet it is Scotland which developed a system of registration of deeds earlier: England has not done so even now except in certain special localities.

42 Middlesex Registry Act 1708 (7 Anne c 20); and now Yorkshire Registries Act 1884 (replacing earlier legislation: 2 & 3 Anne c 4; 6 Anne cc 20, 62; 8 Geo 2 c 6). This Act applied only to the Ridings and Kingston-upon-Hull. York was exempt-ed, not being part of any Riding; and there was also a register (Construction of the Bedford Level Act) 15 Car 2 c 17) for lands forming part of Bedford level: *see* *Willis v Brown* (1839) 10 Sim 127.
43 For details *see* 23 Halsbury's *Laws of England* (3rd edn) paras 892 *et seq.*
44 *See* Chapter 23. Twenty years was the normal period (Conveyancing (Scotland) Act 1924, s 16); it is now reduced to ten years by the Conveyancing and Feudal Reform (Scotland) Act 1970, s 8.
45 By lease and release (*see* Chapter 24).

The registration of assurances is not the only possible way of safeguarding land purchasers: another method is the registration of third party rights, whereby, once the purchaser has discovered the person or persons having the legal estate which he wishes to purchase he can depend on a search of official registers to tell him what rights, if any, exist in favour of others than the vendor. This is also to the advantage of the third party, as he no longer has to depend on such risky doctrines as that of notice where his right is purely equitable. Such a system of registration of third party rights was adopted (with considerable reservations) for the whole of England and Wales by the Land Charges Act 1925. A registered land charge is deemed to be notified to all the world, so that no purchaser can eliminate it by any juggling with the doctrine of notice. Conversely, an unregistered land charge is normally ineffective against a purchaser of the legal estate who has duly examined the register. However, some third party rights are not registrable, for example, those under settlements; but these may now be overreached on a sale.

Yet even a register of third party rights is far from satisfactory. The conveyance of land will never be a simple and straightforward affair until Great Britain adopts the out-and-out system of a registered title to the land which prevails in practically all civilised countries. By this is meant a scheme of conveyancing which no longer envisages the transfer of the title to land by means of deeds or other transactions *inter partes*, but which directs that a register of the title to land shall be kept, just as every company having shares keeps a register of its shareholders. Under such a land system questions of disputed title can hardly ever arise, for the State guarantees the title of the person whose name is on the register as owner, paying compensation, if necessary, if any one is harmed through a mistaken registration. The legal title to land under such a system can only pass by the removal of the name of the vendor and the insertion of the name of the purchaser in his stead. Great simplicity may be introduced by insisting that all third party rights shall be entered in the same register, though in a separate space or column.[46]

46 *See* generally Ruoff and Roper, *Law and Practice of Registered Conveyancing*; Rowton Simpson, *Land Law and Registration*; and Hayton, *Registered Land*; Megarry and Wade, 1057–84; Cheshire 103–12 and 766–83.

England, having tried out the system of registering deeds on a local basis, next proceeded (without interfering with the position in those counties where it had been tried) to experiment with the more fundamental revolution of a system of registered title. This was first done under the Land Transfer Act 1875 on a voluntary basis, and it became compulsory for the London County Council area in 1898.[47] The Land Registration Act 1925, merely restated the law as to this area with some improvements and gave power to the king in council to extend the area of compulsory registration. Many years have elapsed since then, but at first the power was used sparingly, extending compulsory registration to Middlesex,[48] Surrey, Eastbourne, Hastings, Oxford, Oldham, Leicester and parts of Kent. 'Since the end of the war in 1945, many Orders in Council have been made extending the compulsory system, all at the instance of local authorities and,' says Simpson, 'the tide of public opinion appears to have turned decisively in its favour. A plan to extend compulsory registration to the whole country by 1973, announced in August 1964, was thwarted by the economic situation which precluded (or at least made politically undesirable) an increase in the number of civil servants'.[49] However, an accelerated programme was undertaken in 1965, which aimed at including all urban areas with populations over 10 000 by 1973 and the rest of the country by 1980.[50] Progress has been slower than was intended, but nevertheless by the end of 1970 half the population of the country was in compulsory areas.[51]

There is no denying the lack of enthusiasm for registration of title in England. When the legislators of 1925 were carrying out their massive reorganisation in both the theory and the practice of English land law, they had a magnificent opportunity for taking a bold step such as had been taken centuries before in so many continental countries. Cheshire himself remarked that it might well have been

47 By virtue of the Land Transfer Act 1897.
48 The Middlesex Deeds Registry was closed in 1936, having become redundant.
49 Rowton Simpson, *Land Law and Registration*, 49.
50 *See* (1966) 110 *Solicitors' Journal*, 37. The procedure was simplified by the Land Registration Act 1966.
51 Megarry and Wade, 1059. *See* the list of compulsory registration areas in Hayton, *Registered Land*, 159–63.

better if they had taken it.[52] Why, then, was this not done? On this, as on so many points, the English law seems to be unable to make up its mind and hovers between registration of deeds, registration of title, and registration of third party rights. It is no harm to experiment, but it seems less than logical, some would even say less than sensible, to retain the experiments in different parts of so small a jurisdiction. Surely, if registered deeds are effective and desirable in Yorkshire (except York) they are equally desirable in Somerset? Or if they are not a success, why preserve them at all? Again, if a registered title is thought to be efficient and sensible in some areas, why not others?

No British subject should, it may be said, examine the legal institutions of his country on the basis of logic. Many of our greatest and most enduring institutions are illogical and many anomalies must be placed to the credit of our diverse and interesting history. But are these anomalies of registration and non-registration justifiable on historical grounds? Is it not the truth that the same force which prevented the sensible proposal of Henry VIII for a register of deeds is still at work? The general public knows little and, until its purse is touched, cares little for these matters. Only when they have to pay the fees on a transfer of land and wait months while the title is being investigated, do they wonder whether it is all really necessary. Experience from the London area and the rest of the world beyond the British islands suggests that it is not.

Scotland led the way magnificently in her early establishment of registered sasines. But she, too, has so far failed to take this greater step. Again, one may wonder why, when the conveyancing reforms of 1874 – which were most satisfactory as far as they went – came in, a systematic scheme of registered title was not also developed at the same time. It would have been fully in accord with the pioneering spirit in the matter of registers hitherto shown by that country and admirably suited to her logical and civilian approach to legal questions. It will not be long now, however, before a fully developed system of registration of title in Scotland will be introduced: the proposals are discussed in Chapter 31.

---

52 *Modern Real Property* (6th edn), 84.

28 Effects of the Union

The three cardinal principles of English land law (the doctrine of tenure, the conception of estates, the importance of seisin) have now been considered together with their Scots equivalents, so far as these exist. It only remains to consider briefly the effect on the land laws of the two countries of the united constitution which they at present enjoy. A general discussion of the effects of the Union on the legal systems of England and Scotland though highly topical at the time of writing, while the Devolution Bill hovers before Parliament, is worthy of a volume of its own and clearly cannot be attempted here.

THE CROWN

The accession of a King of Scots to the throne of Edward I (one of history's ironies) resulted in a mere personal union. No doubt such a union of the crowns need not of itself have caused the slightest change in the internal law of the common monarch's separate kingdoms; but remembering what happened in Ireland one might reasonably wonder whether Scots law too would be as wholly merged in English law as is the law of Wales if the union had come about in any other way than through the succession of a Stuart to the throne of England.

The legal effect of the personal union was carefully examined by the English Lord Chancellor and twelve common law judges in *Calvin's case*.[1] The point at issue was a land law one, namely whether a Scot born after the accession of James VI to the English throne was

---

1 (1608) 7 Co Rep 1.

an alien born so as to be incapable of holding English land,[2] but the court seized the opportunity of discoursing at great length on various legal aspects of the succession of King James and held that England and Scotland remain several and distinct kingdoms and are governed by several judicial or municipal laws.

There can be no doubt as to the correctness of this decision. Indeed, it is mainly remarkable for the absence of any reference to the alleged ancient unity of the Kingdoms,[3] which might, if the uniting sovereign had been English, well have been used as a pretext for reducing these 'separations yet remaining,' a possibility which is illustrated by the events which followed. As soon as power in England passed from the Scottish Stuarts into English revolutionary hands, a move was made towards a closer union. Without consulting Scotland, the illegally constituted 'parliament' of England declared a union of the two countries, graciously permitting thirty Scots to represent their countrymen at Westminster.[4] When this decree was proclaimed at Edinburgh Merket Cross the Scots 'showed no rejoicing at it.'[5]

The Commonwealth parliament was a weak and short-lived institution and the changes in Scots law and its administration introduced by the force of Cromwell's military power were little more enduring. One of his ordinances completely overhauled most of Scots land law as then understood. It abolished all heritable and other landed jurisdiction and offices, all hosting and personal service to superiors and all casualties of superiority.[6] These were desirable reforms, which have all been achieved by more orderly methods in subsequent centuries, but in thus forcing them on Scotland Cromwell was doing her a great injustice. Inevitably, the abolition of such things became identified with English influence and was consequently abhorrent to patriotic Scots who saw in these antiquities the national characteristics of their own land system, whereas they were

---

2   It became an established principle of both systems in the later Middle Ages that an alien could not hold landed property; this was not so in the period of common development (pre-Edward I), when it was common for landowners to have estates on both sides of the Border.

3   Cf Title to the Throne Act 1603.

4   *Acts and Ordinances of the Commonwealth*, ii, 871–5.

5   Whitelock, *Memorials*, 532.

6   *Acts and Ordinances of the Commonwealth*, ii, 873–4.

by no means especially Scottish, but had existed also in England, although for various reasons they had become obsolete there, for the most part long before the seventeenth century.

Cromwell's main reform was not, however, in the field of land law, but in that of procedure and the organisation of the courts. The Court of Session was abolished and instead a supreme court for Scotland was set up consisting of seven judges, four of them Englishmen.[7] With the suppression of all feudal jurisdictions and the introduction of judicial circuits on the English model the Scots administration of justice became much more centralised that it had ever been before. Other reforms included the use of English instead of Latin in all legal documents, including land charters.[8]

But with the restoration of Charles II's lawful authority all the king's horses and all the king's men succeeded to a remarkable extent in putting Humpty Dumpty together again. Unlike the similar ordinances in England,[9] Cromwells' Scottish land law reforms had been premature and were rescinded. The whole edifice of superiors' jurisdictions, hosting and casualties was miraculously re-erected sufficiently stoutly to last another eighty-five years. The alien intruders on the bench were expelled and the Court of Session restored exactly as before. The Commonwealth was treated as an unfortunate interregnum, to be forgotten as soon as conveniently might be. But nonetheless some important intangibles remained: in particular Scotland had learned the value of a centralised and efficient administration of justice. Her leading jurist, Stair, had been a member of Cromwell's bench,[10] yet shone more brightly than before after the Restoration. Some have ascribed his wide knowledge of English law to his experience of working with English colleagues.[11] Possibly this led also to his taking an interest in legal theory and

---

7   Mackay, *Stair*, 60. Their decisions were not published until a century later (1762) as *the Decisions of the English Judges during the Usurpation 1655–61.*

8   On the Restoration they had again to be put into Latin, but this did not last long, and by the eighteenth century English had superseded Latin in practice, although either language could be used. Crown charters were drawn in Latin for longer than those of subjects. Cromwell had made a similar ordinance requiring the use of English in English legal documents, but there English had already long superseded Latin in legal documents except in forensic conveyances such as the fine.

9   The Tenures Act 1660 was merely a legislation of what had taken place previously.

10   Mackay, *Stair*, 65.

11   *Ibid.*, 66.

therefore indirectly to the publication of his great *Institutions*. This was Scotland's first really national major law treatise, though Professor Walker has pointed out[12] that Stair did not necessarily have his interest in legal theory inspired by his English contacts: he had, after all, previously been a Regent (Professor) of Philosophy in the College of Glasgow.

The experience of political unity was not altogether wasted. Ever since the accession of James I there had been advocates of a complete unification between the two countries and their legal systems, though this movement became an effective force only towards the close of the century. Having neglected an opportunity to dissolve the personal union in 1688,[13] the Scots were becoming gradually more and more used to the idea of a close cooperation with England, which benefited Scotland quite as much as, if not more than, the southern kingdom.

PARLIAMENT

Eventually, in the reign of the last Stuart sovereign, a real, parliamentary union was achieved. England and Scotland with their separate parliaments were no longer to exist, becoming merged in the newer entity of Great Britain. Scotland was henceforward to be North Britain, England presumably South Britain, although the title did not endure for even the century or so that 'North Britain' was officially employed.

By the eighteenth article of union the Scots laws as to customs and excise may be made the same as those in England, but 'all other laws in use within the kingdom of Scotland do after the union and notwithstanding thereof, remain in the same force as before . . . but alterable by the Parliament of Great Britain. . . . But that no alteration be made in laws which concern private right except for evident

12   In reviewing Dr Farran's original edition of this work (1959) 75 LQR 595.
13   William and Mary owed the throne to their election by the English Lords and Commons (see the Bill of Rights 1688), so the Scots could then have elected a new sovereign of their own or adhered to King James VII or his Son. When the Union was being discussed in 1669 the Scots Commissioners would not agree to the words 'and successors' after the mention of the King's heirs, for they said, by the law of England even a usurper is a 'successor' of the King and, as they saw it, the whole point of the Union was that James VI's issue should rule the resulting new State. (Mackay, *Stair*, 89).

utility of the subjects within Scotland.' By the following section the Court of Session is to be retained with all its former powers and privileges. Special guarantees are given that the courts in Westminster Hall and the Chancery will not interfere with it or the other Scottish courts. As has been remarked by Lord Dunedin,[14] it is noteworthy that no guarantees were thought necessary the other way!

During the period of the personal union, from 1603 to 1707, the two systems did not have very much effect on each other. Both countries retained their own parliaments, law courts, great and small, and their own land laws; but it is difficult to agree with the assertion that 'if one excepts the period of the usurpation, there is no indication that English and Scots law made any kind of contact during the seventeenth century.'[15] For example, it seems probable that the Scots entail, with its irritant and resolutive clauses, was modelled on an English pattern (originally invented by an Irishman).[16] Changes in the Scots law of forfeiture may well have been due to a desire to equalise the penalties for similar crimes against a common sovereign.[17] The growing Scots practice of reporting judicial decisions, which had been very rare before 1603, was probably due to English ideas being adopted. The first printed series of reports in Scotland were (significantly) those of Stair (1683–1687), though Durie's reports (first printed in 1690) cover cases back to 1621 and there are a few cases in Morison's *Dictionary of Decisions* (printed 1801–1804) from the sixteenth century.[18]

The Commonwealth judges may have influenced the development of Scots law more than the Scots, at least of a later day, would be ready to admit: not only did they bring the very high standards of the English judiciary before Scottish eyes for at least consideration, and, one suspects, emulation;[19] but their methods of pronouncing judgment and of respecting the precedents of their Scottish forebears

14   *English and Scottish Law*, (Murray Lecture) 8.
15   MacGillivray, 'The Influence of English Law,' *Sources* (Stair Society, Vol 1), 217.
16   *See* Chapter 20.
17   *See* Chapter 12.
18   *See* the lists of reports as Appendix to Native Sources: in Leadbetter, 'The Printed Law Reports,' *Sources* (Stair Society, Vol 1) 47. In 1692 the Advocates Library is known to have contained Coke, Littleton, Selden, Hale and other English works. (MacGillivray, 'The Influence of English Law,' *Sources* (Stair Society, Vol 1) 217).
19   Nicholls, *Recollections and Reflections*, 104.

(so far as these were reported) may have set the Scots courts on a new footing, both of care in examining precedents[20] and of generally considering their judgments in a way probably not common in Scotland before 1650.

It is more difficult to cite examples of results the other way. James I may well have brought his own theories of the state and government with him from Scotland, but, if so, it mattered little, for they did not gain a permanent place in English legal thinking; indeed, if anything rather the reverse, because they caused Coke and his party to clarify both in their own minds and for posterity what the English common law was on these matters.

Paradoxically enough, the effect of the union of 1603 (in so far as it had any effects on private law at all) may lie in the strengthening of Scots law from outside attack. The Scots law of 1707 was a well-established system, based securely on feudal and Roman foundations, but equipped with important sources of its own in Craig, Hope, Mackenzie and, especially, Stair. It own ideas, for example, on entails and the registration of sasines, were clearly defined by legislation. It was therefore in a much better state to ensure its continued independent existence than it had been in 1603. Separate development of Scottish jurisprudence would very probably have come to an end had the full union come about then.

Having regard to the section already quoted by which Scotland was to retain her own laws except on matters of custom and excise, it might be thought that the union of 1707 would have had almost as little effect on the private law of England and Scotland as had that of 1603. Such, however, was not the case, and it is proposed to consider here very briefly some of the factors which led to such convergence as took place, although land law was one field particularly resistant to convergent tendencies. It has been observed that 'There are certain fields which are open to English influence more than others. For instance, in the law relating to land tenure and conveyancing the two systems have diverged so much that there is no possible point of contact.'[21] While this probably overstates the position a little it must be admitted that the convergent tendencies

20 MacGillivray, 'The Influence of English Law,' *Sources* (Stair Society, Vol I) 220.
21 *Ibid.*

were very much greater in such fields as commercial law, which are nowadays governed by almost the same rules in both countries.[22]

It was the express purpose of the Act of Union to create a common legislature. The Act gives this common Parliament power to amend every branch of the public and private law of either country, with the proviso that the Scots law in matters of 'private right' should not be altered 'except for [the] evident utility of the subject within Scotland'.[23] It is often said that the sovereignty of Parliament implies that no restriction can be laid on future parliaments, but this looks very like an attempt to do so. Clearly a change not for such 'evident utility' would be unconstitutional, but what tribunal could pronounce it so?

As the united parliament is composed of representatives from both countries, it is difficult to ascertain where a legislative reform may be said to be directly due to the fact of the Union and not merely to 'progress' and the change of human ideas. Thus probably in the ultimate analysis the most salient features of modern Scots and English land law, as opposed to that of most other countries, are:

1   the absence of a general system of registered title to land;
2   the large measure of protection afforded to tenants by such things as the Rent Acts;[24]
3   the serious restrictions placed on the free use and development of land under the Town and County Planning Acts[25] and the Community Land Act 1976.

Of these, the last two may well be due to the changing times, but if we turn to Ireland, which might have shared in the legislation but for her political intractibility, it can be seen that not all states move in these matters at the same pace. It may therefore not be unreasonable to assume that but for the Union these elements of the utmost practical importance in our land laws might well have been arrived at at different dates, and probably to a different extent, in the two countries. This is emphasised when we consider how in so many

22   E.g. the Sale of Goods Act 1893 was originally drafted to apply in England only, but was subsequently made applicable to Scotland also by means of a number of relative minor adjustments.
23   Eighteenth Article of Union.
24   Though these are not known more widely than was the case a few years ago.
25   But see Garner (ed), *Planning Law in Western Europe*.

branches of land law before the Union Scotland went at a slower pace in sweeping away her long established feudal principles than England, while on the other hand, Scotland led the way with the registration of sasines. Again, England reformed her land law radically in 1925, and Scotland has proposed a system of registration of titles which should no doubt pass freely enough at Westminster now that the Scots lawyers themselves are agreed on the form they will take.[26]

On these general matters, then, the Union may well have had a unifying (and, possibly in the case of Scotland, an expediting) effect. It is not so easy to cite examples of particular changes being effected by legislation in the land laws of the two countries as a direct result of the Union. One, already noticed is the introduction into Scots law of a remainder for the purposes of the forfeiture law for treason.[27] This clearly sprang from the Union, as did the narrowing of the scope of treason in Scots law to the limits of the English act of Edward III.[28] This reduced the circumstances in which a Scottish landowner ran the risk of forfeiture for crime, since, among other things, theft in landed men had formerly been accounted treason in Scotland. Most of the statutes relating to the compulsory purchase of land show signs of English draftsmanship. More important perhaps is the fact that the ancient territorial jurisdictions and the personal attendance of vassals on superiors in time of war, which were some of the most characteristic features of Scottish land-holding, were finally swept away by a parliament essentially antagonistic to everything Scottish, as expressed in the support of Prince Charles Edward Stuart. This led to the ending of the Celtic land-holding which had endured until then in the Highlands. It must be doubtful whether the nineteenth century sweeping away of an entail law to which English lawyers have always been intensely antagonistic, would have passed so readily in a wholly Scottish legislature. With it came the introduction into Scots law of a particularly English conception – a modified rule against perpetuities, of which until then Scotland does not seem to have felt any great need.[29]

26   *See* Chapter 30 and 31.
27   *See* Chapter 12.
28   The Treason Act 1351 is still the basis of the United Kingdom's treason law.
29   *See* Chapter 21.

THE COURTS

The Act of Union made no reference to the carrying of Scots appeals to the new parliament for the simple reason that the commissioners were unable to agree on the point. As early as 1669 the Scottish delegates had made it clear that they wished the old appeal to the parliament of Scotland, whose scope was a matter of dispute, to die with that institution.[30] The English maintained that the House of Lords of Great Britain as the lineal successor of the Scottish House of Lords could not be denied one of its most vital privileges.

For better or worse, however, the House of Lords has exercised the power of hearing civil appeals from the Scots courts as well as those of England and Ireland (Northern Ireland only, since 1921). Scots criminal appeals have never been heard by the House of Lords. If there had been some provision for the presence of members of the House trained in Scots law from 1707 onwards (as there now is), this would have seemed an eminently sensible arrangement, whereby the best judges from both countries would sit together to hear appeals of special difficulty or importance from anywhere in the United Kingdom: but this was not the case. Although the Act of Union made provision for Scottish peers to sit in the House of Lords, no arrangement was made by which one or more of them should be legally trained. Consequently, until the elevation of Lord Colonsay to the peerage in 1867 the ultimate appellate tribunal for Scots cases was composed invariably of English-trained judges, headed by a Lord Chancellor of Great Britain chosen as a matter of course from England.[31] The results of this anomaly have been examined elsewhere at length,[32] so that it is only necessary here to see whether or not it has resulted in any changes of importance being introduced into Scots land laws as a result of the English law lords' prejudices or misconceptions.

The English Law Lords did not try blindly to apply English legal

---

30 Mackay, *Stair*, 90.
31 Lord Bathurst, L.C. was advised by Lord Mansfield on a Scots appeal: Campbell, *Lives of the Lord Chancellors*, v, 457.
32 MacQueen, *Appellate Jurisdiction of the House of Lords*; *see also* Gibb, *Law from Over the Border*.

concepts to Scots cases, but examined their own qualifications to exercise this jurisdiction with some care. Thus Lord Wynford after considering a point of Scots entail law before him and the English rule on the same subject had misgivings about deciding it in a purely English manner. He said:

> I protest against what has been said in another place, namely that English lawyers are not competent to advise your Lordships in a question of Scotch law. As well might they say, that one who has studied logic in Edinburgh would not be able to reason on any question of morality or policy that arose in England, although in possession of all the circumstances connected with the case to be discussed. One who is acquainted with the general principles of jurisprudence, and has been in the habit of investigating legal questions, of interpreting written laws, and weighing the authorities on which unwritten laws depend,[42] will be fully competent to decide points arising under the laws of any country. Such a person would make up for his want of familiarity with the subject brought before him, by the additional caution and attention which the novelty of the case would naturally excite. If he has not so much knowledge of the subject as Scotch lawyers may have, before he has heard and considered the arguments and authorities, he will decide on such as are adduced without any preconveived prejudice . . . I have forgotten that I was ever connected with English jurisprudence. I have formed my opinion on Scotch authorities alone.[33]

High tribute has on occasion been paid to the way in which the English judges have adhered to these principles, even by Scottish writers,[34] but this was not always the case, as may readily be seen by comparing with the last two sentences quoted the following passage from a judgment in which the House of Lords overruled the unanimous decision of the Court of Session. The Lord Chancellor (Lord Eldon) was considering the power of leasing of Scots tailzied fiars. Said he:

> Your Lordships are aware that, according to the law of England (*which appears to me to be much better in this respect than the law of Scotland*), if a person becomes, by limitation, the absolute owner

---

33 *Stewart v Fullarton* (1830) 4 W & S 196 at 232.
34 E.g. MacGillivray, 'The Influence of English Law,' *Sources* (Stair Society, Vol 1) 218–19.

of an estate, if you attempt to restrain him from making leases, you make an attempt which is repugnant to the very nature of the estate given to him, and that will have no effect at all. It is clearly otherwise in the law of Scotland.[35]

The truth is that the English lawyers had certain ideas so firmly instilled in their minds that even their best intentions could not entirely remove them. Thus to take an obvious example, English lawyers traditionally so distrusted and disapproved of entails and especially unbarrable entails, that they could not forget these prejudices even when sitting to hear cases from a system which knew no such prejudice. Indeed the English-staffed House of Lords made radical alterations in the Scots law of entails because they could not entirely put aside that dread of 'perpetuities' which had so long characterised their own jurisprudence. Sometimes these decisions upset longstanding decisions of the Court of Session; sometimes the effect of a contrary decision on English law was made an excuse for the changes which were made.[36]

JUDICIAL PRECEDENT

Another fundamental prejudice or belief of the English judges went even further than this, although on a general point rather than one of special land law interest. Everyone knows that the cardinal feature of English law and its offshoots has always been the very high respect paid to judicial precedent.[37] It is clear that Scotland in 1707 knew no such rule.[38] Thus Erskine tells us that decisions:

> have no proper authority in similar cases because the tacit consent, on which unwritten law is founded, cannot be inferred from the judicial proceedings of any court of law, however distinguished by dignity or character, and judgments ought not to be pronounced by examples or precedents. . . . Decisions, therefore, though they bind the party litigating, create no obligation on the judges to

35 *Duke of Queensberry v Marquess of Queensberry* (1830) 4 W & S 254 at 258.
36 *See* Chapter 21.
37 *See* e.g. Roscoe Pound, *The Development of American Law and its Deviation from English Law* (1951) 67 LQR 49 *et seq*; Cross, *Precedent in English Law*; Dias, *Jurisprudence*, 162–217.
38 Smith, *British Justice: the Scottish Contribution*, 84–7; Gibb, *Law from over the Border*, 55 *et seq.*

follow in the same tract, if it shall appear to them to be contrary
to law. It is, however, certain that they are frequently the occasion
of establishing usages which, after they have gathered force by a
sufficient length of time, must, from the tacit consent of the state,
make part of our unwritten law. What has been said of the decisions
of the Court of Session is also applicable to the judgments pronounced on appeal by the House of Lords: for in these that august
Court acts in the character of judges, not of lawgivers; and consequently their judgments, though they are final as to the parties
in the appeal, cannot introduce any general rule which shall be
binding either on themselves or inferior courts.[39]

Yet at the present day Scotland has the doctrine of precedent as
fully as England.[40] How has this come about? One must not look
for legislation on such a fundamental topic. The change has come
about gradually over the years since 1707, through the operation,
it is suspected, of English prejudices and assumptions in favour of
the doctrine at the highest judicial level. Thus to take but one
example, Lord Brougham, L.C., expressly told the Scots courts that
his decision was binding on them:

> Though our decision overrules their decree, yet it is framed
> according to the principles of the Law of Scotland, adheres to the
> law and declares the law, not permitting it to be altered by judicial
> construction. If it is to be altered, it must be done by authority of
> the legislature. I am far from saying that no change is required,
> but I am very clear that it is not to be made by any court other
> than the High Court of Parliament.[41]

This pronouncement was based on the English conception of the
binding nature of a House of Lords decision, which was not the view
of eighteenth century Scotland. The contest here was more than a
national one. It was one between the Civil law and the Common law.
At one time it looked as if Scotland, taught by Stair and Erskine,
was to pass firmly into the former camp,[42] though for reasons closely
connected with the Union, this was not to be. Consequently Scotland
now finds herself with a foot in each camp, as she has the fundamental
English rule of precedent, but also the general philosophic approach

39 Erskine, I.1.47.
40 Leadbetter, 'The Printed Law Reports,' *Sources* (Stair Society, Vol 1) 43 *et seq.*
41 *Sharpe v Sharpe* (1835) 1 S & M 622 at 627.
42 Lord Cooper, *Scottish Legal Tradition*, 11.

and many of the detailed rules of Roman law. This introduction of precedent into Scots law may be thought not to have much direct bearing on land law, but it seems almost certain that but for the Union Scotland would have suffered, or achieved, a complete reception of Roman conceptions, which would probably have meant an abandonment of feudal land law altogether in favour of a continental style of registration. Curiously enough, without the English doctrine of precedent, Scots land law might not be such a nationally distinct system at the present time; for that doctrine implies conservatism in the law and is an effective barrier to all but legislative changes of a revolutionary character. If the English judges in the House of Lords thus forced some of their own ideas on Scots law, they also probably saved it from a merger in continental law, which might have been annihilating as far as her traditional land law was concerned.

Another English prejudice was to regard citation of the Roman law, even as a persuasive authority, with grave suspicion. Thus Lord Brougham remarked in a Scottish appeal: 'I not only deny the authority of the Civil Law as a direct authority, I deny the weight of it – the general deference to it – in a question of merchantile law, in merchantile times and in a merchantile country.'[43] Had he been hearing an English case, this language might well be justifiable, but it was clearly wrong as a declaration of Scottish principle whereby Roman law has been saluted as 'the great foundation of our laws and forms'.[44] As regard for precedent grew, respect for Civil law declined.

Although the convergence of Scots and English land law has been considerably less than in other fields, it is not true that there has been no convergence at all. Scots land law of 1924 had very much more in common with English land law than was the case in 1706 or 1602. How far this was the result of the Unions must be a matter of conjecture, but to argue that it is wholly due to mere coincidence would be absurd. A new and important divergence between all three land laws of the United Kingdom was caused by the English

---

43 *Thomson v Campbell's Trustees* (1833) 5 W & S 16. *See also Clarke v Carfin Coal Co* [1891] AC 412 where Roman Law had been applied by the Court of Session, whose decision was overruled by the House of Lords.

44 Mackenzie, *Works of Sir George Mackenzie*, ii, 7.

reforming legislation of 1925, which made so much of English land law statutory in form that this is now a sharp distinction between the systems. Its deepening of the distinction between the legal and equitable estate caused a further, new divergence, although in one sense this was a move towards Scottish ways of thinking and away from the traditional English doctrine of estates.[45]

DEVELOPMENT OF THE LAW

Apart from the existence of a common legislature already considered, the influence of Scots law on English law until the late nineteenth century was admittedly very slight. This is not to say that Scots-born judges were not to be found on the English bench. Such names as Cockburn, Blackburn, and Mansfield, spring to mind at once (to say nothing of living examples). Presumably these Scots would not have obtained high judicial posts in England if the Union had not taken place, but would have risen to the highest posts in their native country and enriched its jurisprudence with the ability which they lent elsewhere. But few of those judges had had a Scottish legal training. It is therefore doubtful whether one can view their contribution to the development of English law as a result of the influence of Scots law concepts. To this there is one brilliant exception – Lord Mansfield – who had a considerable knowledge of Scots as well as continental law, although he had no formal Scottish qualifications. The influence of this Lord Chief Justice on English legal development was very extensive, especially in the field of commercial law.[46] We need only glance at the land law to see if it extended there. His attempts to upset the traditional illogicality and unfairness of the English view of seisin by introducing notions of investiture borrowed from the Books of the Feus and Scots law as understood in his day have been discussed earlier.[47] They were not received with much favour, although some judges ventured to follow his lead.[48] He also made strenuous efforts to break the dead hand of

45 *See* Chapter 16.
46 *See* Fifoot, *Lord Mansfield.*
47 *See* Chapter 23.
48 *See* Holdsworth, *H.E.L.*, vii, 56 *et seq.*

the rule in *Shelley's Case*,[49] (notably in *Perrin v Blake*[50]) and even to borrow the Scots concept of the Court of Session as a court of law and equity to float the King's Bench off the venerable rocks of precedent, but to no very great effect.[51] The truth was that English land law was too firmly grounded on the works and outlook of such men as Coke, for whom Mansfield had a deep antipathy. To one of his philosophic make-up the subtleties and archaisms of real property law were not at all congenial. As Fifoot says, 'He was not happy in the role of conveyancer. Common sense was always breaking through.'[51] Consequently, his influence, and through him that of Scots law, was not very strong in the field of land law.

When at length arrangements were made after a hundred and sixty years for permanent Scottish representation at the judicial sessions of the House of Lords, a new opportunity for convergence of Scots and English law was created. Henceforth some of the best Scots lawyers were to sit at Westminster to hear appeals with their English peers. Such names as those of Lord Watson, Viscount Dunedin, Lord Macmillan and Lord Reid speak for themselves. It has undoubtedly been of great benefit to English law to have 'an outside opinion' at the very highest level.

The first peer appointed for this purpose was Lord Colonsay, although the formal status of Lord of Appeal in Ordinary only came in later.[52] He considered that his main duty was to explain the Scots law view and he did not attempt to interfere with the decisions of the House in English cases. The attitude of Lord Gordon (who died in 1879) was the same, when he was appointed the first Scots Lord of Appeal in Ordinary in 1876. Lord Watson of Thankerton (Lord of Appeal 1880–1899) was more interested in English law and took the trouble to 'put himself to school with Blackstone.' Even Equity was not beyond his reach. Lord Sands tells us:

> Since then there has been no 'inferiority complex' among Scots law lords in English cases. The complex has been rather the other way round as regards cases where Scots law was involved. It is perhaps unfortunate that English law lords do not always, to use a

49 (1581) 1 Co Rep 88b.
50 (1770) 4 Burr 2579 cf Fearne, *Contigent Remainders*, 155 *et seq.*
51 Fifoot, *Lord Mansfield*, Chapter 6.
52 Appellate Jurisdiction Act 1876. Lord Colonsay was created a hereditary, not a life, peer.

favourite expression of the late Lord Stormonth Darling, 'lay their lugs into it', in the case of a Scottish appeal . . . I can recall no Scottish appeal since 1875 in which the law of Scotland was involved, where one Scottish Lord of Appeal has sat and the judgment of the Court of Session has been either affirmed or reversed contrary to the opinion of that single law lord.[53]

It is doubtful whether even in the recent epoch during which this arrangement has lasted – and it is one well designed to secure a gradual convergence of the two legal systems on some subjects – there has been much convergence of the two systems so far as land law is concerned. Indeed we have the high authority of one who particularly adorned the position of a Scottish lord of appeal in ordinary for the opinion that:

> in this province of law there has been no convergence. The land systems of the two countries are so different that convergence is impossible. Either you would have to give up the one and introduce the other or else make a clean sweep of both and introduce something quite new. Such an impossible task has never been proposed by anyone.[54]

53   Lord Sands, 'Lord Colonsay and his Island,' (1931) 54 Jur. Rev.
54   Lord Dunedin, *English and Scottish Law*, (Murray Lecture) 19.

29 Mortgages and Heritable Securities

ENGLISH LAW

To the English lawyer a mortgage is simply an arrangement whereby land is used as security for the payment of a sum of money or the discharge of some other obligation.[1]

> The essential nature of a mortgage is that it is a conveyance of a legal or equitable interest in property, with a provision for redemption, that is that upon repayment of a loan or the performance of some other obligation the conveyance shall become void or the interest shall be reconveyed.[2] The borrower is known as the mortgagor, the lender as the mortgagee.[3]

In the twelfth and thirteenth centuries, when usury was a crime as well as a sin,[4] the mortgagor normally let his land to the mortgagee, who took possession of it and either used the income to discharge the debt (*vivum vadium*) or simply kept it (*mortuum vadium*). The Church regarded this latter form as sinful, because the income was taken as interest.[5] More important, however, was the harsh fact that if the money was not repaid before the lease expired, the mortgagee's interest was enlarged into a fee simple under the conditions of the mortgage and the mortgagee effectively lost his property. But as early as the thirteenth century a crude mortgage by conveyance of the fee simple, with a condition for re-entry by the

---

1 *Santley v Wilde* [1899] 2 Ch 474, *per* Lindley, M.R. *See also* Lawson, *Introduction to the Law of Property*, 184. For the current law *see* Waldock, *Law of Mortgages*; Fisher and Lightwood, *Law of Mortgage*; Megarry and Wade, 885–987; Cheshire 636–719; Fairest, *Mortgages*.
2 *Santley v Wilde* [1899] 2 Ch 474 approved in *Noakes v Rice* [1902] AC 24 at 28; *London County and Westminster Bank Limited v Tompkins* [1918] 1 KB 515.
3 Megarry and Wade, 885.
4 Holdsworth, *H.E.L.*, iii, 102; Glanvil, VII. 16.
5 Megarry and Wade, 887.

mortgagor on repayment, overcame other forms because of the unassailable security it gave the mortgagee by granting him seisin.[6] This became the usual form despite the harshness of the rule that a mortgagor even one day late in repayment by law lost his right to re-enter, and so lost his land. As Littleton put it:

> If a feoffment be made upon such condition, that if the feoffor pay to the feoffee at a certain day etc., 40 pounds of money, that then the feoffor may re-enter, etc., in this case the feoffee is called tenant in morgage, which is as much to say in French as mortgage, and in Latin *mortuum vadium*. And it seemeth that the cause why it is called mortgage is, for that it is doubtful whether the feoffor will pay at the day limited such sum or not, and if he doth not pay, then the land which is put in pledge upon condition for the payment of the money is taken from him for ever, and so dead to him upon condition etc. And if he doth pay the money, then the pledge is dead as to the tenant.[7]

Lord Haldane added, speaking of this arrangement:

> what made the hardship on the debtor a glaring one was that the debt still remained unpaid and could be recovered from the feoffor notwithstanding that he had actually forfeited the land to his mortgagee.[8]

By the seventeenth century, although it had become the norm to mortgage land by an outright conveyance of the fee simple with a covenant to recover if the money was repaid on the due date (a form which persisted until 1926), equity intervened to transform the relationship between the parties; for as Lord Nottingham put it:

> In natural justice and equity the principal right of the mortgagee is in the money, and his right to the land is only as a security for the money.[9]

At first, equity intervened only in cases where accident, mistake or special hardship caused default on the due date. But from this beginning the courts of equity developed their rule that the mortgagor must be allowed to redeem his fee simple even if he failed to repay on the appointed day, and this is still the essence of the posi-

6 Holdsworth, *H.E.L.*, iii, 129–30; Barton, *The Common Law Mortgage*, (1967) 83 LQR 229.
7 *Tenures*, s 332.
8 *Kreglinger v New Patagonia Meat and Cold Storage Co Ltd* [1914] AC 25 at 35.
9 *Thornborough v Baker* (1675) 3 Swans 628 at 630.

tion between the parties, even though mortgages are no longer made by conveyance of the fee simple. As Cheshire observes:[10]

> The position, then, is this:
> Upon the date fixed for repayment (which is usually six months after the creation of the mortgage, although in most cases neither mortgagor nor mortgagee intends that the loan shall be repaid on that date) the mortgagor has at common law a contractual right to redeem.
> If this date passes without repayment, he obtains a right to redeem in equity.
> The equity to redeem, which arises on failure to exercise the contractual right of redemption, must be carefully distinguished from the equitable estate, which, from the first, remains in the mortgagor, and is sometimes referred to as an equity of redemption.[11]

The result of the intervention of equity was to make the legal effect of a mortgage much less intimidating than it appeared to be. The documents it is true, provided usually for conveyance of the fee simple to the mortgagee subject only to the proviso for redemption by the mortgagor in six months time – a date by which usually neither party would wish to redeem[12] but equity would prevent the mortgagee's legal rights from being enforced. It was small wonder that Lord Macnaghten made his famous remark that 'no one . . . by the light of nature ever understood an English mortgage of real estate'.[13] The equity of redemption which arose as soon as the mortgage was made was in fact an equitable interest owned by the mortgagor, with which he could deal, like any other interest, and which was destructible only by four events: release by the mortgagor, lapse of time under the Limitation Acts, exercise of the mortgagee's statutory power of sale, or by a foreclosure, that is a judicial decree that the property vested in the mortagagee free of any right to redeem. Both these latter procedures were very strictly controlled. Thus, up to 1925 there were two ways of creating a legal mortgage of a legal interest in land; firstly, by conveying the fee simple to the mortgagee together with a convenant to repay the loan in, say, six months

---

10   *Modern Real Property*, 638.
11   *Kreglinger v New Patagonia Meat and Cold Storage Co Ltd* [1914] AC 25 *per* Lord Parker at 48.
12   Megarry and Wade, 890.
13   *Samuel v Jarrah Timber and Wood Paving Corporation Ltd* [1904] AC 323 at 326.

time, and a proviso that in the event of repayment the mortgagee would reconvey the property to the mortgagor; or, secondly, by granting a lease containing a provision vesting the freehold in the mortgagee in the event of default and with a condition of cesser of the term on redemption of the debt. Leasehold property was normally mortgaged by a grant of a sub-lease on similar terms. Equitable mortgages were created either where the mortgagor himself had only an equitable interest, or in the case of second and subsequent mortgages. Furthermore, an agreement to create a legal mortgage thereupon created an equitable mortgage under the doctrine of equity whereby that which ought to be done was regarded as having been already done, or where an agreement akin to a charge on property was made without any proprietary interest passing to the mortgagee.

In 1925, the whole law of mortgages was recast.[14] Cheshire outlines the problem and the main points of the solution as follows:[15]

> The prevailing practice, by which the legal fee simple was conveyed to a mortgagee, presented a difficult problem to the draftsmen of the 1925 legislation. How were they to bring it into line with the principles that they intended to introduce?
>
> The corner-stone of their policy was that the legal fee simple should always be vested in its true owner and that he should be able to convey it free from equitable interests. In the eyes of the law the true owner is the mortgagor. Yet, all that he held before 1926 was an equitable interest, and unless some alteration were made there could be no question of his ability to convey any kind of legal estate during the continuance of the mortgage.
>
> On the other hand it was important to protect the mortgagee in the enjoyment of certain valuable advantages that he derived from his legal ownership. Pre-eminent among these was the priority which, by virtue of the legal fee simple, he obtained over other mortgages created in the same land, for these were necessarily equitable in nature. Moreover, his possession of the title deeds enabled him to control the actions of the mortgagor in his dealings with the land. He also enjoyed the right to take actual possession of the land, and therefore to grant leases; and lastly, when he exercised his power of sale on failure by the mortgagor to repay the loan, he was able to vest the legal estate in the purchaser.

14 *See* Law of Property Act 1925 Part III, ss 85–120.
15 *Modern Real Property*, 640–1.

The solution contained in the Law of Property Act 1925 is to revert to the old fifteenth-century method of effecting mortgages by means of a lease for a term of years.

Mortgages by which the legal fee simple is vested in the mortgagee are prohibited, and a mortgagee who requires a legal estate instead of a mere equitable interest is compelled to take either a long term of years or a newly invented interest called a *charge by deed expressed to be by way of legal mortgage*. Thus in the first case both parties have legal estates:

the mortgagee has a legal term of years absolute, and
the mortgagor has a reversionary and legal fee simple, subject to the mortgagee's term;

while in the case of a charge by way of legal mortgage the mortgagee has the same protection powers and remedies as if he had taken a legal term of years.

In this way the principle that the legal fee simple should always remain vested in the true owner has been maintained. The mortgagor is owner at law as well as in equity, and the mortgagee has only a right *in alieno solo*. The charge by way of legal mortgage at last provides a method which reflects the reality of the transaction and goes some way towards rebutting Maitland's description of a mortgage deed as one long *suppressio veri* and *suggestio falsi*.[16] We should also notice two important consequences of the change made by the 1925 legislation. First, the mortgagor's retention of the legal estate means that any second and subsequent mortgages which he creates may be legal. And secondly, the rights of the parties remain unchanged, and in particular, the mortgagor's equity of redemption is still of importance. 'This, as before 1926, is an equitable proprietary interest and is in value equal to the value of the land less the amount of the debt secured by the mortgage. . . . The mortgagor retains that interest and keeps a legal estate as well.'[17]

Since 1925 therefore, the following methods of creating mortgages have been available:

1   Legal mortgages are made either by deed expressed to be by way of legal charge, or by lease with a proviso for cesser on redemption.

2   Equitable mortgages are made (a) by agreement to create a legal mortgage; (b) by deposit of title deeds under the doctrine of

16   Maitland, *Equity*, 182.
17   Hanbury, *Modern Equity*, 535.

Russel v Russel,[18] whereby such a deposit by way of security for a loan has been deemed to be evidence of a contract to create a mortgage and as part performance of such a contract;[19] (c) by mortgaging an equitable interest; (d) by equitable charge.

The equity of redemption remains unimpaired and inviolate and has been jealously guarded by the courts in their concern to see that crafty moneylenders do not take advantage of the impecunious who seek their help by insisting on unconscionable terms in mortgage arrangements. Such at least was the view of Lord Macnaghten, who leapt readily to the aid of mortgagors in a series of great cases which set the limit to the rights of the parties,[20] following the clear statement of the situation by Romer, J. in *Biggs v Hoddinott*:[21]

> There is a principle which I will accept without any qualification . . that on a mortgage you cannot, by contract between the mortgagor and mortgagee, clog, as it is termed, the equity of redemption so as to prevent the mortgagor from redeeming on payment of principle, interest and costs.

This principle is usually expressed in the equitable maxim '*once a mortgage always a mortgage*', meaning that the nature of the arrangement could not be changed once a mortgage had been made through, for example, unfair or unreasonable postponement of redemption,[22] or collateral advantages such as an option to purchase the mortgaged property granted to the lender on creation[23] or assignment[24] (though such an option is not deemed objectionable if given in an independent or subsequent transaction[25]). The solus agreement is a modern illustration of the collateral advantage; but the rule is still that the terms of the constraint upon the mortgagor (for example, that he must buy all his petrol from the oil company which lent him the money to establish a garage business) must be reasonable in length and kind and in a reasonable relationship to the size of the

18   (1783) 1 Bro CC 269.
19   *Edge v Worthington* (1786) 1 Cox Eq 211; *Pryce v Bury* (1853) 2 Drew 41.
20   *See Noakes v Rice* [1902] AC 24 *Fairclough v Swan Brewery Co Ltd* [1912] AC 565.
21   [1898] 2 Ch 307 at 314.
22   *Fairclough v Swan Brewery Co Ltd* [1912] AC 565; but only if the postponement is such as to be an unreasonable interference with the mortgagor's rights: *Knightsbridge Estates Trust Ltd v Byrne* [1939] Ch 441; *Davis v Symons* [1934] Ch 442.
23   *Samuel v Jarrah Timber and Wood Paving Corporation Ltd* [1904] AC 323.
24   *Lewis v Frank Love Ltd* [1961] 1 All ER 446.
25   *Reeve v Lisle* [1902] AC 461.

sum of money involved.[26] The general test now for any collateral advantage is that it can be valid if made at arm's length and if it is not oppressive or unconscionable, or calculated to prevent or unduly hamper redemption.[27] Private individuals who mortgage their houses to building societies (probably the most common form of mortgage) enjoy additional protection under the Building Societies Acts 1874–1962;[28] but even so, the courts remain watchful for oppresive or unconscionable terms.[29]

The position of the mortgagee rests upon his powers to use the mortgaged property to secure the recovery of the debt if the mortgagor should fail to make repayment. His main powers are similar to those of the Scots mortgagee under the standard security, but such a major topic cannot be treated here.[30] They may be listed for convenience as:

1   Remedies involving realisation of the mortgaged property:
     (*a*) sale,[31]
     (*b*) foreclosure.[32]
2   Remedies which do not involve such realisation:
     (*a*) action on the mortgagor's personal covenant to repay;
     (*b*) take possession.[33]

Scots Law

The Scots law of heritable securities[34] has developed along very similar general historical lines to the English law of mortgages and

---

26   *Esso Petroleum Co Ltd v Harper's Garage (Stourport) Ltd* [1968] AC 269; *Re Petrol Filling Station, Vauxhall Bridge Road* (1959) 20 P & CR 1. *See also* Cheshire and Fifoot, *Law of Contract*, 338–55 for aspects of 'restraint of trade' in these arrangements.

27   *Biggs v Hoddinott* [1898] 2 Ch 307; *Bradley v Carritt* [1903] AC 253; cf *Kreglinger v New Patagonia Meat and Cold Storage Co Ltd* [1914] AC 25.

28   *See* Waldock, *Law of Mortgages*, Chapter 4; Wurtzberg and Mills, *Building Society Law.*

29   *See* e.g. *Cityland and Property (Holdings) Ltd v Dabrah* [1968] Ch 166.

30   Rights of mortgagees are treated in detail in Waldock, *Law of Mortgages*, 170–223; Megarry and Wade 904–36; Cheshire, 668–86; Fairest, Mortgages, 49–83.

31   Law of Property Act 1925, ss 101–7.

32   *Ibid.*, ss 88, 89.

33   *See Four-Maids Ltd v Dudley Marshall (Properties) Ltd* [1957] Ch 317 *per* Harman J. at 320; cf *White v City of London Brewery Co* (1889) 42 Ch D 237.

34   *See* generally Walker, 1340–75; Gloag and Irvine, *Law of Rights in Security*, 1–86; and, as to the standard security, Halliday, 85–211.

the present position is very similar in both jurisdictions, but heritable securities in Scotland developed late and were not really efficient until the nineteenth century.

The wadset[35] was a security created by disponing the land to the creditor, and was redeemable by the debtor on payment of a specified sum, the lender meanwhile taking the rents of the land as interest on the debt. It was cumbersome and inflexible and went out of use at an early date.[36] The other early form of heritable security was the right of annual rent, a fixed annuity from rents of the land which became redeemable in the sixteenth century. After the Reformation a power of requisition was given to the lender, but it too disappeared fairly early, though more by simply going out of use rather than by being abolished.[37]

The immediate predecessor of the bond and disposition in security was the heritable bond, which allowed the lender a specific annual rent out of the land but no power to enter into possession to collect the rents to enable him to recover the principal sum gradually. Originally it contained an obligation to infeft the lender in the lands, but later a dispositive clause was added to the bond. It was superseded by the bond and disposition in security which contained a power of sale.

Before the Heritable Securities Act 1845[38] and the Infeftment Act 1845[39] the bond and disposition in security contained the following clauses:

1　narrative
2　obligation to repay interest and penalty as in a personal bond
3　disposition of the lands in security
4　clause of redemption in favour of the borrower specifying how premonition was to be made
5　clause of sale on failure of payment in favour of the lender authorising him to sell by group (auction) after specified advertisement
6　clause binding the lender to ratify any sale

35　As to which see Stair, II.120; Erskine, II.8. Bell, *Principles*, 901-7.
36　Bell, *Principles*, 901 *et seq*; Craigie, 924.
37　Bell, *Principles*, 908; Craigie, 925.
38　As to which *see* Craigie, 925.
39　*See* Craigie, 926–98.

7 obligation to infeft the lender *a me vel de me*
8 procuratory of resignation
9 obligation on the borrower to enter the lender's heirs, assignees and singular successors
10 warrandice
11 assignation of writs
12 consent to registration for preservation and execution
13 precept of sasine
14 testing clause

The lender recorded an instrument of sasine within sixty days of the date of the bond and disposition in security to safeguard his interest.

When there was an *a me* or an *a me vel de me* holding a procuratory of resignation was added to enable the lender to enter with the borrower's superior and the date of entry with the superior decided the precedence of the bond and disposition in security, with the result that the lender might find his security postponed to that of a later lender who had entered with the superior ahead of him. The lender had also to make sure that the borrower himself had entered with his superior and had recorded an instrument of sasine on his charter of resignation or charter of confirmation.[40]

The Heritable Securities Act 1845 made the transmission of bonds and dispositions in security easier by virtue of the following provisions:

1 The right of the creditor could be transferred in whole or in part by recording an assignation in the form specified in Schedule 1 of the Act.

2 If the assignation of the heritable security was contained in a deed of conveyance granted for a further purpose and conveying other land, the lender could record a notarial instrument setting forth generally the nature of the rest of the deed and containing at length the part which related to and assigned the security.

3 The creditor's heir could complete title by obtaining an acknowledgement in the form of Schedule 2 of the Act from the person infeft, and recording the acknowledgement.

40 Craigie, 927 *et seq*; *Henderson v Campbell* (1821) 1 S 104.

4   An adjudger for debt could record the abreviate of the adjudication, and an heir duly served or the general disponee of the creditor could record a notarial instrument in the form of Schedule 3 of the Act.

5   Any heritable security completed by infeftment could be discharged in whole or in part by recording a discharge in the form of Schedule 4 of the Act. The above deeds could be recorded at any time during the lifetime of the grantee in the appropriate Register of Sasines; no further procedure was necessary after recording.

The Infeftment Act 1845 provided a form for a precept of sasine in a heritable security and allowed infeftment to be taken without symbolic delivery by recording a notarial instrument within the lifetime of a person in whose favour it was granted.

This Act was followed by a number of statutes which made a number of changes of detail intended to make the conveyancing arrangements easier, but involving no change of principle.

The Heritable Securities Act 1847 introduced a statutory form of a bond and disposition in security which could itself be recorded in the Register of Sasines, and conditions in the borrower's title could be referred to in any recorded instrument or deed forming part of the investiture of the borrower in the form specified in the Act.

More simplified forms were introduced by the Heritable Securities Act 1854 and the Titles to Land Acts 1858 and 1860.

The above Acts were all repealed by the Titles to Land Consolidation Act 1868, but this re-enacted, with some modifications, the changes introduced by those Acts.

The process which had developed between 1845 and 1868 of abolishing instruments of sasine and entry with the superior and substituting the recording of the deed granted or a notarial instrument directly in the Register of Sasines was applied to bonds and dispositions in security and other heritable securities and deeds relating thereto, as well as to feu charters and dispositions.

The disadvantage of the bond and disposition in security was that it only applied to a definite sum of money lent at or before the date of granting the bond and disposition in security: it could not secure fluctuating amounts or future advances.

The bond of cash credit and disposition in security[41] had originally been introduced by statute in 1814 to allow landowners to pledge land in security of cash accounts or credits, provided that interest was limited to a certain definite sum specified in the security (which must not exceed the amount of the principal sum plus three years interest thereon at five per cent). This was dealt with as a heritable security along with bonds and dispositions in security by the nineteenth century legislation, but it was a clumsy deed and posed difficult questions of ranking of future advances if any later heritable security appeared on the Register.

Bonds of cash credit were used almost exclusively by banks or for loans to builders while they were developing a building project, whereas future or fluctuating debts were more commonly secured by *ex facie* absolute dispositions[42] which were generally used by building societies. Under this arrangement the borrower granted a disposition to the lender, who became absolutely infeft in the property. The conditions of the loan, including the personal bond, were written into a separate agreement or back-letter which could be, but never was, recorded in the Register of Sasines. The lender, if unpaid, could then sell the property without the consent of the borrower (who only had a personal right to the land during the period of the loan). The problem was that the lender, being infeft, was absolutely liable to the borrower's superior for any breach of the feudal conditions, and in theory the superior could irritate the feu and would have no liability to repay the borrowers' loan. In practice a superior could easily obtain obedience to the feudal conditions by intimating the breach to the borrower, who very quickly had the breach remedied; but the position was little more satisfactory than the old wadset, because the lender was the infeft and entered owner of the *dominium utile* while the real owner who lived on the land and paid the rates and feuduties and obeyed the conditions of the feu charter had no more than a personal right. Another problem was that although under the Titles to Land Consolidation Act 1868, bonds and dispositions in security were moveable as regards the lender's succession, a loan secured by an *ex facie* absolute disposition was heritable as regards the lender's succession because the lender was infeft.

41 Described in Payment of Creditors Act 1814. *See* generally Craigie.
42 As to which *see* Craigie, 999–1009.

The Conveyancing and Feudal Reform (Scotland) Act 1970 which came into effect on 29 November 1970 abolished all the then existing forms of heritable security, with transitional provisions to deal with existing heritable securities[43] and introduced in their place the standard security,[44] which is now the only document which can be used to create heritable security for what may be broadly described as capital debts.[45] It is a flexible type of security, adaptable for use whether the debt is of fixed or maximum amount or an open-ended obligation, or even an obligation *ad factum praestandum*.[46] The scheme of the Act is that if the obligation secured is a debt within the wide meaning given to that term in the Act, and the security is an interest in land (other than an entailed estate) which is capable of being owned or held as a separate interest, a title to which may be recorded in the Register of Sasines, the use of the standard security is obligatory.[47]

The Act provides what is virtually a new self-contained code with a large number of standard deeds, governed by standard conditions which the parties may vary[48] to suit their own case, except the conditions governing default in making payments and calling up the loan, that is the provisions relating to powers of sale, redemption and foreclosure: any attempt to vary such conditions is void and, ineffective.[49] The reason for making these conditions non-variable is to afford protection to the debtor in fundamental matters in which he may well be at a disadvantage (a sentiment akin to that of Lord Macnaghten in his efforts to define the English mortgagor's equity of redemption[50]), while the powers of sale and foreclosure are non-negotiable because they are intended to enable the creditor to expropriate the debtor from his heritable property in order to satisfy the debt, though it is not unreasonable to write in statutory safeguards upon the exercise of such fundamental powers.

The standard conditions are set out in Schedule 3 to the Convayancing and Feudal Reform (Scotland) Act 1970 and relate to:

43 Conveyancing and Feudal Reform (Scotland) Act 1970, Part III, ss 33–34.
44 *Ibid.*, ss 9 (1).
45 *Ibid.*, s 9 (3) and 8 (c).
46 *Ibid.*, s 9 (c).
47 *Ibid.*, s 9 (3) and 8 (b); and *see* Halliday, 63–4.
48 Conveyancing and Feudal Reform (Scotland) Act 1970, s 11 (3).
49 *Ibid.*
50 *See* p. 317 *supra.*

maintenance and repair of the mortgaged property; completion of building and prohibition of alterations; observance of conditions in title, payment of duties and charges and general compliance with the law relating to security subjects; planning notices; insurance; restriction on letting; general power of creditor to perform obligations on default of the debtor (and consequent power to charge debtor); calling-up; default and the debtor's exercise of the right of redemption.

The Act has greatly simplified the problems which attended the older forms of heritable security. It has, in practical terms, placed the Scots mortgagor in a position very similar to that of his English counterpart and, so far, it has caused few problems.

30 Amendment of the Feudal System in Scotland

THE CASE FOR REFORM

In recent years a great deal of consideration has been given to the amendment of the feudal system and to the possibility of its abolition in Scotland. The main points which gave rise to discontent were:

1 The use of the words 'superior' and 'vassal' (although the word 'feuar' has been used for many years on many estates in place of 'vassal').

2 The enforcement or not of feudal conditions which might interfere with the amenity of the area at the whim of the superior.

3 The practice of some superiors in demanding a money payment for granting a minute of waiver to vary existing feudal conditions. There had been some doubt as to whether this was strictly competent where the superior could not prove any loss, but the matter was clarified in *Howard de Walden Estates Ltd. v Bowmaker Ltd.*[1] In that case it was decided that the superior was entitled to payment for altering the feuing conditions when the feu charters of houses in a street provided that they were to be used only as dwelling-houses, even though in the course of the years many (but less than half) of the houses in the street had been used for various business and commercial purposes.

4 The necessity of one of the feuars to collect unallocated feuduties from his neighbours and to pay the whole *cumulo* feuduty to the superior.

1 1965 SC 165.

5   The fact that the feudal system is fundamentally rigid and autocratic.

6   The deeds used for securing mortgages over land, particularly the *ex facie* absolute disposition, were cumbersome and needed simplification.

In 1964 the Halliday Committee was appointed 'to examine and report on existing conveyancing legislation and practice in relation to heritable and moveable property and to make recommendations with a view to amending or new legislation' and in 1966 produced a wide ranging Report,[2] which in general was found to be acceptable to the legal profession in Scotland.

PROPOSALS FOR REFORM

The Halliday Committee Report was followed in 1969 by a White Paper on Land Tenure in Scotland,[3] which set forth a seven point plan of reform showing the intentions of the government as follows:

1   On an appointed day feudal tenure will be abolished, and existing vassals who are owners of the *dominium utile*, i.e. the present proprietors of the land, will be declared to own their land in terms of the new form of absolute ownership.

2   From the appointed day the feuing or sub-feuing of land will no longer be allowed, nor will any other disposal of land or rights in land subject to any form of annual payment in perpetuity or quasi-perpetuity.

3   The system of land tenure will in future be based on two forms of holding:
     (*a*) a form of absolute ownership; and
     (*b*) enjoyment of occupation for a term (a lease).

4   It will be possible under the new system to create certain types of private condition running with the land.

5   The Lands Tribunal for Scotland, for which provision was made in the Lands Tribunal Act 1949, will be given power to annul or modify unreasonable land conditions.

6   The leasing of land for the purpose of building dwellinghouses will only be allowed in special circumstances and subject to the most stringent safeguards.

2   Conveyancing Legislation and Practice 1966 Cmnd 3118.
3   1969 Cmnd 4099.

7   Leases of land for non-residential purposes will be limited to sixty years.[4]

LAND OBLIGATIONS

The first Act of Parliament to begin to implement these intentions and other recommendations of the Halliday Committee was the Conveyancing and Feudal Reform (Scotland) Act 1970. This Act set up the Lands Tribunal for Scotland, which was given jurisdiction to vary or discharge land obligations but no power to impose any new or additional burden on the land (but without prejudice to any other method of variation or discharge) and to allocate feuduties which had only been apportioned among the vassals, and had not been allocated by the superior.

The power given to the Tribunal to vary or discharge land conditions has effectively prevented superiors from refusing to grant minutes of waiver or charters of novodamus except for payment of substantial sums because the feuar can now go to the Tribunal.

Before ordering the variation or discharge of land conditions the Tribunal must be satisfied that in all the circumstances:

   (*a*)   by reason of changes in the character affected by the obligation or of the neighbourhood thereof or other circumstances which the Tribunal may deem material, the obligation is or has become unreasonable or inappropriate; or

   (*b*)   the obligation is unduly burdensome compared with any benefit resulting or which would result from its performance; or

   (*c*)   the existence of the obligation impedes some reasonable use of the land.[5]

The Tribunal is entitled to order payment to the superior or other proprietor benefited by the obligation of sums under one, but not both, of the following heads:

   (*i*)   a sum to compensate for any substantial loss or disadvantage suffered by the proprietor as such benefited proprietor in consequence of the variation or discharge; or

4 *Ibid.*, 11.
5 Conveyancing and Feudal Reform (Scotland) Act 1970, s 1 (3).

(*ii*) a sum to make up for any effect which the obligation produced, at the time when it was imposed, in reducing the consideration then paid or made payable for the interest in land affected by it.[6]

There have been a number of decisions by the Tribunal which have gradually formed a pattern for the guidance of conveyancers, the most cautious of all legal practitioners. Keeping a nursery school for up to fifteen children in a residential terrace in Edinburgh was reasonable and compensation was refused.[7] The existence of an obligation to use an ice-rink for skating, curling and other recreational and communal purposes and which permitted the supply of liquor on the premises was not unduly burdensome and did not impede some reasonable use of the land. On appeal the Court of Session upheld the Lands Tribunal's decision.[8] A licenced grocer was not allowed to turn his shop into a licenced betting shop.[9]

Feuing conditions which required the maintenance of derelict buildings and prevented the use of the premises as a factory to make computer components were held to be unduly burdensome compared with any resulting benefit to the superior, as they required pointless and expensive maintenance of derelict buildings and impeded a reasonable use of the land for a factory; and it was observed that 'benefit to the superior' did not include the power to extract a sum of money for granting a minute of waiver. Compensation was refused because the superior had not proved that a lower feuduty was charged in 1897 than would have been charged if the conditions had not been imposed.[10]

When the proprietor of a house with a large garden applied to the Tribunal for a variation order because certain neighbours, who were also 'benefited proprietors' with a right to enforce restrictions against buildings, objected except under condition that they should be entitled to approve of the plans it was held that the houses should be built not more than two storeys high according to plans

---

6 Conveyancing and Feudal Reform (Scotland) Act 1970, s 1 (4).
7 *Main v Lord Doune* 1972 SLT (Lands Tr) 14.
8 *Murrayfield Ice Rink v Scottish Rugby Union* 1972 SLT (Lands Tr) 20; 1973 SC 9.
9 *Bolton v Aberdeen Corporation* 1972 SLT (Lands Tr) 26.
10 *West Lothian Co-operative Society v Ashdale Land and Property Co* 1972 SLT (Lands Tr) 30. The principle that the loss of the power to obtain money for the grant of a Minute of Waiver did not entitle the superior to compensation was re-affirmed in *McVey v Glasgow Corporation* 1973 SLT (Lands Tr) 15.

approved by the benefited proprietors and that an existing copse should be preserved.[11]

When four sub-feuars holding under one of the superior's vassals and some of the superior's immediate vassals who were neighbouring proprietors objected to an unlicenced boarding house's being extended and used as a licenced hotel, it was held (*a*) that the Tribunal had powers to decide who are benefited proprietors entitled to enforce undisputed land obligations; (*b*) the feuing condition should be discharged because it impeded a reasonable use of the land to permit the proposed development; and (*c*) the four sub-feuars who lived beside the proposed building extension should be entitled to compensation of £500, £250, £100 and £100 respectively.[12]

An owner of an hotel in Pitlochry applied to vary a condition imposed in 1924 which required the hotel to be used as a temperance hotel only. The objectors were the superior and the proprietor of another hotel to whose predecessors the superior had granted a feu charter permitting the sale of spiritous liquor and binding herself not to permit any other premises owned in the same street to be used for the sale of liquor. It was held (*a*) that the obligations had become unreasonable and inappropriate because Pitlochry had become a major tourist centre; (*b*) that the Tribunal could not consider the financial benefit of affected persons who were not 'benefited proprietors'; (*c*) that the obligations were unduly burdensome and impeded a reasonable use of the land; and (*d*) that the superiors were not entitled to compensation because they had failed to prove that a lower rate of feuduty would have been charged in 1924 if the feuing conditions had not been imposed.[13]

Building two dwelling-houses on a vacant plot of ground was held to be a reasonable use being impeded by a land obligation which the Lands Tribunal discharged with an award to the superior of compensation of £150 because the restricted feuduty charged in 1913 was £10 less than the feuduty on adjoining ground feued in 1888.[14]

In *Cooperative Wholesale Society v Ushers Brewery*[15] a small

11 *Crombie v George Heriot's Trustees* 1972 SLT (Lands Tr) 40.
12 *Smith v Taylor* 1972 SLT (Lands Tr) 34.
13 *Manz v Butter's Trustees* 1973 SLT (Lands Tr) 2.
14 *Gorrie and Banks v Musselburgh Town Council* 1974 (Lands Tr) 5.
15 1975 SLT (Lands Tr) 9.

precinct consisting of a public house, a licenced betting office and a supermarket was constructed within a council housing estate. Each plot had restrictions on use enforceable not only by the superior but also by the proprietors of each plot *inter se*. The proprietors of the supermarket were required to use their plot for the purpose only of a retail shop and were prohibited from selling exciseable liquor therein. The successors of the original feuars were the Co-operative Society who applied for a variation of the feudal conditions to allow the sale of liquor in the supermarket on an off-licence certificate. The owners of the public house opposed the application and claimed compensation if the discharge was granted. It was held that the objectors were 'benefited proprietors' as defined by 1(2) of the Conveyancing and Feudal Reform (Scotland) Act 1970, and as such entitled to claim compensation. The application was granted under s. 1 (3) (c) of the Act because in all the circumstances the restriction impeded a reasonable use of the land. Compensation under s. 1 (4) (i) of the Act was assessed at £4600, representing the estimated diminution in value of the public house resulting from the Tribunal's discharge order, and it was directed that unless the sum was paid within twelve months of the date of the Order the Order itself would become void.[16]

In *McArthur v Mahoney*[17] the applicants were the owners of a shop on the ground floor of a group of buildings in which a separate dwelling-house with a garden in separate ownership were situated. Under the Feu Charter of 1846 a height restriction was imposed for the protection of the neighbouring pier, which had since become disused. The applicants, who lived nearby, applied to the Tribunal for a discharge of the land obligation so as to allow them to construct an attic flat in breach of the height limit. The application was opposed by the proprietors of the dwelling-house both as affected persons and as superiors who had recently purchased the superiority. It was held (*a*) that although the pier had become disused the restriction was still reasonable and appropriate to protect the amenity of the objector's dwelling-house; (*b*) that the land obligation was not unduly burdensome; and (*c*) that the proposed use of the attic as a dwelling-house would seriously affect the house and

16   Lands Tribunal for Scotland Rules 1971, rule 5 (3).
17   1975 SLT (Lands Tr) 2.

dwelling-house occupied by the objectors and the restriction which inhibited the redevelopment of the attic did not, in all the circumstances, impede some reasonable use of land. The case is interesting because the Tribunal decided that it had power under the 1970 Act to take into account the amenity of affected persons who did not have a contractual right to object as 'benefited proprietors' as defined by s 2 (6), and had a discretionary power to consider that although the original purpose of the restriction had disappeared, the restriction still had a continuing value to preserve the amenity of the objectors. The Tribunal considered English cases[18] brought under s 84 of the Law of Property Act 1925 relating to the discretionary powers of the Lands Tribunal in England to modify restrictive covenants.

In *Robertson v Church of Scotland General Trustees*[19] it was held that where superiors did not oppose the discharge of a prohibition against building they were not entitled to compensation therefor. It was also observed that the Lands Tribunal should try to follow its own decisions especially when reached by a large Tribunal.

The 1970 Act also applies to long leases and servitudes. In *McQuiban v Eagle Star Insurance*[20] tenants under a 99-year lease were prohibited from assigning the lease in part. Two houses had been built on the ground and it was held that the leases of each house and garden could be assigned separately and the land obligation discharged.

In *Devlin v Conn*[21] a servitude right of access was reserved when the adjoining ground was retained by the superior, and was then conveyed to a doctor, who constructed an alternative access. The Tribunal discharged the servitude right on the grounds that it had become unreasonable because of changes in the character of the neighbourhood and would not award any compensation.

The general pattern shown from these cases is that:

1 It is difficult for a superior to insist on imposing a land obligation which has become unreasonable as a result of a change in general circumstances, and the most difficult argument to surmount is

---

18 *Truman, Hanbury Buxton & Co Ltd's Application* [1956] 1 QB 261; *Luton Trade Unionist Club and Institute Ltd's Application* (1968) 20 P & CR 1131; and *Driscoll v Church Commissioners for England* [1957] 1 QB 330.
19 1976 SLT (Lands Tr) 11.
20 1972 SLT (Lands Tr) 39.
21 1972 SLT (Lands Tr) 11.

that it impedes a reasonable use of land. In all but the last two cases cited an objection under, *inter alia*, s 1 (3) (c) prevailed.

2   Benefit to the superior does not include the power to obtain a sum of money for the grant of a minute of waiver.

3   The onus of proving that a lower feuduty was charged at the time of the grant of a feu charter because of the imposition of the land obligation is on the superior; and it is often difficult for him to prove that an additional feuduty would have been charged, because the proposed development would not have been contemplated at the time of the original grant.

4   The Tribunal can decide who are 'benefited proprietors', but if these are not the superior they must have a recorded title to enforce the land obligation.

5   The Tribunal itself can protect the interests of 'affected persons'.

6   The amount of compensation awarded has usually been a small sum.

7   The Tribunal will decide on obligations in long leases and on servitudes.

It may be considered that the more the Lands Tribunal for Scotland permits the variation or discharge of land obligations the less certain the feuars are that the area in which they live or work will remain the same as it was when they bought their dwelling-houses or offices. For instance, it would be most annoying to have the dwelling-house next door changed into a public house or club, with only the prospect of a small sum of compensation being awarded, as in *Smith v Taylor*.[22]

ALLOCATION OF FEUDUTIES

The other jurisdiction given to the Lands Tribunal for Scotland was to allocate feuduties which had been apportioned between vassals, usually the owners of flats.[23] Any proprietor of part of a feu may

22   1972 SLT (Lands Tr) 34.
23   Conveyancing and Feudal Reform (Scotland) Act 1970, ss 3–5.

serve on the superior a notice of allocation showing the name of the vassal, the address of the subjects and the amount of feuduty apportioned on the part owned by the vassal.

The form of notice prescribed unfortunately does not make it necessary for the vassal to specify the feu charter which imposes the feuduty; and on a large estate it is often difficult to find the right feu charter, because the original grant will have been of the land upon which the block of flats has been erected.

The superior may also have no means of being certain that the amount of feuduty specified is correct.

The Court of Session decided in *Moray Estates Development Co.*[24] that a superior upon whom an allocation had been served who objected on the ground that it was not known that the amount of the portion of feuduty specified in a notice of allocation had been apportioned by disposition or by any other formal or informal method on any parts of the subjects, was entitled to do so. The Lands Tribunal for Scotland has to do the investigation to show whether or not the notice of allocation is correct, and must then allocate the whole *cumulo* feuduty.

There has been a considerable amount of cooperation between those acting for superiors and the officials of the Tribunal in finding lists of the feuduties collected and checking them against the titles of flats in blocks. It has been found that in many cases the amount collected from the vassals does not conform to their titles.

Section 6 of the 1970 Act applied the same rules to unallocated ground annuals.

MISCELLANEOUS REFORMS (1970)

Part II of the Conveyancing and Feudal Reform (Scotland) Act 1970[25] introduced a new form of mortgage,[26] the standard security, which since November 1970 is the only form of heritable security that can be used. This has removed the troublesome *ex facie* absolute disposition which intruded the lender into the feudal system as the entered vassal, and left the apparent owner of the heritage with

24 1971 SLT 318.
25 Ss 9–32.
26 As to mortgages, *see* Chapter 29.

nothing more than a personal right, even though the balance of capital due to the infeft lender was only a very small sum.

Part III of the Act[27] simplified the discharge of the existing heritable securities.

Two further feudal reforms were made by ss 46 and 48 of the 1970 Act. Section 46 reduced the period of notice by a superior of his intention to exercise a right of pre-emption to twenty-one days and provided that the right could be exercised only on one occasion. This means that the right of pre-emption becomes contractual between the superior and his first vassal and ceases to be feudal. Section 48 finally abolished forms of assignations of unrecorded conveyances which had become unnecessary in 1924.

REDEMPTION OF FEUDUTIES

The second measure enacted to implement the seven point plan of reform, set out in the White Paper on Land Tenure in Scotland[28] which followed the Report of the Halliday Committee,[29] was the Land Tenure Reform (Scotland) Act 1974. Part I of the Act contains four major reforms:

1   No new feuduty can be imposed or existing duty be increased after September 1974.[30]

2   Any vassal has the right to redeem his feuduty by giving not less than one month's notice before any term of Whitsunday or Martinmas at a price calculated on the value of $2\frac{1}{2}\%$ Consols.[31]

3   Any vassal who sells his property must redeem his feuduty if it is allocated, at a price calculated on the value of $2\frac{1}{2}\%$ Consols.[32]

4   An existing feuduty, whether allocated or not, must be redeemed if the property is compulsorily acquired by a local or public authority.[33]

27   Conveyancing and Feudal Reform (Scotland) Act 1970, ss 33–43.
28   1969 Cmnd 4099; *see* pp. 326–75 *infra*.
29   Conveyancing Legislation and Practice, 1966 Cmnd 3118.
30   Land Tenure Reform (Scotland) Act 1974, ss 1, 2.
31   *Ibid.*, s 2.
32   *Ibid.*, s 5.
33   *Ibid.*, s 6.

The above rules apply also to ground annual, skat or other periodic payment for land which is not rent, a payment of a continuing cost related to land or any sum paid in respect of a heritable security.[34]

The feudal system is not abolished by these provisions. However, feuduties can no longer be imposed and existing feuduties will gradually disappear.

Apart from a flurry of voluntary redemptions at Martinmas 1970 very few feuduties are now being redeemed voluntarily. Feuduties on dwelling-houses are being redeemed compulsorily, but do not have to be redeemed if the feuduty has not been allocated. Feuduties payable by firms or companies for business premises are not being voluntarily redeemed because the feuduty is a deductible charge against annual profits, and the turnover of business premises is much slower that that of dwelling-houses, so feuduties will be with us for some time.

One odd side effect of these provisions is that the power to serve a notice of allocation, introduced in 1970,[35] has become unpopular. If one inhabitant of a block of flats serves a notice and the superior asks for an order by the Lands Tribunal for Scotland allocating the feuduty on each of the other owners of flats in the block, they all become liable to redeem the feuduty allocated on each of their flats on sale; but no redemption is compulsory if the feuduty remains unallocated.

If the process of abolishing feuduty is to be hastened, further legislation will be necessary. The majority of feuduties are £10 or less and clearly the vassals of Scotland are reluctant to throw off their chains, preferring to pay a small annual sum to a superior, even if the modern superior is in many cases a developer, an insurance company or a trust.

MISCELLANEOUS REFORMS (1974)

Part II of the Land Tenure Reform (Scotland) Act[36] 1974 introduces restrictions on the creation of long leases of residential

---

34 *Ibid.*, ss 2, 6 (7).
35 Conveyancing and Feudal Reform (Scotland) Act 1970, ss 3–5.
36 Land Tenure Reform (Scotland) Act 1974, ss 8–10.

property, which could be used as substitutes for feus. Long leases of industrial or commercial property are nevertheless permissible.

Part III of the 1974 Act[37] introduces a number of minor amendments. To prevent situations similar to long leases being created in the case of dwelling-houses, a borrower is given a right to redeem a standard security after twenty years,[38] and rights of redemption and reversion must be exercised within twenty years, whether they relate to dwelling-houses or to other property.[39]

The restrictions on rights of pre-emption contained in feu charters are extended to rights of redemption contained in any deed.[40]

The right of irritancy for non-payment of feuduty arises only if the period of non-payment is five years instead of two years.[41]

Casualties stipulated for in long leases (which were always clumsy and anomalous) are abolished. This does not prevent a review of the rent payable under a lease from time to time.[42]

To clarify the position of an interposed lease in a sale and lease-back arrangement a lessor can grant a lease subject to the rights of a sublessee for the whole or part of the period of the sublease. This provision is retrospective.[43]

Leases of a duration exceeding twenty years may now be recorded under the Registration of Leases (Scotland) Act 1857. The period was formerly thirty-one years and over.

PRACTICAL EFFECTS TO DATE

The 1970 and 1974 Acts have gone only a small way towards fulfilling the Seven Point Plan of Reform.[44] The feudal system has not been abolished, and a start only has been made towards the abolition of the payment of feuduty. The Lands Tribunal for Scotland has been given power to amend or modify unreasonable land conditions, and the leasing of land for the purpose of building

37 Land Tenure Reform (Scotland) Act 1974, ss 11–20.
38 *Ibid.,* s 11.
39 *Ibid.,* s 12.
40 Conveyancing and Feudal Reform (Scotland) Act 1970, s 46; Land Tenure Reform (Scotland) Act 1974, s 13.
41 Land Tenure Reform (Scotland) Act 1974, s 15.
42 *Ibid.,* s 16.
43 *Ibid.,* s 17.
44 1969 Cmnd 4099, p. 11. *See* pp. 326–7 *supra.*

dwelling-houses has been stopped, so that only points 5 and 6 of the seven point plan have so far been implemented.

The stumbling block at present is how to cope with land conditions which can at present be enforced only by the superior.

The Green Paper on Land Tenure Reform in Scotland published by the Scottish Home and Health Department in 1972 recognises that the reform of land tenure is a very complex subject. It discusses methods of preserving useful land conditions relating to the upkeep and repair of property in which more than one proprietor has an interest, which are usually in detailed terms and relate to particular properties. It seems that the most favoured proposal is likely to be that existing land conditions should be retained and be enforceable by 'qualified proprietors' who might be co-terminous proprietors, and who could show that they had an interest to enforce the conditions.[45] It is proposed that new land conditions might be created which would be enforceable among proprietors who would agree to the imposition of certain rights and liabilities relating to their properties by recording a deed of conditions in the Register of Sasines.[46] These would have to be enforced by interdict or an action of specific implement.[47]

Practitioners who deal with large feudal estates find that neighbours sometimes get involved in disputes which create considerable hostility; this can be lessened in many cases by the intervention (or the refusal to intervene) of the superior's solicitor, who can take a more detached view of the problem. No solution to the regulation and enforcement of land conditions will be an easy one. It would be a tragedy if the power to create positive conditions running with the land were lost to Scots law simply because the regulation and enforcement of land conditions is often difficult; but until a solution to this problem can be found the feudal system cannot be abolished.[48]

45 Green paper, *Land Tenure Reform in Scotland*, paras. 38–45.
46 *Ibid.*, para. 84.
47 *Ibid.*, para. 85.
48 *See* generally Halliday, *The Conveyancing and Feudal Reform (Scotland) Act 1970* (2nd ed 1977) and Halliday, *Land Tenure Reform (Scotland) Act 1974*.

31 Proposed Scheme of Compulsory Land Registration in Scotland

In 1959 the Reid Committee was appointed 'to consider the case for introducing registration of title to land in Scotland, and, if necessary, the method by which such registration might be effected', and the Reid Report on Registration of Title to Land in Scotland was published in 1963.[1] It recommended that a system of registration of title should be introduced, but also stated the conditions which, in the view of the Committee 'must be fulfilled by any system of registration of title in Scotland if it is to be preferable to the existing system of registration of deeds.'[2] These conditions were set out as follows:

1   It must retain the merits of the present system as regards security, flexibility and publicity.

2   It must in the long run result in a substantial saving in time occupied in legal work and in cost to the public.

3   Its character must be such as to prevent dislocation or substantial practical difficulties during the transitional period while it is being introduced: it must therefore be in the nature of an evolution or development of the present system.

4   The first registration of title of any subjects must not be unduly expensive. In particular we would not favour any system which required intimation to neighbouring proprietors as a preliminary to such registration, because that would inevitably stir up disputes and involve expense in many cases in settling or litigating questions which are at present dormant. So the existing rights of neighbouring proprietors must be adequately safeguarded without their having to intervene.[3]

1   1963 Cmnd 2032.
2   *Ibid.*, para 64.
3   *Ibid.*

They added:

> We have considered in some detail the English system of registration,[4] . . . and we have derived much assistance from English experience. But it is obvious that if the above four general conditions are to be fulfilled, it is impossible simply to copy that system, and we have not attempted to do that. We also received some evidence about the South African system, but conditions there are so different that we have not thought it necessary to consider that system in detail. For the same reason we have not investigated the Torrens system or any of the systems in use in Europe.[5]

In 1965 the Henry Committee was appointed to prepare in the light of the report by Lord Reid's Committee a detailed scheme for the introduction and operation of registration of title to land in Scotland with a view to the preparation of a Land Registration (Scotland) Bill.

The Scheme for the Introduction and Operation of Registration of Title to Land in Scotland (the Report of the Henry Committee) was published in 1969[6] and includes a clear simple draft Bill to establish a public Land Register for Scotland, annexed to which are forms of Land Certificate and Charge Certificate.

If the scheme is adopted, the Land Certificate will be dated and numbered and begin with an Ordnance Survey map on which the subjects of sale are outlined and any servitude rights granted with the lands are shown and coloured with appropriate colours. In built up areas a 1:1250 (50-inch) map will be used; in non built-up areas a 1:2500 (25-inch) map, and in rural areas a 6-inch or the new 1:10 000 map will be used. If a developer proposes to build on open land and so make it into a built-up area the Register House will obtain his layout plans, as finally approved by the planning authority, and will ask the Ordnance Survey to produce a new sheet of 50-inch map showing the new layout.

The Land Certificate will be divided into four sections:

1 The Property Section, which gives the description of the subjects and of any servitude or ancillary rights attached thereto.

2 The Proprietorship Section, which shows the name and address of each successive proprietor, the consideration and the date of

---

4 As to which the standard work of reference is Ruoff and Roper, *Law and Practice of Registered Conveyancing*.

5 1963 Cmnd 2032, para 66.

6 1969 Cmnd 4137.

entry. On each sale the particulars of the previous owner will be deleted in red and the deletion authenticated, and the name and address of the new owner will be added, together with the consideration and date of entry.

3   The Charges Section, which specifies any deed such as a feu charter, bond and disposition in security, *ex facie* absolute disposition or standard security which has burdened the subjects during the period of ten years. When any charge is discharged it will be deleted in red and the deletion authenticated. The result is that at a glance the current charges can be discovered.

4   The Burdens Section will list all deeds which imposed burdens on the enjoyment of the subjects, and the subsisting burdens which cannot be specified in a short memorandum are to be added in a Schedule of Burdens. It would normally be necessary to add a schedule to specify the burdens imposed by the owner's immediate superior which would express in detail what was to be built on the feu and the purposes for which it was to be used as well as details of maintenance of fences and making the roads, footpaths and drains. It might be necessary to include in the schedule conditions imposed if the property were subdivided.

The resulting document would give a purchaser's solicitor all the information which he needs almost at a glance, and the conveyance would become a short deed conveying the subject described under the particular title number.

The Land Certificate specifically excludes the following overriding interests which are not disclosed on the Register of Sasines:

1   unregistered leases

2   rights of crofters, landholders under the Small Landholders Acts and cottars

3   servitudes, which do not appear on the Register of Sasines or the land register, public rights of way and inalienable rights of the public

4   liabilities, claims restrictions orders and reservations under statutory authority enforceable by any local authority or government department

5   coal, coal mines, oil, petrol and generally all rights of ownership created by statute

6 floating charges including those which have become fixed securities, which appear on the Register of Companies

The Charge Certificate corresponds to the Title Sheet in the Land Register and specifies the subjects, the registered proprietor, the registered heritable creditor with the date of registration and the amount secured or to be secured, and a note of any security ranking *pari passu* with the heritable security. It also has annexed a copy of the heritable security.

On the first registration the purchaser's solicitor is required to deliver the titles along with the conveyance in favour of his client and to certify that the title is in order. The titles are examined and the Land Certificate and Charges Certificate issued. When the subjects are resold all that it is necessary to do is to deliver a very short conveyance[7] which refers to the title number, along with the Land Certificate and Charges Certificate to be bought up to date.

The Register House has been operating a pilot scheme in the County of Renfrew since 1967 and has been able to work out practical solutions of all the problems which have been presented in that county during the last ten years or so, including a method of dealing with the separate ownership of flats. As soon as the Land Registers (Scotland) Act is passed the County of Renfrew will become the first county in which all transfers of land for value will be compulsorily registrable in the Land Register; and within nine years the system of compulsory registration will be extended to all the counties of Scotland. Glasgow will be dealt with in the second year and Midlothian in the fourth.

The result will be that both the Register of Sasines and the Land Register will exist as public registers side by side for many years, the first gradually diminishing in size while the second grows correspondingly, until in the end, the Register of Sasines will dwindle away to nothing. Dwelling-houses change hands, on an average, once every seven years; but some offices, shops and factories remain under the same ownership for very long periods. When the process is complete Scotland will have one of the finest public Land Registers in the world, and it would seem that the sooner the system is put into operation, the better.

7 *See* Appendix XII.

32 General Conclusions

When the project of making a comparative study of the historical development of Scots and English land law was first under discussion, Lord President Cooper was inclined to take the view that the two systems of land tenure were too different to make an altogether satisfactory subject for comparison. It would be, he suggested, like comparing the Gothic and the Romantic in architecture. Viscount Dunedin evidently took much the same view when he said that 'there is no more identity between the two systems than there is between chalk and cheese.'[1] He was, however, speaking in 1935 and since then we have learnt that cheese may well bear a close resemblance to chalk and other inedible substances. Similarly, one of the main results which emerges from the present inquiry, is that there is some measure of similarity between the two land law systems under consideration. Thus they share the basic theory of the universal derivative tenure of all land from the king, although Scotland admits at least one limited exception to this in the extremely interesting udal landholding of Orkney and Shetland.[2] Both differ from the majority of the world's land law systems in not having a full system of registered title, although Scotland does have the registration of writs and is likely very soon to have a compulsory and comprehensive system of registration which will greatly expedite conveyancing,[3] while England knows title registration on the foreign model in certain limited but highly important areas.[4] There are thus not the barriers of difference which would make a comparison between, say, German and English land law a possibly less fruitful inquiry.

1 Lord Dunedin, *English and Scottish Law*, (Murray Lecture) 19.
2 Chapter 1.
3 Chapter 31.
4 Chapter 27.

Furthermore there is scarcely an institution or tenure of the Scots or England feudal system of landholding which has not at one time existed in the other system. Thus the supposedly exclusive Scottish tenure of feu farm was once known to England, while Scots equivalents of copyhold are not entirely lacking, though never approaching the importance of the English institution.[5] The Scots entail based on irritant and resolutive clauses followed, if it was not actually derived from, an English attempt to develop a similar institution.[6] Even the rule in *Shelley's Case*[7] had a Scots counterpart; while the smallest details of the services to be rendered in blench farm and serjeanty have been shown to be identical in some instances.[8]

In view of the different racial compositions and histories of the two countries all this is rather remarkable: Scotland was for centuries mainly a Celtic area and unlike England she never knew a specifically Norman conquest. Yet what may be called the Anglo-Norman land law prevailed for long ages in both countries. Indeed, until the English abandoned the full rigour of feudalism in Edward I's reign the two systems were substantially similar,[9] because the Anglo-Norman Lothians and their law gradually obtained a preponderance over the Celtic parts and squeezed out every truly Gaelic element from Scotland's land law system. Had Celtic customs prevailed, the story would have been very different and the differences between Scots and English land law far greater. It is to be regretted that no local instances of Celtic landholding have survived to rival the Norse udal holdings already mentioned. However, much the same occurred in Wales and Ireland and it seems reasonable to conclude that there was something weakly in the constitution of Celtic landholding: everywhere it has yielded to feudalism. The cause is not far to seek: the absence of written records. A land law system, curious as it may seem, may be saved by paper where dirk and claymore fail. Only too late did Scots lawyers wake up to the fact that Celtic landholding had disappeared from the world of living institutions, like so many Gaelic customs, into the not always very accurate world of legend. Traces of Celticism may, however, possibly be

5   Chapters 7 and 8.
6   Chapter 20.
7   (1581) 1 Co. Rep. 88b; *see also* Chapter 25 *supra*.
8   Chapter 6.
9   Chapter 10.

found in the encouragement long given by Scots law to family landholding from generation to generation without power of alienation, anathema to every English lawyer from Littleton on – if not earlier.

Scots law is often supposed, especially by Englishmen, to be largely based on Roman law. This is less true in all fields than might be supposed and in land law Scotland has borrowed little more than some rather inappropriate language about usufructs and *dominium*[10] from Rome. This is not to say, however, that the indirect influence of Rome was not strong; for undoubtedly, until the increasing Anglicising tendencies of the last century or so Scots lawyers were essentially civilian in outlook. The radical difference from the English lawyer's approach is that the civilian looks first of all for fundamental principles and a regular system of legal logic, into which every institution of his law can be securely fixed. English systems draw their inspiration from particular instances, decided cases, and leave the enunciation of principles to the chances of litigation. This is a very fundamental difference of approach, which certainly had a fundamental effect on Scots legal thought. But however hard they searched, the Scots lawyers were not to find the principles of a feudal land system in the Digest or in any other sources of Roman law: they had to look instead to more recent material. At the time when they first had the opportunity to be interested in principles they were most fortunately provided with a classic work, that of Craig, which, although based largely on the *Libri Feudorum* and other continental sources, was to be the basis of Scots legal thought on land law questions. Through his influence Scots land law resembles continental, and particularly French, feudal law much more than does English law. Nor is this mere coincidence. Scotland was a much more truly 'feudal' country right up to 1745 than England ever had been, certainly since the accession of Edward I, as was shown by the far greater importance of land-owners' jurisdiction in Scotland and by the survival of personal military service for so long in that country after it had died out in England in 1166 or thereabouts.[11]

The civilian's love of principle and of logical deduction is shown

10 Chapters 11, 13 and 15.
11 Chapter 5.

in many branches of Scots land law and conveyancing: for example the very long sustained requirement of entry with the superior by purchasers and heirs was clearly based on the logical feudal necessity for investiture and homage.[12] This logical and orderly approach has coloured the whole historical develoqment of Scots conveyancing: indeed it is not surprising that it has been claimed that the Scots system of land law before recent statutory changes was a veritable model of legal logic:

> There were few of the innumerable problems which cropped up before the middle of the nineteenth century which proved incapable of elegant solution by application of, or deduction from, the finished principles which had been elaborated by the old feudalists, and the leading cases of the period contain many judgments which are models of philosophic law.[13]

English lawyers would not deny this, but most of them would probably not feel that it mattered very much.[14] As has been frequently observed, English land law developed from remedy to remedy rather than from principle downwards:[15] a plaintiff could sue only if some writ were available which suited his case. Procedure dominated justice[16] and this was the main reason for the development of Equity; but it too, originally intended to introduce flexibility, became affected by the fundamentals of the English approach to the law, so that Lord Eldon, L.C., was able to say 'nothing would inflict on me greater pain, in quitting this place, than the recollection that I had done anything to justify the reproach that the equity of this court varies like the Chancellor's foot'.[17] In the light of such attitudes it is not surprising that ill fortune attended Lord Mansfield's efforts to bring the illogical law of disseisin into line with principle.[18] English law does not mind whether or not a judgment is a model of philosophic law: it is enough if it is in accordance with precedent.

12 Chapter 2.
13 Lord Cooper, *The Scottish Legal Tradition*, 18.
14 But contra, *see* Lawson, *The Rational Strength of English Law*, 75 et seq., 144.
15 E.g. Megarry and Wade, 110–12; Maitland, *Forms of Action at Common Law*, 2.
16 Maine, *Early Law and Custom*, 389; Maitland, *Forms of Action at Common Law*, 1, 6.
17 *Gee v Pritchard* (1818) 2 Swans 402 at 414. Selden had complained (*Table Talk*, 31b) that equity varied with the conscience of each chancellor and that this was as absurd as making the measurement known as a foot vary with each chancellor's foot.
18 *See* pp. 309–10 *supra*.

This is but one cause for the important difference noted at the outset[19] between Scots and English legal history: the one system is philosophically satisfying, but not historically continuous or uniform; the other is regular and uniform in origin, but uninterested in logical consistency. Of course other factors, including English interference at various times and in various forms, were also responsible for the lack of continuity in Scottish legal development.

Generally speaking it seems permissible to speak of a time-lag between the developments which have taken place in the two systems. The very introduction of feudal landholding into Scotland was later than in England; actual military tenures lasted far longer in the Northern than in the Southern Kingdom, and superiors' jurisdictions, feudal casualties, ward, marriage and so on, tell the same story. It was the same tale, too, with the admission of testamentary alienation, and the ending of unbarrable entails. Even the statutory origin of the latter in Scotland came four hundred years after its nearest English equivalent. This seems to be a marked feature of the two countries' legal development, with one very important and significant exception: Scotland has known the registration of sasines for over three hundred years.[20] England has no universal equivalent yet. This is significant, because it shows the Scots law's willingness to innovate and to borrow ideas from other systems. These have not been marked features of English legal development.

England early modified the results of the feudal system by legislation and other means, 'in the interests of expediency: Scotland claims to have obtained for herself 'the most feudal of any system of land laws in the world.'[21] It has been the aim of this work to show the reader how these two things have been attempted. Which has been the more desirable objective and how far it has proved possible to achieve it, must be left for him to judge.

19 *See* Introduction.
20 Chapter 27.
21 Lord Cooper, *The Scottish Legal Tradition*, 17.

APPENDICES I - XII

APPENDIX I

THE OLDEST EXTANT ENGLISH LAND CHARTER[1]

A GRANT BY HLOTHERE, KING OF KENT, A.D. 679[2]

In nomine domini nostri salvatoris Jhesu Christi.[3] Ego HLOTHARIUS rex
Cantuariorum pro remedium animae dono terram in Tenid quae apellatur
UUESTANAE tibi Bercuald tuoque monasterio cum omnibus ad se pertin-
entibus campis pascuis meriscis silvis modicis fonnis piscaris omnibus ut
dictum est ad eandem terram pertinentia sicuti nunc usque possessa est
juxta notissimos terminos a me demonstratus et proacuratoribus meis
eodem modo tibi tuoque monasterio conferimus teneas possedeas tu
posterique tui in perpetuum defendant a nullo contradicitur cum consensu
archiepiscopi Theodori et Edrico filium fratris mei[4] necnon et omnium
principum[5] sicuti tibi donata est ita tene et posteri tui: quisquis contra
hanc donationem venire temptaverit sit ab omni Christianitata separatus
et a corpore et sanguini domini nostri Jhesu Christi suspensus. manentem
hanc donationis chartulam in sua nihilominus firmitate et pro confirma-
tione ejus manu propria signum sanctae crucis expraessi et testes ut
subscriberent rogavi. actum in civitate Recuulf in mense maio indictione
septima[6] . . . (*another grant*).
  X signum manus Hlothari regis donatoris.
  X signum manus Gumbercti. (*and ten other witnesses.*)

*In the name of our Lord and Saviour Jesus Christ. I, Hlothere, King of Kent,
do grant for the saving of my soul to you, Brihtwold, and your monastery,
the land in Thanet called Westanae, together with all its appurtanencies,
fields, pastures, marshes, small woods, fens and fisheries; everything, as said,
that appertains to the same land; on the same terms of possession as it has*

1 A photograph of the original is in Hodgkin, *History of the Anglo-Saxons*, ii, 453,
   plate 58.
2 There are unlikely to be earlier examples. Written deeds began to be used in the
   seventh century A.D., for donations to the Church. (Spelman, *Feuds and Tenures*,
   12.)
3 These invocations were customary in all early documents. But there is none in the
   Scots deed. Appendix II.
4 Hlothere's heir. He succeeded him in spite of the fact that he had a son. Eadric's
   father had reigned before Hlothere. (Hodgkin, *History of the Anglo-Saxons*, ii,
   Table 2.)
5 'Where the king was donor, the ancient deeds did usually recite that the gift was
   made by the consent of the peers of the land.' (Spelman, *Glossary*, 234.) He cites a
   Kentish example of a deed being avoided for non-consent of peers.
6 The system of dating by the years of Christ only came in later.

had up to the present, within very familiar boundaries indicated by me and my reeves, we do confer it on you and your monastery to hold and possess and for you and your successors to keep in perpetuity. This we do without opposition and with the consent of Archbishop Theodore and Eadric, my brother's son and moreover of all peers; as it is granted, so hold it, both you and your successors. Whosoever should try to contravene this grant, may he be cut off from the Body and Blood of our Lord Jesus Christ. This charter of grants remains nevertheless in its own validity, and in confirmation of it I have signed it in my own hand with the mark of the Holy Cross and have asked witnesses to sign beneath. Transacted in the city of Reculver, in the month of May, in the seventh indiction.

X Sign manual of King Hlothere, donor.

X Sign manual of Gumberht . . .

APPENDIX II

THE OLDEST EXTANT SCOTS LAND CHARTER[1]

A GRANT BY DUNCAN II, KING OF SCOTS, A.D. 1094[2]

Ego Dunecanus, filius regis Malcolumb, constans hereditarie rex Scotiae,[3] dedi in elemosinam Sancto Cuthberto et suis servitoribus, Tiningeham, Aldeham, Scuchale, Cnolle, Hatheruuich et de Broccesmuthe omne servitium quod inde habuit Fodanus episcopus, et haec dedi in tali quitantia cum saca et soca[4] qualem unquam meliorem habuit Sanctus Cuthbertus ab illis de quibus tenet suas elemosinas. Et hoc dedi pro me ipso et pro anima patris mei et pro fratribus meis et pro uxore mea at pro infantibus meis.[5] Et quum volui quod istud donum stabile esset Sancto Cuthberto, feci quod fratres mei concesserunt: Qui autem istud voluerunt destruere vel ministris Sancti Cuthberti aliquod inde auferre, maledictionem Dei et Sancti Cuthberti et meam habeant. Amen.

Crux Dunecani regis X   Scriptoris Grentonis X
    Accard X   Ulf X   *(and eight other witnesses)*

I, Duncan, son of King Malcolm, established by heredity King of Scotland, have given in alms to St Cuthbert and his servants Tyningham, Aldeham, Scuchale, Cnolle, Hatherwick and from Broxmouth all the service which Bishop Fodan had of it; and these I have given in like quittance with Sac and Soc on as good terms as ever St Cuthbert did have from those from whom he holds his alms. And this I have given for myself and for my father's soul and for my brothers and for my wife and for my children. And since it is my wish that St Cuthbert should hold this gift securely, I have made my brothers agree to it. But whosoever should wish to destroy or carry off anything thence from the servants of St Cuthbert, may they be accursed of God and St Cuthbert and my self.

Cross of King Duncan X

1   A photograph of the original is in Hume-Brown, *History of Scotland*, i, 54. The transcription is from Lawrie, *Early Scottish Charters*, 10. The charter is not dated, but Duncan visited Durham in 1094 on his way to seize the throne, which he held only for a year.
2   For a discussion as to its authenticity, see Lawrie, *et seq.*, 240. It is at least very generally accepted as genuine.
3   A very unusual style. Cf William I's grant to Durham: 'Willielmus, dei gratia Rex Anglorum hereditario iure factus.' (Innes, *Scotch Legal Antiquities*, 35.)
4   I.e. with local jurisdiction over their tenants. As to these grants and their absence in England, *see* Chapter 9. For 'Sake and Soke' in England, *see* P. & M., i, 92–3, and *Burrough of Doncaster's Case* (1610) Ley 5.
5   Later granters made even wider demands. *See* e.g. the long list of people mentioned in Walter Fitzalan's Charter. (Innes, *Scotch Legal Antiquities*, 37.)

APPENDIX III

THE ONLY EXTANT GAELIC LAND CHARTER[1]

A GRANT BY MCDONALD, LORD OF THE ISLES, A.D. 1408[2]

In the name of God, Amen.
I, Mac Donald, am granting and giving eleven merks and a half of land from myself and from my heirs, to Brian Vicar Mackay and to his heirs after him for ever and ever, for his services . . .[3] to myself and to my father before me; and this on covenant and condition that he himself and they shall give to me and to my heirs after me yearly, four cows fit for killing, for my house. And in case that these cows shall not be found, the above Brian and his heirs shall give to me and to my heirs after me, two merks and forty for the same above cows. And for the same causes I am binding myself and binding my heirs after me, to the end of the world, these lands together with their fruits of sea and land, to defend and maintain to the above Brian Vicar Mackay, and to his heirs for ever after him in like manner. And these are the lands I have given to him and to his heirs for ever: namely Baile-Vicar Machaire, Learga-riabhoighe, Ciontragha, Graftol, Tocamol, Ugasgog, the two Gleannastols, Cracobus, Cornubus and Baile-Neaghtoin. And in order that there may be meaning and force and effect in this grant I give from me, I again bind myself and my heirs for ever under covenant this to uphold and fulfil to the aforesaid Brian and to his heirs after him, to the end of the world, by putting my hand and seal down here, in the presence of these witnesses here below, and the sixth day of the month of the Beltane,[4] and this year of the birth of Christ, one thousand, four hundred and eight.

Eion Mac Domhaill[5]
his mark
(*and three other witnesses*)

Mc Domhaill

---

1 For the original, *see National MSS. of Scotland*, II, lix, whence the translation is also taken.
2 The lands referred to are in Islay. The Gaelic shows Islay idioms and is nearer to Irish Gaelic than that now spoken in Scotland. (*National MSS.*, Introduction xiii.)
3 There is a word missing here in the MS.
4 This citing of the druidical month is a curiosity. (*See National MSS.*, II, Introduction.)
5 John MacDonald was a nephew of the chief, the son of a deceased brother. Presumably his signature is appended to show his consent to the charter. (cf. Appendices I and II.)

APPENDIX IV

THE OLDEST EXTANT NORSE LAND DOCUMENT IN SCOTLAND[1]

A RECORD OF THE SALE OF UDAL LAND AT UNST, SHETLAND, A.D. 1465[2]

Unto all men who this letter shall see or hear Andrew Williamson sends God's and his own greeting, making known by this my letter patent that I have sold to that worshipful man Symon Hognason one merk burnt (silver) in land which is situated in Walol from me and my heirs unto the said Symon and his heirs for an everlasting possession. Moreover I acknowledge that I have received the first penny and the last and all that lay between, so that I am well-satisfied, to wit six florins in linen for this merk: and whereas I have no seal myself, I have requested the worshipful men who are thus called Magnus Olaussen and Olaf Arnason, to append their seals at my own desire unto this letter, which was done in Unst Anno Domini MCDLXV.[3]

1 For the original, *see National MSS. of Scotland*, ii, lxxviii. There are earlier Scandinavian examples.
2 I.e. four years before this island was pledged to Scotland. This document could not properly be called a charter because it has no feudal nature such as that of the Gaelic grant in Appendix III. It has no words of grant or warranty, being a mere record of an already accomplished translation.
3 The *Scotsman* in reviewing *National MSS*. (6 November 1870), drew the attention of the Lord Advocate and others then engaged in reforming Scots conveyancing to it for its brevity and distinction.

APPENDIX V

Two Examples to show the Similarity of Feudal Documents in Early Medieval England and Scotland[1]

1 A CHARTER OF FEOFFMENT IN FEE BY WILLIAM THE LION[2]

Willielmus, Dei gratia, *Rex* Scotorum, *Episcopis, Abbatibus, Comitibus, Baronibus, Justiciariis, Vicecomitibus, et Ministris, et Omnibus* probis hominibus *totius* terrae suae Clericis et Laicis, *salutem. Sciant* praesentes et futuri me dedisse, *concessisse,* et hac carta mea confirmasse, Waltero de Berkelay Camerario meo, Inverkileder, per rectas divisas suas[3] Tenend(um) *sibi et haeredibus suis, de me et haeredibus meis, in feudo et haereditate, in bosco et plano, in* terris et *aquis, in pratis et pascuis, in molendinis* et stagnis, in moris et stalangis, in viis et semitis, *et omnibus aliis justis pertinentiis suis, cum sacka et socka, cum tel et theme, et infangenethief,* cum furca et fossa *libere et quiete,* plenarie *et honorifice* per servitium unius militis. *Testibus,* etc.

2 A CHARTER OF FEOFFMENT IN FEE BY HENRY THE SECOND[4]

H(enricus) *rex* Anglie dux Norm(annie) et Acquiet(annie) et comes Andeg(evie) archiepiscopis[5] *episcopis abbatibus comitibus baronibus justic-(iariis) vicecomitibus ministris et omnibus* fidelibus suis *totius* Anglie et Normannie *salutem. Sciatis me concessisse* Roberto Foliot totam terram et honorem[6] qui fuit Widonis de Raimecurt cum Margeria filia Ricardi de Raimecurt que inde heres. Quare volo et precipio quod *ipse et heredes sui* terram et honorem illum *teneant de me et heredibus meis in feodo et hereditarie* ita *libere et quiete et honorifice* sicut predictus Wido de Raimecurt melius vel libertius quiecius et honorificentius unquam tenuit et Richardus filius suus post eum *cum soca et saca et tol et teham et infangereteof et cum omnibus* libertatibus et liberis consuetudininibus que honori predicto pertinent *in bosco et plano in pratis et pascuis in aquis et molendinis* in civitatibus et extra et in omnibus locis. *Testibus,* Thoma cancellario et aliis.

1 The words in italic occur in both charters.
2 From Ross, *Lectures,* ii, 126. The date is between 1165 and 1214.
3 Cf. the longer English description. Scots lands often had the privilege of union. This meant that a name would carry the whole estate without further identification.
4 Stenton, *English Feudalism,* 263, 1154 and 1163.
5 There was no archbishop in Scotland until 1474.
6 An honour was a large manor with jurisdictional privileges.

1 *William, by Grace of God King of Scotland, to the Bishops, Abbots, Counts, Barons, Justices, Viscounts, Ministers and all good men and true of his whole land, both church and lay, Greetings!*

Let men present and future know that I have given, granted and by this my charter confirmed Inverkileder, by its proper boundaries, to Walter of Berkelay my Chamberlain, to be held by him and his heirs from me and my heirs in fee and heredity; in wood and plain, in land and water, in mean and pasture, in mill and pool, in moor and market-stall, in road and path and all its other lawful appurtenancies; with Sac and Soc, with Toll and Team and Infangthief,[7] with pit and gallows, freely and peacefully, with the full rights and honours, for the service of one knight.

2 *Henry, King of England, Duke of Normandy and Aquitaine, Count of Anjon, to the archbishops, bishops, abbots, counts, barons, justices, viscounts, ministers and all his faithful lieges of England and Normandy, Greetings!*

Know that I have granted to Robert Foliot the whole land and honour formerly of Wido of Raimecourt and Margery, daughter of Richard of Raimecourt, and their heirs. Wherefore it is my wish and command that he and his heirs should hold that land and honour of me and my heirs in fee and heredity on as good terms of freedom, peace and honour as did ever the aforesaid Wido of Raimecourt and his son Richard after him; with sac and soc and toll and team, and infangthief, and with all the liberties and free customs, which pertain to the said honour; in wood and plain, field and pasture, water and mill, within towns and without and in all places.

Witnessed, Thomas Chancellor and others.

7 On these terms *see* Windeyer, *Lectures on Legal History*, 11.

APPENDIX VI

The Documents Usually Employed[1] at Common Law to Effect a Transfer of Land in England
(from a seventeenth century students' manual[2])

1   A DEED OF FEOFFMENT UPON A SALE

To all Christian People to whom this present Writing shall come, greeting: Know ye, That I *W.B.* of *etc.* in part of performance of the Covenant mentioned in one Pair of Indentures,[3] bearing date, *etc.* made between me the said *W.B.* and *F*, my Wife, of the one part, and *G.H.* of *etc.* of the other part; Have given, granted, enfeoffed, and confirmed; and by these Presents, do give, grant, enfeoff and confirm unto the said *G.H.* all those, *etc.* several Messuages, Tenements or Cottages, *etc.* and the Reversion and Reversions, Remainder and Remainders, Rents, Issues, and Profits of all and singular the Premisses; and all the Estate, Right, Title, Interest, Benefit, Claim and Demand whatsoever of me the said *W.B.* of, in, and to the same: To have and to hold the said Messuages, Tenements, Cottages, and all and singular other the Premises, with their and every of their Appurtenances before-mentioned to be granted unto the said *G.H.* and his heirs. To the use of the said *G.H.* his Heirs and Assigns for ever. And I the said *W.B.* have granted for me and my Heirs, that we will grant unto the said *G.H.* and his Heirs, the said Messuages, Tenements, or Cottages, and Premises, with the Appurtenances, against all People for ever by these Presents. In witness, *etc.*

2   LIVERY AND SEISIN TO BE ENDORSED ON A DEED[4]

Memorandum, That peaceable and quiet Possession and Seisin of the Lands and Hereditaments within mentioned to be granted, was had, and taken by the within-named *A.B.* the Attorney within-mentioned,

---

1 This was only one possibility. A bargain and sale for years followed by a release could be used. (*See* Chapter 24.) No documents was essential.
2 *The Young Clerks Tutor Enlarged* (1670).
3 This contract could have been unwritten until the Statute of Frauds, 1677. An indenture was traditionally made in duplicate on a single sheet with an erased zig-zag between them. Hence the name.
4 No special wording was necessary, still less a notarial instrument. Similarly power to act as attorney could be given informally. There was no need for a written precept. (*Contra*, Scotland, *see* Appendix VII.)

and by him was delivered to the within-named *M.G.* the Bargainee[5] in his own proper person, To hold to him the said *M.G.* and his Heirs, to the use of him the said *M.G.* and of his Heirs and Assigns for ever, according to the tenour, form, and effect of the within-written Deed, in the presence of us.

5   This endorsement is on a bargain and sale, but the form was the same on a deed of feoffment except for this word.

APPENDIX VII

DOCUMENTS NECESSARY AT COMMON LAW TO EFFECT A TRANSFER OF LAND IN SCOTLAND[1]
(FROM AN EIGHTEENTH CENTURY STYLE BOOK[2])

I   A DISPOSITION WITH GRANT DE ME VEL A ME

BE IT KNOWN to all men, *That*, I *A*, heritable proprietor of the lands and others aftermentioned, *in consideration* of the sum of ten thousand pounds *Sterling* instantly paid in to me by *B*, whereof I hereby discharge him, his heirs and executors, for now and ever, *have sold* and disponed, as I at this present sell and dispone, to the said *B*, his heirs or assignees whatsoever, absolutely and irredeemably, all and whole (*here the lands, etc. ought to be described after the same manner they are denominated in the antecedent infeftments*), together with all right and interest that I, my heirs and successors, either have or anywise can claim or pretend thereto or to any part thereof, in time coming. In the which lands above disponed, I bind and oblige myself and mine aforesaid, to infeft and seise the said *B* and his above named, upon their own proper charges and expenses, heritably and irredeemably: and that by two several infeftments and manners of holding: the one whereof to be holden of me, my heirs and successors, in free blench for payment of a penny *Scots* money in name of blench farm, at the term of *Whitsunday* yearly, provided the same be required; and for relieving us, at the hands of the superiors of the forementioned lands and estate, of the duties and services payable to them forth of the same:[3] and the other of these infeftments to be holden from me and mine aforesaid, of my said superiors, by the same tenure that I presently hold of them myself. And for obtaining the above-said infeftment by resignation, I make and constitute   and each of them, jointly and severally, my very lawful and irrevocable procurators, for me and for in my name, to resign and surrender, as I at this present resign, give up, and surrender, all and whole (*in this place, the lands, etc. are repeated*) together with all right and interest that I, my heirs and successors, either have or any wise can claim or pretend thereto, or to any part thereof, in time coming, *in the hands* of my immediate superior or superiors of the same, presently being, or that shall happen to be for the

---

1   Certain alternatives existed, e.g. a confirmation instead of the resignation and regrant (3) and (4). If nothing followed (1) and (2) the purchaser would have a base infeftment (*see* Chapter 24).
2   From McKenzie, *Origin and Progress of Fees*; (4) is from Ross, *Lectures*, ii, 283.
3   This is the old problem of the forinsec services (P. & M., i, 238).

time, or his or their commissioners having power to receive resignations in his or their names,[4] *in favour* and for new infeftment thereof to be reassigned to the said *B*, his heirs or assignees, absolutely and irredeemably, in due and competent form; and thereupon, acts, instruments and documents to call for and receive, and generally, to do every other thing in relation to that affair, that I might do myself if I were present, which I shall hold firm and stable without revocation. Which lands and others above designated with the pertinents, I, the said *A* bind and oblige myself and mine aforesaid, to warrant and maintain to the said *B* and his above named, at all hands and in every event whatsoever: and also, to extricate and disengage the same of all feu, blench and tiend duties, supplies, taxations, ministers stipends, schoolmasters salaries, and of all other public burdens wherewith they shall be incumbered at the term of
next to come, being the period of time at which the said *B* his entry doth commence. *Further*, I make and constitute the said *B* and his above named, my cessionaries and assignees, in all and singular charters, dispositions, retours, precepts and instruments of seisin, procuratories and instruments of resignation, and all other writings and securities whatsoever, granted to me, my predecessors or authors, with relation to the subject-matter of the present right and disposition, or any part thereof, with all that has followed or may follow thereon; and in like manner, in and to all rents, revenues, and casualties of the before mentioned lands, of the crops and year of God   , and in all time thereafter, with all action and pursuit any wise competent for the same; *surrogating* and *substituting* the said *B* in my full and right place of the premises for ever. With power to him and his aforesaid, to intromit with and uplift, and, if necessary, to use all manner of legal diligence for obtaining payment of the rents and duties above assigned; and to remove and put in tenants, and to do every other thing in relation thereto, or towards the recovery of the evidences and securities before written, that I might have done myself before the granting of this assignation: which assignation I bind and oblige myself and mine aforesaid to warrant in the following manner, namely, in so far as it concerns the writs and evidences at all hands and against all other men, and in so far as it relates to the other subjects above mentioned, from my own facts and deeds done in prejudice therewith. *Moreover*, I have delivered up to the said *B* the rights and securities before assigned, according to an inventory thereof of this day's date, to be kept and used by him and his aforesaid as their proper evidences for the time to come. *Furthermore*, I desire and require you   [5] and each of you, jointly and severally, my bailies, to the effect after specified

4   For this procedure *see* (3) *infra.*
5   These spaces were generally left blank throughout.

especially constitute, that, on sight hereof, ye pass to the ground of the said lands and there deliver to the said *B* heritable state and seisin, with possession, corporal, actual and real, of all and singular the lands, mills, tiends and others before enumerated, by delivering to him or his attorney in his name, bearer hereof, a little earth and stone of the ground of the respective lands, the claps and hoppers of the mills, and an handful of grass and corn in place of the tiends, conform to this disposition, and the infeftment to follow thereon, or either of them; and that this on no account ye leave undone: The which to do, I commit to you, jointly and severally, by this precept. And I consent to the registration hereof in the books of council and session, or of any other competent judicature, therein to remain for preservation; and if need be, to have the strength of a decree of any of the judges interponed thereto, that letters of horning and all other execution necessary may be directed thereupon, constituting my procurators for that effect. (*Follows the clause of subscription, setting forth the date, and the writers and witnesses names and designations, in common form.*)

2   AN INSTRUMENT OF SASINE

IN THE NAME OF GOD, AMEN.[6] *Be it known* to all men, That on the   th day of   in the year of our Lord one thousand seven hundred and fifty-nine, and of the reign of our Sovereign, *George* the Second, by the Grace of God, King of Great Britain, France and Ireland, the thirty-second year, *In presence* of me notary-public and the witnesses subscribing, *appeared A,* and passing with us to the ground of the lands and others after mentioned; *having* and holding in his hands an absolute and ir-redeemable right and disposition granted by *B*, whereby, for the reasons therein expressed, he sold and disponed to the said *A*, his heirs and assignees whatsoever, heritably and irredeemably, all and singular (*Here insert the lands, etc. as they are denominated in the conveyance*) together with all right, etc. as the above-said disposition, bearing date, etc. and containing a clause of infeftment *a me* and *de me*, a procuratory of resignation, a precept of sasine, and divers other clauses and obligements, at more lengths sets forth. Which disposition, including the precept of seisin above and under mentioned, the said *A* presented to *C*, bailie in that part by the aforesaid precept specially constitute, requiring him at the same time to set about and perform the duties of his office. In agreeableness to which desire, he received the disposition into his hands, and delivered the same to me the notary, to be read and published to the

6   Cf. Appendices I and III.

witnesses standing by; which accordingly I did, and have hereunto annexed the before-mentioned precept itself, which is as follows: (*Transcribe the precept word for word*). After reading and publishing the above-mentioned disposition (*or other writing*), the said *C*, in consequence of the office thereby committed to him, gave and delivered to the said *A*, heritable state and seisin, with possession, corporal, actual and real, of all and singular the lands, tenements, mills, tithes and others above enumerated; by delivering to him a little earth and stone of the respective lands and tenements, the claps and hoppers of the mills, and an handful of growing corn (*or* stubble) in the place of the tiends, conform to the fore-mentioned disposition in all parts:[7] whereupon the said *A* required instruments concerning the whole matter under the hand of me notary public subscribing. These things were done on the ground of the particular lands, mills and tenements above-mentioned, betwixt the hours of ten and twelve in the forenoon, upon the day of the month, in the year of our Lord and of his Majesty's reign, respectively before written, in the presence of *E* and *F*, witnesses to the premisses specially called and required. (*Follows the notary's attestation*[8] *etc.*).

3 AN INSTRUMENT OF RESIGNATION *IN FAVOREM*

IN THE NAME OF GOD, AMEN. Know all men, That upon the day of   in the year of our LORD   , and of the reign of our Sovereign *George* the Second the   year: in the presence of *A* Chief Baron, and the rest of the Barons of his Majesty's court of Exchequer in *Scotland*, his Highness's commissioners duly authorised for the purpose after mentioned: *and also*, in presence of me notary public, and the witnesses subscribing *appeared B*, as procurator to the effect under written, specially constitute by *C*, conform to the letter of procuratory contained in an absolute and irredeemable disposition of the lands and others hereafter denominated, granted by the said *C* to *D*, of date, etc.: and there the said *B*, with the utmost humility, resigned, gave up, and by staff and baton, as the custom is, surrendered all and singular (*Copy out the lands, etc. from the conveyance*); together with all right and title the said *C*, his heirs or successors, either had or could any wise challenge to the same, or to any part thereof, *in the hands* of the said *A*, for himself, and in behalf of the other Barons of the above-said Court, his Majesty's commissioners as was said, as in the hands of the Sovereign himself, the

7 Great care was necessary here (*see* Chapter 24).
8 This was very long and continued to be in Latin after the rest came to be in English.

said *C* his immediate superior of the lands and others above enumerated: to the end that new infeftment of the same might be reassigned to the above *D*, his heirs, etc. heritably and irredeemably, in due and competent form: on conditions always. etc. (*the conditions if there are any in the warrant, are here reckoned up*). Accordingly, the said *A*, having accepted the resignation by receiving the symbols into his hands, forthwith reassigned and passed over to the same *D*, the whole lands, baronies and others before described, to be possessed and enjoyed by him and his above named, heritably and irredeemably in all time coming; and that by returning the symbols to the above *B*, who at the same time appeared as his attorney in that behalf; and hereupon this *B* required instruments concerning the whole matter under the hand of me notary public subscribing. These things were done in the high exchequer house at *Edinburgh*, betwixt the hours of, etc. (*forma communi*).

4   A CHARTER OF RESIGNATION [9]

To all and sundry to whose knowledge these presents shall come – Charles, Duke of Lauderdale, etc., etc. immediate lawful superior of the lands and others after described, hath given, granted successors, gives, grants, and perpetually confirms to our lovite John Young of Lery, and the heirs-male of his body, whom failing, to his heirs and successors whatever, heritably and irredeemably, all and haill (*etc.*). Which lands and others above described, pertained heritably of before to Sir Andrew Fletcher of Aberlady, Baronet holden by him of us and our noble predecessors, immediate lawful superiors thereof, and which, with all right and title, and interest which the said Sir Andrew Fletcher had or could pretend thereto, were upon the   day of   last, duly and lawfully resigned by Andrew Walker writer in Edinburgh, procurator for the said Sir Andrew Fletcher, for that effect specially constituted, by virtue of the procuratory of resignation after recited, in our hands as immediate lawful superiors thereof, purely and simply by staff and baston, as use is, in favour and for new infeftment of the same, to be made and granted to the said John Young and his aforesaids, heritably and irredeemably, in such due and competent form as effeirs; and that by virtue of, and conform to the said procuratory of resignation contained in a disposition of the said lands and others before described, granted by the said Sir Andrew Fletcher in favour of the said John Young, and the heirs male of his body, whom failing, to his heirs and successors whatever, of date the   day of   as authentic instruments taken

9   I.e. on a resignation. The 'royal' style may be noted.

thereon, under the subscription of John Hamilton, N.P. at more length proports; to be holden, and for to hold, all and haill the foresaid lands and others, with the pertinents, of us, our heirs, and successors, immediate superiors thereof, in fee and heritage for ever, by all the righteous meiths and marches thereof, old and divided, as the same lie in length and breadth, houses, biggings, etc. (*here the long clause*[11] *was engrossed*) with all and sundry other liberties, advantages, profits, easements, and pertinents thereof, as well not named as named, under and above ground, pertaining or belonging, or that may anyways justly pertain and belong to the said lands and others any manner of way in time coming, freely, quietly, honourably, well and in peace, without any revocation, contradiction, or other obstacle whatsomever; Giving therefor, and paying yearly, the said John Young and his foresaids, to us and our noble successors, immediate lawful superiors thereof, one pound of pepper, at the term of Whitsunday, upon the ground of the said lands, in name of blench farm, if asked allenarly, for all other burdens, exaction, question, demand, or secular service, which may be in any shape exacted or required furth of the foresaid lands and pertinents; attour we hereby require   and everyone of you, conjunctly and severally, our baillies, to the effect that, upon sight hereof, ye pass to the ground of the said lands, and there give heritable state and sasine, with real, actual and corporeal possession, of all and haill, etc. to the said John Young, and the heirs-male of his body, whom failing to his heirs and successors whatsoever, and that by deliverance in their hands, or in the hand of their certain attorney or attorneys, bearers hereof, of earth and stone of the ground of the said lands, as use is, to be holden in manner above mentioned; and this in noways ye leave undone. Which to do we commit to you, conjunctly and severally, our baillies, full and irrevocable power, by this our precept directed to you for that effect; saving to us and our successors our own right and the right of all others. In testimony whereof, etc.

5 ANOTHER INSTRUMENT OF SASINE ON THE PRECEPT CONTAINED IN THE CHARTER OF RESIGNATION

This completed the vassal's entry with the superior in the Register of Sasines.

APPENDIX VIII

A Modern Feu Charter

I, *A*, heritable proprietor of the subjects hereinafter disponed (who and my successors in the estate of superiority of the said subjects hereby constituted are hereinafter sometimes referred to as "the Superior') IN CONSIDERATION of the grassum of............[1] Pounds paid to me by *B* of which sum I hereby acknowledge receipt and in consideration of the prestations aftermentioned and with and under the reservations, limitations, restrictions, obligations and conditions and the irritant and resolutive clauses after specified do hereby CONVEY and IN FEU FARM DISPONE to and in favour of *B* and his executors and assignees whomsoever (all of whom are hereinafter referred to as 'the Feuars') but excluding assignees before the recording of these presents heritably and irredeemably ALL and WHOLE that area of ground extending to   situated to the west side of Roman Road, Bothwell Haugh part of the lands of Bothwell Park belonging to the Superior lying in the Parish of Bothwell and County of Lanark delineated and edged red on the plan annexed and signed as relative hereto and bounded as follows:........... which area of ground is part of the lands and estate of Bothwell Park in the said Parish and County described in the Disposition by *X* in favour of the Superior dated............and recorded in the Division of the General Register of Sasines applicable to the County of Lanark on   1949 (which area of ground is hereinafter referred to as 'the Feu') together with all rights of way, wayleaves and servitudes affecting the Feu. Together also with the whole mines, metals and minerals within and under the Feu but subject to the provisions of the Coal Act 1938 and the Coal Industry Nationalisation Act 1946 and the rights of the National Coal Board under the said Acts or otherwise but declaring that the Superior shall not be responsible for any claim or compensation which may arise as a result of past, present or future subsidence or workings either in respect of coal or any other mineral; But the Feu is disponed with and under the burdens, restrictions, conditions, provisions, declarations and others following videlicet: (First) the Feu is disponed only for the purpose of the erection thereon by the Feuars of private dwelling-houses, private motor car garages, garden huts and greenhouses and other erections ancillary to dwelling-houses, (Second) the said dwelling-houses and others to be erected on the

---

1 Feuduties were abolished by the Conveyancing and Feudal Reform Act 1974 but there is no reason why a feu charter should not be granted for a grassum or capital sum.

Feu shall be erected according to plans, elevations, and specifications in accordance with full detailed Planning Permission obtained by the Feuars from the Local Planning Authority and which shall be approved by the Superior which approval shall not be unreasonably withheld, and such dwelling-houses and others shall be maintained and upheld in good order and repair in all time coming: (Third) the Feuars shall pay to the proprietors whose lands adjoin the Feu one half of the value of the existing walls or fences, provided such adjoining proprietors have the right to require such payment in terms of their Feu Charters and thereafter the Feuars and their successors shall be bound to keep up and maintain the said boundary walls and fences mutually with such adjoining proprietors in all time coming. The fence along the boundaries with ground belonging to the Secretary of State for Scotland are wholly outwith the Feu; The fences and walls along the South East and East South East boundaries of the Feu shall be wholly within the Feu and shall be maintained as stock-proof fences and walls but on the adjoining ground being feued or disponed for development the feuar or disponee thereof shall be taken bound to pay to the Feuars half the value at the time of such fences and walls which shall thereafter be maintained as mutual fences and walls; In the event of there being no provision for the fences along the South by East, East by North, South by West, West and West North West boundaries to become mutual, or in the event of any of the proprietors of the ground adjoining the said boundaries refusing to agree to their fences becoming mutual the Feuars shall be bound to enclose the Feu along such boundaries with suitable fences erected wholly within the Feu; All existing boundary walls fences and hedges within or partly within the Feu so far as they belong to the Superior shall become the property of the Feuars and the Superior shall have no responsibility for the erection or maintenance of any boundary wall fence or hedge (Fourth) there is no outstanding obligation on the Superior to construct or maintain any road *ex adverso* or within the Feu and the Feuars shall be bound to construct at their own expense all necessary roads, footpaths, kerbs, water channels, gratings and main sewers over or through or *ex adverso* the Feu; (Fifth) The Feuars will not incur any liability in respect of disturbance of any agricultural tenants or others and all claims for loss of crop, unexhausted manures and generally all claims arising from such disturbance shall be borne by the Superior but the Feuars shall give as much notice of their intention to resume ground and shall not damage growing crops unless absolutely necessary; (Sixth) the Feu is disponed under burden of all rights of way, wayleaves and servitudes presently affecting the same. The Superior will be entitled to a heritable and irredeemable servitude right of way for pedestrians and vehicles along the private road coloured green on the said plan from Bothwell to Bothwell Park Farm provided that the said right of way shall be for pedestrians and farm and private traffic for the tenant of Bothwell Park Farm and for feuars and developers who may purchase land from the Superiors north east of the Feu on the understanding that such feuars or developers or their successors will be responsible for a *pro rata* share of the maintenance of the said private road depending on the number of houses built on the Feu and the number of houses built to the north-east of the Feu which are served by the said private road; (Seventh) The Feuars shall have the right to make connections with any existing drains, sewers, electric cables, gas or water mains belonging to the Superior or provided by the Local or Public Authorities within the Feu or situated within other subjects belonging to the Superior and shall be entitled to pass sewage or drainage water from the feu into the said drains or sewers subject always to the consent of the Superior and appropriate Local and Public Authority with servitude rights of access to the said connecting drains and sewers so far as passing through ground belonging to the Superior for the purpose of inspection, maintenance or renewal of such connecting drains and sewers on payment for all surface damage caused by such operations; (Eighth) The buildings and erections on the Feu shall not be used for commercial premises, factories or workshops of any kind or in any way which might form a nuisance or be injurious to the amenity of the neighbourhood and the Feu shall be kept in a neat and tidy condition so far as not covered by buildings; (Ninth) The Superior shall not be liable for the execution of any general feuing plan of the lands of which the Feu forms a part and the Superior may give any consent, approval or direction referred to in these presents through their duly authorised Factor for the time; All which burdens, restrictions, conditions, provisions, declarations and others herein contained are hereby declared to be real burdens upon and affecting the Feu and, with the irritant and resolutive clauses after written, are hereby appointed to be inserted or validly referred to in all future renovations, conveyances and investitures of the Feu or any part thereof otherwise the same shall be null and void: DECLARING that if the Feuars shall fail to observe and perform or shall act contrary to any of the obligations and conditions hereinbefore expressed, then, in the option of the Superior not only shall this Feu Charter become null and void but the person or persons failing to observe or perform or contravening shall amit and forfeit all right and interest in the said piece of ground and buildings thereon, which shall thereupon revert to the Superior in like manner as if this Feu right had never been granted but without prejudice to the legal rights and remedies of the Superior for performance of the prestations payable by and incumbent on the Feuars under these presents prior to the date of such forfeiture; Declaring however that if after the sale of any dwellinghouse with ground effeiring thereto Notice of Change of Ownership in respect thereof is duly given to the Superior's Factor for the time on the Superior's behalf such dwelling-house with the ground effeiring thereto shall thereafter be considered as a separate feu in respect that as regards the formation and maintenance of roads, footpaths, water channels, kerbs and gratings, the liability of the purchaser of such house and ground effeiring thereto and his successors shall extend over the area up to the centre line of the road or roads *ex adverso* the ground effeiring to such dwelling-house and the purchaser and his successors shall have no liability in respect of obligations relating to other parts of the feu: WITH ENTRY as at the............TO BE HOLDEN the Feu by the Feuars of and under the Superior as immediate lawful Superior thereof in feu farm fee and heritage forever, And I assign the writs but to the effect only of maintaining and defending the Feuars in the right of the *dominium utile* of the Feu and for that purpose I bind myself and my foresaids to make the same to the extent of a legal progress or so far as in my or their possession at the time furthcoming to the Feuar in the office of my Solicitors on all necessary occasions; And I assign the rents; And I bind myself to free and relieve the Feuars of all feuduties payable to my Superior and of all public burdens due at and prior to the said date of entry: And I grant warrandice:

(Stamp clause if necessary)

IN WITNESS WHEREOF

Register on behalf of the within named *B* in the Register of the County of Lanark

Hamilton, Solicitors Agents.

Docquet for Plan:

This is the plan referred to in the foregoing Feu Charter dated..........

APPENDIX IX

EXTRACT OF SIGNATURE OF RESIGNATION[1] of Lands of Ormistoun[2] in the Parish of Innerleithen and County of Peebles in favour of Joseph Gillon, Writer, Edinburgh. Dated 8 July 1804.[3]

Our Sovereign Lord – with the special advice and consent of Robert Dundas Esquire of Arniston Lord Chief Baron of His Majesty's Court of Exchequer in that part of Great Britain called Scotland, Sir John Dalrymple Baronet Fletcher Norton Archibald Cockburn and George Buchan Hepburn Esquires, remanent Barons of His Majesty's said Court of Exchequer ordains a Charter to be made and passed under the Seal appointed by the Treaty of Union to be kept and used in Scotland in place of the Great Seal thereof formerly used there; giving granting and disponing and for His Majesty and his Royal successors perpetually confirming Likeas His Majesty with advice and consent foresaid by these presents gives grants and dispones, and for him and his Royal successors perpetually confirms to His Majestys Lovite Joseph Gillon Writer in Edinburgh in trust for behoof of the Creditors of the late W. John Scott Writer to the Signet All and whole the Ten pound land of old extent of Ormistoun with the Tower, Fortalice, Manor place, Houses, Biggings, Yards, Orchards parts pendicles and pertinents thereof whatsoever part of the Barony of Traquair lying within the Parish of Innerleithen and Sheriffdom of Peebles, together with the tiends parsonage and vicarage thereof, and the Salmon Fishings in the river Tweed pertaining thereto, and all and sundry minerals of Gold, Silver, copper, lead, and other minerals whatsoever lying within the bounds of all and whole the said Lands and others above written with the pertinents conform to Trust Disposition dated the thirty-first day of December in the year one thousand eight hundred and three, and recorded in the Books of Council and Session (office H.F.) the fourth day of February last granted by William Scott Writer in Edinburgh only son of the said deceased Mr. John Scott and heir to his said father served and retoured entered and infeft

1 This 'Signature of Resignation' (an unusual title) was no doubt properly a Charter which was in turn followed by an Instrument of Sasine.
2 The subjects are the 'Ten pound land of old extent at Ormistoun', a reference to a sort of Valuation Roll made up by Alexander III in the thirteenth century. Large areas of the South of Scotland have no better description than the size of an old extent land. A One pound land was the same as two ox-gaits, which was fifty-two acres Scots (being the amount that an ox could plough in two days). A Two pound land gave the proprietor a vote in an election to the Scottish Parliament.
3 Published with the Approval of the Keeper of the Records of Scotland.

cum beneficio Inventarii; But with and under the conditions and provisions and to the ends and purposes following viz: providing and
declaring always as it is thereby provided and declared that the said
Trust Disposition was granted by the said William Scott with full
power to the said Joseph Gillon without any farther advice and consent
of the said William Scott or his said fathers Creditors to sell and dispose of
the said Lands and other's above written thereby disponed either by
private Sale or publick voluntary roup and either in whole or by parcels
on such conditions and at such prices as he should think fit publick
notice being always given of such sale at least two months previous
thereto by advertisement in the Edinburgh Evening Courant Edinburgh
Advertiser and Kelso Mail; and with power to the said Trustee to receive
payment of the price or to take Bonds or other Securities for the same
from the purchasers with one or more Cautioners reputed responsible
at the time: And for rendering effectual such Sale or Sales with power
to the said Trustee to grant Dispositions and other writings necessary,
with all clauses needful to the purchaser or purchasers of the said lands
and that simply, so as the purchaser or purchasers of the said Lands may
be no ways concerned with the application of the prices thereof nor be
burdened or affected with any of the provisions or conditions contained/in
the said Trust Disposition, but should only be obliged to pay his or their
respective prices to the said Trustee or to the said Mr. John Scotts'
Creditors in such manner as the said Trustee should direct; As also it is
thereby farther provided and declared that the said Trust Disposition
was granted for and to this special end and effect that the said Joseph
Gillon as Trustee foresaid might and should apply the prices of the said
Lands and others thereby disponed and Rents thereof preceding the
Purchasers entry (after deduction of the publick burdens affecting the
said Estate) and also the proceeds of the moveable goods and debts therein
conveyed (after deduction of all necessary charges and expences to be
debursed by him in forming and executing the said Trust Right and all
other expences incurred or to be incurred in relation thereto) for payment
to the said Mr John Scotts' Creditors of all debts resting owing to them
out of his Estate, and that according to their several rights and preferences
conform to a scheme of division to be made thereof among them according
to their respective rights and interests duly authorised by the said
Trustee, and after deduction and payment of the said debts that the said
Trustee should make payment to him the said William Scott his heirs or
assignees of the residue of his said Funds if any should remain: as also
it is thereby provided and declared that the person or persons who shall
happen to purchase the said Lands and others with the pertinents thereby
disponed or any part thereof from the said Trustee should not be obliged
to repeat in the Rights and Infeftments to follow in favours of the pur-

chasers any of the above mentioned conditions and provisions, as the same relate only to the execution of the said Trust right and do by no means concern the purchasers. Which Lands and others above written purtained heritably of before to the said William Scott heir *cum beneficio Inventarii* of the said deceased Mr. John Scott as aforesaid holden by him of His Majesty and the Royal predecessors immediate lawful superior thereof and were together with all right, title, interest claim of right property and possession as well petitory as possessory which he the said William Scott his predecessors and authors or heirs and successors had or could pretend thereto by him and his lawful Procurators in his name to that effect specially constituted by virtue of the Procuratory of Resignation contained in the Trust Disposition above narrated duly and lawfully resigned upon the day and date of these presents in the hands of Fletcher Norton Esquire for himself and in name and behalf of the remanent Barons of His Majesty's said Court of Exchequer as in the hands of His Majesty immediately lawful Superior thereof purely and simply by staff and baton as use is in favour and for new Infeftment of the same to be made and granted to the said Joseph Gillon as Trustee foresaid in due and competent form as effeirs, and that conform to and in terms of a Procuratory of Resignation contained in the Trust Disposition before narrated: as authentick Instruments and documents taken thereupon in the hands of William Riddell Notary Public at more length proport: Moreover His Majesty wills and grants and for himself and his Royal Successors decerns and ordains that one sasine to be taken by the said Joseph Gillon and his assignees purchasers of the Lands and others herein before specified now and in all time coming at the manor place of Ormistoun or upon the ground of any part or portion of the said lands, by deliverance of earth and stone of the ground thereof allenarly without any other symbol is and shall be as valid and effectual a sasine for the said whole Lands, Tiends, Fishings and others herein before specified as if a particular Sasine were taken on each part and portion thereof and by delivery of all the usual symbols, albeit they be separate tenements of different denominations lie discontiguously and might require separate Sasines and different symbols whereanent and with all that might be objected against the validity of any such Sasine so to be taken His Majesty has dispensed and hereby for himself and his Royal Successors dispenses for ever: To be holden and to hold. All and whole the said Lands, Tiends and others with the pertinents above written, by the said Joseph Gillon as Trustee foresaid, of His Majesty and his Royal Successors immediate lawful Superiors thereof, in blench farm, fee and heritage by all the righteous meiths and marches thereof, old and divided, as the same lie in length and breadth etc. with houses biggings etc. freely quietly etc. without any revocation or obstacle whatever. *Giving therefor yearly the said Joseph Gillon, to His Majesty and his Royal Successors, immediate lawful Superiors thereof*, one Red rose at the Feast of the Nativity of Saint John the Baptist yearly, if asked only, and that for all other burden, execution, demand, or secular service, which can be executed or required, furth and from the foresaid Lands of Ormistoun with the Tiends, fishings, minerals, and others above mentioned, any manner of way in all time coming. And that the said Charter be extended in ample form, with all clauses needful, and precepts be directed thereupon. Given at Edinburgh the Fifth day of July in the Forty-Fourth Year of His Majestys Reign, One thousand eight hundred and Four Years.

APPENDIX X

A Modern English Conveyance on Sale[1]

THIS CONVEYANCE is made the 1st day of January 1975 BETWEEN ADAM SMITH of Balliol College, Oxford, Gentleman, (herinafter called the vendor) of the one part, AND WILLIAM BLACKSTONE of All Souls College, Oxford, Knight (hereinafter called the purchaser) of the other part.

WHEREAS the vendor is seised of the hereditaments intended to be hereby conveyed for an estate in fee simple absolute in possession free incumbrances and has agreed to sell the same to the purchaser for the sum of £50,000;

NOW THIS DEED WITNESSETH that in consideration of the sum of £50,000 paid to the vendor by the purchaser (the receipt of which sum the vendor hereby acknowledges) the VENDOR AS BENEFICIAL OWNER HEREBY CONVEYS unto the purchaser

ALL and singular the hereditaments known as Blackacre and situate at Kidlington in the County of Oxford and containing 24 acres 2 roods or thereabouts,

To hold unto the purchaser in fee simple.[2]

In witness whereof the said parties hereto have hereunto set their respective hands and seals the day and year first above written.

Signed sealed and delivered by the vendor in the presence of John Roe of 200 St Aldates, Oxford, solicitor.

1 From Cheshire, 765–6. This example is chosen to be as simple as possible.
2 The English habendum clause does not state of whom the purchaser is to hold, unlike Scottish feudal dispositions.

APPENDIX XI

A MODERN SCOTTISH DISPOSITION

I, *A*, heritable proprietor of the subjects hereinafter disponed IN CON-SIDERATION of the sum of   Pounds paid to me by *B*, of which sum I hereby acknowledge receipt, have sold and hereby DISPONE to the said *B* and his executors and assignees whomsoever heritably and irredeemably ALL and WHOLE that dwelling-house on the second flat above Street level part of the tenement known as Number One High Street, Edinburgh in the County of Midlothian together with part of the garden ground and cellar appropriated thereto and with all common rights, pertinents and others, described in the Disposition by *C* in favour of *D* dated . . . . and recorded in the Division of the General Register of Sasines for the County of Midlothian on   1948, Together with (First) the whole parts privileges and pertinents thereof: (Second) the whole fittings and fixtures in and upon the said subjects so far as belonging to me and (Third) my whole right title and interest, present and future, in and to the said subjects: BUT ALWAYS WITH AND UNDER insofar as still valid, subsisting and applicable, the burdens, conditions and the whole other clauses contained in (One) Instrument of Sasine in favour of *E* dated . . . . and recorded in the Particular Register of Sasines *et cetera* for the Sheriffdom of Edinburgh *et cetera* on . . . . 1810: (Two) Feu Charter by *F* in favour of *G* dated . . . . and recorded in the said Division of the General Register of Sasines on . . . . 1893 (Three) Minutes of Waiver by *F* in favour of *G* dated, ... and recorded in the said Division of the General Register of Sasines on . . . . 1947 and (Four) the said Disposition WITH ENTRY at the term on Whitsunday 1976: And I assign the writs: And I assign the rents: And I bind myself to free and relieve the said disponee of all feuduties and public burdens: And I grant warrandice: (Stamp Clause if necessary)
IN WITNESS WHEREOF

Register on behalf of the within named *B* in the Register of the County of Midlothian.

. . . . W.S.
Edinburgh   Agents

APPENDIX XII

Disposition of Land Comprised in a Registered Title

.THE LAND REGISTER OF SCOTLAND

Title No: PSP 4702

I, JOHN SMITH of Fourteen Thornley Park Drive, Paisley, IN CON-SIDERATION of the sum of TEN THOUSAND POUNDS hereby DISPONE TO HAMISH McTAVISH of Forty-two Duke Street, Cambuslang, Glasgow ALL and WHOLE the subjects registered under the Title number above mentioned: With entry on the first June Nineteen hundred and Seventy-eight: And I grant warrandice: (Stamp Clause) IN WITNESS WHEREOF etc.

Index

(Only main references have been indexed)